Applied Sport Psychology

Practical Guidelines from Behavior Analysis

Fourth Edition

Garry L. Martin

Sport Science Press
Winnipeg, Manitoba, Canada

Printed in Canada by Hignell Printing Limited

ISBN 978-0-9681995-8-9

Orders for this book may be directed to:
Sport Science Press
43 Bright Oaks Bay
Winnipeg, Manitoba, Canada
R2M 2L9
Telephone: (204) 254-5086
www.sportsciencepress.com

To Joseph Pear, Gray Osborne, and Dennis Hrycaiko

Colleagues and co-authors of the first order.

This "solo" effort was made possible by their modeling and collegiality.

Contents

Preface

The goal of this book is to describe how behavior analysis principles and techniques can be applied to enhance the performance and enjoyment of athletes and others associated with sports. For half a century, behavior analysis techniques have been successfully applied to help thousands of individuals of wide-ranging age and ability. Target behaviors have ranged from simple motor skills to complex intellectual activities. Because of their success, applications are occurring with an every-increasing frequency in education, social work, clinical psychology, psychiatry, community psychology, medicine, rehabilitation, business, industry, and sports. A common theme has been the emphasis on practical techniques that work. However, this is not just a cook book. This book deals equally with both the principles and the tactics of behavioral sport psychology consulting – what it is and how to do it.

This book is addressed to two audiences: (a) sport psychology consultants who want to learn about the "nuts and bolts" of behavioral analysis techniques for enhancing their service to athletes and coaches; and (b) undergraduate and graduate students in psychology, counseling, and physical education programs who are interested in learning about a behavioral approach to sport psychology consulting. This book evolved out of my work during the past 35 years as a behaviorally-oriented practitioner and researcher helping coaches and athletes of all ages and levels. I have used the book as the major vehicle for guiding graduate students working with athletes in sport psychology practica. I've also used it as the major text in an undergraduate sport psychology course. It has served well for both audiences.

For the practitioner, the book contains many illustrations of sport-specific questionnaires, behavioral checklists, self-monitoring forms, and practical interventions that have been used successfully to help athletes improve performance. For students, basic behavioral principles and procedures are illustrated with numerous examples to enhance understanding, and to increase the ability of readers to generalize to situations not described in the text. Study questions at the end of each chapter promote the reader's mastery of the material, and can be used for examination purposes in formal courses. For both practitioners and students, the material is presented in such a way that it will serve as an easy-to-use handbook for enhancing the performance and enjoyment of athletes and others associated with sports.

Changes in the Fourth Edition

First, many chapters have received considerable revision in accordance with reviewers' comments and recent developments in the field. Second, in previous editions, principles of respondent and operant conditioning were described in Chapter 2; in this edition, to better help students understand some of the differences between the two types of conditioning, respondent conditioning is presented in Chapter 2 and operant conditioning is presented in Chapter 3. Third, considering that there has been a surge of interest in recent years in objective feedback as a technology for improving performance in business and industry as well as sports, a new chapter has been added titled "The ABCs of Performance Feedback" (Chapter 5). Fourth, in the previous edition, there were two chapters on motivation; in this edition those chapters have been streamlined and combined (now Chapter 7). Fifth, a behavioral analysis has been added of additional topics commonly discussed by sport practitioners, including "choking" (Chapter 9) and "mental toughness" (Chapter 15) Sixth, the last two chapters (ethical issues and developing a consulting practice) from the previous edition have been combined into a single chapter (Chapter 18). Seventh, throughout the book, I have added many new references to reflect recent developments in the field.

Acknowledgements

I want to express my sincere acknowledgement to the many athletes and coaches with whom I have had the opportunity to work during the past 25 years. I especially want to acknowledge the helpful feedback from: Coaches Don Wells, Rod Small, Roger LePage, Lou Bettess, Jean Keedwell, Marilyn Partrick, Russ Salter, Jamie McGrigor, Gordon Linney, and Rick Suffield; basketball player Jennifer Beauchemin; dancer Giana Sherbo; figure skaters Jeff Partrick, Kerrie Smyth, Kara-Lynne Radics, Robin Johnstone, Maryam Ahsan, Lisa Scharf, Kristen Nickel, Kerri Robinson, Robin Forsyth, Alison Harack, Darcia Hainsworth, Danielle Henzel, Cory Krentz, Katrena Holowchuk, Ryan Hamilton, Jenilee Rauch, Sarah Beavis, Erin Carter, Jennifer Gaba, Anita Lloyd, David Schultz, Rachel Siemens, Jason Smith, Courtney Sokal, Amy Whalen, Chris Ali, Stephanie Cousins, Cadfan Edwards, Lauren Flinn, Leif Gislason, Jessica Fontaine, Brady Greening, Sara Hall, Gillian Horne, Claire Legace, Heather Michie, Nicholas Onischuk, Tiffany Smith, Amanda Loacono, and Tamara Palaniuk; gymnasts Monica Goerman and Jodi Gray; curlers Kevin Martin, John Bubbs, Dave Iverson, Cliff Lenz, and Dan Hildebrand; ice hockey players Pat Elyniuk, Stu Barnes, Freddie Olausson, Jon Cara, Jamie Dowhayko, Kris Draper, and Jon Rempel; tennis player Hart Pollock; diver Lisa Irvine; golfers Derek Ingram, Tom Kinesman, Rob McMillan, and Mario Tiziani; cyclist Erin Carter; swimmers Suzie Murray, Bart Wells, Luke Small, (and my sons) Toby Martin and Todd Martin; football player, soccer player, and basketball player and coach (and my son) Scott Martin; and field hockey player, runner, and curler (and my daughter) Tana Martin.

Grateful acknowledgement is also expressed to former graduate students Sandi Koop, Suja Srikameswaran, Siri Ming, Tracey Sewell, Gregg Tkachuk, Adrienne Leslie-Toogood, Jackie Walker, Lisa Schwartzman, and Kendra Thomson and to Dr. Jon Bailey and Dr. Tom Welsh for their constructive feedback on drafts of previous editions. I also want to thank the Manitoba Section of the Canadian Figure Skating Association for their ongoing support of a sport psychology program over many years. A special thanks to Kendra Thomson for her editorial guidance and help in the preparation of this edition.

Finally, I want to acknowledge the leadership provided for behaviorally-oriented sport psychologists by Drs. Brent Rushall, Daryl Siedentop, Ronald Smith, and Frank Smoll.

Part I
The Foundation for Behavioral Sport Psychology Consulting

Chapter 1

Introduction

What is a common element in each of the following?

- *A figure skater has lots of jumping ability. But she gets extremely nervous at important competitions, rushes her jumps, and usually skates below her potential.*

- *An ice hockey player is in a scoring slump. The coach thinks that it must be a mental problem.*

- *A coach of a youth football team wants some suggestions for a better way to teach beginning players how to block.*

- *A college basketball player hits 90% of her foul shots at practice, but less than 40% during games.*

- *Two of the players on a youth soccer team can't get along. The other players have taken sides, and the dissension is destroying the team's chances of winning the league championship.*

- *A baseball team is playing well below potential. According to the coach, "Being too tight is the team's biggest problem right now."*

- *A valuable member of a college football team is easily upset by the opponents. And when they make him mad, he takes "dumb" penalties.*

- *A member of a youth competitive swim team has a basic flaw in her freestyle stroke. But she has been swimming competitively for two years and the flaw is a well-rehearsed part of her technique. Both the coach and the swimmer want to get rid of the flaw, but nothing seems to be working.*

- *A young gymnast performs her routines extremely well at practices. But she's easily distracted at competitions, has trouble focusing, and usually performs below potential.*

- *A ski academy has agreed to provide a range of support services for its members. They would like someone to design and implement a season long mental preparation program.*

- *A young golfer has all the shots, and is touted as an "up and comer". But the golfer continues to make sufficient mental errors during a round to prevent him from entering the winners' circle.*

A common element in these examples is athletic behavior. Collectively, they illustrate many of the behavioral problems which specialists in applied sport psychology are trained to help. This book presents a behavioral approach for overcoming such problems.

What is Behavior?

In general terms, **behavior** is anything that a person says or does. Technically, behavior is any muscular, glandular, or electrical activity of an organism (Martin & Pear, 20011). Some commonly used synonyms for behavior include "performance," "reaction," "response," and "activity." Skating, shooting a hockey puck, throwing a baseball, doing a forward somersault in gymnastics, yelling at a referee, and arguing with a teammate - all are **overt** behaviors and can be easily monitored by observers. The term *behavior* can also refer to **covert** (private, internal) activities that cannot be readily monitored by observers. Just before a golfer is about to attempt an important putt, for example, she might think to herself, "I hope I don't miss," and she is likely to feel nervous (increased heart rate, etc.). Thinking and feeling are conceptualized as private behaviors.

Many traditional psychologists use quite general terms, such as "intelligence", "attitudes", "motivation", and "personality," as though they refer to causes of behavior. You may have heard statements such as the following: "Mary does well in school because she has high intelligence," or "Jack is disruptive at practices because he has a bad attitude," or "Jason doesn't try to do his best because he's not motivated," or "Sue won't make decisions on her own because of her dependent personality." From a behavioral perspective, however, these terms are viewed as summary labels for behavior, not as some "thing" within us that causes behavior (Martin & Pear, 2011).

2

Consider, for example, the concept of attitude. Suppose that Jack's coach, Ms Johnson, reports that Jack has a bad attitude at Little League baseball practices. What does Ms Johnson mean by this? Perhaps she means that Jack frequently shows up late for practice, talks to the other kids when Ms Johnson is giving instructions, and frequently throws the ball high over the head of another player. Why does Jack display such behaviors? Perhaps Ms. Johnson gives him extra attention when he acts that way. Perhaps such behaviors lead to laughter from the other kids. Whatever the cause of such behaviors might be, the term "bad attitude" is at best a summary label for them, it is not an explanation.

Personality, motivation, and intelligence also refer to the kinds of behavior which a person displays. One's personality generally refers to one's characteristic mode of interacting with others. Someone described as displaying a dependent personality is likely to seek the approval of others before buying new clothes, always let friends choose leisure activities, and in various ways, display excessive dependence on others. An athlete described as highly motivated is likely to arrive early at practices, do all the drills suggested by the coach, and spend a great deal of time practicing. (A behavioral interpretation of motivation is discussed further in Chapter 7). Perhaps a college athlete described as "intelligent" readily learns plays from the team playbook, performs well on most course examinations, and enjoys spending time on the computer surfing the Internet. Behaving intelligently can refer to any or all such behaviors.

Summary terms or labels for behavior patterns may be useful for quickly providing general information about how a labeled individual might perform. A high school athlete who has been labeled as intelligent, for example, will likely maintain a grade point average sufficient to maintain eligibility for college athletics. However, use of summary labels also has disadvantages. One disadvantage is that they may lead to pseudo-explanations of behavior. For example, a young athlete who frequently arrives late for practice and rarely completes all of the practice drills might be labeled as "unmotivated". If we ask, "Why does that person show up late for practices?" and we are given the answer "because he is not motivated," then the summary label for the behavior has been used as a false explanation for the behavior. A second disadvantage of labeling is that it may influence coaches to blame young athletes for inferior athletic performance. If young athletes do not perform to expectations, and if those athletes are described as unmotivated, lacking desire, lacking determination, or lacking the "will to win," then the problem appears to be within the athlete. However, as described in later chapters, there are a variety of coaching strategies that might be applied to change the behaviors that are likely to be labeled as unmotivated, lacking desire, etc.

In this book, rather than using general summary labels from traditional psychology, emphasis is placed on identifying the specific behaviors that characterize athletic performances. There are two main reasons for doing so. First, regardless of the labels attached to an athlete, it is *behavioral deficits* (too little behavior of a particular type) or *behavioral excesses* (too much behavior of a particular type) that causes athletes to seek help from a sport psychologist. If you examine each of the reasons for referral listed at the beginning of this chapter, you will find that they involve either behavioral deficits or behavioral excesses. Here are some additional examples.

Examples of Behavioral Deficits

1. A hockey player does not arrive at practice on time and does not complete assigned drills.

2. A tennis player does not practice the forehand shot (instead she frequently works on her serve).

3. A figure skater does not write out a precompetiton plan that would describe her specific mental preparation activities during the last half hour before she skates her program at a competition.

4. A coach rarely praises young athletes after good plays.

Examples of Behavioral Excesses

1. A baseball player frequently swears at the umpire and throws his bat.

2. A gymnast experiences considerable anxiety (i.e., heart pounding, palms sweating, etc.) just before competing.

3. A young soccer player frequently grabs the ball with her hands.

4. A golfer often thinks negatively (e.g., "If I miss this one, I'll lose!") just before important shots.

Second, specific procedures are available that can be applied at practices and competitions to overcome behavioral deficits and excesses. These procedures evolved from **behavior analysis** - an approach to the scientific study and practical applications of laws that govern behavior (Pear, 2001). Applications of behavioral techniques to help individuals in everyday living are referred to collectively as **behavior modification** or **applied behavior analysis** (Martin & Pear, 2011). **Behavioral sport psychology** involves the use of behavior analysis principles and techniques to enhance the performance and satisfaction of athletes and others associated with sports. For a brief review of the early history of behavioral sport psychology, see Martin & Thomson (2011).

The main purpose of this book is to describe, in a user-friendly and practical manner, how principles and techniques of behavior analysis can be applied to help coaches and athletes improve athletic performance.

Characteristics of Behavioral Sport Psychology

The first characteristic of a behavioral approach is *a strong emphasis on defining an athlete's goals and/or problems in terms of behavior that can be measured in some way, and using changes in the behavioral measure as the best indicator of the extent to which the athlete is being helped* (Martin & Pear, 2011). This characteristic is discussed further in Chapter 6, Behavioral Assessment, and in Chapter 17, Evaluating Your Interventions.

The second characteristic of a behavioral approach is that *its treatment procedures and techniques are ways of rearranging antecedents and consequences of an athlete's behavior* to help the athlete perform to his or her full potential. The antecedents and consequences that are typically manipulated are called **stimuli** (plural of **stimulus**), which are the specific physical variables in one's immediate surroundings that impinge on one's sense receptors and that can affect behavior (Martin & Pear, 2011). For example, the coach, the playing field or facility, other athletes in the immediate vicinity, the referee, and spectators are all stimuli in an athletic setting. When a stimulus precedes and influences behavior, it is often called a "cue," "signal," or "prompt." As will be discussed in Chapter 3, many stimuli that follow behavior can strengthen or weaken future instances of that behavior, and such stimuli are referred to as rewards or punishers accordingly. Behavior analysis procedures do <u>not</u> involve such things as traditional psychological and personality assessment, hypnosis, or use of drugs.

A third characteristic is that *behavioral psychology treatment procedures and techniques are based on the principles and procedures of respondent conditioning (discussed in Chapter 2) and operant conditioning (discussed in Chapter 3).* It is argued in later chapters that a thorough knowledge of these principles is necessary to fully understand how an athlete's experiences, thoughts and emotions influence athletic performance. These principles and procedures also provide valuable tools for designing effective interventions for helping athletes to enhance their performance.

A fourth characteristic of this approach is that *it interprets cognitive techniques in terms of operant and respondent conditioning of covert and overt behaviors.* As used by many psychologists, the word *cognition* means "belief," "thought," "expectancy," and "attitude." Psychologists referred to as cognitive therapists focus on how our cognitions can affect our behavior. In simple terms, many cognitive behavior therapists believe that faulty thinking is the cause of emotional and behavioral problems. The field known as *cognitive behavior therapy* has yielded useful techniques for helping individuals to overcome problem behavior and troublesome emotions by getting rid of unproductive, debilitating thoughts or beliefs, and adopting more constructive ones. Cognitively-oriented sport psychologists have helped many athletes to identify inappropriate thinking that can lead to poor performance, and to learn to think positively in order to achieve good performance (Brown, 2011; Donohue, Dickens, & Del Vecchio III, 2011; Williams, Zinsser, & Bunker, 2010). However, I believe that there are practical and theoretical advantages to looking at such procedures from a consistent behavioral viewpoint (see also Martin & Pear, 2011, Chapter 27). Thus, while empirically validated techniques from cognitive psychologists are included in this book, they are given a behavioral interpretation. More specifically, cognitions are assumed to be covert behaviors, and it is assumed that the behavioral principles and techniques that apply to overt behaviors are also applicable to covert behaviors. Consider, for example, a statement made by a coach of an NHL hockey team when asked about the team's losing streak. "We get down a goal and we lose our confidence," the coach replied. "It's a mental thing." Self-confidence does appear to be an important component of successful athletic performance, and it could be examined from a cognitive perspective. In Chapter 15, however, I suggest that confidence can be analyzed into several behavioral components, all of which are teachable (e.g., see Figure 1-1). Consider another example of statements from the same coach after his team lost the first two games in the play-offs. In the post-game interview, the coach suggested, "It's a case of nerves which currently plagues the team. They're afraid to make a mistake." In Chapter 9, you'll read about operant and respondent components of emotions. You'll also discover several behavioral strategies that the coach might have used to help his team overcome their "case of nerves." Some of those strategies have been researched by cognitive psychologists, and they are discussed in terms of a behavioral perspective.

A final characteristic of a behavioral approach is that *it places high value on accountability for everyone involved in the design, implementation, and evaluation of a sport psychology program* (Martin & Pear, 2011*).* In behavioral psychology, the term **social validity** refers to procedures to ensure that techniques employed by a practitioner are selected and applied in the best interests of the clients. Social validation in applied sport psychology requires that the practitioner constantly seek answers to three questions (Hrycaiko & Martin, 1996; Martin & Hrycaiko, 1983):

1. What do the athletes (and perhaps the coach and parents) think about the *goals* of the intervention?

2. What do they think about the *procedures* suggested by the consultant?

3. What do they think about the *results* produced by those procedures?

Strategies for obtaining answers to these questions are discussed further in Chapters 16, 17, and 18.

Figure 1-1. Recalling one's past successes is one of the behavioral components of confidence.

The Approach of This Book

This book is <u>not</u> meant to provide you with a broad understanding of various approaches to sport psychology. Several excellent, broadly-based texts are available for that purpose (e.g., see Weinberg & Gould, 2011; Williams, 2010). Rather, this book focuses specifically on a behavioral approach to sport psychology consulting. The overall goal of sport psychology consulting is to enhance the performance and enjoyment of athletes and others associated with sports. The remaining chapters of Part I describe how to analyze, interpret, and understand athletic performance in terms of principles and procedures of behavior analysis. The chapters in Parts II, III, IV, and V provide numerous examples and how-to-do-it guidelines for the sport psychologist to help athletes to: a) get more out of practices; b) transfer performance from practices to competitions; c) maximize competitive performance; d) decrease problem behaviors; and e) acquire self-management and other life skills. Finally, the chapters in Part VI focus on additional areas of importance for successful sport psychology consulting, including making contacts and getting started, evaluating your service, and following professional standards of ethics.

Study Questions

1. What is behavior, generally and technically? Describe three sport examples that are not in this chapter.

2. What are three synonyms for *behavior*?

3. Using sport examples that are not in this chapter, distinguish between covert and overt behavior.

4. How do many traditional psychologists use general terms such as intelligence, attitude, and personality? Illustrate with an example.

5. What is a behavioral perspective of such traditional psychological terms as intelligence, attitude, and personality? Illustrate a behavioral interpretation of one of the terms with reference to an example.

6. Discuss, with examples, two disadvantages of using summary labels for human behavior.

7. What is a behavioral deficit? Give two sport examples that are not in this chapter.

8. What is a behavioral excess? Give two sport examples that are not in this chapter.

9. For what two reasons does this book place emphasis on identifying specific behavioral deficits and excesses rather than using general summary labels for

behavior?

10. What is behavior modification?

11. What is behavioral sport psychology?

12. What do behavior modifiers mean by the term *stimulus*? Give three sport examples that are not in this chapter.

13. What are three synonyms for *stimulus* when a stimulus precedes and influences behavior?

14. According to many psychologists, what does the word "cognition" mean?

15. What is cognitive behavior therapy?

16. What assumptions does the author make concerning cognitions?

17. List five characteristics of a behavioral approach to sport psychology consulting.

18. In a sentence, what is social validation?

19. What three questions does social validity address?

20. What is the overall goal of sport psychology consulting?

Chapter 2

Behavioral Principles and Techniques:
Respondent Conditioning

An Application

Learning Feelings of Fear, and Then Eliminating Them

Susan, a 12-year-old novice competitive figure skater, was working on her double axel jump. She skated around the rink at a skating practice, approached the take-off position, initiated the jump, and was rotating in the air when she realized that she was on a tilt and was falling. She immediately felt strong feelings of fear, and then hit the ice, and felt considerable pain. This was Susan's third bad fall on a double axel attempt during the past week. She got back up, brushed herself off, and was determined to try the double axel a few more times before leaving it for the day. But each time that she approached the take-off position, she experienced strong feelings of fear, and could not bring herself to attempt the jump during the rest of that practice.

Susan's coach arranged for the skaters' sport psychologist to attend the next practice. In a couple of previous team sessions, the psychologist had been teaching the skaters a relaxation technique referred to as *deep center breathing*. When practicing this technique, a skater would breathe low down in his/her stomach instead of high up in the chest. Instead of a skater's chest rising and falling when breathing, the skater's stomach would bulge out when inhaling and collapse while exhaling. Also, each time they exhaled slowly, the skaters had been encouraged to say to themselves, "R-e-l-a-x." At the next practice, when Susan was getting ready to attempt a double axel, the psychologist called her over to the side of the rink and asked her to practice deep center breathing for several breaths, each time telling herself to "R-e-l-a-x" while exhaling. The psychologist then prompted Susan to skate around and approach the take-off position for the double axel, and just before getting to the place where she would normally initiate the jump, to do a deep center breath, and to tell herself to "R-e-l-a-x" on the exhale, but not to attempt the jump. Susan did this five times in succession. After the fifth time, she told the psychologist that, on the fifth trial of this routine, when she was approaching the take-off position, she did not feel nearly as nervous as during the first trial. She felt that she was ready to try another double axel, including repeating the preceding routine while approaching the take-off position. Susan successfully attempted the jump, and although she two-footed the landing, she indicated afterwards that she felt much less fear

```
on the take-off, and that she could now continue practicing
double axels.

*This application is based on a consultation by G. Martin (1996).
```

Behavioral Principles and Techniques

Behavioral principles and techniques are essentially ways of manipulating stimuli in order to influence behavior. Principles are procedures that have a consistent effect, and are so simple that they cannot be broken down into simpler procedures (Martin & Pear, 2011). Behavioral principles are like laws in science. Behavioral techniques are combinations of behavioral principles. In order to become skillful at designing sport psychology interventions for helping athletes, it is necessary to be conversant with basic behavioral principles and techniques. These principles and techniques will be described under two broad categories; respondent conditioning (in this chapter) and operant conditioning (in Chapter 3).

Respondent Conditioning

Imagine some thoughts and feelings of Mary, a young figure skater just before stepping onto the ice to compete in her first National Championship. She thinks to herself; "I hope I don't fall on my combination. What will everyone say if I don't skate well?" These thoughts cause her to feel anxious, and to experience tension in her arms and shoulders. These reactions are very likely to interfere with her ability to skate to her full potential. As another example, consider Peter, a college hockey player who is given a penalty that he doesn't think he deserves. He feels so angry that he slams his stick on the ice and swears at the referee, and is given an additional penalty for unsportsmanlike conduct. Obviously Mary wasn't born such that thinking about a National Championship caused her to have anxious feelings, and Peter wasn't born such that being told to go to the penalty box would cause angry feelings. Any athlete will tell you that an athlete's internal feelings, whether they be feelings of anxiousness, anger, confidence, or something else, can have an impact on an athlete's athletic performance. How is that we learn to experience various internal feelings to some situations and not others? The answer lies with a type of learning or conditioning that began with our bodys' *unlearned reflexes*.

Unlearned (or unconditioned) reflexes involve stimuli and responses. An **unconditioned reflex** is a stimulus-response sequence in which a stimulus elicits a response without prior learning or conditioning. For instance, you wake up in the morning, open the curtains, and look out on a bright day - and your pupils constrict. The bright light was a stimulus; pupil constriction was a response to the stimulus. The light and pupil constriction together formed an unconditioned reflex. Such a reflex is inborn or *un*conditioned. We are born such that a number of stimuli elicit responses without prior learning. Some examples of unconditioned reflexes are as follows: an object in an infant's hand elicits grasping; a sudden loss of support (i.e., falling) elicits increased heart rate and body stiffening (i.e., fear); food elicits salivation; inhaling pepper elicits sneezing; sticking your finger in your throat elicits vomiting; a high temperature elicits sweating; a low temperature elicits shivering; and after we have reached puberty, genital stimulation elicits vaginal lubrication or penile erection.

Learning a Conditioned Reflex

Ivan Pavlov, a distinguished Russian physiologist, is generally given credit for discovering a type of learning involving unconditioned reflexes. You may recall from introductory psychology that, in one of his experiments, Pavlov noted that a dog would salivate when food was presented, but it would not salivate when a tone was presented. The food was an *unconditioned stimulus* (US) - a stimulus that elicits a response without prior learning. The salivation to the food was an *unconditioned response* (UR) - a response elicited by an unconditioned stimulus. The tone was a *neutral stimulus* (NS). Then, over several trials, Pavlov paired the sound of the tone with food many times by placing a plate of food powder in front of the dog just after making the sound of the tone. In the final part of his experiment, Pavlov presented the tone by itself (without pairing it with the food powder), and the tone now caused salivation (Pavlov, 1927). Because the salivation that occurred to the tone was learned and not inborn, Pavlov called it a **conditioned reflex**, which is a stimulus-response sequence in which a stimulus elicits a response because the stimulus was paired with a different stimulus that elicited that response. The tone was now referred to as a *conditioned stimulus* (CS) - a stimulus that did not originally elicit a response, but has come to do so through appropriate pairings with a stimulus that did elicit that response. The salivation to the tone was called a *conditioned response* (CR) - a response elicited by a conditioned stimulus. With this type of reflexive learning, also referred to as **classical, Pavlovian, or respondent conditioning**, two stimuli are appropriately paired, and the response elicited by one stimulus is transferred to the other.

Consider a plausible example of reflexive learning in sport. Let's suppose that a beginning gymnast experiences several bad falls while practicing a back flip on the balance beam, each fall causing both feelings of fear and considerable pain. The **principle of respondent conditioning** states that if a neutral stimulus (practicing a back flip on the balance beam) is closely followed by an unconditioned stimulus (a bad fall), which elicits an unconditioned response (feelings of fear), then the previously neutral stimulus (practicing a back flip on the balance beam) will also tend to elicit that response (feelings of fear). Now, when the young gymnast is about to practice the back flip on the balance beam, she is likely to become fearful and tense (respondent conditioning of emotions is discussed further in Ch. 9). The model for respondent conditioning is shown in Figure 2-1.

Model for Respondent Conditioning

Procedure: Pair neutral stimulus and unconditioned stimulus

Several Pairings {

NS (practicing back flip on balance beam)

US (bad fall) ⟶ UR (feelings of fear)

Result: Neutral stimulus acquires ability to elicit response that was elicited by the unconditioned stimulus.

CS (practicing back flip on balance beam) ⟶ CR (fear)

NS = neutral stimulus
US = unconditioned stimulus
UR = unconditioned response
CS = conditioned stimulus
CR = conditioned response

Model for Respondent Extinction

Procedure: Present conditioned stimulus repeatedly without further pairings with the unconditioned stimulus.

Repeated Trials { CS (practicing back flip on balance beam) ⟶ CR (fear)

Result: Conditioned stimulus loses ability to elicit conditioned response

NS (practicing back flip on balance beam) ⟶ (No fear reaction)

Figure 2-1. Models for respondent conditioning and respondent extinction.

Extinction of a Conditioned Reflex

After a conditioned reflex is formed, does it stay with you forever? No! Pavlov demonstrated a process of "unlearning", which he referred to as extinction. **Respondent extinction** refers to the procedure of the repeated presentation of a conditioned stimulus by itself (without further pairings with the US), with the result that the CS loses its ability to elicit a conditioned response. In the above example, if the gymnast repeatedly practices the back flip on the balance beam a number of times in succession across each of several practices and does not fall, then practicing the back flip on the balance beam will lose the ability to elicit fear. The model for respondent extinction is shown in Figure 2-1.

Counterconditioning

Respondent extinction is one way to eliminate a conditioned response. A more effective way to cause a CS to lose the ability to elicit a CR is to condition a new "and very different" response to the CS at the same time that the former CR is being extinguished. This process is called **counterconditioning**. Let's reconsider our young gymnast who has learned to fear practicing the back flip on the balance beam. As indicated previously, the fear might gradually be overcome if the child simply practices the back flip on the beam repeatedly without falling. This process might be hastened if, each time just before the child is about to practice the back flip, the child is given a lick of an ice cream cone, which influences the child to relax and enjoy the taste of the ice cream. These positive responses to the ice cream become associated with practicing the back flip on the balance beam, and can help to counteract the fear reaction previously elicited by practicing the back flip, and thus more quickly and effectively eliminate those fear responses.

As another example of counterconditioning, consider the case of Susan, the figure skater, described at the beginning of this chapter. As illustrated in the top half of Figure 2-2, the bad falls that Susan experienced while approaching the take off position for her double-axel jump established approaching the take off position as a CS that caused feelings of fear as a CR. However, when she went through five trials of practicing deep center breathing while approaching the take off position (without jumping), that established approaching the take off position as a CS for the CR of feeling relaxed. Because feeling relaxed is incompatible with feeling fear, approaching the take off position for the double axel lost the ability to elicit the CR of fear (at least to the degree that it had done so prior to the counterconditioning procedure; see bottom half of Figure 2-2).

Factors Influencing Respondent Conditioning

There are several variables that influence the development of a conditioned reflex. First, *"the greater the number of pairings of a CS with a US, the greater the ability of the*

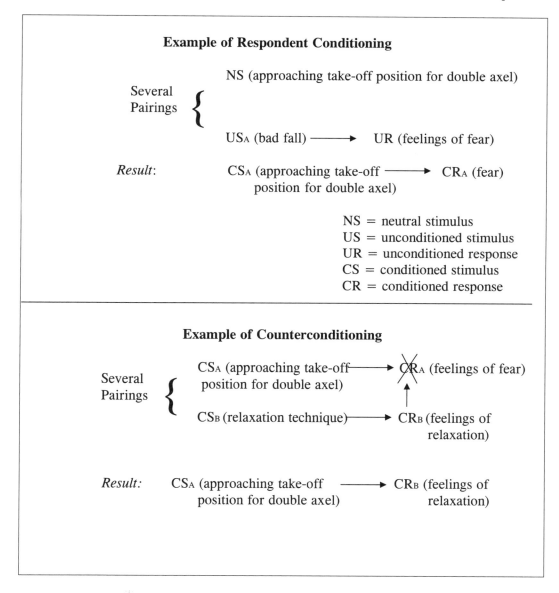

Figure 2-2. An illustration of respondent conditioning, and counterconditioning, of fear in a figure skater.

CS to elicit the CR, until the maximum strength of the conditioned reflex has been reached" (Martin & Pear, 2011, p. 170). Suppose that a first-year little league baseball player faces a wild pitcher. If the player has been hit several times by wild pitches from that pitcher, then the player will experience stronger fear when approaching the plate than if he/she had just been hit once.

Second, *"stronger conditioning occurs if the CS precedes the US by just a second, rather than by a longer time, or rather than by following the US"* (Martin & Pear, 2011, p. 170). Conditioning in the latter case is difficult to attain. Suppose that a child is taken to a skeet shooting competition for the first time. (At such competitions, a target, called a clay pigeon, is propelled into the air by a machine, and a contestant attempts to hit the target by shooting at it with a shotgun.) If the child sees a clay pigeon propelled into the air, and then is immediately scared by the loud sound of the shotgun, the sight of a clay pigeon is likely to become a CS for fear as a CR. On the other hand, if the child heard the blast of the shotgun, and a few seconds later saw a clay pigeon released into the air, the fear caused by the noise of the gun would be less likely to be transferred to the sight of the clay pigeon.

Third, *"a CS acquires greater ability to elicit a CR if the CS is always paired with a given US, than if it is only occasionally paired with the US"* (Martin & Pear, 2011, p. 170). Consider, for example, a gymnast who spends two minutes each day practicing a breathing technique (deep center breathing, as discussed in the case of Susan) that elicits relaxation. Let's suppose that, each time the gymnast exhales while deep center breathing, she repeats the word, "e-a-s-y" slowly to herself. After several days, simply reciting the word, "e-a-s-y" will elicit the feelings of relaxation normally elicited by deep center breathing. On the other hand, if the gymnast had said, "e-a-s-y" on some instances of deep center breathing, but not on others, then saying, "e-a-s-y" would be a weaker CS for relaxation.

Fourth, *"when several neutral stimuli precede a US, the stimulus that is most consistently associated with the US is the one most likely to become a strong CS"* (Martin & Pear, 2011, p. 170). Suppose that the gymnast in the above example consistently pairs the word, "e-a-s-y" with each exhalation during deep center breathing. On some occasions, when doing her breathing exercises, she also clasps her hands together. Reciting the word, "e-a-s-y" will become a stronger CS for relaxation than clasping hands because clasping hands is less consistently paired with deep center breathing (for an explanation of this effect, see the description of a phenomenon called blocking in Pear, 2001).

Fifth, *"respondent conditioning will develop more quickly and strongly when the CS or US or both are intense, rather than weak"* (Martin & Pear, 2011, p. 170). In the example given previously involving the child at the skeet shooting competition, the child will acquire a stronger fear of the clay pigeon if the clay pigeon is painted bright colors and the shotgun blast is exceptionally loud, than if the clay pigeon was a bland color and the shotgun blast was muffled.

You can see that this type of learning involves unconditioned reflexes - responses that are inborn and involuntary, like feeling scared or startled when you hear a loud noise, or shivering in a cold wind, or feeling relaxed when deep center breathing. And you can also see that a variety of factors determine whether or not respondent conditioning will occur - whether or not the reflexive responses become attached to novel stimuli in a given situation.

Respondent Conditioning and Athletic Performance

Respondent learning is especially important in determining how previously neutral stimuli come to influence the internal functioning of your body. In this chapter, we have described how respondent learning can be involved in learning to feel fear in various situations. In Chapter 9, we will discuss in considerably more detail how respondent learning is involved in the "feelings" component of all of our emotions. Because of respondent conditioning, previously neutral stimuli (such as approaching the take-off position for a double axel) can influence the reflexes controlled by the part of our nervous system referred to as the *autonomic nervous system,* such as an individual's heart rate, breathing, digestion, and glandular activity. Respondent learning is also important in enabling us to understand aspects of athletes' thinking- the control of aspects of their imagery. We will discuss this aspect of respondent learning in more detail in Chapter 8. But before learning about the importance of respondent learning in understanding aspects of an athlete's thinking (Chapter 8) and emotions (Chapter 9), it is necessary for you to understand a different type of learning, referred to as operant conditioning, which we will focus on in the next chapter.

Study Questions

1. Define unconditioned reflex. Give two examples of an unconditioned reflex.

2. What was the unconditioned reflex experienced by Susan, the figure skater, at the beginning of Chapter 2.

3. Define conditioned reflex, and describe the example of a conditioned reflex illustrated in the case of Susan, the figure skater at the beginning of Chapter 2.

4. What are two other names for respondent conditioning?

5. State the procedure and result of respondent conditioning.

6. Describe the procedure and result of extinction of a conditioned reflex (i.e. respondent extinction), and describe an example that is not in Chapter 2.

7. Describe the details of how the sport psychologist helped Susan, the figure skater, to overcome her fear of attempting the double axel jump in Chapter 2. (If you prefer, you can simply diagram this example of counterconditioning.)

8. Suppose that a young child who can't swim was dunked underwater by friends at a swimming pool party and is now afraid of going into the water at a pool or at the beach. Describe the details of how you might use counterconditioning to help the child overcome this fear.

9. In respondent conditioning, what does each of the following stand for: NS, US, UR, CS, and CR?

10. In a sentence each, briefly state five variables that influence the development of a conditioned reflex.

11. Suppose that a child hears loud barking from a dog, hidden behind a car, and several seconds later the dog appears in view to the child (but the dog has not been barking for several seconds before appearing). Is that sequence likely to cause the child to fear the sight of a dog? Explain why or why not based on one of the variables that influences the development of a conditioned reflex.

12. What is the name of the part of our nervous system that is influenced by respondent conditioning?

Chapter 3

Behavioral Principles and Techniques: Operant Conditioning

An Application

Behavioral Chaining to Improve Steve's Pre-Putt Routine[*]

Steve was a young professional golfer playing on the Canadian PGA Tour for the second consecutive year. Although he had had several top ten finishes, he had not yet won a tournament on the tour. Steve felt that his inability to win thus far was due in part to inconsistent putting. Steve knew that top-ranked golfers have more consistent pre-putt routines than golfers who are less successful. After thinking about his performance in the last couple of tournaments, Steve realized that his own pre-putt routine was somewhat inconsistent. If it was an especially important putt, for example, he tended to stand over the ball for a longer period of time than usual before stroking the ball toward the hole. Steve decided to improve the consistency of his pre-putt routine.

Putting is typically divided into two parts. The first part involves deciding where to aim and how hard to hit the ball so that it will follow the contours of the putting green as it rolls towards the hole. Once the golfer has decided where to aim the ball, then the pre-putt routine is followed. Steve's pre-putt routine included the following steps:

1. While standing behind the ball, Steve would look at the spot that he was aiming at, take two practice strokes, and visualize the ball rolling in the hole.
2. He then moved beside the ball, placed his putter head behind the ball, and adjusted it so that it was aiming at the desired spot.
3. He next adjusted his feet so that they were parallel to the putting line, gripped the putter in the usual way, and said to himself, "stroke it smooth."
4. Steve then looked at the ball, looked at the spot at which he was aiming, looked back at the ball, and then stroked the putt.

Steve practiced this routine on the practice green for a number of putts. He first practiced short putts so he would be reinforced by making them. He then practiced his routine with

<u>putts of different lengths</u>. He especially focused on being consistent with the timing of the four steps of the pre-putt routine. On each trial, a friend checked off the steps on a checklist as they were performed. After completing a number of trials at the practice green, Steve and his friend played a practice round of golf during which Steve consistently practiced the above routine. During subsequent tournament rounds, Steve's caddy reminded him frequently to follow his pre-putt routine. Three weeks after implementing the procedure, Steve won his first tour event. He felt that one of the contributing factors was his improved putting due to a more consistent pre-putt routine.

*This application is based on a consultation by G. Martin (1999).

Operant Conditioning

Reflexes! That's what Pavlovian learning is all about - automatic responses to prior stimuli. But much of our behavior appears to be voluntary rather than reflexive; behavior that is influenced by its consequences (rewards and punishers) rather than by prior stimuli (CSs and USs). Examples of voluntary behavior include running in a race, high jumping, hitting a baseball, ice skating, shooting a hockey puck, swimming, listening to a coach, and talking to friends. Skinner (1953) referred to such activity as **operant behavior** - behavior that affected or "operated on" the environment to produce consequences, and which was, in turn, influenced by those consequences. **Operant conditioning** is a type of learning in which behavior is modified by its consequences. One important type of consequence that influences our behavior is referred to as positive reinforcement.

Positive Reinforcement

A stimulus, the presentation of which <u>immediately</u> after a behavior that causes the behavior to increase, is called a **positive reinforcer**. The term *positive reinforcer* is roughly synonymous with the term *reward.* Application of a positive reinforcer to strengthen a behavior is called positive reinforcement. More specifically, the principle of **positive reinforcement** includes a *procedure*, the presentation of a reinforcer immediately after a behavior, and an effect or *result*, the behavior is strengthened. In the example of Steve practicing his pre-putt routine for short putts, at the beginning of this chapter, the completion of Steve's fourth step (the behavior) was reinforced by the sight of the ball dropping in the hole. The model for positive reinforcement is shown in Figure 3-1.

Positive Reinforcement

Procedure: In a certain situation, a response is immediately followed by a reinforcer.

S (end of baseball ⟶ R (little leaguer helps ⟶ Cons. (coach thanks
   practice)   coach pick up equipment)   little leaguer for
                                           helping)

Result: The response is more likely to occur in similar situations

(the Little Leaguer is more likely to help the coach pick up the equipment after practice)

S = stimulus
R = response
Cons = consequence

Figure 3-1. Model for positive reinforcement.

Unconditioned and Conditioned Reinforcers. Because of our genetic structure and our biological needs, we are capable of being reinforced by some stimuli without prior learning, provided that we have been appropriately deprived of those stimuli. Such stimuli or events are called **unconditioned reinforcers** (that is, stimuli that are reinforcing without being conditioned). (They are sometimes also called primary, or unlearned reinforcers.) Examples include food, water, warmth, and sexual contact. Other stimuli acquire reinforcing value. A stimulus that was not originally reinforcing can acquire reinforcing value through appropriate pairings with other reinforcers. Stimuli that acquire reinforcing value are called **conditioned reinforcers** (or secondary or learned reinforcers). A common example of a conditioned reinforcer is praise. Parents who praise their child's good behavior are also likely to smile at the child, play with the child, or give the child a toy. Praise is normally established as a conditioned reinforcer during childhood, and it continues to be maintained for one as adults. That's because when people praise us, they are generally more likely to favour us in various ways than when they do not praise us. Other examples of conditioned reinforcers include money, the opportunity to watch our favourite sport on television, books that we like to read, and our favourite clothes. Examples of conditioned reinforcers in sports include seeing a golf ball drop in the cup (for golfers), getting a safe hit in baseball, scoring a touchdown in football, and winning a competition.

Natural vs. Deliberately-Programmed Reinforcers. Consider the examples in

Table 3-1. In those examples, no one was deliberately applying the principle of positive reinforcement. The reinforcing consequences just naturally followed the responses - that is, no one specifically or deliberately programmed the reinforcers to increase or maintain behavior. In each of those examples, it might take several repetitions before there would be an obvious increase in the reinforced response. Nevertheless, the effect is still there.

	Table 3-1 Examples of Natural Reinforcers	
Response	*Naturally Occurring Consequence*	*Effect on the Response*
You open the door at a store for a person carrying several parcels	The person says, "Thanks"	You are more likely to open a door for someone on the next opportunity
When experiencing difficulty unlocking your door, you wiggle the key up and down	The key works and your door unlocks	You are more likely to wiggle a key up and down on the next occasion that it doesn't unlock a door
A golfer tries a new style of gripping the golf club just before a shot	The golfer makes a good shot	The golfer is more likely to try that grip on future shots

Reinforcers that immediately follow behavior in the normal course of everyday living are called **natural reinforcers**, and the settings in which they occur are called the *natural environment* (Martin & Pear, 2011). Reading signs is naturally reinforced by reaching desired destinations. Eating is reinforced by the taste of food. Social behaviors are reinforced by the natural reactions of others. Many of our actions are followed by natural reinforcers. However, as we will see in later chapters, it is also possible to deliberately arrange for reinforcers to follow behavior in order to strengthen that behavior. Coaches can deliberately use various reinforcers to improve the skills of athletes. Athletes themselves can learn how to rearrange reinforcers in self-control programs in order to work harder at practices or accomplish other objectives. When reinforcers are deliberately manipulated in order to change behavior, then the reinforcers are referred to as **arbitrary, contrived, or deliberately-programmed reinforcers.** The pros and cons of using natural (sometimes called intrinsic) reinforcers versus deliberately-programmed (sometimes called extrinsic) reinforcers are discussed further in Chapter 7.

Direct Effect Versus Indirect Effect of Reinforcers. The **direct effect** of the principle of positive reinforcement is the increased frequency of a response because of its immediate reinforcing consequences (at least within approximately 30 seconds) (Martin & Pear, 2011). In each of the examples of natural reinforcement in Table 3-1, the reinforcer had a direct effect. Sometimes, however, it's possible to influence individuals to work for delayed reinforcement. An effective strategy for a coach of young competitive swimmers, for example, might be to tell the athletes at the start of practice, that if they practice their racing turns consistently during the practice then they can play water polo (an enjoyable activity for the swimmers) during the last 10 minutes of practice. Moreover, some people do work toward very long-delayed consequences, such as college degrees or making the Olympic team. But it is a mistake to attribute such results to the direct effects of the principle of positive reinforcement. A reinforcer is not likely to have much direct effect on a behavior that precedes the reinforcer by anything much longer than 30 seconds with animals (Lattal & Metzger, 1994), and we have no reason to believe that humans are any different (Michael, 1986). Knowledge of this fact can help prevent misinterpretations of the causes of behavior change. In the case of the young swimmers mentioned above, for example, the opportunity to play water polo (a reinforcer) is considerably delayed following the practicing of racing turns at the beginning of practice. The **indirect effect** of positive reinforcement is the strengthening of a response (such as the swimmers practicing racing turns) that is followed by a reinforcer (playing water polo) even though the reinforcer is delayed. Delayed reinforcers do not always influence prior behavior. In Chapter 4 we'll discuss conditions under which delayed reinforcement can be effective, as well as conditions under which it is not likely to be effective. The distinction between direct and indirect effects of reinforcement has important implications for practitioners. If reinforcers can't be presented immediately following desired athletic behavior, then practitioners must know how to arrange conditions to increase the likelihood that delayed reinforcement will be effective (as discussed in Chapter 4).

Operant Extinction

Positive reinforcement is a powerful technique for strengthening behavior. But what happens when a response is no longer followed by the usual reinforcer? That response is then weakened - a process referred to as **operant extinction**. The operant extinction *procedure* is withholding of a reinforcer following a previously reinforced response. The *result* is that the response decreases in frequency when reinforcement for that response ceases. However, the effects of an operant extinction procedure are not likely to be noticed immediately. If a golfer has been positively reinforced (by hitting the ball further) after trying a new way of gripping the golf club over several rounds of golf, then the golfer is not likely to go to a different grip after just one mediocre shot. However, if many mediocre shots occur, then the golfer's use of the new experimental grip may decrease. In general terms, behaviors that no longer "pay off" gradually decrease. The model for operant extinction is shown in Figure 3-2.

Operant Extinction

Procedure: In a certain situation, a previously reinforced response is not followed by a reinforcer.

S (golfer setting up   →   R (golfer grips club   →   Cons. (a good shot does
    for a golf shot)   in a way that was   not occur)
                              previously followed
                              by good shots)

Result: The response is then less likely to occur in similar situations

            (the golfer is less likely to grip the club in that way when setting up for a golf shot)

                                             S = stimulus
                                           R = response
                                           Cons = consequence

---

Figure 3-2. Model for operant extinction

Schedules of Reinforcement

When positive reinforcers are used deliberately to influence behavior, they are usually presented each time that the appropriate behavior occurs. After all, the goal is typically to strengthen the desirable behavior as quickly as possible. However, it's often impractical to continue to promptly reinforce each occurrence of a desired response. And most real life activities are reinforced irregularly. Golfers make some good shots, but also some poor shots. In baseball, a batter who gets a hit in four out of ten times at bat has a good batting average. And students don't always get good grades after studying. Fortunately, we've learned that, sooner or later in such cases, persistence pays off. Experiments on the effects of various strategies for rewarding behavior have been studied under the topic of schedules of reinforcement. In addition to a **continuous schedule**, in which every occurrence of a specified response is reinforced, there are many types of partial or **intermittent schedules** in which responses are reinforced only occasionally. Research on intermittent schedules has revealed two surprising results (Martin & Pear, 2011): (1) Individuals are likely to work much more consistently on certain intermittent schedules of reinforcement than on continuous reinforcement; and (2) A behavior that has been reinforced intermittently is likely to take much longer to extinguish than a behavior that has been reinforced continuously. If a behavior takes a long time to extinguish, we say that it is *resistant to extinction.*

One type of intermittent reinforcement is called **fixed ratio** reinforcement: reinforcement occurs after a fixed number of a certain response is emitted. If a person exercising, for example, does 10 push-ups before pausing for a refreshing drink, then that person is being reinforced on a fixed ratio schedule. We would refer to this particular example as an FR (Fixed Ratio) - 10 schedule. A student who reads 20 pages of a book before getting a cup of coffee is performing on an FR-20 schedule, and so on. In general, fixed ratio reinforcement generates high rates of responding, and high resistance to extinction.

A **variable-ratio** schedule is like a fixed-ratio schedule, except that the number of responses required to produce reinforcement changes unpredictably from one reinforcer to the next. Slot machines and other gambling devices are programmed according to variable-ratio schedules such that gamblers have no way of predicting how many responses they must make (that is, how many times they must play the machine) for reinforcement (hitting the jackpot). Someone casting for fish is reinforced on a VR schedule in that one must cast an unpredictable number of times in order to get a bite. A salesperson working on commission who makes a sale about every 10 clients is working on a VR (variable ratio) - 10 schedule. That is, although the salesperson can never predict exactly when a sale will be made, that individual knows that the average success rate is 1 in 10. Sometimes a sale is made to two customers in a row. At other times, the salesperson may have to approach 20 or more customers before making a sale. Because success can come at any time, the salesperson is likely to be very persistent. Each new customer could be "the one". Many activities in sport are reinforced on variable-ratio schedules. Making a good serve in tennis, hitting a good shot in golf, hitting the bulls eye on a dart board, or making a field goal from 40 yards at football practice, all occur on an intermittent and somewhat unpredictable (at least for many athletes) basis.

Ratio schedules do not have a time requirement. The reinforcer follows a certain number of responses (either fixed or variable), and the more often the individual responds, the greater is the likelihood of being reinforced. That's one reason why such schedules generate high rates of responding; the higher the rate, the faster that reinforcers will be earned. Another type of schedule doesn't require that a certain number of responses occur, but rather it requires that a response be practiced for a certain period of time. A common example of this is a **fixed-duration** schedule, in which a reinforcer is presented if a behavior occurs continuously for a fixed period of time. For example, a swim instructor might require swimmers to tread water continuously, without touching down, for three minutes, before taking a reinforcing break. That would be an example of an FD (fixed-duration) three minute schedule.

Another type of schedule requires only one response (rather than a certain number), but that response must occur at an unpredictable period of time. Technically, the schedule is referred to as a **variable-interval schedule with a limited hold**. Consider the following strategy for managing the behavior of kids on a family car trip. When my two boys (2 1/2 years apart) were children, family car trips usually involved my wife and I sitting in the front seat and the boys in the back seat. With that arrangement, minor bickering between the boys frequently occurred (e.g., "Move over," "I want that," "You're on my side," etc.). In an attempt to increase cooperative play, we applied the following strategy. First, we purchased a timer that produced an audible "ding" when it reached a preset time, and that could be preset at values up to 25 minutes. Then, at the beginning of a car trip, my wife explained the rules of the "timer game" to the boys. "Whenever this timer goes 'ding', if you're playing nicely, you can stay up for an extra five minutes to watch TV in the motel room (a strong reinforcer for the boys). But if you're bickering, you lose that five minutes. We'll play the game until we get there." Thereafter, my wife set the timer at random intervals for the duration of the trip. Because the boys couldn't see the timer, they never knew when it would go "ding." And although they had to be playing cooperatively only briefly to earn a reinforcer, they never knew when that opportunity might occur. The procedure was immediately effective. Bickering rarely occurred, and car trips became much more pleasant for Mom and Dad. (For a review of research on the "Timer Game", see Tingstrom, Sterling-Turner, and Wilczynski, 2006).

Technically, the schedule described in the preceding paragraph is a variable-interval schedule because, after an unpredictable period of time, a response is reinforced. It also included a limited hold - a limited time after a reinforcer is available that a response will produce the reinforcer. For the boys and the timer game, the limited hold was 0 seconds because they had to be behaving appropriately at the instant the "ding" occurred to receive reinforcement. (This intervention also included rule-governed control over behavior, which you'll read about in the next chapter.) A variable-interval schedule with a 0-second limited hold is a very useful strategy for a coach to maintain on-task behavior in a group of young athletes. At unpredictable intervals, the coach can check to see if the athletes are on-task with various assigned drills. If they are, they can earn points towards a back-up reinforcer (perhaps a scrimmage at the end of practice, or an opportunity to compete against the coach, etc.) Other types of schedules of reinforcement are discussed in Martin & Pear (2011).

Stimulus Control

Positive reinforcement provides one explanation for how operant behavior is increased and maintained. However, a newly acquired behavior is valuable only if it occurs at the right times and in the appropriate situations. For instance, at an intersection it is desirable if you stop the car when the light is red, not when the light is green. Performing 50 push ups may earn one valuable points on a fitness test, but it won't have the same effect if performed by a golfer just before a crucial putt. As we learn new operant behaviors, we also learn to emit those behaviors at the right time and place. A key factor in this process is something called stimulus control.

Let's consider how stimulus control comes about. Suppose that a golfer is standing on a putting green and is about to hit a 5-foot putt toward the hole. In the presence of the stimuli provided by a flat putting green, the golfer who responds by aiming directly at the hole will be rewarded by making the putt (assuming the ball is hit with appropriate force). However, in the presence of the stimuli provided when there is a slope on the green, the golfer who aims directly at the hole will not make the putt; the ball will curve off in the direction of the slope. After several trials, the golfer learns to hit the ball directly at the hole only when the putting green is flat. This sequence of events is diagrammed in Figure 3-3. In general terms, an operant behavior is likely to occur in the presence of stimuli that were present when previous instances of that behavior were reinforced; an operant behavior is not likely to occur in the presence of stimuli that were present when previous instances of that behavior were not reinforced.

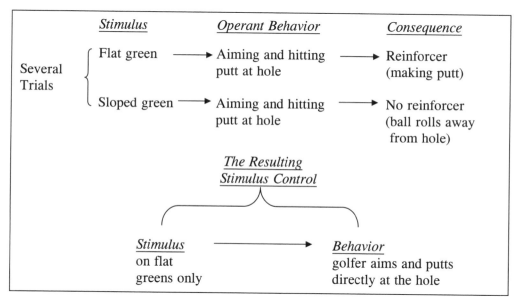

Figure 3-3. An example of the development of stimulus control.

We use the term **stimulus control** to refer to the degree of correlation between a stimulus and a behavior. **Good stimulus control** (or effective stimulus control) refers to a strong correlation between the occurrence of a particular stimulus and the occurrence of a particular response; i.e., when the stimulus occurs, the response is likely to follow. Good stimulus control develops as a result of a behavior having been reinforced in the presence of a particular stimulus. In the previous example, after enough practice trials, the slope of the green comes to exert control over where the golfer aims when putting. The stimulus of a flat green exerts control over the behavior of aiming at the hole. The stimulus of a sloped green exerts control over the behavior of aiming away from the hole (so the ball will curve in the direction of the slope towards the hole).

For an athlete to be successful in any sport, certain stimuli must exert control over certain operant behaviors of that athlete. The stimulus of an open receiver must control the passing behavior of a quarterback in football, even in the face of charging linemen from the opposing team. An effective counterpuncher must be able to detect and avoid a punch (the stimulus) from an opponent boxer, and to throw the correct counterpunch (the response). The distance and terrain on the holes of a golf course must exert appropriate stimulus control over the correct selection of clubs in order for a golfer to hit the ball the correct distance consistently. Basketball players must know when to shoot versus when to pass. All of these examples involve stimulus control, situations in which specific stimuli control the occurrence of specific operant behaviors because of those behaviors having been reinforced in the presence of those stimuli.

Through experience, a wide range of stimuli - such as objects in the environment, the behavior of others, even our own behavior - can acquire control over aspects of our operant behavior. A word spoken by a coach might be a stimulus for an athlete to perform a particular skill. The expression on a coach's face can provide a stimulus for athletes to show attentive listening behavior. The tactile or kinesthetic feeling of muscle movement can serve as a stimulus for further muscle movement for an athlete in order to successfully perform a skill (discussed further in Chapter 5).

While some stimuli indicate that certain behaviors will be reinforced, other stimuli indicate that certain behaviors will not be reinforced. The sound of the referee's whistle to stop play in an ice hockey game is a cue that shooting the puck into the net will not count as a goal. The feeling that the lace on an ice skate is loose (because of a broken skate lace) is a signal to a figure skater that attempting a difficult jump will not likely be successful. Through experience, we learn not to emit certain behaviors in the presence of certain stimuli because we have learned that those behaviors will go unreinforced. Thus, stimulus control also exists when a particular stimulus controls the absence of a particular operant behavior.

Discriminative Stimuli and Extinction Stimuli

There are names for the two types of stimuli associated with reinforcement and nonreinforcement of a particular response. If an event has been correlated with the availability of a reinforcer for a particular operant behavior, then that event is called a **discriminative stimulus (S^D)** for that response. Loosely speaking, an S^D is a signal that a particular response will pay off. In the example of a golfer attempting to make a putt (see Figure 3-3), the appearance of the flat green was an S^D - a cue that aiming the ball at the hole would be reinforced by the golfer making the putt. If an event has been correlated with extinction trials for a particular operant behavior, then that event is called an **extinction stimulus (S^E)** for that response. Thus, an S^E is a signal that a particular response will not pay off*. In the example of a golfer attempting to make a putt, the stimulus of the sloped green was an S^E for the response of aiming at the hole, it was cue that aiming at the hole would not pay off.

A stimulus can simultaneously be an S^D for one response and an S^E for another; that is, in the presence of a particular stimulus, one response will be reinforced while another will not be reinforced. While eating dinner with a guest, for example, the stimulus, "Pass the salt please" spoken by your guest is an S^D for you to pass the salt (and probably be reinforced by a "Thank you"), and it is simultaneously an S^E for you to pass the pepper (passing the pepper would probably not lead to a "Thank you"). This may be diagrammed as follows:

An Instance of Positive Reinforcement

S^D ⟶   Response ⟶   Reinforcer

("Pass the salt please", spoken by your guest)   (Your behavior of passing the salt)   ("Thank you", spoken by your guest)

An Instance of Extinction

S^E ⟶   Response ⟶   No Reinforcer

("Pass the salt please", spoken by your guest)   (Your behavior of passing the pepper)   (Your guest does not say "Thank you")

Stimulus Discrimination

Stimulus discrimination training refers to: (a) the *procedure* of reinforcing a response in the presence of an S^D and extinguishing that response in the presence of an S^E; and (b) the *result* that the response occurs to the S^D, and not to the S^E. When the latter occurs, the individual is showing a **stimulus discrimination.** In the example in Figure 3-3, when the golfer learned to aim at the hole on a flat green but not on a sloped green, the golfer was demonstrating a stimulus discrimination. The opposite of stimulus discrimination is something called stimulus generalization.

---

* In behavior modification books, an S^E is commonly referred to as an ess-delta (S^Δ).

Stimulus Generalization

Imagine what life would be like if you could not perform a newly learned skill in a new situation that is somewhat different than the situation where you originally learned the skill. You would have to "relearn" how to put mustard on a hotdog with each different mustard dispenser; when playing racquetball, you would learn to hit a forehand shot and have to be taught that shot again when you switch to playing squash; you would learn to hit a golf ball with one club, but be unable to do so when you try to hit a ball with a different club. Fortunately, we have not evolved with such limitations to our adaptability.

If we're conditioned to respond to one particular stimulus, we are more likely to respond to a whole range of similar stimuli. For example, an infant learns to say "kitty" to a furry, four legged creature with a long tail. Later, the infant sees a different kind of cat and says "kitty". This is an instance of what is called stimulus generalization. **Stimulus generalization** refers to: (a) the *procedure* of reinforcing a response in the presence of a stimulus or situation; and (b) the *result* that the response becomes more probable not only in that situation but also in the presence of another stimulus or situation. In other words, stimulus generalization and stimulus discrimination are opposites in that with the former, an individual responds in the same way to two different stimuli, while with the latter, the individual responds differently to two different stimuli. In the above example of the child with the cat, the child showed stimulus generalization because a previously reinforced response (kitty) was emitted in the presence of a new stimulus (a new kind of cat). Still later, the infant sees a dog and again says "kitty". This is another instance of stimulus generalization, even though the response in this case is incorrect, which proves that not all instances of stimulus generalization are favourable and illustrates why it is necessary to teach discriminations (Martin & Pear, 2011).

In order for an athlete to be successful, skills acquired in practices must transfer to competitions. Strategies for programming stimulus generalization from practices to competitions are described in Chapters 14 through 16.

Modeling and Imitation

Modeling is a procedure whereby a sample of a given behavior is presented to an individual to induce that individual to engage in a similar behavior (e.g., see Figure 3-4). As with other behavioral procedures, modeling is common in everyday life. Parents frequently tell their children, "Do it like this" while modeling the desired behavior. Youth athletes see how the "pros" talk and act, and the youngsters are soon behaving the same way. All of us in our daily lives have frequent opportunities to observe the actions of others, and we frequently imitate their behaviors.

The well-known psychologist, Albert Bandura (1986) and others have identified several factors that influence the effectiveness of modeling as a behavior modification

<u>Figure 3-4.</u> Modeling can be an effective instructional tactic.

technique. First, people are more likely to imitate someone who is similar to them in various ways (such as in age, socioeconomic status, physical appearance, etc.) than someone who is quite different from them. Thus, whenever possible, coaches should use athletes as models to influence the behavior of other athletes. Second, one is more likely to imitate individuals perceived as competent or proficient at obtaining consequences than individuals who are seen as less proficient at doing so (Schunk, 1987). To capitalize on this factor when using modeling, one should arrange for an athlete to observe a skilled model emit the desired behavior and receive a reinforcer. Third, the number of individuals modeling a particular behavior is a factor determining whether or not that behavior might be imitated. A young athlete is more likely to attempt a skill if it is modeled by three or four peers than if it is just modeled by one peer. Finally, modeling as a behavior modification strategy is most effective when combined with appropriate instructions. As discussed further in Chapter 10, "show and tell" is more effective than just "showing" or "telling" alone.

Shaping

If a behavior occurs once in a while, then it can be strengthened by following it with a positive reinforcer. But what if you want to increase a behavior that doesn't presently occur? And if you have worked with beginners in any field, you will know that they rarely execute a skill perfectly the first time they try to perform it. One possibility is to capitalize on modeling and imitation, as described previously. Another possibility is a technique called **shaping** - the reinforcement of successive approximations of, or increasingly close attempts at, correct execution, one approximation at a time, until the desired response occurs.

Shaping can be used to modify several aspects or dimensions of behavior. One dimension is the form (or topography) of a behavior. For example, suppose that an ice hockey coach has a young defenseman who continually plays the puck rather than taking the man on a one-on-one basis, even though he has been told frequently to play the man ("playing the man" involves player X making body contact with player Y to a sufficient degree so that player Y is no longer involved in that particular play). During a series of one-on-one drills, the coach might begin by praising the defenseman for simply moving back and forth in the same direction as the oncoming puck carrier. Over the next few trials, the coach might then praise the young defenseman only if he moves in the same direction as the puck carrier and makes some body contact. Finally, the coach might withhold praise on subsequent one-on-one drills until the young defenseman not only makes body contact but makes contact sufficiently to take the oncoming forward out of the play. Note the differences between shaping in this instance and alternative strategies that the coach might have followed. The coach could have told the young player, "Take the body or you'll sit on the bench" (control by threat), or the coach might have had the young defenseman observe a skilled defender model the correct behavior on several trials and have given the young player an opportunity to imitate the skilled player (control by modeling), or the coach might have used some other strategy. With shaping, the coach simply reinforced successive approximations to the final desired behavior. (Discussion of shaping to improve the topography of the serve in tennis is presented in Chapter 10.)

Shaping can also be used to modify the <u>frequency</u> of a behavior (such as the number of repetitions that a golfer practices a particular golf shot), the <u>duration</u> of a behavior (such as the length of time spent treading water in a swimming practice), the <u>intensity</u> (or force) of a behavior (such as the force with which a hockey player can shoot a slap shot), or the <u>latency</u> of a behavior. A common term for latency is "reaction time," such as the time between the firing of the starters pistol until the runner leaves the blocks.

Shaping is so common in everyday life that most people aren't even aware of it. Becoming more skillful at using the keyboard on your computer, learning to shoot a basketball more accurately, changing gears smoothly when driving a car with a stick-shift - all involve shaping across successive trials. Sometimes the shaping procedure is applied systematically, such as during a driver training course, and sometimes non-systematically, such as when the natural reactions of the members of the football team at Florida State University gradually shape the pronunciation of a new player from Canada to talk with a southern drawl. And sometimes your behavior is shaped even though no one else is involved, such as when you perfect your method for making your favourite spaghetti sauce.

Applications of shaping typically follow three steps:

1. Identify the final desired behavior in terms of one or more of its dimensions, i.e., its form (such as the defenceman making body contact sufficiently to take the oncoming forward out of the play), frequency, duration, intensity, or latency;

2. Identify a starting behavior that the individual currently emits and that approximates the target behavior (such as the defenceman moving in the same direction as the forward);

3. Reinforce successive approximations from the starting behavior to the final desired behavior across trials (as indicated previously with the young defenceman).

Chaining

In shaping, some aspect of the behavior (form, force, etc.) is gradually changed. But sometimes an individual is capable of performing each individual response that make up a particular routine, but the responses are not consistently performed in the appropriate sequence. In a procedure called **chaining**, an individual is taught to perform a specific series of steps that are linked together, one after the other. A **behavioral chain** is a consistent sequence of stimuli and responses that follow each other closely in time, and which terminates in a reinforcer. In the behavioral chain of serving in tennis, having the ball in one hand and the racquet in the other provides the cues for the server to stand appropriately at the service line. Standing at the line provides the cues for glancing at the position of the opponent and bouncing the ball once. The next step is for the server to throw the ball in the air above his/her head at the appropriate level for serving, which provides the cue for swinging the racquet at the ball. This final response leads to the reinforcer (hopefully), of making a good serve.

If a new desired behavior does not currently occur, then shaping might be appropriate. However, if the components of a sequence of behaviors are in an individual's repertoire, but they do not occur consistently in the appropriate sequence, then chaining might be appropriate. This was the case with the application of behavioral chaining to improve Steve's pre-putt routine described at the beginning of this chapter. Although there are several alternative strategies for developing a behavioral chain (e.g., see Martin & Pear, 2011), the **total task chaining strategy** is commonly used. This approach was used with Steve and it consists of the following steps:

1. List the sequence of responses (or components or stimulus-response links) in the order in which they should occur in the chain.

2. Arrange practice opportunities in which the athlete is instructed to perform the entire sequence in the proper order on each occasion.

3. Provide corrective feedback and positive reinforcement as needed until the chain occurs correctly several times in succession.

Punishment

A stimulus, the presentation of which *immediately* after a behavior causes the behavior to decrease, is called a **punisher**. Application of a punisher to weaken a behavior is called punishment. More specifically, the principle of **punishment** includes a *procedure*, the presentation of a punisher after a behavior, and *a result*, the behavior is weakened.

Like positive reinforcement, punishment has affected our learning throughout life. The immediate consequences of sitting too close to a campfire, for example, teaches us not to do that again. An infant learns to walk with better balance partly because of the bruises from a few falls. A strong reprimand from your parents may have taught you as a child, not to take candy from the corner store without paying for it. And we have all had our behavior affected by ridicule or unpleasant reactions of others.

Many kinds of events, when delivered as consequences of behavior, fit the definition of punisher given above. Events that act as punishers without prior conditioning or learning are called *unconditioned punishers*. A stimulus paired with punishment becomes itself a punisher. Such a stimulus is called a *conditioned punisher*.

The various events that act as punishers (whether conditioned or unconditioned) can be classified into four categories (Martin & Pear, 2011). *Physical punishment* includes all punishers, contingent on behavior, that activate pain receptors or other sensory receptors which typically evoke feelings of discomfort. Physical punishers are unconditioned punishers and are also referred to as aversive stimuli. Some examples of physical punishers include spankings, cold showers, and maintaining uncomfortable positions for long periods of time. *Reprimands* are strong negative verbal stimuli contingent upon behavior. Reprimands are conditioned punishers. Examples include "No!", "Stop it!", or "Don't be an idiot!" *Timeout* involves transferring an individual from a more reinforcing to a less reinforcing situation following a particular behavior. If a hockey coach makes a child sit on the sidelines while all the other players enjoy participating in a scrimmage, then the child would be experiencing timeout punishment. Timeout might also be thought of as timeout from the opportunity to earn positive reinforcement, and it is a conditioned punisher. *Response cost* involves the removal of a specified amount of reinforcer following a particular behavior, and is a conditioned punisher. Examples of response cost in sports include player fines for violating team rules, a referee taking away points from an amateur boxer during a match because of low blows, and a referee disallowing a goal in ice hockey because the player was inside the goalie's crease when the goal was scored.

In sports, coaches can try to influence their athletes in a positive way by liberally reinforcing desirable behaviors, or they can attempt to control their athletes with a negative approach that emphasizes punishment. Most coaches employ a mixture of these two methods. Unfortunately, the mixture often favours the negative (Rushall, 1983). It is understandable that a coach might occasionally criticize, and generally disapprove of mistakes. However, should punishment be *deliberately and frequently used* to decrease problem behaviors of young athletes?

As a behavior management technique, punishment leaves a great deal to be desired and has a number of troubling side effects. First, punishment can cause frustration and aggressive behavior on the part of the person being punished. We should not be surprised to observe individuals who have just been punished attacking other individuals. Second, strong punishment can produce undesirable emotional side effects such as nervousness and general fearfulness, which, among other things, interfere with skilled performance. Third, punishment does not establish any new behavior; it only suppresses old behavior. In other words, punishment does not teach an individual what to do; at best, it only teaches what not to do. Fourth, children are likely to model or imitate others who use punishment. In one study, for example, a group of 7- and 8-year-old boys who watched a violent TV program were much more aggressive later during a game of floor hockey than were boys who had watched a TV program that did not contain violence (Josephson,

1987). If a coach frequently uses punishment, the coach may be inadvertently providing a model for young athletes to follow in showing aggression toward others. Fifth, and especially important when coaching young athletes, punishment may cause the situation and people associated with the aversive stimulus to become conditioned punishers. Thus, if a young athlete experiences a lot of punishment while participating in a sport, he or she may decide not only to quit the sport but to avoid other similar sports. This may account for many of the nonparticipants in sports among adults. Performance in youth sports or school sports may have been made aversive by overzealous coaches and/or parents, and the avoidance may have generalized to a large number of sports.

Does this mean that coaches should not correct errors because it might be unpleasant to the athlete? Of course not. However, a coach should pay careful attention to the ratio of instances of positive and negative feedback that he or she issues to a young athlete. For a coach of young athletes, the following exercise can be quite informative. The coach might purchase or borrow two wrist counters used for keeping count of golf scores, and wear one on each wrist during a typical practice. Throughout the practice, each time that the coach praises or speaks positively to an athlete, it should be counted on one of the wrist counters. Each time that the coach disapproves, yells, criticizes, reprimands, or shows sarcasm, it should be counted on the other wrist counter. Many coaches will find that they give more negative feedback than positive feedback to young athletes. Some research, however, indicates that a desirable ratio of positive to negative feedback with children in educational settings is 4 to 1 (4 positive, 1 negative) (Madsen & Madsen, 1974; Stuart, 1971). Although no research has examined the most effective ratio for coaching young athletes, a goal of providing positive feedback versus negative feedback at a ratio of at least 3 or 4 to 1 is consistent with recommendations of experts on learning (e.g., Siedentop & Tannehill, 2000; Smith, 2010).

Escape and Avoidance Conditioning

Punishment involves the presentation of an aversive event *after* a behavior in order to *decrease* future instances of that behavior. Aversive events can also be involved in strengthening of responses. In many situations, we have learned behavior to escape from an aversive event. For example, in the presence of an obnoxious odor, we have learned to escape the unpleasant smell by holding our nose. When we walk from a dark room into bright sunlight, we escape the intensity of light by squinting or shading our eyes. When a room is too cold, we escape the chill by turning up the thermostat. The principle of **escape conditioning** (also referred to as negative reinforcement) states that we learn to do things that terminate aversive events, or that allow us to escape them. Note that escape learning is the opposite of punishment: in punishment, the likelihood of certain behavior is *decreased* as a result of *presenting* a punisher after instances of that behavior. In escape learning, the likelihood of certain behavior is *increased* as a result of *terminating* or *removing* a punisher after instances of that behavior. If a certain move by a wrestler, for example, enables the wrestler to escape from a painful hold applied by an opponent, the wrestler is more likely to try that move the next time an opponent applies the painful hold.

In addition to learning behavior that enables us to escape from an unpleasant event that has already occurred, we also learn behaviors that prevent unpleasant events from occurring at all. This latter type of learning is called **avoidance conditioning**. Like escape conditioning, avoidance conditioning is common in everyday life. We take an umbrella to work on cloudy days to avoid getting wet. We put money in parking meters to avoid getting a ticket. We have the oil changed in our car to avoid a costly malfunction. And avoidance learning is also common in sports. A forward in ice hockey learns to keep his/her head up to avoid getting knocked down by an opponent. A football player may learn to work hard at practice to avoid having to do extra wind sprints. And a golfer learns to line up properly when addressing the ball in order to avoid hitting the ball out of bounds. (For a discussion of immediate consequences that may be responsible for avoidance learning, see Martin & Pear, 2011, p. 162.)

Because escape and avoidance learning involve punishers or aversive stimulation, they suffer from many of the same disadvantages as punishment. An individual tends to avoid or escape any situation or person associated with the use of punishers. You probably know people who are often quite antagonistic during conversations, negative in their outlook, and frequently in a bad mood. Chances are that you avoid such people. In sports, if a coach frequently hollers at, criticizes, and ridicules athletes, the athletes are likely to avoid the coach as much as possible. And if the coaching tactics become too aversive, some athletes might quit the sport entirely. While deliberate use of escape or avoidance learning may be defensible in certain cases (Martin & Pear, 2011), the primary emphasis should always be on positive reinforcement for desirable behavior.

Respondent and Operant Conditioning Compared

In Chapter 2, we described principles of respondent conditioning that influences learning of involuntary or reflexive behavior. With respondent conditioning, involuntary behaviors come to be elicited by previously neutral stimuli when those neutral stimuli are paired with unconditioned stimuli that elicit the involuntary behaviors. In this chapter, we described principles and procedures of operant conditioning. With operant conditioning, operant or voluntary behavior is strengthened or weakened by its consequences, and we learn to emit operant behaviors to prior cues (S^Ds or S^Es) because of the consequences of doing so. Major differences between respondent and operant conditioning are summarized in Table 3-2. A thorough knowledge of the principles and procedures of respondent and operant learning are invaluable for the successful application of sport psychology.

Table 3-2

Respondent and Operant Conditioning Compared

	Operant	Respondent
Type of Behavior	-controlled by consequences - referred to as voluntary behavior - usually involves skeletal muscles - is said to be *emitted* by an individual	-automatic responses to prior stimuli - referred to as reflexive or involuntary - usually involves smooth muscles and glands that control our gastrointestinal tract and blood vessels - is said to be *elicited* by prior stimuli
Conditioning Procedure	- in the presence of a stimulus, a response is *followed by* a reinforcer*	- pairing of a neutral stimulus with an eliciting stimulus *prior to* a response
Results of Conditioning	- response is more likely to occur to prior stimulus, now called an S^D**	- response is more likely to occur to the neutral stimulus, now called a CS**
Extinction Procedure	- a response is no longer followed *by* a reinforcer	- the CS is no longer paired with the US
Results of Extinction	- response is less likely to occur to the former S^D	- the CS loses the ability to elicit the CR

*Positive reinforcement is only one of the operant conditioning procedures. Others, discussed earlier in this chapter, are escape conditioning, avoidance conditioning, and punishment.

**Responses to CSs seem to be more automatic and consistent (i.e., involuntary) than responses produced by S^Ds. In an attempt to capture this distinction, behavior analysts consistently talk about operant behavior as being emitted, and respondent behavior as being elicited, and S^Ds are said to evoke responses, while CSs are said to elicit responses.

Study Questions

1. In a sentence each, distinguish between operant conditioning (Chapter 3) and Pavlovian conditioning (Chapter 2).

2. Describe the procedure and result of positive reinforcement.

3. Describe a sport example of positive reinforcement that is not in this chapter. Does your example illustrate the direct effect or indirect effect of positive reinforcement? Justify your choice.

4. Define conditioned reinforcer. Describe two sport examples of conditioned reinforcers that are not in Chapter 3.

5. Distinguish between a natural reinforcer and a deliberately-programmed reinforcer. Illustrate each with a sport example that is not in Chapter 3.

6. Define the procedure and the result of operant extinction, and illustrate with a sport example that is not in Chapter 3.

7. What are two differences between the effects of continuous versus intermittent reinforcement?

8. Define fixed-ratio schedule of reinforcement, and give a sport example that is not in Chapter 3.

9. Define variable-ratio schedule of reinforcement, and give a sport example that is not in Chapter 3.

10. Define fixed-duration schedule of reinforcement, and give a sport example that is not in Chapter 3.

11. Define variable interval schedule with a limited hold and give a sport example that is not in Chapter 3.

12. Define stimulus control and give a sport example that is not in Chapter 3.

13. Define or describe each of the following and give a sport example of each that is not in Chapter 3.
    a) good stimulus control
    b) S^D
    c) S^E

14. Distinguish between stimulus generalization and stimulus discrimination. Give an example of each that is not in Chapter 3.

15. What is modeling? Describe an example in which you were influenced by modeling.

16. List five dimensions of behavior that can be shaped. Illustrate each with a sport example that is not in Chapter 3.

17. List the three steps typically followed in an application of shaping.

18. What is a behavioral chain? Describe a sport example that is not in Chapter 3.

19. Distinguish between the types of target behaviors that are typical for shaping versus chaining.

20. List the three steps typically followed in the total task chaining strategy. Were these steps followed by Steve to improve his pre-putt routine (see the beginning of Chapter 3)? Defend your answer.

21. Describe four categories of punishers. Give a sport example of each.

22. List five troubling side effects of the use of punishment.

23. Define escape conditioning and give a sport example that is not in Chapter 3.

24. Define avoidance conditioning and give a sport example that is not in Chapter 3.

25. Describe two differences between punishment and escape conditioning.

26. List two differences between operant behavior and respondent behavior (any two of the differences listed in Table 3-2).

27. What is the procedure for establishing an S^D? For establishing a CS?

28. Describe the procedure and result of both operant and respondent extinction.

Chapter 4

Rules and Goals: Important Strategies for Influencing Behavior*

```
An Application

Tiger Woods' Drill for Improving his Putting**

     In 2005, Tiger Woods won two major championships after not
winning a major in the previous two seasons. One of the reasons
for his resurgence was his awesome putting, especially for short
putts of approximately 3-feet in length. Here is one of the
practice drills that he used to ensure his success at making
short putts.

     First, at the practice green, he chose a level place on the
green approximately 3-feet from the hole. Next, he placed two
tees in the ground slightly wider than his putter. Next, he
placed a ball in between the two tees, and hit it with his right
hand only, making the putter "go through the gate." He did this
until he made 12 putts in a row. Then he practiced making the
putt six times with both hands on the putter. After making 18
putts (12 with one hand and 6 with both hands), he repeated the
process until he had made 100 putts in a row. If he missed a
putt, he started the drill over again. In Tigers' words, "It is a
great drill to keep you paying attention. You'd be surprised how
sharp your focus becomes when the consequence is starting over."

**This example is based on a report in Golf Digest (November, 2005).
```

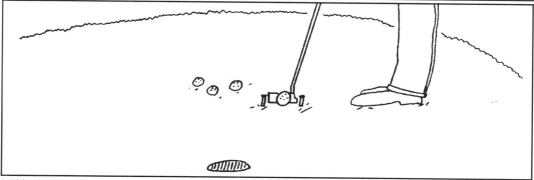

* This chapter is modeled after a chapter on rules and goals in Martin and Pear (2011).

Rule-Governed Control Over Behavior

Superficially, Tigers' successful performance of his drill might be considered as an application of positive reinforcement. After extensive practicing, the reinforcer would be making the 100th putt. However, a careful analysis suggests that something else had to be involved. Making the 100th putt would occur much longer than 30 seconds after making the first few putts. Clearly this was <u>not</u> an example of the direct effect of positive reinforcement for completing the first part of the drill. To fully understand the principles responsible for the behavior improvement in this example, you need to know about rule-governed control over behavior and goal setting.

In behavioral psychology, a **rule** is a statement that a specific behavior will pay off in a particular situation. When we were infants, rules were meaningless to us. But as we acquired language, we learned that following rules often led to reinforcers (e.g., "If you clean your room, you can watch TV"), or enabled us to avoid punishers, (e.g., "If you don't do your homework, you'll have to stay in after school."). Thus, a rule can function as an S^D, a cue that emitting the behavior specified by the rule will lead to the reinforcer identified in the rule (or a cue that not following the rule will lead to a punisher) (Martin & Pear, 2011). As described in Chapter 7, rules can also function as motivating operations.

Sometimes rules clearly identify reinforcers or punishers associated with following the rules, as illustrated in the above examples. In other cases, consequences are implied. If a head coach at a practice calls to an assistant in an excited voice, "Wow! Come and look at this!" going immediately to the head coach will likely enable the assistant to see something interesting. Reinforcers are also implied for rules stated in the form of <u>advice</u>. For example, the advice, "You have to see this movie, you'll love it," implies that doing so will be very entertaining. On the other hand, rules given in the form of a <u>command</u> or a <u>threat</u> imply that noncompliance will be punished. For example, the command by a football coach at a practice, "I want everybody to hustle on and off the field. Don't let me catch you poking along!" implies that not hustling will lead to unpleasantness (such as running extra laps after practice).

Rules that do not identify all three aspects (antecedent, behavior, and consequence) of a reinforcement situation are called <u>partial rules</u>. Some partial rules specify only the behavior (e.g., "Don't touch the ball with your hands"), while the antecedent (when playing soccer) and the consequences (or the referee will blow the whistle) are implied. Other partial rules identify the antecedent (e.g., "Out of bounds" area in golf), while the behavior ("hitting the ball into the out of bounds area") and the consequences ("a penalty stroke and the ball must be hit from the original location") are implied. In other instances, partial rules identify the consequences (e.g., "$500,000 1st prize"), while the antecedents ("at our golf tournament"), and the behavior ("play better golf than the other competitors") are implied. Because of our various learning experiences, partial rules also control our behavior.

Contingency-Learned Versus Rule-Governed Behavior

Some of our behaviors are acquired through trial and error. Consider, for example, the first time a person attempts to play miniature golf. Sometimes that person doesn't' hit the ball hard enough to get it to the hole. At other times, the ball is hit much harder than is necessary. Eventually, that person gets better and better at hitting the ball just hard enough to get it to the hole. In this example, we would refer to the behavior of hitting the ball as **contingency-learned behavior** - behavior that has been strengthened (or weakened) in settings by the direct effects of consequences in those settings. Now consider a different example. Suppose that a coach of a youth hockey team says to players at the beginning of a passing drill, "If everybody makes five accurate passes, we'll have an extra five minutes of scrimmage at the end of practice." During the drill, the players meet the goal and earn the reinforcer. In this example, accurate passing would be referred to as **rule-governed behavior** - behavior that is controlled by the statement of a rule.

Contingency-learned behavior and rule-governed behavior typically differ in at least two ways. First, contingency-learned behavior is typically strengthened gradually through trial and error, while the presentation of a rule frequently leads to immediate behavior change. Secondly, contingency learned behavior involves immediate consequences, while rule-governed behavior often involves delayed consequences.

Knowledge of rule-governed behavior enables us to explain applications involving reinforcers in which the reinforcers are quite delayed following the occurrence of the critical behaviors, such as in Tiger Woods' putting drill. In Tigers' drill, the reinforcer of making the 100th putt was quite delayed following the first few putts of the drill. It's likely that part way through the drill, Tiger rehearsed a rule such as, "I've made 50 putts in a row, only 50 more to go." It's likely that this type of statement functioned as a conditioned reinforcer for completing the first part of the drill, and it likely exerted rule-governed control over completion of the last part of the drill.

Why Do Rules Control Our Behavior?

Rule-governed behavior is so common in most of us that it is almost impossible for us to imagine anyone responding simply on the basis of contingency-learned behavior. Early in our lives, however, our operant behavior was entirely contingency-learned. For example, most parents use the shaping procedure while teaching their children to talk. When an infant first begins to babble, the parents usually reinforce the behavior with hugs and smiles. English-speaking parents are likely to be especially attentive to the sounds "maa" and "daa". When such children eventually say, "Mama" and "Dada", these approximations are strongly reinforced. At a later stage, reinforcement is given after the child says "mommy" and "daddy". The same process also occurs with other words. And while this description greatly oversimplifies the way in which a child learns to talk, it does illustrate the importance of the direct effect of reinforcement in the process by which normal children gradually progress from babbling to baby talk and finally to speaking in accordance with prevailing social conventions. As our language skills improved, we learned to follow rules (Hayes, 1989; Skinner, 1957, 1969).

It's easy to understand why people learn to follow rules that describe direct-acting consequences. Following the rule, "Try this dessert, it's delicious," will be reinforced immediately by the taste of the dessert. Failure to follow the rule, "Wait a couple of minutes before drinking your coffee, it's extremely hot," will likely lead to a fairly immediate punisher. But why do we follow rules that identify very delayed consequences? There are several possibilities (Martin & Pear, 2011). First, although the reinforcer identified in a rule might be delayed for an individual, other people might provide immediate consequences if the individual follows (or does not follow) the rule. In the example of the hockey coach who provided the rule for the players to earn extra scrimmage time for good passing, the coach might also have said immediately following a pass, "Good pass! Keep it up and you'll earn extra scrimmage time."

Second, an individual might follow a rule and then immediately make reinforcing statements to him or herself. In the case of the passing drill, for example, after making a good pass, a player might have thought to himself, "The scrimmage is going to be fun." Alternatively, failure to comply with a rule might lead to self-punishment. Suppose, for example, that an individual makes a resolution to exercise before dinner each evening. If, upon arriving home from work, the individual sits in front of the TV set instead of exercising, the individual might think, "Don't be such a couch potato. Stick with your plan; get up and exercise!" (Note that, while this self-statement might serve as a conditioned punisher for sitting in front of the TV set without exercising, it also contains the ingredients of a new rule, "If I exercise, I won't be a couch potato.")

A third possibility is that our learning history with respect to emotions (discussed further in Chapter 9) is such that following rules is automatically strengthened and failure to follow rules is automatically punished by what we feel. Suppose, for example, that a student gives herself the rule, "I'd better start studying my sport psychology text now or I'll fail the exam tomorrow." Because of her history of being punished for failing to meet deadlines, such a statement might elicit some anxiety. When she starts studying, her anxiety decreases, and her rule-following is maintained by escape conditioning. Stated more generally, because of our past experiences, an approaching deadline causes us to feel anxious, and following a rule to meet the deadline then makes us feel a lot better (Malott, 1989).

Situations Where Rules are Especially Helpful

For positive reinforcement to increase an individual's behavior, it is *not* necessary that the individual be aware of or indicate an understanding of why he or she was reinforced (Greenspoon, 1951). After all, the principle has been shown to work quite effectively with animals that can't talk (at least not in human language). However, the addition to reinforcement programs of instruction in the form of rules will increase the effectiveness of such programs in the following situations (Baldwin & Baldwin, 2001; Skinner, 1969, 1974).

<u>When rapid behavior change is desirable</u>. Correct use of rules can produce behavior change much more rapidly than trial and error experiences with reinforcement and extinction (Martin & Pear, 2011). Consider, for example, the case of a young figure skater who is extremely nervous just before skating her program at an important competition. While talking to her sport psychologist, the skater expresses her concerns: "I hope I don't fall on my double axel. I hope I don't come in last. What if I don't skate well?" How can the sport psychologist help the skater? The psychologist might ask the skater to repeat self-talk such as, "I've landed all of my jumps in practice and I can land them all here," "I'll focus on the things that I do when I'm skating well, and I"ll take it one step at a time," "I'll smile, have fun, and play to the judges," and so on. In this example, the psychologist is essentially capitalizing on rule-governed control over behavior. The skater was given a rule (i.e., "If I focus on the things that I think about when I'm skating well at practice, then I'll land all the elements in my program, just like I do at practice."). Rehearsing the rule might help the skater to focus on the cues that normally enable her to land her jumps, rather than worrying about falling. (The statement of the rule might also function as a conditioned stimulus to elicit the relaxed feelings that were typically experienced at practices, as described in Chapter 9.)

<u>When consequences that might be provided for a behavior are too delayed to directly reinforce that behavior</u>. In Tiger Woods' putting drill, making the 100th putt in a row was considerably delayed following completion of the first few putts of the drill. By adding a rule, "If I miss a putt I have to start the drill over again," Tiger focused carefully on each putt and increased the chances of the delayed reinforcer of the 100th putt having an indirect effect on making the first few putts.

<u>When you would like to maintain a behavior for which natural reinforcers are immediate, but highly intermittent</u>. Suppose that a figure skater is learning several new jumps. When a new jump is landed, the skater feels great (i.e., the reinforcer is immediate), but the skater may land only one jump in ten or fifteen attempts. In other words, the schedule of reinforcement is highly intermittent. The coach might increase the persistence of the skater by encouraging her to rehearse the rule, "Be persistent! The very next time I try the jump I might land it."

When a specific behavior will lead to immediate and severe punishment. Rules can help people learn appropriate behavior in situations where learning "the hard way" can be extremely costly. In ice hockey, for example, if a player aggressively touches or pushes a referee, the player can be ejected from the game and can receive a lengthy suspension. Most hockey players learn at a very early age to follow the rule, "Never touch a referee."

Effective and Ineffective Rules

In the preceding section, I described several situations where use of rules might influence athletic performance. Many additional examples are presented in Chapter 8, which presents guidelines for helping athletes to use self-talk to improve their performance. But in order to be maximally effective in helping athletes, it is useful to understand five conditions that affect the likelihood of rule-following behavior.

Specific versus vague behavior. Suppose that you tell a golfer, "If you concentrate more, you will improve your putting." Is that rule likely to be helpful? Probably not, because the behavior - concentrating more - is extremely vague. A rule that describes a behavior vaguely is less likely to be followed than a rule that describes a specific behavior, provided that there is adequate reinforcement for rule-following. A more effective rule for the golfer would be, "When putting, keep your eyes down and your head still until after you have stroked the ball."

Sizeable versus small consequences. Suppose that a university professor announces to students in a course, "Next Monday we will have an exam that will be worth 50% of your final grade." Would most students in that course study for the exam? Probably yes! On the other hand, suppose that the professor announces, "Next Tuesday, we will have an exam that will be worth 1% of your final grade." Would the students likely study for such an exam? Perhaps some would, but many wouldn't. Rules that describe behavior that leads to large consequences are more effective than rules that describe behavior that leads to small consequences, even if the consequences are delayed.

In some cases, each instance of following a rule leads to small, immediate consequences, and it is often necessary to follow the rule many times in order for the consequences to accumulate and become noticeable (Malott, 1989, 1992). Such rules are usually not effective. Suppose, for example, that an individual resolves, "I'm going to exercise several times a week and get in better shape". In this case, the benefits (e.g., better blood circulation, extra energy, etc.) from a single instance of exercising aren't noticeable. It is only after that person has exercised regularly over several weeks that the benefits would become noticeable. In other cases, punishers for failing to follow a rule are small and only cumulatively significant. Such rules are also not effective. One reason that many people fail to follow the rule, "I'll cut back on my food intake and lose some weight", is that the immediate, negative effects of a single instance of excessive eating are too small to be noticeable. It is the cumulative effects of excessive eating on numerous occasions that causes excessive weight and other health problems. Rules that describe small consequences that are harmful or beneficial only after they have accumulated are likely to be ineffective unless complimented by additional self-management strategies such as modeling, self-monitoring, and behavioral contracting (see Chapter 13).

Probable versus improbable consequences. Rules that describe sizeable consequences for specific behavior are likely to be followed only if those consequences *are* *likely* to occur. Stated differently, rules that describe consequences that are highly improbable are not very effective. For example, most people know that it is wise to wear a life jacket when canoeing. However, they also know that a serious boating accident while canoeing is highly unlikely. Therefore, many people don't wear a life jacket while canoeing. Thus, if a rule that describes improbable consequences is to be effective, that rule may need to be complemented by additional self-management strategies (see Chapter 13).

Consequences might act against rule-following. Some rules are difficult to follow because the opposite behavior is immediately reinforced. Suppose, for example, that you give yourself the rule, "I'm going to stop eating desserts in order to lose some weight". That rule is difficult to follow because the opposite behavior, eating desserts, is immediately reinforced by the good taste of the food. Other rules are difficult to follow because following the rule leads to fairly immediate punishers. For example, a person might decide, "If I wear my safety helmet while cycling, I can avoid the possibility of serious brain damage from an accident." But wearing a helmet is often hot and uncomfortable, which is one of the reasons that many people cycle without wearing a helmet. When there are consequences that act against rule-following, it may be necessary to compliment the rules with additional behavior management strategies (see Chapter 13).

Deadlines. Suppose that a swim instructor says to a group of children at the swimming pool, "If you put all the equipment away, I'll bring you a treat next week." Are the children likely to put the equipment away for such a delayed reinforcer? What if the swim instructor says to the children, "If you put all the equipment away *right now*, I'll bring you a treat next week." Would specifying "right now" make a difference? Surprisingly, it would. Braam and Malott (1990) found that, with young children, rules to perform behavior with no deadline and a one-week delay of the reinforcer were relatively ineffective, while rules to perform behavior with a deadline and a one-week delay of the reinforcer were quite effective. By the time that most of us were in elementary school, we had learned that failure to meet deadlines often leads to unpleasantness, and meeting deadlines is often reinforced.

Figure 4-1. When providing instructions (i.e., rules) coaches should clearly identify sizeable and probable consequences that will occur for specific behavior of athletes.

To summarize, *rules that describe **deadlines** for **specific behavior** that will lead to **sizeable** and **probable outcomes** are often effective, even when the outcomes are delayed.* On the other hand, *rules that describe behavior vaguely, do not identify a deadline for the behavior, lead to small or improbable consequences for the behavior, and/or have consequences that act against rule-following are often ineffective.*

A Summary of Guidelines for Using Rules Effectively

Here are some guidelines for the effective use of rules (Martin & Pear, 2011, p. 211):

1. The rules should be within the understanding of the individual to whom they are applied.

2. Rules should clearly identify:
   a. The circumstances in which the behavior should occur;
   b. The specific behavior in which the individual is to engage;
   c. A deadline for performing the behavior;
   d. The specific consequences for complying or not complying with the rules.

3. Rules should describe probable and sizable outcomes, rather than improbable and small outcomes. (Rules that describe improbable and/or small consequences should be supplemented by the additional behavior management strategies described in Chapter 13.)

4. Complex rules should be broken into easy-to-follow steps.

5. Rules should be gradually faded out if you want other stimuli that are present to take control of the behavior.

Goals

In sports, goal setting programs have led to improvements in many areas (e.g. kicking field goals in football, making jump shots in basketball, punches landed in boxing, fielding without errors in baseball, and making putts in golf) (Gould, 2010; O'Brien, Mellalieu, & Hanton, 2009; Ward, 2011; Weinberg, & Gould, 2011). A precisely stated **goal** describes a target behavior or outcome, the situation in which it should occur, and the consequences for achieving it. In the previous section, a rule was described as a statement that a specific behavior would pay off in a particular situation. Thus, from a behavioral perspective, a goal is a rule. For example, in the Tiger Woods drill described in the beginning of the chapter, Tiger said, "I'll practice putting until I make 100 in a row from 3-feet." Tiger identified the situation (at the practice putting green), the behavior (practicing 3-foot putts), and the consequences (making 100 in a row, with the implication that he would putt better on the course). As is the case with the use of rules, goal-setting is used to influence athletes to improve performance when reinforcers are delayed (e.g., Tiger might have to practice for a considerable period of time before making 100 in a row) or are immediate but highly intermittent (e.g. a figure skater might initially land only one out of every eight attempts at a particular jump).

Effective and Ineffective Goal Setting

The efficacy of goal setting as a performance improvement strategy is well established, provided that a number of conditions are met (Locke & Latham, 2002; Ward, 2011; Gould, 2010).

Specific goals are more effective than vague goals. Rather than a goal of "having a better relationship," for example, a figure skating dance pair might agree to tell each other on a daily basis at least three things that they appreciate about the other person, and to focus on what they want to do rather than on what they don't want to do in their relationship. As another example, it would be more effective for a middle-distance runner to set a goal of training sufficiently to run the 1000-meters 20 seconds faster than his/her current best time, rather than setting a goal of "getting faster".

Goals with respect to learning of specific skills should include mastery criteria. A **mastery criterion** is a specific guideline for performing a skill such that if the guideline is met, the skill is likely to be mastered. A mastery criterion should identify a particular quantity, level, or standard of performance. Examples might include making 10 tennis volleys in a row alternating left and right corners, making three one-handed catches in a row of a 15-yard pass in football, making 10 jump shots in a row from 10 feet in basketball, or making five goals out of 10 shots from 20 feet in soccer with the goalie free to move. A mastery criterion is typically formulated to make it likely that two assumptions will be met. First, once the athlete has achieved the mastery criterion, it is likely that he or she has learned the skill well enough so that, if asked to do it sometime later, the skill would be performed correctly. Second, if the athlete has met a mastery criterion during practice, there is a high probability that the skill will be executed correctly during a competition.

Goals should identify the circumstances under which the desirable behavior should occur. A goal for a basketball player to "practice jump shots" is somewhat vague. A goal to "practice jump shots until you can make five in a row from 10 feet, with a defender standing three feet in front of you" identifies the circumstances surrounding the performance.

<u>Realistic, specific, challenging goals are more effective than "do your best" goals</u>. A number of studies have found that specific, challenging goals lead to better performance than a goal of "do your best" (Locke & Latham, 2002). Why do you suppose that is? One reason that "do your best" goals for young athletes at competitions may not be effective is that the advice, "Just do your best" may not be interpreted by a young athlete in the way that the advice is meant when offered by a well-meaning parent or coach. In my work with young figure skaters, for example, I observed that parents providing such advice to a skater just before a competition meant to convey that the skater should try to perform like they had been doing in practice, have fun, and not put too much pressure on him or herself. But the young skaters interpreted "do your best" advice from parents as meaning, "I have to try to skate the best that I've ever skated in my life," and that frequently influenced the young skaters to feel unnecessary pressure and tension, which disrupted their performance. The reason that "do your best" goals at practices may be less effective than specific challenging goals is that individuals instructed to simply "do their best" may set relatively easy goals, and as suggested by Locke and Latham, difficult or challenging goals at practices may produce better performance than easier goals.

Whether one is setting goals for a practice, or just before a competition, is a factor to be considered when attempting to assess whether or not a goal is challenging. For practices, athletes should be encouraged to challenge themselves to show some improvement on their previous best performance. For example, a figure skater who has recently learned to land a double axel, and has landed one out of three attempts at a practice, might set a goal of landing two out of three for the next practice. But just before a competition, setting "challenging" goals may not be the best strategy, depending on the sport. In figure skating, for example, it is totally unrealistic to expect a figure skater to land a jump in a competition that has never been landed in a practice. If a skater can skate as well in a competition as he or she has skated during the last couple of weeks leading up to that competition, then that would be considered a highly successful performance. Realistic goal setting for competitions is discussed further in Chapters 15 and 16.

<u>Public goals are usually more effective than private goals</u>. In many areas of behavior modification, public goals have been demonstrated to be more effective than private goals (e.g., Hayes et al., 1985). Public goals for a person are goals that at least one other person, and usually several or more other people, are aware of. Hayes and colleagues theorized that setting a public goal provides a public standard against which performance can be evaluated, and that it implies social consequences for achieving or not achieving the goal(s).

<u>Goal setting is more effective if deadlines are included</u>. As indicated previously, we all have a history of being reinforced for meeting various deadlines, and for

encountering aversiveness when deadlines are not met. Capitalizing on this history increases the effectiveness of goal setting. Suppose, for example, that a figure skater sets a goal of adding a new triple jump to his program during the coming season. Shorter term goals might include landing the triple jump by itself at practices by the end of the spring season, landing that jump when the entire program is skated at a practice during the summer season, and landing that jump during the program at a competition by the second month of the fall season.

Goal setting plus feedback is more effective than goal setting alone. Goals are more likely to be met if feedback indicates degree of progress toward the goal. One way of providing feedback is to chart the progress being made. Individuals who chart their progress toward a goal are likely to find improvements on the chart to be reinforcing.

Goal setting is most effective when individuals are committed to the goals. Goals are likely to be effective only if there is continuing commitment to them by the individuals involved. From a behavioral perspective, **commitment** refers to statements or actions by a person setting a goal that imply that the goal is important, that he or she will work toward it, and that he or she recognizes the benefits of doing so (Martin & Pear, 2011).

Researchers in the area of self-management have identified several strategies for helping individuals to keep their commitment strong. First, making one's commitment public to work toward specific goals increases the number of people who can remind one to stick to the program, which increases chances of success (Hayes et al., 1985; Shelton & Levy, 1981). Second, an athlete can be encouraged to rearrange his or her environment to provide frequent reminders of their commitment to their goal (Watson & Tharp, 2007). Examples include writing one's goals on 3x5 cards and leaving them in conspicuous places, such as taped to the door of one's fridge or on the dashboard of one's car, and creatively using photographs to remind them of their goals. Third, one can frequently review the benefits of achieving the goal. Fourth, because individuals undoubtedly encounter temptations to give up on their goal, they should plan ahead for various ways to deal with those temptations (e.g., see Martin & Pear, 2011).

A Summary of Guidelines for Goal Setting

There are clearly some ways of setting goals that are more effective for influencing behavior than others. If, for example, a goal is vague, with no deadline or timeline for meeting it, and without a feedback mechanism for monitoring progress, then it is not likely to influence behavior. If, on the other hand, you practice goal setting according to the following guidelines, then goal setting can be an effective behavior modification strategy (Martin & Pear, 2011).

1. Set goals that are specific, realistic, and challenging.

    a. If the goal concerns learning a skill, then mastery criteria should be included.

    b. Goals for practices should include some "stretch" beyond the individual's current capabilities, while goals for competition should be within the individual's optimal practice performance range, especially for sports like figure skating, gymnastics, diving, and golf.

2. The circumstances in which the behavior (that leads to the goal) is to occur should be identified.

3. There should be sizeable and probable consequences for meeting the goal, or not meeting the goal.

4. Longer term goals should be broken down into several shorter term goals.

5. If the goal is complex, the process should include an action plan for meeting it.

6. There should be deadlines for goal attainment.

7. Individuals involved in goal setting should demonstrate clear commitment to the goals.

8. There should be a system for monitoring progress toward goals.

9. Positive feedback should be provided as progress toward goals is achieved.

Study Questions

1. Define a rule, and give a sport example that was not in this chapter. Does your example illustrate all 3 aspects of a complete rule?

2. What is a partial rule? Describe a sport example that is not in this chapter. Which of the three aspects of a rule does your example specify?

3. Define contingency-learned behavior, and give a sport example that is not in this chapter.

4. Define rule-governed behavior and give a sport example that is not in this chapter.

5. Did Tiger Woods' drill for improving putting involve contingency-learned behavior, or rule-governed behavior, or both? Defend your answer.

6. Describe two typical differences between contingency-learned versus rule-governed behavior.

7. Describe three plausible explanations of why we learn to follow rules which have delayed consequences.

8. Identify four situations where rules are helpful. Give a sport example of each situation.

9. Why is it that the rule, "I'm going to exercise more so that I will feel better," often is not effective for a person?

10. What is a reason that many people do not wear a helmet when riding a bicycle even though doing so could prevent brain damage from a serious accident?

11. What are two reasons that the rule, "I'm going to eat healthier and lose some weight," is so difficult to follow for many people?

12. What are four characteristics of rules that are often effective in controlling behaviour?

13. What are five characteristics of rules that are often ineffective in controlling behavior?

14. What is a mastery criterion? Give a sport example that is not in this chapter.

15. A mastery criterion is typically formulated so that what two assumptions are likely to be met?

16. With young athletes, why is it that "do your best" goals may not be effective at competitions? Why might they not be effective at practices?

17. According to Hayes and colleagues, why is public goal setting likely to be more effective than private goal setting?

18. From a behavioral perspective, what is the meaning of commitment in the context of goal setting? Give a sport example that illustrates all three components of commitment.

19. List four strategies for helping an individual to maintain commitment to meet specific goals.

Chapter 5

The ABCs of Performance Feedback

An Application

Influencing Speed Skaters to Work Hard at Practices[*]

Twelve speed skaters ranging in age from 12-17 years made up the Manitoba Provincial Speed Skating Team that was preparing for the Canada Winter Games. The team typically skated 5 times a week for 1-hour each time. Three of the skaters, however, showed considerable off-task behavior such as not paying attention when the coach was talking, fooling around with other skaters, and continuing to stand and stretch while they were supposed to be skating. In a typical practice the 3 skaters averaged completion of approximately 32 laps per practice of the oval skating rink, and approximately 85% of the skating drills assigned by the coach.

With the help of Connie Wanlin, a Masters student at the University of Manitoba, the skaters agreed to participate in a **goal-setting, self-monitoring,** and **performance feedback** project. Skaters were encouraged to set written weekly goals for number of laps skated and drills completed, and to use their weekly goals to set written daily practice goals for each behavior. They recorded their daily performance in their log books, evaluated their performance at the end of each practice, and met with Connie once per week to discuss their progress and receive feedback. During the intervention which lasted for several weeks, the 3 skaters showed an average of 73% improvement in the number of laps skated per practice, and they averaged 98% completion of the drills assigned by the coach. Racing times obtained in practice and competitions also improved for all three skaters. The coach rated the performance feedback package very highly and observed that, during the intervention, the 3 skaters were more motivated, more attentive and more focused.

[*]This application is based on a report by Wanlin, Hrycaiko, Martin & Mahon (1997).

Performance feedback is a commonly used strategy to improve athletic performance. But, from the point of view of behavior analysis, what is performance feedback? Why is it an effective behavior management strategy? And what are the components of an effective performance feedback system? Those questions will be addressed in this chapter. But first, let's consider the ABCs of behavior management.

Antecedents, Behavior, and Consequences

You will recall from Chapter 3 that operant behavior is prompted by antecedents (S^Ds or S^Es) and is strengthened or weakened by its consequences (reinforcers, or the lack of them during operant extinction, and punishers). Identifying the antecedents and consequences that influence a particular operant behavior is sometimes referred to as an ABC (antecedents, behavior, and consequences) assessment. If we want to know why a particular behavior is occurring or not occurring, we would examine the current antecedents and consequences for that behavior. In the case of Connie and the speed skaters at the beginning of this chapter, Connie had observed, prior to implementing her program, that the typical practice conditions had become an S^D for off-task behavior by the three skaters (which had been reinforced by fooling around with the other skaters), and an S^E for the three skaters to be attentive and focused (which apparently had not been sufficiently reinforced). The implementation of the goal setting, self-monitoring, and performance feedback system rearranged the contingencies so that the speed skaters experienced S^Ds for desirable practice behaviors and positive reinforcement for emitting those behaviors. Now let's consider how performance feedback fits into an ABC assessment of the control of operant sport behavior.

What is Performance Feedback?

In general, **performance feedback** is a consequence of an operant behavior that can influence: (a) future instances of that behavior; and/or (b) future instances of an alternative behavior. One type of performance feedback is the internal stimulation generated from movement, and that is referred to as **proprioceptive feedback** (also referred to as kinesthetic sensations). These are the internal sensations generated by the position and movement of the body in space, and by the position and movement of parts of the body with respect to other parts. Learning to be responsive to proprioceptive cues is a part of the process of becoming aware of our body positions and movements (Martens & Collier, 2011). This type of feedback, following successful and unsuccessful instances of a particular behavior, enables an individual to learn to successfully repeat a behavior. Suppose, for example, using modelling and praise, an adult teaches a young child to close her hand into a fist when the adult says, "Make a fist," and to show her hand open when the adult says, "Open your hand." After these two responses have been learned, the adult would then be able to say to the child, "Close your eyes, now make a fist without looking at your hand," and the child would be able to do so because she has learned to respond to the proprioceptive feedback that is generated when her hand is closed to make a fist. Now consider some sport examples. After a young athlete has learned a sport skill (either through trial and error or through instruction from a coach), then proprioceptive feedback enables the individual to successfully repeat that skill, such as shooting a basketball accurately from the free throw line, or swinging a bat at the coming pitch in baseball, or jumping high enough to clear the bar in high jumping, or accurately returning a serve in tennis.

A second type of performance feedback might be called **external sensory**

feedback, which consists of the natural sights, sounds, and smells that occur as consequences of our behavior. For example, when a basketball player makes a shot, the player can *see* the ball going through the hoop, and *hear* the sound of the ball swishing through the net. Alternatively, if a player misses the shot, he/she will have different sensory feedback (such as seeing and hearing the ball bounce off the backboards).

A third type of performance feedback might be referred to as **external informational feedback,** which is a judgment provided to an athlete about the quality of performance that the athlete has just displayed. This type of feedback is often provided to athletes by coaches or judges or timers. For example, a figure skater will know, from the proprioceptive feedback, whether or not a jump has been landed, but the figure skater will have difficulty judging the quality of his/her choreographed presentation until the skater hears the presentation score from the judges. As another example, a swimmer will not know how fast he/she has just completed a 100-meter race until the time is posted. Informational feedback is often provided to an athlete after the athlete has been following a particular practice routine for a period of time, and it lets the athlete know whether or not his/her practice routines are paying off.

An interesting example of informational feedback was described by Stokes, Luiselli, Reed, and Flemming (2010). They worked with a coach of a high school football team to improve pass blocking of offensive linemen. The coach first informed each player about specific steps to be performed to try to successfully block a pass. Then, during a practice, when a player successfully implemented the pass blocking strategy, the coach sounded a bull horn that produced a siren lasting one second. This combination of instruction and acoustical feedback was very effective for improving the performance of the players.

External informational feedback for effort can encourage athletes to put a high level of effort into the execution of various practice routines. Although assessment of effort is subjective, one possible strategy is for the coach and the athletes to use a rating scale with behavioral "anchoring" points. For example, coaches and beginning swimmers in the Manitoba Marlins Swim Club each assessed effort at the end of practices (Martin et al., 1983). Swimmers were encouraged to assess themselves on a scale of 1 to 10. A 10 meant, "You have worked hard to swim each of the sets without resting during the set, you started each of the sets when I asked you to, without wasting time adjusting your goggles or fooling around, you practiced your racing turns, and you completed all of your sets within the times." A 5 meant "You fooled around a lot, skipped some laps on three or more sets, stopped at the end of the lane at least five or six times during practice, and took two or three bathroom breaks." Athletes who gave themselves a score of 6, 7, 8, or 9, were somewhere in between. At the end of each practice, the swimmers and coaches sat down as a group, and one of the coaches asked, "OK, how many would rate yourself as at least a 5? How about a 6?" and so on. By a show of hands, each swimmer indicated their self-rating. The coaches then indicated what they considered the overall team rating to be. If the swimmers wanted coaches to indicate their assessment of individual ratings, this was done privately. In general, there was considerable agreement between the ratings assigned by the coaches and the ratings assigned by the swimmers. Before implementing this system, the coaches had rated approximately half of the swimmers as showing an effort of 8 or more at a typical practice, while the other half were typically rated only 7 or less. After the rating system was implemented, almost all of the swimmers both swam (according to the coaches' ratings) and self-rated somewhere in the neighbourhood of 8, 9, or 10.

A fourth type of feedback might be referred to as **external instructional feedback,** which consists of instructions presented to an athlete about a skill that was just performed. The instructions might identify aspects of the skill that were performed correctly, aspects of the skill that should be performed differently, or both. For example, a basketball coach might tell a young player, "You're not following through enough when you're shooting free throws." As another example, a figure skating coach might tell a young skater who is working on her double axel, "You're stepping too far on your take off foot, set your take off foot closer to your back foot." Instructional feedback is very important for teaching athletes about the aspects of a particular skill that they are performing correctly, and about those aspects that need to be changed and improved.

Why Does Performance Feedback Lead to Improved Performance?

Performance feedback to an athlete can lead to improved future performance by that athlete for one or more of three reasons.

1. Positive Reinforcement or Punishment of the Preceding Behavior.

Independent of whether the feedback is internal or external, it can function as a reinforcer or a punisher for the preceding behavior, and strengthen or weaken the behavior accordingly. Here are some examples. The internal sensations experienced by a young figure skater who has just landed his/her first triple jump are highly reinforcing. The internal sensations experienced by a pole vaulter who hits the bar and has a bad fall are highly punishing. The external information provided by a track coach can be highly reinforcing (e.g., "Great run, you beat your previous speed by two seconds.") or very punishing (e.g., "That was a bad run; you were two seconds slower than your best speed.")

Sometimes, following a behavior, there will be more than one source of feedback that will have a reinforcing or a punishing effect on the preceding behavior. For example, if a basketball player follows through on a free throw and sees the ball going through the basket, the visual feedback increases the likelihood that the player will follow through on the next shot. If the player's coach, immediately after the ball goes in, hollers out, "Great follow through," that external feedback will also have a reinforcing effect on the player's follow-though. Alternatively, if the same player does not follow through on a free throw, and misses the shot, then the visual feedback and a shout from the coach ("You didn't follow through") will both serve as punishers.

2. Rule Control Over Future Performance

When an athlete is given instructional feedback, that feedback can exert rule-governed control over future attempts to perform that behavior. In the previous example of the basketball player making the free throw and the coach shouting "Great follow through," the coach was essentially giving the player a rule (e.g., "If I follow through on my free throws I am more likely to make them."). This function of feedback is especially important when an athlete performs a skill inappropriately, and the coach points out what was wrong and also explains what should be done in order to perform the skill correctly. Many coaches have experienced considerable success with this type of feedback. For example, one of the most successful college basketball coaches of all time was UCLA's John Wooden. Psychologists Ronald Gallimore and Roland Tharp (2004) attended 15 of Wooden's practices and recorded and categorized his comments to his players. Seventy-five per cent of Wooden's comments to his players contained instructional feedback, most of which focused on what the players should be doing and whether or not they were doing it.

3. Motivation

In Chapter 7 you will read about a behavioral analysis of motivation and athletic performance. After reading that chapter, it will be very clear to you that performance feedback can play a powerful role in motivating and directing athletes' behavior towards the accomplishment of particular tasks. This was illustrated by the feedback package implemented by Connie with the speed skaters at the beginning of this chapter.

Putting it All Together: A Performance Feedback System

The task of improving the performance of a group of athletes in practice can be difficult. The coach must consider the nature of the sport (team vs. individual), the various reasons that the athletes are participating, the developmental level of the individuals involved, and a host of other things. The following is a general system that can be applied to improve athletic performance in a number of different sports, either group or individual. The components of the system include goal-setting (rule-governed control over behavior), performance monitoring, display of results, and frequent feedback for goal attainment. (For an additional discussion and examples of these components, see Ward, 2011.) These components can also be used in self-management programs, as described in Chapter 13.

1. Identify Behaviors that You Wish to Improve

The first step is to identify specific, measurable behaviors of the athlete(s) to be increased and/or maintained. Examples include the number of laps to be swum per hour, the total distance to be run each day, the number of correct jumps to be performed in a figure skating practice, the time required to complete a set exercise routine, the number of correct executions of backfield plays, the percentage of correct blocks by linemen in football, or the percentage of accurate serves in tennis.

Sometimes it might be helpful to assign points to particular behaviors so that each individual can be given a total score at the end of practice. For example, a point system for evaluating player performance during ice hockey scrimmages at the college level is shown in Figure 5-1. Other examples include performance indicators for high school basketball and football practices (Siedentop, 1980), age group swimming practices (Cracklen & Martin, 1983; Martin et al., 1983; McKenzie & Rushall, 1974), play execution of the offensive backfield on a youth football team (Komaki & Barnett, 1977), exhibition games for a barn-storming baseball team (Heward, 1978), service accuracy in volleyball (McKenzie & Liskevych, 1983), volleying skill of collegiate tennis players (Landin & Hebert, 1999), defensive skills of collegiate football players (Ward & Carnes, 2002), and offensive skills of high school soccer players (Brobst & Ward, 2002).

Goals for	+4	Goals scored against	-2
Assists	+4	Losing turnover	-1
Goals scored for (but didn't get goal or assist)	+2	Penalty in offensive zone	-1
Shots on goal	+2	Penalty when on power play	-1
Shots at goal	+1	Face-off lost	-1
Going to aid of teammate	+1		
Headmanning puck to open player	+1		
Forcing turnover	+3		
Finishing check	+2		
Face-off won	+1		
Prepared by Paul Milton			

Figure 5-1. A point system for evaluating player performance during ice hockey scrimmages.

2. Arrange for the Behaviors to be Recorded and Charted

In order to evaluate the effectiveness of a performance feedback program, and to provide additional feedback to the athletes, the behaviors to be improved should be recorded and charted over time. At the beginning of Chapter 7, I describe how Coach Dawson and Daryl Siedentop taught student managers to record various statistics at practices of the Clinton Junior High basketball team. Parents or other volunteers might also be enlisted to record behavior during repeated practices and to make that information available to the participants, as requested by the coach.

Another possibility is for the athletes to self-record. For example, McKenzie and Rushall (1974) designed a self-recording system to influence young competitive swimmers to swim greater distances during practices. A program board like that shown in Figure 5-2 was placed at the end of each of the lanes of the pool. A transparent pocket along the top edge of each board enabled the coaches to write the practice requirements on program unit cards. The cards, indicating a set of repeats, were then inserted along the top of the board. The coaches were able to insert any training program they wished, and could easily alter the training program content between practices by changing the work unit cards. At a given practice, the names of swimmers in a lane were written along the left side with a grease pencil. As a swimmer completed a work unit (e.g., a 400 meter free style swim consisting of 16 lengths), that swimmer placed a check beside his or her name with a grease pencil. After each practice, the checkmarks and swimmers' names were erased from the boards with a solvent. The swimmers took turns assuming the responsibility of caring for and preparing the board for practice.

How effective were the program boards as performance improvement devices? When the distances swum before the program boards were compared with the distances swum after the program boards were introduced, there was an average increase for all swimmers of 27%. This represented an additional 566 meters per practice for each swimmer. In addition, use of the program boards allowed swimmers to continue with practice activities on an independent basis; they did not have to wait at the end of the pool for instructions from coaches. This freed the coaches to monitor swimming skills, to provide more frequent feedback on individual strokes, and to praise swimmers for stroke performance and for completing activities. In other words, coaches were better able to function as effective behavior modifiers. Finally, most of the swimmers preferred to use the program boards. There were one or two exceptions, however. One girl was overheard saying, "I don't like them. They make me work too hard" (McKenzie & Rushall, 1974, p. 205).

Why should a program board of the sort used by McKenzie and Rushall (1974) exert a positive influence on the swimmers? In theory, there are several possibilities. First, as soon as a swimmer completed a set, there was a clear prompt to perform the next set. This allowed swimmers to proceed at their own independent rates rather than waiting for all to finish before beginning the next set. Second, because the swimmers finished sets at different times, peer attention for fooling around at the end of the lane was no longer present because other swimmers were not there. Thus, there were fewer disruptive behaviors. Third, the coach's instructions may have functioned as a conditioned motivating operation (see Chapter 7) to establish the self-recording checkmarks as a conditioned reinforcer for appropriate behavior of swimmers. Fourth, swimmers received intermittent attention and praise from the coaches as they completed sets and recorded checkmarks. Finally, the public aspect of the program board may have added additional delayed reinforcers and/or punishers such as peer recognition for completing the sets and/or negative comments from peers when sets were not completed.

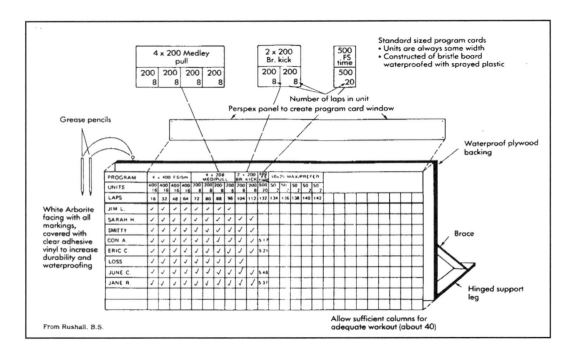

Figure 5-2. A program board for self-monitoring by competitive swimmers during practice. Reprinted with permission from Rushall (1975).

The program boards used by McKenzie and Rushall required that the swimmers self-monitor their performance during practice. Another possibility is to have athletes complete self-evaluation checklists after practices (discussed further in Chapter 13). An example of such a checklist that we have used to prompt figure skaters to work hard at practices is presented in Figure 5-3 (Martin & Thomson, 2010). Note that the checklist also incorporates feedback from the coach.

Other examples of self-monitoring by athletes to improve practice performance include self-monitoring of jumps and spins performed by figure skaters (Hume et al., 1985), repetitions of skills by gymnasts (Wolko et al., 1993), laps and drills completed by speed skaters (Wanlin et al., 1997), and correct tags during relay races of inline roller speed skaters (Anderson & Kirkpatrick, 2002).

An important part of recording and charting is that the recorded behaviors be displayed in a way that provides meaningful feedback to the athletes. This is a critical component of a performance feedback system. If an athlete can see a simple set of checkmarks on a graph that is easy to interpret and that clearly displays progress, then opportunities arise for factors such as self-praise, coaches' praise, and peer feedback to play a role in motivating that athlete.

Frequently, feedback can be enhanced if the measure of behavior is *publicly* displayed on a chart (e.g., see Brobst & Ward, 2002; Ward & Carnes, 2002). Public posting of performance can be effective in stimulating peer interactions to reinforce increased output. Public posting can also serve as an important reminder to coaches to provide praise for progress (e.g., see Hume et al., 1985). However, the coach must not lose sight of the fact that public posting might be embarrassing and aversive to some young athletes. If public posting is to be used, it should be designed so that it encourages teammates to praise each other and to focus on how each athlete has improved in comparison to his/her prior performance. Care should be taken to ensure that the public posting procedure does not bring positive attention to some at the cost of excessive embarrassment to others.

3. Set Performance Goals

After a recording and charting strategy has been designed, and after it has been used in several practices to obtain current measures of performance, then goal-setting should be used to help the athletes to improve on the specific behaviors being monitored, as described at the beginning of this chapter for the speed skaters. As described in Chapter 4, goals capitalize on rule-governed control over behavior and should therefore follow the guidelines for effectively using rules.

4. Provide Positive Feedback for Goal Attainment

There are several ways that a coach can ensure that athletes receive frequent positive feedback for accomplishing various practice goals. These might include some of the strategies described previously such as self-monitoring of improvements, publicly posted feedback, setting and meeting performance goals, frequent informational and instructional feedback from coaches that includes statements about aspects of skills

Figure 5-3. A self-monitoring checklist for encouraging young figure skaters to follow good practice habits.

Homework Checklist **Monitoring Good Practice Habits** Use this checklist at two or three practices each week to ensure that you follow good practice habits.													
Dates →													
a. I set a practice goal for quantity.													
b. I set a practice goal for quality.													
c. I set a practice goal for sport psychology.													
d. I deliberately put myself in a good mood at the start of practice.													
e. At least half of my practice was done with 100% effort and concentration.													
f. I tried to do at least one thing in practice the best I have ever done it.													
g. I practiced instant mental replays of several difficult jumps just after I landed them.													
h. I asked my coach to give me a "grade" on how hard I worked (record the grade).													
i. Before leaving the ice, I told the coach about one thing that I thought I did really well and really liked about the practice.													
j. Initialled by coach													

performed correctly, videotaped feedback that shows skills performed correctly (e.g., Stokes et al., 2010), and any of the strategies for using reinforcers described in Chapters 7, 10 and 11.

An additional option is to encourage an athlete to recruit positive feedback. *Recruitment of positive feedback* is a strategy to improve performance that involves an individual emitting a desirable behavior, and then telling someone about it in order to receive positive feedback. This strategy has been used in settings to increase work rates. For example, in a study by Hildebrand, Martin, Furer, and Hazen (1990), some of the developmentally disabled workers in a sheltered workshop usually showed very low productivity. On the few occasions when they worked at a higher rate, they received very little feedback from the busy staff. Hildebrand and colleagues taught the workers to meet a productivity goal, and then to call staff members' attention to their good work. This led to increased feedback for the workers from the staff, and helped to maintain a higher level of productivity by the workers. Although this approach has not been researched in sport settings, it may have considerable potential for motivating young athletes to work hard at practices. It may be especially appropriate when coaches are too busy to ensure that they appropriately praise each of the young athletes. Aspects of recruitment are contained in Figure 5-3 in which the figure skater recruited feedback from the coach in two different ways.

Study Questions

1. Describe the three main components of the motivation package that Connie applied to improve the practice performance of the speed skaters.

2. What is an ABC assessment?

3. In general, what is performance feedback?

4. What is proprioceptive feedback? Describe an example that was not in this chapter that illustrates how proprioceptive feedback could enable an athlete to successfully repeat a previously learned athletic skill.

5. What is external sensory feedback? Describe a sport example that was not in this chapter.

6. What is external informational feedback? Describe a sport example that was not in this chapter.

7. In two or three sentences, describe a strategy that coaches and young athletes might use to assess the effort of young athletes at practices.

8. What is external instructional feedback? Describe a sport example that was not in

this chapter.

9.   Briefly state four factors that influence the effectiveness of rule-governed control over behavior (you may want to review Chapter 4).

10.   In a sentence each, list three reasons why performance feedback can lead to improved athletic performance.

11.   List the 4 main steps of a performance feedback system for use with young athletes at practices. Describe a specific sport example of each step that was not in this chapter.

12.   What were three positive outcomes of using the program boards at swimming practices?

13.   Describe five plausible reasons why the program boards used by McKenzie and Rushall exerted a positive influence on the swimmers.

14.   What are two reasons that public posting of practice performance might be more effective as a motivator than the athlete's private monitoring of performance?

15.   What is meant by "recruitment of positive feedback"? Illustrate with a sport example that is not in this chapter.

16.   Describe the two ways that recruitment of positive feedback was incorporated into the figure skating self-monitoring sheet in Figure 5-3.

Chapter 6

Behavioral Assessment

An Application

Selecting Target Behaviors to be Improved*

    Coach Keedwell, one of the coaches of the Manitoba Marlins Swimming Team, coached two lanes of swimmers who ranged in age from 8 to 13 years, and who attended at least four practices per week. Coach Keedwell had taught the swimmers how to execute correct racing turns for each of the four basic swimming strokes: backstroke, breaststroke, butterfly, and freestyle. In spite of frequent prompts by Coach Keedwell to execute their turns on all opportunities at practices, the swimmers frequently swam to the end of the lane, touched the bulkhead with their hands, and began swimming again without executing a proper turn. The swimmers were also encouraged during a practice to swim each set (typically from four to eight laps of the 25m pool) without stopping. However, the swimmers were frequently observed to touch down during the middle of a set, stop and adjust their goggles, fool around with the other swimmers briefly, and so forth. With help from Clayton Cracklin, a University of Manitoba Psychology student, **Coach Keedwell selected these two problem behaviors – failing to execute a racing turn and stopping momentarily during a set – as the target behaviors for study.** For the next four practices, Clayton recorded instances of the two target behaviors for the six swimmers who swam in one of the lanes. The total number of missed turns and unscheduled stops averaged approximately 140 per practice, approximately 23 instances for each of the six swimmers.

    Consistent with recommendations in books for coaches of young age-group competitive swimmers, Coach Keedwell had been scheduling a fun activity at the end of every practice. During the last 10-minutes of a typical practice, the swimmers would choose teams and compete in a relay race, an activity they thoroughly enjoyed. Coach Keedwell decided to change the rules. At the beginning of a practice she announced to the swimmers in lane 1, "You've been averaging a total of 140 missed turns and unscheduled stops per practice for everybody in the lane. From now on, to earn relays for both lanes, you have to keep your total number of missed turns and stops below 40 for the rest of the practice." The swimmers were easily able to meet the goal and earn relays. Across the next several practices, the problem behaviors decreased dramatically, and the swimmers showed approximately 150% improvement.

*This application is based on Cracklin & Martin (1983).

Behavioral Assessment

Suppose that a coach or an athlete has called you and asked for help. At your first meeting a number of questions will arise. What is the nature of the problem? Can the problem be easily translated into specific behaviours to be increased or decreased? Is the problem one that would appear to be easily manageable? Is the problem one of long standing, and if so, will it be resistant to change? How rapidly does the problem need to be solved? Are there significant individuals (such as other athletes, coaches, parents, etc.) who might manage controlling stimuli and consequences? Can the client be taught self-management skills to solve the problem, or is it necessary for you to spend time in the athlete's world to work with the athlete and others (such as the coach)? The purpose of this chapter is to help you to answer such questions. Additional discussion of your few first sessions with a client is presented in Chapter 18.

The behavior to be changed in a behavioral program is often referred to as the **target behavior**. **Behavioral assessment** is concerned with identifying and describing a target behavior, identifying possible causes of the behavior, selecting an appropriate treatment strategy to modify the behavior, and evaluating treatment outcome. This chapter focuses primarily on the first concern. Some causes of problem behaviors were described in Chapters 2 and 3 and are discussed further in Parts II, III, IV, and V. Strategies for selecting appropriate treatments are also presented in Parts II, III, IV, and V. Guidelines for evaluating your interventions and your service are presented in Chapters 17 and 18.

Behavioral assessment began to emerge in clinical psychology during the 1970s as an alternative to traditional psychological tests, such as the *Wechsler Adult Intelligence Scale*, the *Minnesota Multi-Phasic Personality Inventory*, and the *16 Personality Factor Inventory*, that focus on global aspects of intelligence, personality, and abnormal tendencies. For a discussion of behavioral versus traditional psychological assessment in sport psychology, see Tkachuk, Leslie-Toogood, and Martin (2003). Behavioral assessment was developed, in part, because traditional standardized psychological tests do not aid the behavior modifier in helping clients identify specific target behaviors that occur under specific circumstances (Martin & Pear, 2011). For this reason, as expressed by Terry Orlick (1989), standard psychological tests are of little practical value in working with high performance athletes. Rather, sport specific behavioral checklists and/or direct monitoring of specific sport behaviors in specific situations are more likely to provide the assessment information necessary to design effective interventions for athletes. But before illustrating such assessments, let's review some topics to cover in your first session with an athlete.

Some Topics During the First "Session"

As described in Chapter 18, referrals for sport psychology consultation are likely to come from a variety of sources. Moreover, your first meeting with an athlete could just as easily be at a sport facility as in your office. But let's assume that you are meeting in a comfortable setting with no distractions, and that your introduction, body language, and seating arrangements have helped the athlete to feel comfortable. You might then proceed through the following topics.

Explain Confidentiality

Although best results are likely obtained when the athlete, psychologist, and coach (and sometimes parents and others) work as a team, the athlete must understand your guidelines on confidentiality. My personal approach is to explain to the athlete that our discussions are completely confidential, and that I will relate aspects of our discussion to the coach or others only with prior approval from the athlete.

Briefly Describe Your Background

In my experience, most athletes like to know something about the individual from whom they are seeking guidance. They also typically appreciate an overview of how the first session is likely to unfold. I usually say something like, "Perhaps we can start by my telling you a little about myself so that you'll know where I'm coming from. Then we'll talk about sport psychology in general, and then we'll focus on why you came to see me." You might also briefly mention some examples of the different sports in which you've helped athletes in the past, and, with prior permission, you might mention one or two of the athletes with whom you've worked if they are likely to be known to your client.

Talk About Sport Psychology

Early during the first session, I usually ask the athlete if they have ever talked to a sport psychologist before, or if they have read anything about sport psychology. If the athlete has had minimal contact with sport psychology, then you might explain that sport psychology has become increasingly popular during the past 30 years, cite examples of professional sport teams that have utilized the services of sport psychologists, give examples of work that sport psychologists have done with Olympic athletes, and indicate that sport psychology consultations are becoming increasingly popular for top-level youth athletes. You might also briefly mention several areas in which sport psychologists have helped athletes, such as getting the most out of practices, improving confidence and concentration, and performing up to potential at competitions.

Clarify Misconceptions About Sport Psychology

Occasionally, quotes in newspapers by famous coaches and athletes make sport psychologists cringe. Perhaps the coaches and athletes are misquoted. Or perhaps some of the coaches and athletes quoted are misinformed about sport psychology. And perhaps some sport psychologists themselves have been misleading the athletic community about the benefits of sport psychology. Whatever the reasons, some statements that athletes might hear about sport psychology are clearly myths or misunderstandings. It is sometimes helpful to clarify such misconceptions in your first session. Some of the more common misunderstandings are as follows:

"To do well in competition, you have to get yourself really psyched up." Usually such a statement implies that athletes have to learn to increase their physiological arousal and to show the sorts of behaviors that are likely to be described as "pumped up." That may be true about certain individuals in certain sports, but it certainly does not apply across the board. A swimmer about to swim a 50-meter race should be physiologically aroused. A swimmer about to swim a 1500 metre race, however, should be reasonably relaxed. Excessive physiological arousal for the 1500 metre race will take away from the energy needed to swim such a long distance. Behavioral assessments might demonstrate that some people are simply too "laid back" in sporting situations, and their performance might be improved by increasing their physiological arousal. Other individuals, however, might show an improvement by learning how to relax before important sport events.

"Sport psychology alone can make one a super athlete." Many years ago I was asked to provide a seasonal sport psychology program for a youth competitive swim team. We began with weekly group meetings. At the first meeting, one of the swimmers asked, in all seriousness, "If we attend these psychology sessions can we skip some of our practices?" Athletes need to understand that exceptional athletic performance requires preparation in four main areas: **physical** - they must be in excellent physical condition; **technical** - their technical skills must be correct, highly practiced, and second nature to them; **tactical** - they must have a game plan for dealing with certain opponents, running certain races, skiing certain courses, etc.; and **psychological** - this refers generally to mental preparation and is discussed in Chapters 15 and 16. To be a "super athlete", an athlete needs extensive preparation in all four of these areas.

"Sport psychologists only consult with athletes at competitions." When I first received a call from the President of the Manitoba Figure Skating Association, I was pleased to learn that they were interested in the possibility of a seasonal sport psychology program for their skaters (rather than a "quick fix"). I was surprised to discover, however, that in the eyes of the executive of the association, a sport psychology program was thought to involve the availability of a psychologist to talk to the skaters at competitions - nothing more. It is certainly true that, of all of the services provided by sport psychologists, helping athletes with their mental preparation at competitions gets most of the popular press. However, as illustrated in later chapters, sport psychology interventions can enhance athletic performance in all four areas of physical, technical, tactical, and psychological preparation. Athletes, coaches, and others associated with sports need to understand that psychological strategies can help them to improve performance in all aspects of practices and competitions.

"To get really good at mental preparation, all you have to do is talk to a sport psychologist." Athletes need to appreciate that mental skills are like physical skills - they are behaviors that occur in certain settings, and to be good at them they must be learned and practiced. Mental skills are not mystical or magical, and they cannot enable one to

perform miracles. What they can do is help an individual to perform consistently at or near his/her potential, given that individual's level of preparation in the physical, technical, and tactical areas. Athletes know that it's not enough to sit on the sidelines and watch a coach demonstrate various skills. They know that they have to practice those skills themselves, over and over and over. Similarly, they need to understand that they can't get good at mental preparation just by listening to a sport psychologist. Rather, they have to practice the mental skills themselves, over and over and over.

At some point during the first session, you will begin to discuss the presenting problem. Usually the first step involves a broadly based behavioral assessment. Subsequent steps include choosing target behaviors and devising ways to monitor them, a functional assessment of the causes of problem behaviors, prioritizing problem selection, and developing and implementing a treatment plan. We will now discuss each of these areas.

Broadly Based Initial Information Gathering

Initial information gathering in behavioral assessment can be accomplished using behavioral interviewing, across-sport behavioral checklists, within-sport behavioral checklists, performance profiling, and assessment for slump-busting.

Behavioral Interviewing

As described previously, I like to begin a behavioral interview with an athlete by explaining confidentiality, talking about sport psychology in general, and clarifying misconceptions about sport psychology. As is the case with traditionally oriented therapists, an important component of the behavioral interview is to establish and maintain rapport and mutual trust with the athlete and any significant others who may be included in the interview.

After presenting general information in the first session, as described previously, I then typically ask the athlete something like, "Tell me a little about your background in your sport, your goals for this season, and why you would like some help from a sport psychologist." Some athletes are comfortable talking at length about their current situation and the presenting problem. Others may find it somewhat threatening, at least during the initial session, to discuss their reasons for seeking assistance. When athletes appear to be somewhat reluctant to discuss their needs, I have found it useful to ask the athlete to complete an Athlete Information Form (see Martin, Toogood, and Tkachuk, 1997). The information obtained provides a useful starting point for subsequent behavioral assessment discussions and decisions.

Another interviewing strategy for conducting a broadly-based assessment is to ask the athlete about the details of their own best and worst recent performances during competitions (Orlick, 1986a, 1986b, 1989). This will provide some hints as to what the athlete already does well, and areas in which the athlete needs to improve mental preparation for competitions. This approach is discussed further, with examples, in Chapter 16.

Sometimes an athlete might come to you seeking help with a specific problem. In such cases, you and the athlete might focus on a few specific target behaviors and then devise a system for initial evaluation of those behaviors for monitoring progress. Other cases are likely to benefit from an additional, broadly based behavioural assessment.

Across-Sport Behavioral Checklists

An **across-sport behavioral checklist** lists performance aspects of practices and/or competitions that apply to a number of different sports. For example, in the *Precompetition and Competition Behavior Inventory* developed by Rushall (1979), an athlete is presented with such statements as, "I get nervous and tense before an important competition," "I mentally rehearse my competition plan before contests," and "When I am tired during a competition, I concentrate on my technique." For such statements, the athlete is asked to circle the alternative that best applies from the options of Always, Occasionally, or Never. Such an inventory is designed to assess an athlete's current physical and mental behaviors that comprise his/her preparation for competitions. This information can then be used to detect preparation activities that may interfere with optimal competitive performance, and to introduce new preparation activities to maximize competitive performance. Other examples of across-sport behavioral inventories include Orlick's (1986b) *Post Competition Evaluation Form*, the *Psychological Skills Inventory for Sport* (Mahoney, Gabriel, & Perkins, 1987), and the *Athlete Coping Skills Inventory-28* (Smith, Schutz, Smoll, & Ptacek, 1995). Also, for a review of protocols and instruments that can be used by sport psychologists for helping athletes to make decisions for preparing for and participating in competitive events, see Donohue, Dickens, and Del Vecchio III (2011).

In my view, across-sport behavioral inventories are more valuable for working with athletes than are traditional psychological tests and personality inventories because they aim to tap into athletes' sport related behavior rather than personality dimensions or hypothetical constructs such as self efficacy. However, instruments that may be even more useful for broadly based initial information gathering are within-sport behavioral checklists.

Within-Sport Behavioral Checklists

A **within-sport behavioral checklist** lists performance aspects of practices and/or competitions for a particular sport. Completing such a checklist, has the benefits of providing a quick, and reasonably thorough, identification of areas in which the athlete already performs well, as well as areas in need of improvement. An example of such a checklist that I have used at the beginning of the season with basketball players is shown in Figure 6-1. Such checklists differ from across-sport behavioral checklists in that they apply only to a particular sport. They differ from traditional psychological tests such as the *16-Personality Factor Inventory* in that the within-sport behavioral checklists do not have norms and they are not designed to measure character or personality traits. A major advantage of using such checklists over other self-report measures, including across-sport behavioral checklists, is the increased face validity in the eyes of the athlete involved, which can often enhance rapport and lend credibility to the consultant. Martin, Toogood, and Tkachuk (1997) published within-sport behavioral checklists for 21 different sports. The items included in these checklists were selected by reviewing the literature on the psychological skills of exceptional athletes (Greenspan & Feltz, 1989; Mahoney et al., 1987; Orlick & Partington, 1988).

The within-sport checklists by Martin et al. (1997) were positively reviewed (Smith & Little, 1998). Also, research on the checklists for basketball and swimming (Lines, Schwartzman, Tkachuk, Leslie-Toogood, & Martin, 1999) and running and volleyball (Leslie-Toogood & Martin, 2003) found them to have high face validity and high test-retest reliability.

Following the completion of a within-sport checklist with an athlete, I like to go to some practices and competitions of that athlete in order to gain some validation of their strengths and their needs. As another alternative, to obtain validation of the areas identified by the athlete as needing improvement, you might, with the permission of the athlete, request that a within-sport checklist be completed independently by the athlete's coach and/or parents (assuming that the athlete is under 18 and still living with his/her parents). Athletes are not always aware of their mental strengths and limitations, and information from independent sources can often be quite helpful. This was illustrated in a study of a group of young figure skaters for whom I had provided a seasonal sport psychology program (Martin & Toogood, 1997). At the beginning of the season, a questionnaire for figure skaters (see Martin & Thomson, 2010) was independently completed by 13 figure skaters (average age 16 years), their coaches, and their parents. The coaches and parents agreed with skaters on the scoring of just over half of the 34 items. However, they clearly disagreed with skaters on their scoring on an average of 5.7 items (parents) and 7.2 items (coaches) (Martin & Toogood).

Although more research is needed, the results of the needs assessment at the beginning of the season for this group of skaters supported three generalizations which likely hold for youth athletes in other sports as well. First, the individual variation from skater to skater indicated that psychological skills training for athletes should be individualized. Second, differences in the perceived needs from the points of view of the skater, coach, and parent underscored the importance of involving the athletes in the planning of the sport psychology program. Third, differences in the perceived needs from the three sources demonstrated the value of obtaining behavioral assessment information from more than just one source.

Figure 6-1. Sport Psychology Questionnaire for Basketball Players*

This questionnaire was designed to help you to identify areas in which you would like some help and/or need to improve. All the information will be kept confidential.

Name: _____   **Date:** _____

GAMES **Would you say that, just before or during a game, you need to improve at:**	Not Sure	Definitely Not	Somewhat	Definitely Yes	Check here if you would like help to improve
1. Thinking positive thoughts? *(e.g., "An easy 2 points", "I'm going to can this one", etc.)*	_____	1 2	3	4 5	
2. Tuning out negative thoughts? *(e.g., thinking, just before a game-tying free throw, "I hope I don't blow this one!" etc.)*	_____	1 2	3	4 5	
3. Staying relaxed and not getting too nervous: a) just before the game? b) in pressure situations?	_____ _____	1 2 1 2	3 3	4 5 4 5	
4. Maintaining/regaining your confidence in difficult situations? *(e.g., you have a bad warm-up, you make a mistake, your coach subs you off, your shot gets blocked, the ball gets stolen from you, your check beats you, etc.)*	_____	1 2	3	4 5	
5. Maintaining your concentration on the task at hand? *(e.g., focusing on the front rim before each shot, taking it one play at a time, etc.)*	_____	1 2	3	4 5	
6. Blocking out distractors over which you have no control? *(e.g., who you are playing against, who you are checking, the gym where you are playing, the fans, etc.)*	_____	1 2	3	4 5	
7. Blocking out what people might say if you lose or don't perform well? *(e.g., comments from parents, coach, friends, or spectators)* Other? _____	_____	1 2	3	4 5	

*An initial draft of this questionnaire was prepared by Adrienne Toogood.

Figure 6-1 (cont'd)

	Not Sure	Definitely Not	Somewhat		Definitely Yes	Check here if you would like help to improve
8. Block out distractors that don't involve basketball? *(e.g., school, family, or relationship problems)* Other? _____	____	1	2	3	4	5	
9. Refocusing after you get distracted for any reason? *(e.g., an opponent tries to put you off your game, you have a bad first half, the referee makes a bad call, etc.)*	____	1	2	3	4	5	
10. Staying energized in difficult situations? *(e.g., when you feel fatigued or ill, you have a bad warm-up, nothing else is going right, etc.)*	____	1	2	3	4	5	
11. Communicating tactically with teammates? *(e.g., "You've got helpside", "Take away the baseline", "Take the ball", etc.)*	____	1	2	3	4	5	
12. Identifying and reacting to your opponents' weaknesses and making adjustments as the game progresses? *(e.g., your shot is not going in, your opponent is taking away the right-hand drive, etc.)*	____	1	2	3	4	5	
13. Being assertive when the opportunity presents itself? *(e.g., driving for the basket when you get a step on your opponent, etc.)*	____	1	2	3	4	5	
14. Managing troublesome emotions? *(e.g., excitement, anger, disappointment, etc.)*	____	1	2	3	4	5	
15. Giving 100% effort when there are excuses not to? *(e.g., you are playing a team you play often, you are losing by a large margin, etc.)*	____	1	2	3	4	5	
16. Setting challenging yet attainable goals for each game?	____	1	2	3	4	5	
17. Having a better health management plan before games? *(e.g., getting enough sleep, drinking enough water, eating properly, etc.)*	____	1	2	3	4	5	
18. Preparing and following a detailed precompetition and competition plan?	____	1	2	3	4	5	
19. Communicating your precompetition needs to others? *(e.g., parent(s), coach, teammates, and friends, etc.)*	____	1	2	3	4	5	
20. Staying supportive of and praising teammates' performance? *(e.g., "Good job", "Nice shot", etc.)*	____	1	2	3	4	5	

Figure 6-1 (Cont'd)

IMMEDIATELY AFTER A GAME **Would you say that you need to improve at:**	Not Sure	Definitely Not	Somewhat	Definitely Yes	Check here if you would like help to improve
1. Evaluating your mental preparation and playing performance for that game?	_____	1　　2	3	4　　5	
2. Putting aside a poor performance and focusing on the next game?	_____	1　　2	3	4　　5	
3. Remembering the good things that happened, and incorporating them into mental preparation for the next game? *(e.g., "I blocked out well", "I saw the ball at all times", etc.)*	_____	1　　2	3	4　　5	
4. Communicating with your coach? *(e.g., "What can I improve upon?" "What did I do right or wrong?", etc.)*	_____	1　　2	3	4　　5	
5. Learning from your mistakes in order to improve? *(e.g., "I will fill the lane harder next time", "I will follow through on my shot more", etc.)*	_____	1　　2	3	4　　5	
Additional Concerns about Games _____ _____ _____ _____					
PRACTICES **Would you say that, at practices, you need to improve at:** 1. Setting specific physical, technical, tactical, and mental goals for every practice?	_____	1　　2	3	4　　5	
2. Keeping a written record of progress in meeting your goals?	_____	1　　2	3	4　　5	
3. Arriving at practice totally committed to do your best?	_____	1　　2	3	4　　5	
4. Maintaining your concentration, especially when practice gets long, repetitive, or uninteresting?	_____	1　　2	3	4　　5	
5. Maintaining your effort and focus, especially when you are tired or don't feel like being there?	_____	1　　2	3	4　　5	

Figure 6-1 (Cont'd)

	Not Sure	Definitely Not	Somewhat		Definitely Yes	Check here if you would like help to improve
6. Making better use of full practice time? *(e.g., shooting between drills, ball handling if you're subbed off, etc.)*	____	1	2	3	4	5	
7. Staying positive when you're having a bad practice?	____	1	2	3	4	5	
8. Remaining positive when an injury forces you to stop training?	____	1	2	3	4	5	
9. Improving your consistency and fine tuning the skills you can already perform, rather than just going through the motions? *(e.g., making sure your crossover dribble is low & fast, etc.)*	____	1	2	3	4	5	
10. Working more on skill deficiencies?	____	1	2	3	4	5	
11. Practicing mental skills, as well as physical skills?	____	1	2	3	4	5	
12. Forgetting about what other players are doing, or how much playing time they are getting? *(i.e., concentrating on what you have to do to improve)*	____	1	2	3	4	5	
13. Using key words and self-talk to improve your skills? *(e.g., "See the ball", "Follow through", etc.)*	____	1	2	3	4	5	
14. Making better use of visualization/mental rehearsal to improve skills?	____	1	2	3	4	5	
15. Giving 100% effort and concentration to the task at hand, in order to have quality practices? *(e.g., if ball handling, do it accurately and precisely, etc.)*	____	1	2	3	4	5	
16. Doing serious game simulations, and making them as realistic as possible? *(e.g., visualizing what the defence does when you headfake and adjusting your move accordingly, etc.)*	____	1	2	3	4	5	
17. Using mental imagery, self-talk, and key words before and during game simulations?	____	1	2	3	4	5	

Additional Concerns about Practices

_____
_____
_____
_____

Performance Profiling

Performance profiling is a strategy for discovering an athlete's perspective of his/her own strengths and weaknesses (Butler & Hardy, 1992; Butler, Smith, & Irwin, 1993). The strategy involves three main steps. First, an athlete is asked to identify the qualities and characteristics of a top athlete in their sport. Next, the athlete is asked to evaluate his/her current level of mastery with respect to each of those qualities and characteristics. Third, areas in which the athlete is deficient in terms of those qualities and characteristics are used to identify specific target behaviors for improvement. For example, Butler and Hardy (1992) described a performance profile of an amateur boxer in which they identified areas for improvement such as faster punches, being able to slip punches, and improved counter-punching. Although some questions about the value of performance profiling have been raised (Doyle & Parfitt, 1997), it has been successfully used (e.g., Mellalieu & Juniper, 2006), and theoretical underpinnings of the technique have been described (Gucciardi & Gordon, 2009).

Assessment For "Slump-Busting"

A problem that calls for broad-based behavioral assessment is "slumpbusting". A **slump** is an unexpected decline in athletic performance that occurs for a sufficient length of time to be of serious concern to the athlete and coach. As expressed by Taylor (1988, p.39), "Slumps are a significant source of concern, confusion, and frustration for athletes and coaches." Because slumps are often thought to be psychologically caused, they frequently lead to referral to a sport psychologist. In an insightful analysis of the causes of slumps, Taylor (1988) suggested that they require broad-based assessment. Before analysing psychological factors that might cause a slump, other possible causes should first be ruled out.

First, some slumps may have a physical cause. Loss of visual acuity, for example, could certainly affect a batter's ability to hit a ball. Second, slumps may be the result of some slight change in the athlete's technique. A golfer may be unaware of the fact that the way that she grips the golf club has changed subtly over time, and yet that change in grip could cause considerable change in the outcome of golf shots. Third, slumps might be caused by slight changes in the equipment used in a particular sport. Taylor (1988), for example, described a case of an alpine ski racer who experienced a significant deterioration in performance during the latter half of the season. The cause was eventually determined to be worn ski boots that affected the way that the racer stood on his skis.

Fourth, if an athlete in a slump comes to you for help, and if you can rule out physical, technique, and equipment causes of the slump, then a sport-specific behavioral checklist might be appropriate to determine if a slump is due to inadequate mental preparation. An example of such a checklist is the basketball checklist presented in Figure 6-1. As indicated previously, similar checklists are available for 20 other sports (Martin et al. 1997).

Most athletes experience a slump at some point in their athletic career, and slump-busting will be discussed further in Chapter 15. An excellent source of strategies for overcoming slumps is the book by Goldberg (1998).

Choosing Target Behaviors and Devising Ways to Monitor Them

Broadly based information gathering can be useful for helping an athlete to identify general problem areas. The next step is to identify a few specific target behaviors, to describe them specifically, and to devise ways to monitor them.

When specifically describing behavior, there are **six objective dimensions** or characteristics to consider: topography, frequency (or rate), duration, intensity (or force), stimulus control, and latency, as described in Chapter 3. Concern about the *quality* of a behavior is frequently encountered in sports. In judgmental sports like diving, gymnastics, and figure skating, the athletes receive points based on the quality of their performances. And in all sports, athletes regularly make resolutions to do various activities better. But quality is not a new characteristic beyond the six mentioned previously. Rather, it is a refinement of one or more of those characteristics. Sometimes, differences in judgments of quality are based on topography, such as when a figure skating jump that is landed on one foot is considered better than when that jump is landed on two feet. With respect to frequency, many general evaluations of whether or not an athlete is good or poor at something relate to how many times the athlete tends to emit some behavior in a given period of time. For example, someone who is considered a good offensive basketball player is someone who shows a high frequency of making baskets in a game. An athlete who is said to be a good "team player" is likely someone who shows high frequencies of doing whatever it is that the coach asks and displaying supportive behavior to teammates. In terms of latency, a runner who leaves the blocks very quickly after the firing of the starter's pistol, might be considered to have a "good" start while a runner who shows a longer latency had a "poor" start. Thus, quality of response is essentially a refinement of one or more of the six previous characteristics of behavior that have been identified as having value in a sport setting.

As indicated in Chapter 1, a behavioral approach emphasizes identification of specific behaviors. By being specific in the identification of target behaviors, you: (a) help to ensure the reliability of detecting improvements in the behavior (the yardstick by which one judges the effectiveness of a treatment program); and (b) increase the likelihood that your treatment program will be applied consistently. Target behaviors are typically monitored by one of the following strategies.

Direct Observation Of A Single Behavior

In some cases, a target behavior of an athlete is directly monitored by an observer. Examples of directly observed target behaviors include swimming stroke errors with beginning age-group swimmers (Koop & Martin, 1983), skating speed of speed skaters

(Wanlin, Hrycaiko, Martin, & Mahon, 1997), performance of a defensive basketball tactic during basketball games (Kendall, Hrycaiko, Martin, & Kendall, 1990), serving accuracy in volleyball (McKenzie & Liskovitch, 1983), inappropriate on-court behavior of tennis players (Galvan & Ward, 1998), and defensive skills of collegiate football players (Ward & Carnes, 2002).

Behavioral Checklists To Record Multiple Behaviors

In some cases, consultants or researchers have designed checklists that enable observers to easily monitor multiple behaviors of an individual. Examples include the Coaching Behavior Assessment System for monitoring coaching behaviors of Little League baseball coaches (Smith, Smoll, & Curtis, 1979), a checklist with picture prompts to help evaluate the topography of the backstroke of youth competitive swimmers (see Figure 6-2), the Self-talk and Gestures Rating Scale for Systematic Observations of the on-court behavior of junior tennis players (Van Raalte, Brewer, Rivera, & Petitpas, 1994), checklists of components of moves in classical ballet (Fitterling & Ayllon, 1983), a checklist of components of correct form of sprinters in track (Shapiro & Shapiro, 1985), a checklist for recording coaches interactions with players during timeouts in basketball, volleyball, and ice hockey (Hastie, 1999), and a task analysis for tackling in high school football (Stokes, Luiselli, & Reed, 2010).

Athlete Self-Monitoring

Often, athlete self-monitoring is an effective way to track the behavior of interest. Examples include self-monitoring laps swum during swimming practices (Critchfield & Vargas, 1991); jumps and spins performed by figure skaters (Hume et al., 1985); and good shots in golf (Kirchenbaum, Owens, & O'Connor, 1998).

Videotaping Of Target Behaviors

Coaches in a number of sports have used videotapes to assess the strengths and weaknesses of their opponents. While videotaping of target behaviors of athletes for sport psychology consulting is less common, it is nevertheless a useful way of monitoring target behaviors, and provides a permanent record of that behavior for observational analysis. Examples include videotaping of a defensive skill during basketball games (Kendall et al., 1990); offensive rebounds, defensive rebounds, steals, and turnovers of basketball players (Swain & Jones, 1995); pass blocking of offensive linemen in football (Stokes et al., 2010); and correct "reads", "drops", and tackles of linebackers in football (Ward & Carnes, 2002).

Let's suppose that you have identified several target behaviors, and you've assessed their current level of performance. You are ready to design a treatment.

Hands: Fingers together
Arms: Roll shoulder into your ear
(Recovery) Arm comes over straight
Arm comes over close to ear
Little finger enters water first

Arms: Lower arm bends to almost 90 degrees under shoulder
(Pull) As arm straightens underwater, snap wrist at thigh and down

Legs: Leg action begins at the hips
Knees move up and down very little
Knees don't break the surface
Toes point down at bottom of kick
Toes just break surface at top of kick

Body: Hips kept high in the water
Hips kept as flat as possible
Head: Tilted up slightly, ears in water
Head kept stationary, don't rock

Figure 6-2. A checklist for the backstroke (reprinted with permission from Martin & Pear, 1996).

Designing a Treatment Plan

Information obtained in the broadly based information gathering and the monitoring of target behaviors is used in treatment planning to change a client's target behaviors. Detailed strategies for planning treatments are described in subsequent chapters. In many cases, it will also be necessary to include strategies to program generalization from practices to competitions, as described in Chapter 14.

Evaluating Treatment Effects

A successful behavioral treatment program typically involves at least three phases during which behavior is recorded: a baseline phase, a treatment phase, and a follow-up phase. During the *baseline* phase, the target behavior is assessed in order to determine its level prior to the introduction of the intervention. In the application described at the beginning of this chapter, Clayton and Coach Keedwell obtained a baseline of the number of missed turns and unscheduled stops of the swimmers. Ideally, you and/or the athlete will have the luxury of monitoring the target behavior across several practices and/or competitions. In my experience, however, this is a rare luxury.

Most often, the athletes are eager to begin an intervention program, and are reluctant to continue to monitor performance under current circumstances. Sometimes, objective data will already exist that can provide a baseline measure. Such was the case with a professional hockey player who approached me after eighteen games of the regular season. At that time, the player, one of the teams "goal scorers" from the previous year, was averaging only one goal in every six games. This information served as an 18-game baseline even though I had not been involved with him during that time.

The *treatment* phase involves that period of time, after the initial baseline assessments, during which you intervene in various ways to attempt to help the athlete. In Coach Keedwell's program, the treatment consisted of requiring the swimmers to meet a practice goal to earn the fun activity at the end of practice, and the swimmers improved considerably. With the professional hockey player described above, treatment consisted of a detailed mental preparation plan (a recent version of that plan can be found in Martin, 2010). During the remaining 42 games of the regular season after implementing the plan, the player tripled his output, averaging one goal in every 1.9 games.

Finally, the *follow-up* phase is carried out to determine whether the improvements achieved during treatment are maintained after the termination of the program. This is also the typical time that social validity assessments are conducted to assess the subjective value of your service to the client(s) (as discussed in Chapters 1 and 18). In the example of the professional hockey player cited previously, it was at the end of the season that a follow-up questionnaire was administered by the Assistant General Manager of the hockey team to evaluate the hockey player's view of the mental preparation program and its potential benefits. Sometimes additional research phases are conducted to more thoroughly evaluate whether or not improvements observed were really due to the treatment or to some uncontrolled variable. These typically involve formal research projects, and are discussed further in Chapter 17.

Benefits of Behavioral Assessments

Why are behavior analysts so concerned with devising ways to accurately identify and monitor target behaviors? There are several reasons (Martin & Pear, 2011). First, accurate records of a behavior on a few occasions prior to the introduction of a treatment program may help you to identify the best treatment strategy. That is, monitoring aspects of an athlete's problem behavior may help to identify features of the environment that are contributing to the problem, and that may therefore be changed during a treatment program. Second, accurate records of a behavior provide a means for clearly determining whether your treatment program has produced, or is producing, the desired improvement. Third, recording and charting behavior may lead to improvements apart from any further treatment program. For example, as described in Chapter 5, a group of youth competitive swimmers increased their work output at practices by an average of 27% by recording, on a chart located at the end of the pool, the number of laps swum (McKenzie and Rushall, 1974). Fourth, visual demonstrations of improvement through the use of checklists and graphs can provide a powerful incentive for athletes to continue to implement the treatment, and to maintain the progress that they have gained. Numerous examples of this effect are described in later chapters. Finally, as discussed in Chapter 18, frequent discussions between an athlete and a sport psychologist concerning the data that assesses progress throughout a program is an important accountability mechanism to ensure that the psychologist provides ethical treatment of the athlete.

Study Questions

1. Define behavioral assessment.

2. Define "target behavior." What target behaviors for the swimmers were selected by Coach Keedwell?

3. Why are traditional, standardized psychological tests of little practical value for working with high performance athletes?

4. Briefly list four general topics that might be discussed by a sport psychologist in the first "session" with an athlete.

5. Describe four misconceptions that many people have about sport psychology. Explain why each is a misconception.

6. Describe the four main areas of athletic preparation. For each area, list a relevant item from the Sport Psychology Questionnaire for Basketball Players.

7. What is an across-sport behavioral checklist?

8. What is a within-sport behavioral checklist? What are the benefits of such checklists, and how do they differ from traditional psychological assessments?

9. Describe the three steps in developing a "performance profile" for an athlete.

10. Using sport examples, distinguish between a broadly-based behavioural assessment vs. assessment of a specific target behavior.

11. What is a slump in sports? Describe an example that is not in this chapter, and that illustrates all aspects of the definition.

12. What are the four possible causes of slumps identified by Taylor? Briefly describe a specific sport example of each.

13. List six objective dimensions for describing behavior.

14. Using sport examples, explain how the quality of a behavior is no different from other behavioral dimensions such as topography, frequency and latency.

15. What are two reasons for being specific in the identification of target behaviors?

16. Briefly describe four strategies for monitoring target behaviors.

17. Name and describe the three minimal phases of a behavioral treatment program.

18. What is a baseline? Briefly describe the baseline conditions in Coach Keedwell's program with swimmers.

19. List five reasons why behavior modifiers emphasize the importance of accurately monitoring target behaviors.

Part II
A Behavioral Analysis of Motivation, Thinking, and Emotions

Chapter 7

Motivation and Athletic Performance

An Application

A Motivational System to Improve Practice Performance[*]

Jim Dawson, coach of the Clinton Junior-High Basketball Team in Columbus, Ohio, was concerned about the players' poor performance and their bad attitude during a series of drills that he used to open each practice. Most of the players didn't seem to try while doing the drills, and they weren't supportive of each other. With the help of Dr. Daryll Siedentop of Ohio State University, Coach Dawson designed a new motivational system. He explained it to the players at the beginning of the practice.

"From now on you can earn points for performing the lay-up drills, jump-shooting drills, and free-throw drills. You can also earn points by encouraging your teammates. If I see a lack of 'hustle' or a 'bad attitude' you lose points. The points will be recorded by student volunteers and after each practice I'll let you know how many points you've earned. Also, players who earn a sufficient number of points will have their names posted on the 'Eagle Effort' board in the hall leading to the gymnasium, and those players will receive an 'Eagle Effort' award at the post-season banquet".

At the end of each practice, while telling each of the players how many points they had earned, Coach Dawson also praised those who earned a lot of points, and/or more points than in the previous practice. At the first couple of practices with the new system, the players' positive comments were "pretty phony" as they overly exaggerated their support of each other. But as the season progressed, their support of their teammates became increasingly sincere. Equally important, their performance during lay-up drills improved from an average of 68% before the system to an average of 80%. Jump-shooting performance improved from 37% to 51%. Free-throw shooting improved from 59% to 67%. By the end of the season, in Coach Dawson's words, "We were more together than I ever could have imagined."

[*]This application is based on a report by Siedentop (1980.)

Motivation

The instructions given by Coach Dawson in his description of the motivational program established the points as conditioned reinforcers for the players, and it influenced them to emit behavior to earn points. This example illustrates one way that the term motivation has been used, namely, as an adjective to refer to something that changes what you "want" and tells you what to do to get whatever it is that you now "want". The term has also been used in two other ways, one of which is useful and one of which is not. In this chapter we will review some ways in which the concept of motivation has been commonly used in sports, and will describe strategies for capitalizing on motivation to influence athletic performance in desirable ways.

Motivation as a Noun: An Internal Cause

Ricky consistently arrives early for practices, works hard during various fitness drills, listens attentively to the coach, and practices basic drills on his own. According to Ricky's coach, "Ricky works hard *because* he's highly motivated." Ryan, on the other hand, is the opposite of Ricky. Ryan is frequently late for practices, rarely finishes the fitness drills, fools around while the coach is talking, and doesn't appear to try during games. Ryan's coach feels that Ryan is lacking motivation. As illustrated by these examples, many people conceptualize motivation as some "thing" within us that causes our actions. Consistent with this traditional view, Webster's unabridged dictionary defines motive as "some inner drive that causes a person to act in a certain way." And many people attribute an outstanding athletic performance to the athlete's internal drive to achieve.

A conceptual limitation of the traditional view of motivation is that it involves circular reasoning. The causal "thing" (drive, motive, etc.) is usually inferred from the very behavior that it is supposed to explain (e.g., Why does Ricky work hard? Because he's highly motivated. How do we know he's highly motivated? Because he works hard.). There are also practical limitations to conceptualizing motivation as an internal cause of behavior. First, the suggestion that the causes of behavior lie within us might influence some coaches to blame athletes for inferior athletic performances (e.g., "they just weren't motivated"), rather than examining the principles and procedures for changing behavior described in Chapters 2, 3, 4, and 5 and the enormous amount of data demonstrating that application of those principles can effectively modify behavior (Martin & Pear, 2011). Second, it may influence some athletes to blame themselves for inferior athletic performances (e.g., "I just couldn't get up for the game."), rather than examining potential self-management strategies (see Chapter 13) for improving their performance.

To Motivate: A Verb

How did Tiger Woods motivate himself to practice the putting drill (described at the beginning of Chapter 4) until he made 100 putts in a row? How can any athlete motivate him or herself to practice long hours so that they will achieve athletic excellence? How can a coach motivate athletes to work hard at practices and to perform to their potential at competitions? As illustrated by such questions, a second use of the concept of motivation in sports is its' verb form, **to motivate**, *which generally means to influence individuals to behave in various ways*. An implication of this perspective is that motivational strategies are to be found primarily in environmental contingencies concerning behavior, not within the individual. Thus, with respect to young athletes like Ricky described previously, we might speculate that Ricky shows motivated behavior because he has come under the control of natural reinforcers for listening attentively to the coach, practicing skills and drills, and showing many of the behaviors characteristic of "motivated" athletes. On the other hand, we might speculate that athletes like Ryan might not have experienced much reinforcement for such "highly motivated" behaviors.

If we interpret "to motivate" as generally referring to strategies to influence an athlete's behavior in various ways, then we can capitalize on introducing antecedents and consequences to manage behavior according to the principles and procedures described in Chapters 2, 3, 4, and 5. Let's start with antecedents.

Manage Antecedents to Motivate Athletic Behavior

I will now list and briefly describe several antecedents to motivate athletic behavior. Detailed strategies for applying them to motivate desired athletic behaviors are described in other chapters.

Goals. As described in Chapter 4, goals can be a powerful tool to improve performance. Goals commit an athlete to the work, time, pain, and the dedication that is necessary to achieve success. They give the athlete a sense of purpose and help to keep the athlete on target. Goal-setting should be practiced as described in Chapters 4, 13, and 16.

Models. All young athletes have their heroes, such as Sidney Crosby for young hockey players or Steve Nash for young basketball players. And all athletic settings typically include athletes who stand out among their peers. Encouraging a young athlete to imitate a skilled model can be an effective motivational strategy, such as described in Chapters 3 and 13.

Imagery. To become a top athlete in any sport requires hundreds and hundreds of hours of quality practices. A strategy that is sometimes used to motivate practice performance is to use imagery to create pressure games. For example, when practicing putting, one of the young golfers with whom I worked would frequently imagine that he was leading the tournament on the final day of the Masters. For each of 18 practice putts, he would pretend that he needed the putt to maintain the lead. Using imagery in this way motivated him to approach his putting practice with a maximum of concentration, and increased his desire to make each and every putt. As described in Chapter 8, imagery can also be used to energize before practices, and to elicit emotions that have been associated with successful performances.

Picture Prompts. Posted pictures of past success can often be used to motivate desired behaviors. For example, many years ago, when my wife and I were visiting Brazil, I took a photograph of her, looking very slim and in great shape, while she jogged on the beach in Rio de Janeiro. When we returned to Canada, she posted an enlargement of the photo on the inside door of our bedroom closet. For several years thereafter, viewing the photo as she dressed each morning motivated her to continue her jogging program.

Posted Records of Progress. An important component of many motivational strategies is a system to record and chart the behaviors to be motivated. Considerable evidence indicates that public posting of charted progress over time is an effective motivational strategy (Watson & Tharp, 2007). Strategies for doing so are illustrated in Chapters 5, 11, 12, and 13.

Announcements of Friendly Competitions. Suppose that two golfers are practicing putting. One says to the other, "I'll bet I can make more 10-foot putts than you. We'll each take five putts. Loser buys the soft drinks." Although winning the bet involves a consequence (a free soft drink), the announcement of the bet is an antecedent that would motivate high practice effort among the participants. Announcements of friendly competitions can be an effective motivational strategy.

Schedule Cross Training for Variety. It is difficult for athletes to consistently show motivated behaviors when they follow the same training routine, day in and day out, for weeks on end. An effective motivational strategy is to plan a training schedule that includes different kinds of drills, exercises, and even different sports. The benefits of cross training (improved conditioning, different fun activities, etc.) are consequences. However, the announced schedule is an antecedent.

Train with a Partner. Whether an athlete participates in a team sport or an individual sport, training with a partner with similar goals and routines can motivate improved practice performance. A training partner can prompt an athlete to perform activities with maximum effort, and reinforce such activities when they occur.

Rules. The various antecedents listed above can serve as prompts to motivate desired athletic behaviors. Each of the antecedents should be accompanied by a rule that clearly identifies the desired sport behaviors, the situations in which they should occur, and the consequences for performing those behaviors. Guidelines for using rules effectively were described in Chapter 4.

Manage Consequences to Motivate Athletic Behavior

There are several different categories of reinforcers that motivate participation in sports. First, some people enjoy sports because winners get lots of attention. Ribbons, medals, the "roar of the crowd," having others look up to you, and congratulations from fans are all reinforcers that occur when athletes perform well and win. These reinforcers have a powerful effect on many athletes.

Second, a powerful reinforcer for most young athletes is the coach's praise. Useful guidelines for helping a coach to utilize his/her praise to motivate young athletes include:

a. Praise each athlete several times during each practice, contingent upon desireable practice behavior;

b. Ensure that the praise/reprimand ratio favours praise;

c. Be sensitive to each athlete's work volume across practices and praise an increase in output across practices in order to motivate young athletes to continue improving their output.

Third, some people participate mainly because of the consequences that result from self-improvement. For them, it is reinforcing to be able to swim faster this month than they did last month, or to make progress in lifting heavier weights, to tone up flabby muscles, or simply to experience the satisfaction of mastering a new skill.

A fourth kind of reinforcer derives from the sensory stimulation that is experienced while participating in a given sport. Practicing skills provides participants with visual, tactile, and auditory sensations, which can be rewarding to many athletes. For a cyclist it might be the sensation of speed and movement as he or she cycles at a fast pace. Or it might be the exhilarating sensations of "flying" for a young diver. A variety of sensory experiences can be reinforcing to a particular individual and may, as a result, go a long way toward influencing that person to persist in practicing his or her chosen sport.

Fifth, many athletes just "love to compete". We can explain this tendency by examining their reinforcement history. As described above, winning is paired with a variety of reinforcers. Therefore, cues associated with winning (e.g., scoring goals in ice hockey, receiving a high score from the judges in gymnastics, etc.) become strong conditioned reinforcers for most athletes (conditioned reinforcement was discussed in Chapter 3). Similarly, because competing is paired with winning (and the backup reinforcers associated with winning), cues associated with competing become conditioned reinforcers for athletes. In basketball, for example, a player who might be described as "loving to compete" is likely to be a player who finds it highly reinforcing to beat the opponents to a loose ball, make a good pass, and block a shot. Stated differently, given an appropriate reinforcement history, many athletes enjoy participating for the sake of the competition.

Sixth, peer approval and attention can be a powerful motivator. Unfortunately, peer attention often strengthens undesirable practice behaviors. It is possible, however, for a coach to capitalize on positive peer interaction to motivate desirable practice performance. One such example was described at the start of this chapter. You may recall that Coach Dawson was concerned about the kind of effort that he was getting from his players at practices. In particular, he expressed concerns about the degree of support and encouragement among teammates. He was also concerned about the apparent lack of motivation for the players to perform a series of lay-up drills and jump shooting drills to open each practice, and the team's freethrow shooting during practices.

The motivational system that he developed, with help from Daryll Siedentop, capitalized on positive peer interactions. You might recall that it included a point system and public recording of those points by volunteer students who served as managers for the team. Players could earn points for performance on various practice drills, and by encouraging their teammates. Not only was the system highly effective for improving the basketball skills (e.g., lay-ups, jump-shooting, etc.) but it also improved peer encouragement - an additional motivator. In Siedentop's words:

> ...the most dramatic improvement was in the "team player" category. Before implementation, 4 to 6 instances of criticism were detected during each practice session. Approximately 10 to 12 instances of peer encouragement were detected. The management system "required" that players encourage one another in order to win their points. During the first practice session after implementation, the managers recorded over 80 statements of encouragement among teammates, and also reported that they probably didn't record more than 1/3 of what actually happened. There were simply too many supporting comments to monitor them all. Coach Dawson reported that for several days the supporting comments were "pretty phoney." There was much laughter following comments and it all seemed to be pretty much "put on." But then a funny thing happened. The laughter slowly subsided. The boys got more comfortable saying nice things to one another. The comments got more genuine. At one point, according to Coach Dawson, the mood of his practices changed dramatically. He calls it the most amazing transformation he has seen in his coaching career. Teachers would stop Jim and ask him, "What in the world is going on in your practices?" He could reply in all honesty, "We have started to really help each other" (1980, p. 53).

It's also important for coaches to be aware that not all young athletes participate in sport as a function of reinforcers for doing so. We cannot ignore the fact that some kids play a sport because of pressure from their parents. And for some, ridicule or rejection by peers is an aversive consequence that may be escaped or avoided by that person's participation in sport. When participation is governed primarily by avoidance and escape conditioning, it is especially important for a coach to capitalize on reinforcers to motivate those athletes at practices and competitions in order to counteract the negative side-effects of aversive control (see Chapter 3).

An implication of a behavioral approach to motivation is that a coach can increase the likelihood of highly motivated behaviors in all young athletes by appropriately managing consequences. Steps to do so include determining reinforcers for specific athletes, and then deliberately managing those reinforcers to motivate desirable performance (e.g., see Figure 7-1), as described in detail in Chapters 10 through 12. Alternatively, athletes can be taught to manage consequences to motivate their own behavior, as described in Chapter 13.

Is deliberate use of reinforcement bribery?

Some critics of a behavioral approach to sport psychology have suggested that encouraging coaches to use reinforcers to deliberately motivate athletes is nothing more than bribery. In my view, such critics have not bothered to look up the definition of **bribery**, which is a reward or a gift offered to induce one to commit an immoral or illegal act. Suppose that a gambler offered $200,000 to the goalie of one of the soccer teams in the finals of the World Cup if he would let in a couple of easy goals. We would probably agree that that fits the definition of bribery. However, suppose that a coach of a youth ice hockey team offers the players the opportunity to earn an extra 15 minutes of scrimmage time at the end of practice if they each make five accurate passes during a passing drill. Is that bribery? Of course not. It is the use of a rule about a reinforcement program to strengthen desirable rule-governed behavior, not to commit an illegal or immoral act. As another example, the administration at the University of Manitoba tells the professors, at the beginning of each year, how much their salary will be for teaching, but nobody claims that the professors are being bribed to teach. Obviously, if critics accuse coaches of using bribery because coaches apply reinforcers deliberately to increase desirable athletic behaviors, then those critics have failed to distinguish between the promise of reinforcers for immoral or illegal deeds versus the promise of reinforcers for desirable behaviors.

Do Extrinsic Reinforcers Undermine Intrinsic Motivation?

As described in Chapter 3, reinforcers that immediately follow behavior in the normal course of everyday living are called natural reinforcers. Eating, for example, is naturally reinforced by the taste of food. As another example, when you meet an acquaintance, you might say "Hi. How are you?" and you are typically naturally reinforced by their response such as, "Fine, thank you. How are you?" Natural reinforcers are sometimes referred to as intrinsic reinforcers. On the other hand, also described in Chapter 3, when reinforcers are deliberately manipulated in order to change behavior, they are referred to as arbitrary, contrived, deliberately managed, or extrinsic reinforcers.

Figure 7-1. Fun scrimmages can be scheduled as reinforcers to motivate practice behaviors

In the example described at the beginning of this chapter in which Coach Dawson awarded points to his junior high basketball team for their performance on certain practice drills, and for being good team players, the points were extrinsic reinforcers.

Some people suggest that the use of extrinsic reinforcers to strengthen a behavior will undermine the intrinsic motivation to perform that behavior (Deci & Ryan, 1985; Kohn, 1993). What do these authors mean by the term *intrinsic motivation*? As described by Deci (1975), *intrinsically motivated behaviors* are those in which there is no apparent reward except for the activity itself. In sports, athletes who appear to participate in their chosen sport for no other reason than "the love of the game" might be described as intrinsically motivated. Beginning in the 1970s, Deci and others conducted experiments that seemed to imply that the use of extrinsic (or deliberately managed reinforcers) to increase a behavior may undermine intrinsic motivation to perform that behavior (Deci & Ryan, 1985; Deci, Koestner, & Ryan, 1999). This led some individuals (e.g., Kohn, 1993) to suggest that tangible rewards should not be given to children to perform desired activities. Kohn would argue, for example, that if parents give money to a child for reading, then the child will be less likely to "read for reading's sake." As another example, Kohn's argument would imply that Coach Dawson's program involved extrinsic reinforcers which would (in theory) undermine the players' intrinsic motivation to display the reinforced behavior. This implies that when Coach Dawson stopped giving points to players for specific practice behaviors, those behaviors would decrease to an even lower level than before the points program was initiated.

In my view, coaches can confidently ignore the advice of Deci, Kohn, and others that extrinsic reinforcers undermine intrinsic motivation. I say this for several reasons. First, their definition of intrinsically motivated behaviors does not take into account probable natural reinforcers that are likely to influence athletic behaviors. Just because a behavior is not followed by obvious deliberately managed reinforcers does not mean that there are no external reinforcers involved in its maintenance. As described earlier in this chapter, there are many natural reinforcers that strengthen participation in sports, including the roar of the crowd, "high fives" from team mates, sensory feedback inherent in performing a skill, the conditioned reinforcement of winning, etc. Second, when young people first begin to participate in a sport, they usually lack the skills to perform sufficiently to experience such natural reinforcers. Extrinsic reinforcers (such as deliberate praise from the coach, a points program like Coach Dawson's, etc.) may strengthen athletic behavior sufficiently in its early stages so that it can subsequently come under the control of natural reinforcers. And there is considerable evidence that use of deliberately programmed reinforcers with young athletes can greatly enhance athletic performance (Martin, 1992; Martin, Thompson, & Regehr, 2004; Martin & Tkachuk, 2000). Third, a careful review of more than 100 experimental studies conducted on this topic indicates that reward contingencies do not have pervasive negative effects on intrinsic motivation (Cameron, Banko, & Pearce, 2001). Fourth, observations indicate that rewards offered in everyday settings contingent upon specific behaviors do not negatively affect intrinsic motivation to perform those behaviors. For example, in a retrospective study of the effects of extrinsic rewards offered to children for reading, the rewards did not negatively affect the children's desire to read in later life (Flora & Flora, 1999). Finally, the notion that extrinsic reinforcers undermine intrinsic interest flies in the face of common sense (Flora, 1990). If extrinsic reinforcers undermine intrinsic motivation, for example, then those fortunate people who genuinely enjoy their jobs should refuse to be paid for fear that their paycheques will destroy their enjoyment of their work.

For the reasons outlined above, it is my view that *the notion that extrinsic reinforcement undermines intrinsic motivation is a myth.* Nevertheless, there are situations where it might appear, based on a superficial analysis, that extrinsic reinforcement undermines intrinsic motivation. Suppose, for example, that a coach of a youth basketball team is concerned that the players are not adequately practicing foul shooting on their own. Suppose further that the coach introduces the following program: At each practice, every player will shoot 10 foul shots; any player who makes all 10 shots will be reinforced with a bottle of Gatorade; any player who misses one or more of the 10 shots will have to sprint four lengths of the gym. Now this program does involve a reinforcement component. But it also involves a punishment component. And the difficulty of the criterion for reinforcement will mean that most of the players will experience punishment far more than they will experience reinforcement. The long term effect of such a program may be that practicing foul shots will become aversive, and when the program terminates, the players may practice foul shots on their own even less than they did prior to the program. However, most people would recognize that this outcome is an illustration of the side effects of aversive control (as discussed in Chapter 3). Most people would <u>not</u> conclude that this type of program is evidence that extrinsic reinforcement undermines intrinsic motivation.

Motivating Operations

As indicated previously, coaches and athletes can increase motivated behaviors by reinforcing them when they occur. But what if available reinforcers do not appear to be effective? The solution is to introduce motivation operations. **Motivating operations** (MOs) are events or operations that (a) temporarily alter the effectiveness of consequences as reinforcers or punishers, and (b) influence behaviors that normally lead to those reinforcers or punishers (Laraway, Snycerski, Michael & Poling, 2003; Michael, 1993). Consider, for example, the unconditioned reinforcer of food. When we are deprived of food, food becomes a powerful reinforcer and we engage in food seeking behavior. Just after eating a big meal, however, food temporarily loses its effectiveness as a reinforcer, and we are less likely to emit behaviors that have been reinforced with food. Thus, deprivation and satiation of food are MOs. Because deprivation and satiation alter the effectiveness of unconditioned reinforcers or punishers, and they do so without prior learning, they are called **unconditioned MOs (UMOs)**.

Some MOs alter the effectiveness of consequences as reinforcers or punishers, and they do so because of prior learning. In other words, they are not UMOs. Consider, for example, Coach Dawson's points program with the basketball players described earlier. Coach Dawson's explanation of the program was an MO because it established the points as reinforcers, and it increased the likelihood of desirable practice behaviors to earn those reinforcers. However, his explanation of the program would be described as a **conditioned MO (CMO)** - an MO that alters the effectiveness of conditioned reinforcers or punishers because of prior learning. Consider another example of a CMO. In the example described previously in which a golfer used imagery to create a pressure game by imagining himself competing in the Masters, he was administering a CMO to himself. The pressure game increased the reinforcing value of making a putt as a conditioned reinforcer, and increased the likelihood of focusing appropriately to make the putt. In both of these examples of CMOs, an antecedent variable altered the reinforcing effectiveness of behavioral consequences, and increased behavior that led to those consequences.

In addition to temporarily increasing the effectiveness of reinforcers, MOs can also temporarily abolish the effectiveness of reinforcers. As described previously, satiation of food temporarily abolishes the effectiveness of food as an unconditioned reinforcer. Consider another example. Suppose that a coach initiates a new set of drills to open practices at the beginning of a season. Initially, the players perform the drills enthusiastically, presumably in part because of some of the natural reinforcers for doing so (the drills are novel, challenging, etc.). But after several weeks of performing the same drills, the coach notices that the players have begun to delay the start of the drills, terminate the drills more quickly than they should, and the players are not nearly as enthusiastic. Presumably, the repetitive nature of the drills, day in and day out, has abolished the effectiveness of natural reinforcers for performing the drills, and has functioned as an MO to motivate escape and avoidance behaviors that are incompatible with productively completing the drills. An obvious solution for the coach is to introduce more variety in the opening drills. Posting a new schedule listing different types of drills would function as a CMO in that it would temporarily increase the extent to which aspects of the drills are conditioned reinforcers, and would influence behaviors that increase drill competition. Consider another example of an MO involved in the cause of problem behaviors. At football practices in the southern USA during excessively hot fall days, the heat may function as a UMO to increase the reinforcing value of inactivity, and to evoke counterproductive complaining among the players about the practice drills. Rather than introducing potential negative consequences for such behaviors, the coach might decrease the effectiveness of the heat as an MO for problem behavior by introducing more frequent than usual water breaks, or the occasional opportunity for the players to briefly sit in the shade. Further discussion of treatment implications of MOs in non-sport areas can be found in Martin & Pear (2011) and Sundberg (2004).

Students of behavior analysis sometimes confuse the concept of discriminative stimulus or S^D and the concept of CMO. In everyday language, an S^D is a cue that tells you what to do to get what you already want. Suppose, for example, that a football team has been practicing for a half an hour in the hot sun without water. The statement by the coach to one of the players, "Here are the keys to my car, bring the jug of ice water from the trunk," would be an S^D for the behavior of the player to go and get the ice water. The statement told the player how to get what he already wanted. In everyday language, a CMO temporarily changes what you want, and tells you how to get it. Thus, Coach Dawson's explanation of the points program was a CMO - it increased the likelihood that the players would want to earn points, and it told them how to do so.

In summary, this chapter has outlined a behavioral approach to the topic of motivation and athletic performance. In order to motivate athletic performance, coaches and athletes are encouraged to arrange antecedents to prompt motivated behavior, manipulate MOs to maximize the effectiveness of reinforcers for motivated behavior, describe the environmental arrangements in appropriately stated rules prior to practices and competitions, and provide reinforcers following motivated behavior.

Study Questions

1. How do many people conceptualize motivation? Illustrate with a sport example that is not in this chapter.

2. What is a conceptual limitation of the traditional conceptualization of motivation? Illustrate with a sport example that is not in this chapter.

3. List two practical limitations to conceptualizing motivation as an internal cause of behavior.

4. What is a general meaning of the verb "to motivate" as used in sports? What is an implication of this approach?

5. Describe an example that is not in this chapter to illustrate how an athlete might use imagery to motivate practice performance.

6. Describe an example that is not in this chapter to illustrate how an athlete might use picture prompts to motivate practice performance.

7. Recording and charting practice behaviors, and posting charted progress involves management of both antecedents and consequences to motivate practice

performance. Explain how both antecedents and consequences are involved.

8. Briefly describe four different categories of reinforcers that influence participation of athletes in sports. Give an example of each.

9. Many athletes appear to participate in sport for the sake of the competition. How might we explain that observation in terms of a reinforcement analysis? Illustrate with an example.

10. Is it likely that some young athletes participate in sports because of avoidance and/or escape conditioning? Justify your position.

11. How did Coach Jim Dawson go about encouraging the members of the junior high basketball team to be team players?

12. Is deliberate use of reinforcement by coaches bribery? Defend your position.

13. What does it mean to suggest that extrinsic reinforcement undermines intrinsic motivation? Illustrate with an example.

14. Describe any three of the five problems that were presented regarding the view that extrinsic reinforcement undermines intrinsic motivation.

15. What is a UMO? Illustrate with an example.

16. What is a CMO? Illustrate with an example.

17. Explain how Coach Dawson's program with the basketball players involved a CMO.

18. How does a CMO differ from an S^D? Illustrate with examples that are not in this chapter.

19. In a sentence, summarize, from a behavioral perspective, four steps that a coach might follow to motivate athletes.

Chapter 8

Thinking and Athletic Performance

An Application

Improving Execution of a Basketball Skill by Thinking about it[*]

Gail Kendall, assistant coach of the University of Winnipeg Women's Basketball Team, was concerned about he execution of the team's zone defense. When an opponent player attempted to dribble toward the basket, Gail wanted her player to execute a defensive skill called "cutting off the baseline." Specifically, Gail wanted her defender to cut-off the offensive player's path to the basketball hoop in such a way as to force the offensive player to pass back out, or to force a missed shot, or to create a turn-over and get the ball. In a research project, the performance of four of the defenders was videotaped and evaluated after games. The four players executed the defensive strategy correctly on an average of 60%, 59%, 49% and 54% of the opportunities respectively.

In an attempt to increase the percentages that the players "cut off the baseline", each player agreed to **mentally rehearse** correct execution of the strategy for approximately 15 minutes each day. Specifically, a player, while relaxed in a quiet setting, would visualize an opponent bringing down the ball. The defender would then say to herself "cut her off", and imagine herself successfully executing the "cutting off the baseline" strategy. After a brief pause, this would be repeated against another imaginary player. Each player was required to practice the strategy against five imaginary opponents each day, record the times that they practiced the **self-talk** and **mental imagery** strategy in a log book, and hand it in to Gail each week. The results were very positive with all four players. During the remaining games of the season, the players correct execution of the defensive strategy averaged 73%, 76%, 71% and 74% respectively. When asked about the procedures after the research, all four players indicated that they would not hesitate to suggest these self-talk and mental rehearsal techniques to other elite athletes.

[*]This application is based on a report by Kendall, Hrycaiko, Martin & Kendall (1990).

Thinking

One type of thinking used by the basketball players involved imagining themselves in a game situation – imagining so vividly that it seemed almost like the real thing. A second type of thinking practiced by the basketball players involved self-talk – telling themselves to "cut her off." In order to help athletes make their thoughts work for them, it is beneficial to thoroughly understand these two different types of thinking. Let's consider them in more detail.

Thinking As Imagery

All of us, at one time or another, have had the experience of thinking in images, not in words. And having a good imaging ability can be a valuable trait. Albert Einstein, for example, attributed many of his successes to his ability to think in images. People who score high on tests of creativity also tend to have a good imagination (Shaw & Belmore, 1983). And many highly successful athletes have learned to imagine specific aspects of their performance in considerable detail before they perform. Legendary golfer Jack Nicklaus, for example, attributed much of his success to his ability to form a mental picture of a golf shot just before hitting the ball (Nicklaus, 1974).

How is it that we learn to think in images? Why is it, for example, that you can close your eyes and imagine vividly the flag of your country? A part of the explanation may lie with respondent conditioning (see Chapter 2). As you grew up, you experienced many trials in which the words "our flag" were paired with actually looking at and seeing the flag of your country. As a result, when you now close your eyes and imagine that you are looking at your country's flag, the activity in your visual system enables you to experience the behavior of "seeing" the flag (see Figure 8-1). This has been referred to as **"conditioned seeing"** (Skinner, 1953).

Although we tend to form mental pictures when imagining things, all of our senses can be involved. In a broader sense, we might think of "conditioned sensing." That is, just as we acquire, through experience, conditioned seeing, we also acquire conditioned hearing, conditioned smelling, and conditioned feeling. Consider the example described by Martin & Osborne (1993) in which an individual experienced numerous passionate sexual encounters with a partner who consistently used a very distinctive perfume. Then one day someone walked past that individual in a department store wearing that same perfume. The individual immediately imagined seeing the partner (conditioned seeing), felt "tingly" all over (conditioned feeling), and even imagined that he heard the partner's voice (conditioned hearing).

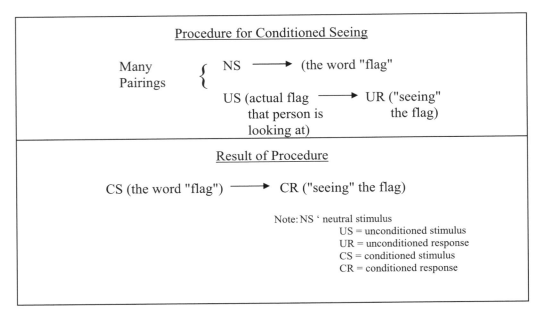

Figure 8-1. An example of conditioned seeing (or conditioned imagining).

This sort of thing is also a part of what goes on during fantasy. To experience a fantasy or to read or to listen to a story is, in some sense, to be there. It's as though you can see what the people see, feel what they feel, and hear what they hear. We're able to do this because of many instances of conditioned sensing. Our long histories of associating words with actual sights, sounds, smells and feelings enables us to experience the scenes which an author's words describe. The inside actions that occur when we're thinking are real - we're really seeing, or feeling, or hearing, when we respond to the words (Malott & Whaley, 1983).

As described above, when you imagine your country's flag, it is assumed that the imagery involves respondent conditioning. But what about the process of imagining yourself performing some action? That is, rather than "seeing" yourself perform a skill, you might "feel" yourself perform it. It is assumed that this latter type of imagery involves operant conditioning. As described in Chapter 3, our motor movements involving our skeletal muscles are learned through operant conditioning. As described in Chapter 5, one type of internal stimulation generated from movement is referred to as *proprioceptive feedback* (also referred to as kinesthetic sensations). Learning to be responsive to proprioceptive cues is a part of the process of becoming aware of our body positions and movements (Martens & Collier, 2011). For example, if I asked you to close your eyes and raise your left arm to shoulder level, you would be able to do so because you have learned to respond to the proprioceptive feedback that is generated when your arm is moved to that position. If I then asked you to close your eyes and to simply imagine raising your left arm to shoulder level, and to try to recapture the feelings as though you were actually performing that act, you would likely be able to do so. Presumably, such covert operant behavior is similar, in terms of its controlling variables, to the behavior of overtly moving your arm to that position (Skinner, 1953). While there are likely considerable individual differences in the clarity with which people can imagine themselves performing various skills that they have learned, the ability to do so is highly valued by top level athletes (Hardy, Gammage, & Hall, 2001; Orlick & Partington, 1988). In a survey of 235 Canadian Olympic athletes, 99% claimed to use mental rehearsal to enhance their performance (Orlick & Partington, 1988), and a number of studies have shown that imagery can enhance athletic performance (Vealey and Greenleaf, 2010).

Learning Mental Rehearsal

Before athletes can use imagery to improve athletic performance, they must become skillful at mental rehearsal. **Mental rehearsal** or **mental practice** refers to the process of imagining and feeling oneself performing an activity. An instance of mental rehearsal, if performed as recommended by experts on imagery training for athletes (Martin, Moritz, & Hall, 1999), is likely to include both respondent imagery and operant imagery. Consider, for example, a golfer imagining herself performing a golf shot. First, she might imagine the feeling (the proprioceptive cues) from assuming the proper knee-bend, etc. of the stance (operant imagery), she might imagine "seeing" the club head behind the ball (respondent imagery), she might recall the "feelings" of the proper backswing (operant imagery), and so forth. Mental rehearsal can involve all of the senses that are typically used while actually performing the skill that is being mentally rehearsed.

Guidelines for teaching mental rehearsal. Sport psychologists usually recommend that the first step in teaching athletes about mental rehearsal is to help them to relax (Gould & Damarjian, 1996). A review of early research using mental training in competitive settings found that procedures combining relaxation and imagery were, in general, superior to either relaxation or imagery alone (Greenspan & Feltz, 1989). However, the recommendation to include relaxation in mental rehearsal procedures has not been unanimous (Murphy, 1994). The primary reason for encouraging athletes to relax prior to engaging in mental rehearsal is to increase the likelihood that they will be responsive to cues that might be experienced during mental rehearsal. If a person is anxious or excited, it's difficult for that person to imagine all of the cues and sensations typically experienced while performing a skill.

While in a relaxed state, the athlete should be provided with specific prompts - auditory, visual, and tactual cues - concerning the conditions that normally surround the skill or performance to be mentally rehearsed, in order to elicit respondent conditioned sensing of the typical environment where the skill normally occurs. Suppose, for example, that a synchronized swimming coach wants a synchronized swimmer to mentally rehearse a particular sequence of movements to be performed during her routine. The coach might say, "Imagine that you are in the pool, waiting near the edge for your event to be announced.

You can see out of the corner of your eye that the judges have just raised the scores of the previous swimmers. Feel the water lapping gently against your arm, "and so on. If music is a part of the routine, such as in figure skating, then the music could be played in the background.

After setting the mood, athletes should then be asked to feel all aspects of the particular skill or performance exactly as though they were performing, in order to experience operant imagery. Encouraging athletes to feel themselves performing is often referred to as **internal imagery**, while encouraging athletes to imagine that they are watching themselves performing is often referred to as **external imagery**. Research that has attempted to evaluate which of the two types of imagery is most successful has yielded equivocal findings, causing some reviewers to recommend that athletes flexibly adopt training in both strategies (Gould & Damarjian, 1996, or that they be free to choose whichever strategy best suits them (Hall et al., 1994; Vealey & Greenleaf, 2010). From a behavioral analysis perspective, both types of imagery should be involved. Athletes should be encouraged to feel themselves performing (i.e., operant imagery). Additionally, the visual sense should be involved during mental rehearsal, but the athletes should see what they normally see while performing (i.e., respondent imagery), rather than watching themselves. A figure skater, for example, might imagine seeing the crowd and the judges just before mentally rehearsing her routine. A golfer might imagine looking at and seeing the golf ball on the grass just before mentally rehearsing the golf swing. Following a mental rehearsal of a skill, the athlete might be asked several questions to determine if the mental rehearsal was realistic. The athlete might be asked, for example, "What do you usually focus on when you perform that skill?" "What were you focusing on during your mental rehearsal?" "What body sensations did you feel?" "What did you imagine that you were looking at?" "Did it feel like you were actually performing the skill?" The athlete's answers will likely enable you to make additional suggestions to help make the mental rehearsal seem like the real thing.

Several additional guidelines have been recommended for teaching athletes to use mental rehearsal (Martin et al., 1999; Moritz, Hall, Martin, & Vadocz, 1996; Orlick, as expressed in Botterill, 1988; Vealey & Greenleaf, 2010). Athletes should start practicing imagery with skills that they already do well. The imagined skill or event should approximate the rate or speed of actual performance. They should try imagery with more advanced skills only after practicing it on easier skills. The athletes should always imagine themselves being successful when performing a skill. Practitioners suggest that the ability to use imagery can be enhanced considerably by devoting from 10 to 15 minutes per day to practicing successful imagery.

Mental Imagery to Enhance Practice Performance

There is no question that physical practice of a skill is more effective than mental practice of that skill. Nevertheless, there are some conditions under which mental rehearsal might enhance performance. We'll draw on principles of operant and respondent conditioning to help understand and capitalize on these conditions for improving the performance of athletes.

Imagery practice sessions to improve a skill. Suppose that a beginning basketball player, each evening before bedtime, imagines shooting ten shots from the free-throw line. Will such imagery practice improve that player's free-throw shooting during games? Many studies indicate that imagery practice can enhance the learning and performance of motor skills (Martin et al., 1999; Vealey & Greenleaf, 2010). However, we must be cautious about our explanations of why imagery practice might improve a skill. I say this because, when athletes are mentally rehearsing a particular task, they might also be rehearsing rules that exert stimulus control over improved athletic performance, and this latter possibility might account for performance improvement observed after instances of mental rehearsal (rule-governed control over behavior was discussed in Chapter 4). This possibility has rarely been assessed in research studies on mental practice, and one should be cautious about endorsing a technique without a solid understanding of the mechanisms that underlie its effectiveness. Nevertheless, many athletes have endorsed imagery practice sessions for improving skills.

Imagery to energize before practices. Committed athletes devote hundreds of hours to practicing sport skills. It stands to reason that, at the beginning of some practices, an athlete will feel sluggish, or be in a bad mood, and probably would prefer being elsewhere. Top-level athletes have indicated that they often use imagery to energize before practices. When in a bad mood just before a practice, for example, one young figure skater imagined the money that he would make in endorsements if he won a world championship. Thinking about using the money to buy a condo in Florida, another condo in Aspen, and travelling with friends elicited pleasurable feelings that put the skater in a positive mood. Another figure skater might imagine that she is about to experience the final practice before competing at the national championship. A hockey player might imagine that there is one more practice to go before the championship game, or he might visualize a particular opponent that he will face in the opening face-off. Other examples of the use of imagery to energize before practices are contained in the sport psychology video entitled, *Visualization: What you see is what you get* (Botterill, 1988).

Instant mental replays to learn the feelings of correctly-performed skills. If an athlete is unable to perform a skill, that athlete will be unable to imagine the appropriate feelings and kinesthetic sensations (or muscle memory) for that skill. But once a skill has been performed correctly a few times by an athlete, then mental rehearsal might be used to increase the athlete's consistency at performing that skill correctly (Vealey & Greenleaf, 2010). In my work with young figure skaters, for example, I suggested to them that they use **instant mental replays** to help them learn the muscle memory for a new jump. An instant mental replay is a mental rehearsal strategy to learn the feelings of a correctly-performed skill. Right after a skill has been performed correctly, an athlete might take a few seconds to mentally rehearse the skill, trying to feel everything exactly like it felt when the skill was performed. The skaters were instructed as follows:

1.   Pick a jump that you've been working on. It should be one that you've landed a few times, but that is not yet very consistent. The next time that you land that jump at practice, and feel good about it, immediately skate over to the side boards.

2.   While standing along the side, take a few deep breaths, close your eyes, and try to imagine what it felt like when you landed that jump. In other words, relive the jump in your mind. But imagine doing the jump three times in a row, and each time focus on a different part of it as follows:

   a)   The first time that you imagine it, think about what it felt like during the entry. Think about your balance, shoulders, and hands and leg position when you were skating into it and preparing to jump.

   b)   The second time that you imagine yourself doing that jump, think about the take-off. How did it feel when you brought your arms and legs in close? Was your back straight and your head up?

   c)   The third time that you think about the jump, focus on the landing. Did you bend your knee and use your free leg and arms to firmly check the rotation?

3.   After imagining the different parts of the jump in the three instant mental replays as described above, then take a few seconds and look around the rink. Now close your eyes and try to imagine the jump one more time. This time, don't worry about any particular part of it, just try to feel yourself performing the jump at the speed at which it actually occurred when you landed it.

In a study of 17 skaters who participated in a seasonal sport psychology program skaters were asked to rate a number of components of the program on a 5 point scale where 1 meant "No", 5 meant "Yes", and 3 meant "Somewhat". In terms of a question concerning use of imagery at practices to improve jumps, skaters gave it an average rating of 3.8 for being helpful (Martin & Toogood, 1997).

The main reason for recommending that athletes practice an imagery rehearsal immediately after performing a skill correctly is that it is easier for the athlete to recapture the feeling of doing it correctly immediately after the skill has been performed rather than at some later time. And being able to mentally rehearse a skill correctly might then be used to enhance performance at practices as described below, and at competitions (as described on the next page).

Imagery at practices before performing a previously-learned skill to increase the likelihood of performing it correctly. In many sports, such as figure skating, diving, and gymnastics, the athlete's goal is to perform flawlessly in front of the judges. Therefore, a typical goal is to get to the point where the routines can be performed flawlessly on the first attempt at practices. To increase the likelihood that this will occur, a figure skater might mentally rehearse a particular jump before attempting it, in order to experience the proper feeling. Olympic gold medal diver, Sylvia Bernier, mentally rehearsed her dives before performing them at practices. World champion synchronized swimmer, Carolyn Waldo, mentally rehearsed difficult artistic moves before performing them in the pool at practices. Many top-level athletes use mental rehearsal of a previously-learned skill before performing it at practices in order to increase the likelihood of correctly performing the skill on the first attempt (for other examples, see Botterill, 1988).

Visualization to simulate the competitive environment (to promote generalization to competition). Obviously, the ultimate goal for an athlete, after considerable practice, is to perform successfully at a competition. The more similar that the practice environment is to the competitive environment, the more likely it is that skilled athletic performances will generalize from practices to competitions. In Chapter 14, I discuss ways to physically arrange practice conditions to simulate competition conditions. An alternative is for athletes to use imagery to visualize a competitive environment during a practice, and to then attempt to perform successfully at that practice (e.g., see Figure 8-2). Suppose, for example, that the first hole that a golfer must play during a tournament has a narrow fairway with water on the left and trees on the right. While hitting some practice shots at the driving range before teeing off on the first hole, the golfer might imagine standing on the first hole, and looking down the fairway. The golfer might visualize where the water will be on the left, and what the trees on the right will look like. The golfer could then go through the normal preshot routine and practice hitting a ball down the middle of this imaginary fairway. The use of imagery to simulate competitive conditions during practices is discussed further in Chapter 14.

The term **visualization** is sometimes used interchangeably with the term *mental rehearsal*. However, because visualization is likely to be interpreted by many to refer to visual imagery, it should be restricted to situations where use of visual imagery (as opposed to experiencing kinesthetic feelings) is the primary objective.

Mental Imagery At Competitions to Enhance Competitive Performance

There are several ways that many highly successful athletes have reported use of mental imagery to enhance their performance at competitions. Three possibilities are described below.

Imagery for emotional control. In Chapter 2, I described how stimuli that are paired with emotion-causing events come to elicit those same emotional feelings through Pavlovian conditioning. Suppose, for example, that a child reaches out to touch a large dog just as the dog barks very loudly, which scares the child. As a function of the pairing of the loud bark with the sight of the big dog, the sight of the big dog alone can come to cause feelings of fear (increased heart rate, crying, trembling, etc.) by the child. Because our emotions come under the control of various stimuli, and because our images of those

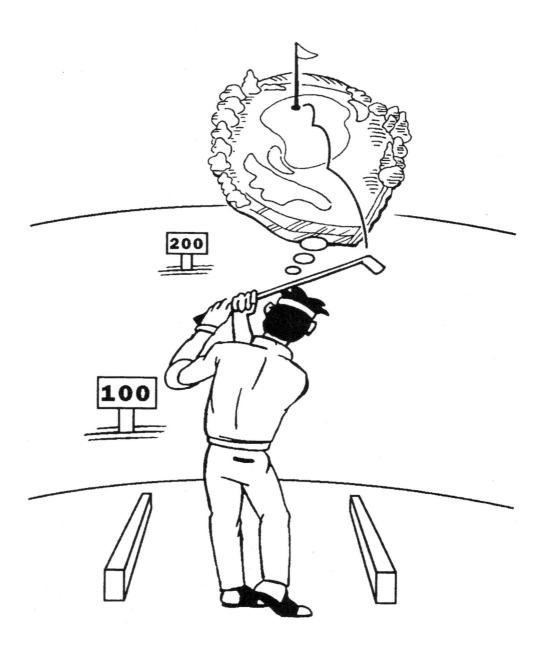

Figure 8-2. At a driving range, a golfer can visualize a particular hole on the golf course on which he/she will be competing, and then practice the shot for that hole.

stimuli are similar to the real thing, we can conjure up images of those stimuli to elicit various emotions. Just thinking of a big dog is now likely to cause the child to feel fear. As another example, think of the last time that you got really mad while arguing with someone. Try to imagine where you were, who was there, what was said, the expressions on the person's face and how you felt in the situation. As you relive the scene, are you beginning to feel angry all over again? If you imagine a previous situation in which you experienced a strong emotion, the imagery will likely cause you to reexperience some of that emotion.

Now consider an example in sport. Suppose that a golfer is standing over a crucial 4-foot putt on a fast green with a steep downhill slope. Looking at the putt, the golfer realizes that the ball could easily roll 6 feet past if the putt is missed. That image is likely to elicit feelings of nervousness and tension, which may interfere with the golfer executing a smooth putting stroke. On the other hand, while looking at the ball before putting it, the golfer might imagine the path of the ball as it rolls slowly towards the middle of the cup, and might "see" the putt drop into the hole. Such imagery is likely to elicit quite different feelings. The obvious message here is for the golfer to use imagery to imagine positive outcomes of shots in order to elicit emotions that are likely to enhance appropriate execution, rather than imagining negative outcomes of shots which would likely elicit emotions that would hinder performance.

Consider another example from golf. Suppose that a golfer is about to play an important match. It's approximately 15 minutes until the scheduled time to begin, and the golfer is feeling quite nervous. This is an ideal time to use imagery for emotional control. The golfer could sit in the locker room, or on a bench just outside the club house, close his/her eyes, and visualize a relaxing scene that had been previously experienced. The golfer might imagine, for example, that he/she is sitting on a deserted beach on a warm summer day, watching the waves. The golfer might imagine feeling the warm sun, and seeing the waves break on shore, over and over and over. When the golfer feels quite relaxed, he/she could then proceed to the tee box to begin the match.

Mental rehearsal of a skill(s) just before performing. Jack Nicklaus still has the best record of any golfer in major tournaments (although Tiger Woods might surpass that record). Nicklaus suggested that success on any one shot in golf depends 10% on technique, 40% on set-up (e.g., club selection for the particular shot, etc.), and 50% on mental rehearsal of the correct form for the shot (Nicklaus, 1974). Of course, we don't know if the percentages accurately identify determinants of his success. We do know, however, that during a typical round, Nicklaus indicated that he mentally rehearsed every shot before performing it. First he pictured the target spot where he wanted the ball to land (i.e., respondent imagery). Then he visualized the arc of the ball flying through the air to land on that target spot (again, respondent imagery). Next he imagined himself executing the swing needed in order to produce a shot that would give the ball that particular flight pattern.

When imagining himself performing the swing, he imagined how it felt to him when he was addressing the ball, on his backswing, on his follow through, weight transfer, and so forth (i.e., operant imagery). In other words, he did not mentally picture how someone else might see him from the outside; he imagined how he felt from the inside while executing the shot.

Many highly successful athletes have learned to mentally rehearse specific aspects of performance in considerable detail just before performing. A figure skater is likely to do a mental rehearsal of an entire program during the last fifteen minutes or so before competing. An ice hockey player might visualize himself/herself in a variety of game situations before putting on his equipment on game day. He/she might visualize on-ice situations, and try to feel finishing a check, forechecking and creating a turnover, winning a battle for a loose puck, and so on. A basketball player, just before a game, might mentally rehearse successfully performing a defensive tactic against an opponent (as described at the beginning of this chapter). Hundreds of athletes have endorsed mental rehearsal as an effective technique for helping them to prepare to compete to the best of their ability (Orlick & Partington, 1988).

Why should mental rehearsal of a well-learned skill at a competition enhance the likelihood of that skill being performed optimally? First, imagery can help to recall the kinesthetic sensations associated with a skilled performance. Presumably that increases the likelihood of reexperiencing those sensations while attempting to perform the skill correctly. Here is an example. Suppose a golfer is about to tee off on a very tight driving hole on a course that she frequently plays. If she hits it to the right, the ball will go out of bounds. The desire to hit it to the left causes her to shorten her swing, exaggerate an outside-in swing path (for a right-hander), and hit a big fade that ends up where she doesn't want to be - in trouble on the right. Now imagine the very next time that the golfer will play that hole. What thoughts are likely to enter her head just before teeing off? Probably the memory of her last shot on that hole when she hit into trouble on the right. But of course that's not the memory that she wants. A solution? The golfer might think of the last time that she hit a great shot with the club that she is now using. She could picture the hole and feel the swing that she took, imagine her set-up, the tempo, and the feel of a smooth swing and the excellent result. Now she could set up and hit the shot on a tight hole with that imagery in mind. In this way, she is using mental rehearsal to recall the feelings and muscle memory of a successful shot with that same club. A second explanation of the benefits of mental rehearsal of a skill just before performing that skill at a competition is that the mental rehearsal might help to minimize distractors.

Imagery to help tune out distractors. Just before an athlete is about to perform, distractors can be especially disruptive to skilled performance. Such things as psych-out attempts by the opposition, worrying about performing poorly, worrying about what others will say if the athlete loses, and the like, have caused havoc with many athletes. Mental rehearsal of a skill just before performing that skill at a competition might help to minimize distractors. The athlete who is mentally rehearsing a particular past successful performance is less likely to experience negative thoughts that can cause excessive nervousness and tension that would detract from performance. Stated differently, an athlete who is mentally rehearsing a past successful performance of a skill is focusing on what he/she wants to do, rather than worrying about what not to do, which is one of the components of self-confidence (discussed further in Chapter 15). Examples of athletes' use of mental rehearsal to minimize distractors can be seen in the video narrated by Botterill (1988).

Thinking as Self-Talk

Have you ever watched a 3- or 4-year-old child play alone with a toy truck in a sand pile? Chances are that you observed the child talking out loud while playing. "Now I'll put my truck in here," the child might say. "Darn, my truck got stuck!" The child is thinking out loud in words. Much of our thinking is made up of things that we say to ourselves - called **self-talk**. Thinking out loud is something that we learn to do as children, perhaps in part because it helps us to perform tasks more efficiently (Roberts, 1979). When children first start attending preschool, they often say rules out loud to themselves to adjust to difficult tasks (Roberts & Tharp, 1980). By the time that kids are about the ages of 5 or 6 years old, however, they have learned to talk silently to themselves (Vygotsky, 1978). Children learn to talk silently to themselves at an early age because they encounter punishers when they think out loud, such as when nearby adults tell them to "be quiet" (Skinner, 1957). Also, teachers in school prompt children to think to themselves because the classroom would be extremely noisy if all the children "thought out loud". Also, as we grow older, we learn to keep certain thoughts to ourselves because of the distressed reactions from others when we think out loud. When you see someone that you haven't seen for several years, for example, your first reaction might be, "Wow, have you let yourself go!" But you probably won't say it out loud; instead you will "say it to yourself" or "think" it. Because much of our thinking goes on at a level that is not observable to others, we refer to it as *private behavior*. Although private self-talk is more difficult to study in that it can not be directly observed, we assume that it is the same as speaking out loud; that is, that the operant conditioning principles described in Chapter 3 apply to private self-talk in the same way that they apply to public operant behavior.

Often, an instance of what we would refer to as thinking includes both imagining and self-talk. To illustrate, consider the possible thinking of a figure skater just before stepping onto the ice to skate her program in a competition. And let's suppose that the figure skater fell on her triple toe jump in the previous competition. The skater might say to herself, "I hope I don't fall on my triple toe again!" (operant thinking or private self-talk). The skater can picture herself clearly at the previous competition (respondent thinking or conditioned seeing or imaging). Thoughts of the aversive experience would likely elicit unpleasant feelings (a respondently conditioned response as described in Chapter 2).

Athletes can be taught to use their self-talk to improve performance in five areas: controlling their emotions and/or mood, stopping negative thoughts, improving their focusing or concentration skills, problem solving and planning, and improving skill acquisition and performance.

Self-Talk to Control Emotions and/or Mood

Imagine a weight-lifter mentally preparing to lift a heavy weight. The weight lifter thinks, "Energy! Power! Super strength!" That kind of self-talk is likely to help the weight-lifter feel energized. Or consider a gymnast who thinks, "Easy, Balance, Graceful" in order to relax just before stepping on the balance beam. As discussed in more detail in Chapter 9, our self-talk can serve as conditioned stimuli to elicit various emotional feelings (Staats, 1968; Staats, Staats, & Crawford, 1962).

Words that elicit emotional feelings which have been associated with past successful performance are referred to as **mood words**. In ice hockey, for example, use of mood words can help a player to maintain intensity at the right level. When skating onto the ice for a shift after a whistle or when waiting for the players to get set for a face-off, a player can quickly rehearse some mood words. Mood words used by some of the professional hockey players with whom I have worked include "be aggressive," "fast feet," "kick ass," "play mean," "maximum overdrive." Such words are likely to help the players play with the desired level of intensity. Professional golfers with whom I have worked, on the other hand, usually want to create a very different mood. They want to feel relaxed and in control. They are more likely to use self-talk like, "swing smooth," "enjoy the moment," "stay in control," and "feel the tempo."

Some words might function as both mood words and as partial rules. For example, when an ice hockey player thinks, "fast feet," those words might elicit some of the feelings associated with skating fast and performing well in the past. But they also imply a partial rule. The complete rule might be, "If I keep my feet moving quickly, I'll keep my speed up and create opportunities for a shot on goal."

Self-Talk to Stop Negative Thoughts

As illustrated previously, self-talk can be used to increase desirable emotions. But sometimes the opposite problem occurs. Sometimes an athlete will experience negative emotions or disturbing thoughts that he/she would like to get rid of. An ice hockey player in a scoring slump, for example, might be so obsessed with scoring that he/she forgets about focusing on the actions (such as getting into the open, cushioning a pass, etc.) that result in goals. Or a figure skater who fell on a particular jump during an important competition might frequently relive that experience, which produces anxiety and interferes with future performance. Or a gymnast at a practice might get so obsessed and angry (over a difficult move that he/she is unable to perform) that the entire practice is ruined.

One strategy for helping athletes to terminate such thoughts is called thought-stopping. **Thought-stopping** is a procedure designed to temporarily disrupt whatever it is that a person might be thinking about. One way to do this was developed by behavior therapist Joseph Wolpe (1958) to help a person who engages in persistent, disturbing, private thinking that he or she can not control. The procedure involves teaching an athlete to yell "Stop!" silently in order to disrupt the unpleasant thoughts. To teach this technique, you first instruct the athlete to close his/her eyes and to imagine a particular scene, such as sitting on the sand at a beach watching the waves roll up on shore. When the athlete has the scene clearly in mind, you yell loudly, "Stop!" Of course, your loud yelling serves to disrupt the thoughts of the athlete (and probably startle him/her in the process). Next, explain to the athlete that you wish him/her to close their eyes and to yell "Stop!" when you tap the athlete's shoulder. Then, instruct the athlete to imagine another scene, such as looking up at a clear blue sky with a few white fluffy clouds. After allowing the athlete a few seconds to vividly imagine the scene, tap the athlete lightly on the shoulder. Repeat this process a couple of times. After three such trials, repeat the process again, except this time instruct the athlete to yell "Stop!" silently to him or herself, rather than out loud (they are able to do so with their mouth closed). After several such attempts, the athlete will be able to temporarily disrupt any thought by "silently yelling" "Stop!" to him or herself.

Other thought-stopping procedures involved inflicting mild pain on oneself. One strategy is to wear a rubber band on your wrist, and whenever disturbing thoughts occur, you simply snap the rubber band. Another strategy is to disrupt undesirable thoughts by using your fingers to give the hair on your arm a quick yank. A third possibility is to give your thigh a sharp slap

Thought-stopping by itself is not likely to have much longterm success because, although it temporarily interrupts the negative thoughts, they are likely to return. However, thought-stopping combined with substitution of desirable alternative thoughts can be quite successful in eliminating problem thoughts (Wolpe, 1990), as illustrated by the following case. Rob McMillan, a professional golfer, had been in contention several times to win tournaments on the Canadian tour, but each time had fallen short (although he had won on the tour as an amateur). One of his goals during tournament play was to take it one shot at a time. In Rob's words, "When I'm playing well, I think of nothing but each shot - not looking ahead or behind. I put everything outside my mind and ignore everything when I get up to the shot. During the round, I try not to think about what's going on in the tournament. I try to focus on one shot at a time and what I need to do with that shot. Then I just go ahead and hit it. In between shots, I work on staying relaxed. I joke around with my caddy and stay loose." However, Rob had trouble maintaining this type of focus when he was in contention to win on the final day of a tournament. Instead, he found himself thinking about what it would mean to win, what score might be necessary to win, who was making a move on the leader board, and so on. To help him maintain his focus when he was in contention, we worked on a two-component strategy. The first component was thought-stopping. He decided that, on the final day of a tournament when he was in contention, if negative thoughts popped into his head, he would immediately grab the hair on his arm and give it a yank. This served to disrupt the negative thoughts. Second, he immediately followed that up with desirable alternative thoughts. If he was in the middle of his pre-shot routine, he would simply remind himself, "Stick with your routine," and start his pre-shot routine all over again. If he was walking down the fairway in between shots or waiting for his playing opponents to hit the ball, he would follow thought-stopping by talking to his caddy about one of several predetermined topics, such as their favourite movies. The next time that he was in contention was in a Canadian Tour event in British Columbia, which he won. When I talked to him after the tournament and asked him how the thought-stopping routine went, Rob replied, "It worked great, but I don't have much hair left on my arm."

Self-Talk for Attention Control or Focusing

The ability to *concentrate* during an athletic competition, to *attend* to the proper cues while competing, and to stay *focused* throughout an athletic competition are widely recognized as important determinants of success. But how do we define such terms?

Concentration (discussed further in Chapter 15) refers, in part to the extent to which relevant cues in the athletic environment exert stimulus control over skilled athletic behaviors. The terms, attending and focusing, can be used interchangeably, and refer to the behavior of orienting to relevant S^Ds (as discussed in Chapter 15). Robert Nideffer (1985; Williams, Nideffer, Wilson, Sagal, & Pepper, 2010) developed a useful strategy for analyzing an athlete's attending in terms of four major categories of stimulus control as illustrated in Figure 8-3.

The dimensions of stimulus control (broad vs. narrow and internal vs. external) should be thought of as continua, rather than as four discrete categories. Nevertheless, they provide a useful way of isolating some of the S^Ds that exert control over athletic performance. *Broad external stimulus control* indicates that, in some athletic situations, the athlete must attend to a number of different external cues in a short period of time. Examples would include a quarterback in football trying to pick out a receiver while at the same time being aware of onrushing opposing linemen, a defensemen setting up a power play in hockey while attending to the location on the ice of teammates and opponents, and a point guard in basketball attempting to set up a play when the opponents are running a zone defense.

Narrow external stimulus control refers to an athletic skill under the stimulus control of a specific external stimulus, and the ability of the athlete to ignore a variety of potential distracting cues. Examples would include a batter focusing on the baseball from the point when it leaves the pitcher's hand until it arrives at the plate, a tennis player watching the ball as it leaves the opponent's racquet until the player makes contact with the ball in an attempted return, and a goalie in ice hockey focusing on the puck rather than being distracted by the movement of the players milling around in front of the net.

Broad internal stimulus control refers to instances of thinking about complex problems in the absence of any obvious external S^Ds; such thinking is often referred to as analyzing, planning, and problem solving. A football coach at half-time, for example, might mentally review the different defensive formations of the opponents, and recall the offensive plays that were executed successfully and unsuccessfully against those formations.

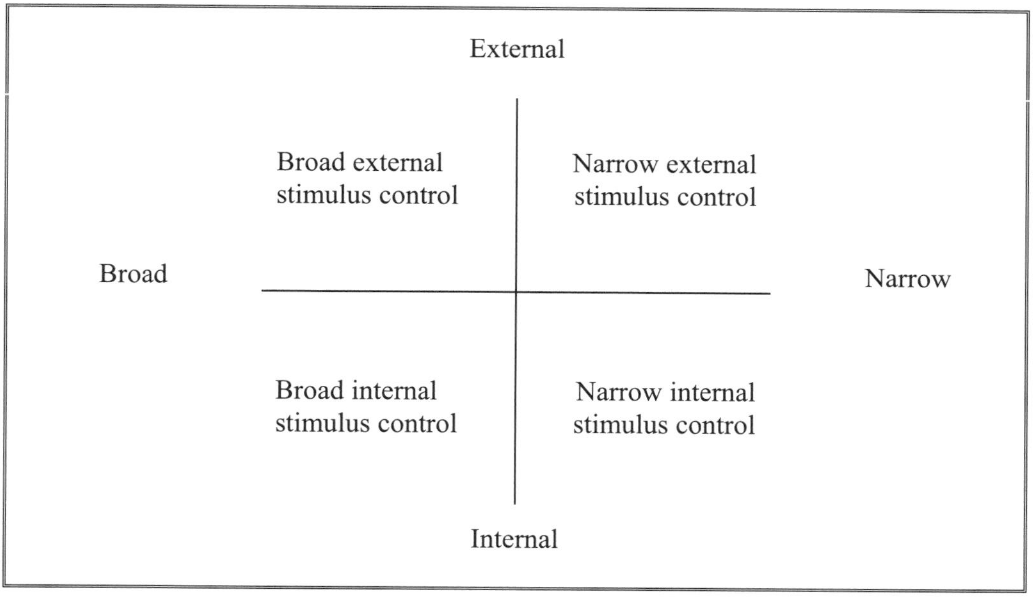

```
                            External

              Broad external        Narrow external
              stimulus control      stimulus control

   Broad     _____|_____     Narrow

              Broad internal        Narrow internal
              stimulus control      stimulus control

                            Internal
```

Figure 8-3. Categories of attentional control devised by Robert Nideffer (1981)

The final category, *narrow internal stimulus control*, refers to situations where an athletic skill is under the control of a specific internal cue. A diver, for example, might focus on achieving a particular kinesthetic sensation or "feel" as a prompt for coming out of a forward somersault just before hitting the water. A figure skater might focus on the feeling of being directly over the take-off foot at the beginning of a jump.

During an athletic performance, an athlete is likely to shift between the different categories of stimulus control, and self-talk can be used to facilitate proper shifting of attention. We'll examine how a golfer can use self-talk to shift between the four categories of stimulus control during the execution of a shot (also, see Williams et al., 2010).

Suppose that the golfer has hit the ball off the tee. As the golfer approaches her ball as it lies in the fairway, her attention needs to be under broad external stimulus control in that she needs to consider a wide range of external cues - the hazards, the safe areas, the wind, the lie, the distance for the next shot, etc. In the presence of these broadly-based external cues, she needs to choose the proper club for the shot. Simply saying "LWLD" while approaching the ball would remind the golfer to always check the landing area, the wind, the lie, and the distance before selecting the club for the shot. Next, while standing behind the ball to take a practice swing, her behavior might switch to broad internal stimulus control. That is, she might remind herself of a similar shot that she performed successfully on an earlier hole. She might then focus on a couple of swing thoughts while taking a practice swing. She might remind herself to swing smooth, and she might take a couple of deep breaths to help herself relax. The phrases "just like before" and "feel the swing" might remind the golfer to focus on the appropriate muscle sensations during the practice swing. Then, when setting up for the shot, her attention switches to narrow external control. She needs to focus primarily on the line on which she wants to hit the ball, and the proper placement of her feet for the stance in order to hit the ball along that line. The phrase "set it up" would prompt the proper set-up. Finally, her behavior is likely to switch to narrow external control. Just before swinging, she needs to focus on the direction that she wants to hit the ball. At that point, she is also likely to use only a single thought such as, "straight flight" in order to focus on starting the ball in the desired direction (e.g., see Bell & Hardy, 2009).

Self-talk can be used to help an athlete bring his/her behavior under the appropriate type of attentional control. A golfer, for example, is likely to improve consistency by having set reminders for each of the four parts of the preshot routine described above. A figure skater can use self-talk for narrow internal stimulus control during a program to focus attention on setting up particular jumps in a certain way, and for broad external stimulus control to remind herself to present the program to the judges and the audience in order to maximize artistic marks. An ice hockey player might use self-talk between shifts to help focus his/her attention for the next shift. Examples might include: "I'll stay with my check until we have control;" "In our end, I'll be aggressive and strong down low;" and, "In their end, I'll apply quick pressure on the opposing puck carrier."

Self-Talk for Skill Acquisition and Performance

Just before a jump in figure skating, or a serve in tennis, or the kicking of a field goal in football, or a drive in golf, should the athlete use instructional self-talk? Experts do not agree on the answer to this question. On the one hand, some athletes have reported that their best sport performances occurred automatically without consciously thinking during the action (Krane & Williams, 2010). On the other hand, many psychologists (e.g., Williams, Zinsser, & Bunker, 2010) argue that athletes usually do think before and during sport performances but they are often unaware of it. And many athletes report using self-talk at practices and during competitions (Hardy et al., 2001). While more research is needed on this issue, most experts agree that it is not thinking itself that causes problems, but rather improper thinking.

In order to maximize the success of your recommendations to an athlete to use self-talk to enhance performance of a skill, you should begin by clarifying the nature of the problem. What function do you hope that the self-talk will serve? There are several possibilities. *First*, if you want to help the athlete recapture feelings and emotions associated with past successful performances, then you might recommend mood words (such as a golfer thinking, "s-m-o-o-t-h" to elicit feelings of a relaxed, easy swing). And in order to ensure that mood words are functioning as a CS, you should follow guidelines for respondent conditioning. *Second*, if your task is to help an athlete persist in the practice of a repetitive, previously-learned skill, then you might focus on self-talk which the athlete could use as a reinforcer following desirable actions (such as a golfer thinking, "Good work, keep it up," after successfully executing several good shots at the driving range). Guidelines for using reinforcement effectively are presented in Chapters 10, 11 and 12. *Third*, if you want to help an athlete improve the quality and consistency of skills at practices and competitions, then you might recommend technique words or **key words** that would serve as S^Ds to prompt particular body positions or focus of attention (such as a golfer thinking, "shoulder turn" to prompt a full shoulder turn on the back swing). Research has demonstrated that key words, just before performing a skill, can enhance skill acquisition at practices (Garza & Feltz, 1998; Johnson, Hrycaiko, Johnson, & Halas, 2004; Masser, 1993; Ming & Martin, 1996; Smith & Johnston, 2000; Ziegler, 1987), lead to improvements in speed of performance and volume of work output (i.e., endurance training) involving previously learned skills during practices (Landin & MacDonald, 1990; Mallett & Hanrahan, 1997; Rushall, 1984; Rushall, Hall, Roux, Sasseville, & Rushall, 1988; Rushall & Shewchuk, 1989), enhance accurate repetition of previously learned skills at practices (Bell & Hardy, 2009); enhance transfer of previously learned skills from practices to competitions (Kendall et al., 1990; Hamilton & Fremouw, 1985; Hill & Borden, 1995), and enhance endurance performance (Hamilton, Scott, & MacDougall, 2007).

At the Vancouver Olympics in 2010, Tess Virtue and Scott Moir took home Canada's very first ice dancing gold medal, and at ages 20 and 22, they are the youngest ice dancers ever to win a gold medal in the Olympics. Shortly after their compulsory dance on February 19, the first of the three dance programs that they completed, a sportscaster asked them, "How did you cope with the excitement and the crowd?" Tessa replied, "Just before our program, we focused on our key words for the dance: relax, calm, knees."

A behavioral analysis and available research support four rules for using key words and rules to improve performance of a skill at practices and competitions.

Rule #1: *An athlete's self-talk should help the athlete to focus on what he/she wants to do, not what he/she doesn't want to do.* Consider the example of a golfer who says, just before hitting a shot, "Don't swing too hard," or "Don't lift your head," or "Don't lose this one to the right," or "Don't jab it (while putting)." There are two problems with that type of self-talk. First, as indicated previously, it focuses on negative outcomes and is therefore likely to function as a CS to elicit excessive nervousness. Second, that type of self-talk is almost impossible to follow. If I tell you, for example, not to think of a pink elephant, what is the first thing that you will think about? A pink elephant. On the other hand, if I tell you to think of a white rabbit, chances are that you will think of a white rabbit (and it's unlikely that thoughts of a pink elephant will pop into your head). Thus, an athlete's key words should always focus on what he/she wants to do, not what he/she doesn't want to do.

Rule #2: *When an athlete is learning a skill, the athlete should use a few key words to prompt specific positions or movements in order to perform the skill properly*. If an individual is learning the golf swing, for example, a beginning right-handed golfer might think the words "balance" to prompt the proper weight distribution and set-up, the words "push back" to prompt starting the backswing with the left side, the words "shoulder to chin" to prompt a full shoulder turn on the backswing, and so forth. Only one or two of these key words might be used on any given swing. If practicing at a driving range, the beginner might think the first couple of key words on the first two shots, the next couple on the next two shots, and so on in order to improve the swing.

Rule #3: *After a skill has been mastered, an athlete can use self-talk just before executing a skill at practices and competitions, in order to help transfer that skill from practices to competitions*. As described in Chapter 14, one strategy for transferring skilled athletic performance from practices to competitions is to bring the desired athletic behavior under the control of specific stimuli in practices that can be taken to the competition. In the behavior modification literature, this strategy for programming stimulus generalization is referred to as "programming common stimuli." An athlete can use self-talk to remind him or herself of the sorts of things that are usually focused on in practice, and then by focusing on some of those same things at a competition, skilled performances that occurred in practice are likely to transfer to the competition.

Consider the case of Damian, a twenty-year-old sophomore college basketball player. In practices, he rarely missed a foul shot. But during games, his foul shooting percentage was less than 40%. Obviously, the problem was not lack of skill, rather it was a problem of transferring a previously learned skill from practices to games. To solve the problem, Damian consistently rehearsed specific self-talk just before foul shooting at practice. Before every shot, he would say, "relax," and take a deep breath; he then said "bounce" and bounced the ball once; he then said "set up, and focus," and then set up for the shot, focused on the rim, and shot the ball. After using this strategy consistently across several practices, he then used it in games. His foul shooting in games improved to approximately 70%. Although Damian's case is fictitious, similar results have been reported for foul shooting (Hamilton & Fremouw, 1985) and a defensive basketball skill (Kendall et al., 1990) with college-level basketball players.

After a skill has been mastered, should the self-talk that an athlete uses, just before executing that skill, focus on body positions or external cues? Some research suggests that the latter may be more effective. In one study, skilled male golfers were divided into two groups while practicing 20-meter chip shots (hitting the ball from just off the putting green to the flag stick). One group was instructed, just before hitting a chip shot, to focus on the motion of the arms and wrists and to use the key words "wrist hinge" in order to prompt a proper wrist release. The other group was instructed, just before each shot, to focus on the flight of the ball after it left the club face and to use the key words "straight flight" in order to prompt themselves to maintain an external focus. Some of the golfers in each group were also told that their performance would be examined by golf professionals, in an effort to increase their anxiety. The results indicated that, regardless of anxiety conditions, those who maintained an external focus of attention performed more accurately (Bell & Hardy, 2009). Whether or not this finding will hold up in future research with athletes in other sports remains to be seen. Also, subjective reports from some top athletes counteract the above finding that self-talk should maintain an external focus rather than an internal focus. For example, consider reports of some professional golfers. When asked about his swing thoughts, Jack Nicklaus replied, "At the driving range before a tournament, I hit a few balls to see how my swing feels, then I choose two or three swing thoughts to use during the round." Sometimes the swing thoughts of professional golfers are mood words that help golfers to focus on the desired feeling that goes along with having a good rhythm, such as the late Payne Stewart's "Keep it smooth." Sometimes they are key words that focus on the speed of the swing, such as Jack Nicklaus' "Slow takeaway." And sometimes the key words of professional golfers focus on swing mechanics or technique, such as Nick Price's thought of "Sit" at the top of his backswing to focus on "sitting" on his right knee during the downswing (to keep himself from sliding laterally). Thus, based on the limited research thus far, in conjunction with reports of top athletes, I would encourage skilled athletes to experiment with both focuses of attention, and to use the strategy that appears to work best.

Of course, sports like golf, figure skating, gymnastics, and diving where the timing of the performance is under the control of the athlete, are more amenable to the use of key words than sports like ice hockey, basketball, and football, where the action is extremely fast-paced and includes reactions to opponents. In ice hockey, for example, if a defenseman pauses to rehearse his key words while superstar Sidney Crosby streaks toward him with the puck, the defenseman will be left standing while Crosby is long gone with a clear shot on goal. But even in fast-paced reactive sports, there are typically pauses in the action where key words and self-talk can be used to enhance performance. Earlier, we described how a basketball player might use self-talk to enhance foul shooting during games. And in ice hockey, many players could make better use of the time between shifts on the ice. While sitting on the bench, some players become spectators. Their thoughts and emotions are controlled by what they see happening on the ice. That can be good if the player's team is playing well. But sometimes it's not good, especially when things are not going well on the ice. Other players let their minds wander between shifts (e.g., they think about their agent, contract, love life, etc.) and they lose their concentration. Still other players get down on themselves after a bad shift, or after missing a chance to score. And players who are not on the specialty teams sometimes have trouble staying in the game when there are a lot of power plays or penalties, and they have to sit on the bench for quite a while. Hockey players could use self-talk between shifts to help them play the best game that they are capable of. Some of the professional hockey players with whom I worked used the strategy of "relax, regroup, refocus." (A similar strategy has been used by Wayne Halliwell [1990] in his work with professional hockey players and by Ken Ravizza [Ravizza & Osborne, 1991] in his work with college football players.)

After a shift, the hockey player would:

a) Relax - they relaxed during the first 30 seconds or so after a shift
b) Regroup - they rehearsed general self-talk to put the last shift behind them and get ready for the next shift
   e.g., "That one's gone forever,"
         "The rest of my game starts now,"
         "Get ready for the next shift."

c) Refocus - they reviewed some key words to help them be properly focused for the next shift
   e.g., "I'll jump on loose pucks,"
         "I'll finish my checks,"
         "I'll shoot quick."

Rule #4: *Too much self-talk can cause "paralysis by analysis"*. Can you imagine a golfer trying to hit a ball while thinking, "Arms straight, full shoulder turn, pause briefly, don't hurry, move your hips laterally, hit down, no peeking, and follow through." If the golfer tries to think about too many details in the middle of a swing, the swing will be jerky and forced, not smooth and rhythmic. Thus, while an athlete might identify a number of key words to help achieve the proper focus and feelings while performing a skill, only two or three of them should be used on any given attempt in order to guard against "paralysis by analysis" - thinking about so many things during performance of a skill that the performance is disrupted.

When Recommending Self-Talk for Athletes, Capitalize on Guidelines for Using Rules Effectively

Self-talk to control emotions (as described in Chapter 9) or mood capitalizes on words as CSs to elicit respondent components of emotions. Thought-stopping involves silently yelling "Stop!" as a conditioned punisher to decrease and disrupt thoughts. All of the remaining strategies listed above can be analyzed in terms of rule-governed control over behavior. Recognizing that the various types of self-talk involve use of rules (either complete rules or partial rules) as a strategy for influencing the behavior of athletes is an important step for aiding a sport psychologist to enhance the effectiveness of his/her advice. When recommending that athletes use self-talk in various ways, the sport psychologist should constantly keep in mind strategies for effective rule-governed control of behavior (see Chapter 4).

Study Questions

1. How might stimulus generalization have been involved in the application with basketball players described at the beginning of this chapter?

2. Using the model for Pavlovian conditioning, diagram a sport example of "conditioned seeing" that is not in this chapter.

3. What is proprioceptive feedback?

4. In a sentence or two, describe what is meant by "mental rehearsal."

5. Distinguish between internal vs. external imagery.

6. List five ways that athletes might use mental imagery to enhance practice performance.

7. In two or three sentences, describe what is meant by "instant mental replays."

8. What does the term visualization refer to? Should that term be used interchangeably with the term mental rehearsal? Why or why not?

9. Describe an example (that was not in this chapter) to illustrate how an athlete might use visualization at practices to promote generalization of a skill to competitions.

10. List three ways that athletes might use mental imagery and/or visualization to enhance competitive performance.

11. Using an example that is not in this chapter, describe how an athlete might use imagery to elicit feelings of relaxation, so as to enhance athletic performance.

12. Why should mental rehearsal of a well-learned skill just before a competition enhance the likelihood of that skill being performed optimally (there are two reasons)?

13. What is meant by the term "mood words"? Illustrate with a sport example that is not in this chapter.

14. Describe an example that is not in this chapter that illustrates how a word might

function as both a mood word and as a partial rule.

15. In several sentences, describe the main steps of a strategy for teaching athletes to use thought-stopping to decrease negative thinking, plus prompts to increase alternative desirable thoughts.

16. Briefly describe each of Nideffer's four major categories of stimulus control of athletic performance, and illustrate each with a sport example that is not in this chapter.

17. Using an example that is not in this chapter, describe how self-talk might be used to help an athlete focus on the appropriate external stimuli at a particular point during an athletic performance.

18. Describe three different functions which self-talk might serve for enhancing an athlete's performance of a skill. Illustrate each with a sport example.

19. What is meant by the term "key word?" Describe a sport example that is not in this chapter.

20. List four rules for using key words to improve performance of a skill at practices and competitions.

21. What are two problems with an athlete thinking about what he or she doesn't want to do just before performing a skill?

22. List the three components of a strategy used with professional hockey players to help them stay focused when sitting on the bench in between shifts on the ice. Describe examples of self-talk for the last two components.

23. What is meant by the phrase "paralysis by analysis"? Illustrate with a sport example that is not in this chapter.

Chapter 9

Emotions and Athletic Performance

An Application

Helping Seth control his anger during tennis matches[*]

"Seth, you idiot! That was a stupid shot!" Seth yelled loudly as he smacked his tennis racket on the court. Seth was a 14-year-old tennis player who had just lost a point. He had a long history of angry outbursts during tennis matches that interfered with his tennis performance, and were especially embarrassing to his parents. Seth and his parents approached Dr. Keith Allen, a Psychologist at the University of Nebraska Medical Center, for help.

The treatment designed by Dr. Allen combined three components: awareness training, teaching a competing response, and arranging supporting contingencies. **Awareness training** involved teaching Seth to identify the earliest signs of his angry outbursts. When Seth began to experience an anger episode, the earliest sign was that he started talking to himself and waving his racket. Whenever Seth's parents saw such behaviors, they operated an audible clicker as a prompt for Seth. Next, when Seth detected an early sign of an outburst, he engaged in a **competing response**: a relaxing, breathing procedure referred to as deep-centre breathing(described in Chapter 2 and later in this chapter). After standing still and taking 2 to 4 deep breaths, Seth continued the tennis match. Finally, the **supporting contingencies** involved a motivational program in which Seth received praise and points for observable use of the competing response during matches, and the points could be cashed in for new stereo compact discs. Also, a punishment procedure was added in which outbursts that were not immediately terminated by practicing the competing response resulted in Seth's removal from the current non-tournament or tournament match and forfeiture of the next non-tournament or tournament match.

The program was very successful. Prior to implementing the treatment, Seth averaged approximately 10 outbursts per tournament match. Following the introduction of the treatment, his outbursts during tournament matches averaged less than 1 outburst per match. At a 12-month follow-up, Seth's parents reported that some of the outbursts had returned, but were sufficiently subtle that others were unlikely to notice them, and that Seth had recently won his first State-Wide age-group tournament.

[*]This application is based on an article by Allen (1998).

Emotions

Like Seth, all of us have experienced anger at one time or another. Anger and other emotions are a fundamental part of the experience of being human, and they play an important role in the lives of athletes. To help you to understand this important topic, this chapter will examine three major characteristics of emotions, some major causes of emotions, and strategies for controlling the emotions of excessive nervousness and anger.

Three Major Characteristics of Emotions

In spite of their obvious importance, emotions have caused a great deal of difficulty for behavioral scientists. Emotions cannot easily be defined and measured, they can be classified in a number of different ways, and the terms commonly used to describe them are often so vague that psychologists are hard-pressed to talk about them precisely. Martin and Osborne (1993) analyzed this important topic in three components: a) the reaction that one feels inside during the experiencing of an emotion (such as the "butterflies" that an athlete feels just before the start of a competition), which is influenced by respondent conditioning; b) the way that one learns to outwardly express an emotion (such as talking fast in an animated fashion when nervous), which is influenced by operant conditioning; and c) how one becomes aware of and describes one's emotions (e.g., "I'm a little nervous," as opposed to "I'm really mad."), which is also influenced by operant conditioning.

The Respondent Component: Our Feelings

As stated in Chapter 2, the respondent component of emotions involves that part of our nervous system referred to as the autonomic system. Our *autonomic nervous system* is involved in the activities of our internal functioning, such as heartbeat, breathing, digestion, and glandular activity. These physiological activities are also involved when we experience what we label "emotional behavior." What happens inside you, for example, in a moment of great fear? Your body reacts in such a way to enable you to fight or to flee. You breathe more rapidly, providing more oxygen to your blood. Your heart rate increases, which increases the supply of oxygen to your muscles. Your adrenal glands secrete adrenalin, which gives you extra energy. Blood vessels to your stomach and intestines constrict and digestion is interrupted, which gives you a "queasy" or "butterflies" feeling in your stomach, and diverts extra blood to your muscles. All of these reactions prepare you to deal with the cause of your fear. We learn to describe these physiological components of our emotions as our **feelings**. These reactions helped our prehistoric ancestors to survive. However, they are not always useful in athletics (e.g., when it is necessary to perform a skill that requires relaxed composure, such as making a putt in golf or shooting at a target in archery).

The internal autonomic reactions that make up our feelings initially occur as part of unconditioned reflexes, that is, they are unconditioned or inborn responses to unconditioned stimuli. Although such autonomic responses are internal and cannot be readily detected by others, they are often accompanied by visible reactions such as blushing, trembling, crying, etc. In studies of unconditioned emotional reflexes in newborn infants, Watson (1930) observed that the USs of a sudden loss of support, loud sounds, and a sudden push elicited the URs of a sudden catching of breath, a clutching or grasping response, and crying that he labelled as *fear*; the US of hampering an infant's movements elicited the URs of crying, screaming, and body stiffening, that he labelled as *anger*; and the USs of tickling, gentle rocking, and patting elicited the URs of smiling, gurgling, and cooing, that he labelled as *joy*. Cross cultural evidence suggests that such unconditioned emotional reactions are universal for humans (Ekman, 1993).

In some studies of respondent conditioning of emotions with humans, experimenters have directly measured the internal autonomic responses (e.g., Staats, Staats, & Crawford, 1962). In other studies, experimenters have relied on the visible signs (such as blushing, trembling, and crying) of the internal feelings to demonstrate that conditioning has occurred. Consider, for example, the classic experiment by Watson and Rayner (1920). In order to demonstrate that fears could be learned through Pavlovian conditioning, they conducted an experiment with Alittle Albert, an 11-month old infant. Albert was first placed on a rug on the floor with several toys. A white rat was then placed just in front of Albert. While Albert was watching the rat, Watson snuck up behind him and banged a steel bar with a hammer. The loud noise startled little Albert, causing him to cry. In two separate sessions approximately one week apart, Albert experienced a total of seven pairings of the loud noise with the sight of the rat. Then, at the end of the second session when the white rat was reintroduced, Albert cried, trembled, and showed the facial expression characteristic of fear. Albert's fear also generalized to several other items, including a rabbit, a dog, a sealskin coat, and a piece of cotton. Watson fully intended to extinguish little Albert's newly acquired fear in a subsequent session. Unfortunately, Albert's parents moved away before Watson was able to do so. Today, it is unlikely that such an experiment would be approved by a university ethics committee. Procedural questions about the Watson and Rayner study have also been raised (Harris, 1979). Nevertheless, the finding that fears can become attached to previously neutral stimuli by Pavlovian conditioning is well established. Also, Mary Cover-Jones (1924) demonstrated that fear reactions to CSs in infants could be eliminated with respondent extinction.

Respondent conditioning of feelings of fear frequently occurs in athletic situations. At the beginning of Chapter 2, I described the example of Susan, the young figure skater. Susan experienced several bad falls while approaching the take-off position for the double-axel jump. Approaching the take-off position became a CS that elicited feelings of fear as a CR.

The feelings associated with other emotions are also influenced by respondent conditioning. At a sporting event, for example, photos are often taken of the winners receiving their medals or trophy. A few weeks later, when viewing the photos, pictures of the occasion will likely be CSs eliciting "happy" feelings. But the reactions that you feel inside constitute just one component of emotions. Another component consists of our accompanying words and actions - which are influenced by operant conditioning.

An Operant Component: Our Words and Actions That Express our Emotions

When we encounter an emotion-causing event, we experience internal autonomic responses (our feelings) which are often accompanied by blushing, trembling, etc. But we are also likely to show an ongoing external reaction that depends on our operant learning experiences. In a situation that causes me to feel anger, for example, I tend to become very quiet and somber. My wife, on the other hand, in similar situations, is likely to shout and swear. In the case of little Albert, the white rat elicited the respondent components of fear of crying and trembling. But Albert also showed the operant response of crawling away as fast as he could.

As indicated previously, certain respondent unconditioned emotional reactions may be universal. The operant displays of emotion, however, depend on the culture in which we have been raised, and tend to vary from culture to culture and from person to person. Fans at a sporting event in Europe, for example, tend to display their displeasure towards unsportsmanlike play by whistling, while fans in North America are likely to react by booing. In the example of Seth at the beginning of this chapter, his operant display of his anger included calling himself an idiot and smacking his tennis racket on the court. In general, we learn to overtly react to emotion-causing events in ways that have been modelled and positively reinforced, or that have enabled us to escape or avoid aversive events. Now let's see how operant conditioning is involved in the third characteristic of our emotions - the way that we become aware of them.

Another Operant Component: Our Awareness of our Emotions

When we displayed emotional behavior while growing up, the people around us typically asked questions like, "Did something scare you?" or "What made you so mad?" or they offered comments about our reactions, such as, "You sure seem to be happy today!" or "Don't feel so sad." From such experiences, we learned to be aware of and to label our emotions, and to recognize emotional expressions of others (Izard, 1991). Thus, becoming aware of and describing emotional behavior in ourselves and others is operant behavior that is prompted and reinforced by those around us. Because others don't always have access to the emotion-causing events or the inside feelings of individuals experiencing emotions, there are sometimes inconsistencies in the ways that we talk about emotions.

To summarize, emotions have three important characteristics: a) the physiological reaction that you feel inside during the experiencing of an emotion (and which is typically accompanied by visible signs such as frowns or smiles), which is influenced by respondent conditioning; b) the way that you learn to overtly express an emotion (such as shouting, jumping up and down, etc.), which is influenced by operant conditioning; and c) the way that you become aware of and describe your emotions, which is also influenced by operant conditioning (Martin & Osborne, 1993).

Some Major Causes of Emotions

Presentation and withdrawal of reinforcers and presentation and withdrawal of punishers are four major causes of emotions (Martin & Osborne, 1993). Presentation of reinforcers causes the emotion called **happiness**. Winning a race, receiving praise from a coach, scoring a basket in basketball, getting a hit in baseball - all involve the presentation of positive reinforcers.

Withholding or withdrawal of reinforcers causes the emotion called **anger**. Athletes have experienced such anger-causing events as hitting a golf ball out of bounds, striking out in baseball, being thrown for a loss in football, and missing a penalty kick in soccer. Unpleasant occurrences, such as foul odours, high temperatures, and even disgusting scenes can also cause one to feel anger (Berkowitz, 1990). A common operantly-learned reaction in many such cases is the occurrence of aggression. Consider that drivers of cars without air conditioning in Phoenix, Arizona, are more likely to honk at a stalled car on hotter days than on cooler days (Kenrick & MacFarlane, 1986). And pitchers in major league baseball games are more than twice as likely to hit the batters with a pitch for games played outdoors on hot days as compared to games played in cooler temperatures (Reifman, Larrick, & Fein, 1988).

The various ways in which we have learned to display anger are not always problematic. When people feel angry, they often experience a surge of vigour and energy, which can sometimes be channelled quite usefully, such as by helping to unscrew a frustratingly sticky top on a pickle jar, or by helping an offensive lineman in football to knock the defensive lineman out of the way and create an opening for a rush up the middle. In other cases, however, angry behavior is disruptive to athletic performance, such as when an angry hockey player takes an unnecessary penalty.

Anxiety or **fear** is the label given to the emotional experience when we encounter dangerous events that may cause us to experience pain. For example, consider the case of Kevin. When he was only four years old, he fell into the neighbour's swimming pool. Unable to swim, he almost drowned before he was hauled out. Since then, he has been deathly afraid of water. What's the difference between *anxiety* and *fear*? Beck, Emery, & Greenberg (1985) suggest that fear is a label for the cognitive appraisal of a danger, while anxiety is a label for the consequence of the appraisal (Beck, 1991). That is, many people use the term fear when they are talking about danger (e.g., "I'm afraid of dogs."). Having made such an appraisal - perhaps in the presence of a dog - the consequence of the appraisal is anxiety. When the appraisal generates intense, irrational, and incapacitating anxiety, it is referred to as a phobia. Many people, however, use the terms anxiety and fear interchangeably, and they are used interchangeably in this text.

Finally, withdrawal of aversive or punishing events causes an emotion that is called **relief**. For example, imagine that you have just arrived at your winter cabin after driving for two hours in a blinding snowstorm. Without any place to stop along the way, you had to continue despite the ever-present danger of slipping off the road, or worse yet, having a head-on collision. Now, sitting safely in front of the fireplace, relief and relaxation slowly settle in.

Each of these causes of emotions occur on a continuum from very mild to very strong. Presentation of rewards, for example, can cause emotions ranging from mild pleasure to happiness to ecstasy. Withdrawal of rewards can cause emotions ranging from mild annoyance to anger to rage. Presentation of aversive events can cause mild apprehension, anxiety, or stark terror. And the effects of withdrawal of aversive events can range from mild relief to an emotional collapse. Other emotions may represent a mixture of some of these basic emotions. Consider the case of a golfer who has been punished with penalty strokes for moving his ball a couple of inches to set up a more favourable shot. Now imagine that the golfer finds himself all alone, with his ball behind a tree. Moving it a few inches would give him a shot. At that point, the golfer might think, "What if someone sees me and I get penalty strokes, or even disqualified?" This amounts to the presentation of an aversive stimulus causing anxiety. At the same time, the golfer might think, "If I move it a couple of inches and make this shot, then I could win the tournament." This represents the presentation of a reward causing happiness. The resulting combination of anxiety and happiness might be experienced as *guilt*.

As another example, consider the emotion of *pride*. Martin and Osborne (1993) described an example involving a coach giving a locker room pep-talk to his high school football team just before the big game. The coach said, "This is the big one. One more to go and we've won the championship. Just think how good you're going to feel if you get to wear those championship jackets." This represents the presentation of rewards. The coach continued, "Are you going to let their team take it away from you? Are you going to let them win the championship?" This represents the withdrawal of rewards. While the players shouted in unison "Nooo," they were probably feeling a sense of pride - an emotion that may represent a combination of happiness from the presentation of rewards and anger from the potential withdrawal of rewards.

With this preliminary discussion of emotions in mind, let's now examine some effects of emotions on athletic performance, and some emotion-management strategies.

Effects of Excessive Nervousness or Fear on Athletic Performance

Reference to excessive nervousness (or anxiety or fear) is often made by coaches and athletes to account for poor athletic performance, as illustrated by the following statements:

"Being too tight is the team's biggest problem right now;"

"He's afraid to make a mistake;"
"It's a case of nerves which currently plagues the team;"
"She was a great golfer until she got the 'yips' on her putts."

As indicated previously, anxiety or nervousness is caused by the presentation of aversive stimuli. Examples include thoughts of falling on a figure skating jump or a gymnastics move, getting "reamed out" by the coach after dropping a crucial pass in football, thoughts of striking out in baseball, being knocked into the boards in ice hockey, and thoughts of negative comments from teammates, coaches, friends, or family for poor athletic performance or losing (e.g., see Figure 9-1).

Why does excessive nervousness or fear interfere with athletic performance? There are four main reasons. <u>First</u>, as indicated earlier in this chapter, we have evolved such that exposure to threat causes physiological changes within us to prepare us to deal with that threat. One of those changes is a narrowing of attention (when a sabertooth tiger was threatening your ancestors, they were less likely to survive if they continued to gaze absentmindedly at the mountains off in the distance). But because of this narrowing of attention, a nervous or fearful athlete is less likely to attend to important external cues. A nervous quarterback might have difficulty picking out the receivers. A nervous figure skater might skate too close to the end boards. And a nervous golfer might be less aware of the trouble spots on the next shot. A <u>second</u> effect of excessive nervousness is that it consumes energy in the process of all those physiological changes. Although a burst of energy can enhance performance in short-term athletic activities, such as a 50-meter sprint in swimming, the extra energy consumption can be problematic in endurance activities. A nervous swimmer just before a 400 meter race is likely to "die" during the last couple of laps. A nervous cross-country skier "won't have the legs" to accelerate during the home stretch. A <u>third</u> effect of excessive nervousness is that it causes the adrenal gland to secrete adrenalin, which will cause the athlete to rush a skilled routine, so that timing is thrown off. A nervous tennis player is likely to have a shorter backswing, a choppier stroke, a rushed shot, and often devastating results. The <u>fourth</u> effect of excessive nervousness or fear is that it adds additional stimuli to the competitive environment that were not likely present in the practice environment, which interferes with stimulus generalization of a skill from practice to competition. In Chapter 14, we identify several categories of stimuli present at practices and competitions, one of which is the state of the athlete's physiological arousal. The more similar those categories of stimuli are between practices and competitions, the greater is the likelihood of transfer of performance from practices to competitions. Most athletes are likely to be relatively loose and relaxed at practices. If they are nervous or fearful at a competition, that adds different stimuli, and there is less likelihood of successful stimulus generalization of skilled performance from practices to the competition.

Figure 9-1. A golfer's negative thoughts can cause excessive nervousness.

Strategies for Coping with Excessive Nervousness or Fear

There are five commonly used strategies for coping with excessive nervousness and tension; two of these minimize the causes of nervousness, and three of them change the body's reactions to stressful events.

Minimize Causes of Nervousness or Fear

Recognize and change negative thinking. Imagine a golfer, standing on the first tee, thinking, "I hope I don't embarrass myself," "I hope I don't hit this into the water," "If I hit a bad shot, I'll look like an idiot." Or imagine a young gymnast just before performing her beam routine, thinking, "What if I fall on my dismount?" "If I miss a single element I won't have a chance." Or imagine a boxer thinking about the exceptional knockout record of his next opponent. Such thoughts are likely to elicit nervousness. A first step for an athlete to control excessive nervousness or fear is to recognize and change the negative thoughts that cause the athlete to be tense or fearful.

One way of reducing the stress caused by thinking negatively about an event is referred to as **cognitive reappraisal** - changing the way you view that event. Consider, for example, a study of two groups of surgical patients. Prior to undergoing an operation, one group was given no special counselling. The second group of patients, however, was taught that it is often one's view of an event that causes stress rather than the event itself. These patients were encouraged to view surgery positively by concentrating on the improved health that they would experience afterward and on the fact that hospitalization would give them a break from outside pressures. Both groups of patients then underwent surgery. Afterward, the group that had received cognitive reappraisal counselling requested pain medication only one-third as often as the control group, and they also recovered more rapidly (Langer, Janis, & Wolfer, 1975).

If an athlete experiences excessive nervousness because of negative thoughts at a competition, the athlete might reappraise the situation in terms of a realistic challenge. Suppose that a golfer, when approaching a crucial shot, experiences excessive nervousness while thinking, "If I miss this shot, I could lose the tournament." The golfer might reappraise the situation by thinking, "I've made this shot hundreds of times when practicing. I've worked hard to get in this position. I'll just go through my usual routine." Additional examples of self-talk to control emotions were provided in Chapter 8.

If negative thoughts are causing an athlete to be tense, the athlete should be encouraged to practice at least one of the following *guidelines in order to eliminate the negative thoughts*:

- Use cognitive reappraisal to view a situation as an opportunity for a realistic challenge;

- Focus on what you can control, don't think about what you can't control;
- Think about what you want to do, not what you don't want to do;
- Just before performing, mentally review past instances of successful performance; (Use of imagery for emotional control is discussed in more detail in the next chapter.)
- Focus on the process of competing, not the possible outcomes.

Of course, recommending these guidelines to an athlete is one thing, getting them to practice them consistently is something else again. Detailed strategies for helping athletes to change negative thinking were presented in Chapter 8 and are discussed in Chapter 15 (also see Brown, 2011).

Structure the environment to "tune out" and prompt relaxing thoughts. In athletics, anxiety-causing events do occur. World class figure skaters and gymnasts do experience bad falls. The best golfers in the world do miss easy shots occasionally. And favoured athletes or teams sometimes lose to the underdogs. Although we might encourage athletes not to think about such possibilities just before or during a contest, that may be easier said than done. Sometimes an effective strategy is to help the athlete structure the environment to "tune out" and prompt relaxing thoughts.

Professional athletes in various sports have developed strategies for "taking their mind off the game." For example, I had the opportunity to follow the pairing of professional golfers Patty Sheehan and Laura Davies at an LPGA event when they were both "in their prime". On a Par 3 where there was a fairly long wait, Patty took her mind off the game by pouring sand into some of the divots on the tee-box. On a Par 4 with a long wait, Patty and Laura began reciting nursery rhymes to each other. Richard Zokol, one of the Canadians who played on the PGA tour used to be known as "Disco Dick" for his strategy of bopping along to music on his walkman (before there were iPods) between shots. Golf legend Lee Trevino frequently relaxed by joking with the crowd. Even in fast-paced sports, naturally occurring pauses (in between periods, changing sides of the court, time-outs, changing ends, etc.) might provide opportunities for athletes to take a "mental breather" to help them relax. In the previous chapter I described a strategy of "relax, regroup, and refocus" that might be used by athletes to momentarily tune-out during natural breaks in play.

Change the Body's Reactions to Stressful Events

The previous two strategies focus on minimizing the causes of nervousness and tension. But sometimes stressful events are experienced. The stressors are there and the athletes can't ignore them. What can they do about it? One possibility is to change their bodies' reactions to the stressors.

Controlled breathing: Centering. An effective way of combating mild levels of anxiety is to practice **deep centre breathing** - a martial arts procedure that emphasizes thought control, a particular way of breathing and muscle relaxation (Nideffer, 1985). Deep centre breathing was described at the beginning of Chapter 2, involving Susan, the figure skater, and I will repeat the description here. When centering, the athlete should first consciously relax the neck (by gently rolling one's head) and shoulder muscles (by gently rolling the shoulders). Next the athlete should breathe low down in his/her stomach instead of high up in the chest. Instead of the chest rising and falling when breathing, the stomach should bulge out when inhaling and collapse while exhaling. Also, when practicing this manner of breathing, the athlete should slow down the exhaling part. Each time the athlete exhales, he/she should slowly whisper to him/herself: "r-e-l-a-x" or "e-a-s-y". Breathing in this manner for several breaths can help an individual to relax. Also, because it takes some concentration to do it correctly, centering is also a thought-stopping procedure. While focusing on the procedure of centering, an athlete is less likely to be thinking anxiety-eliciting thoughts. As an example of its applicability, centering just before shooting foul shots by youth basketball players improved the accuracy of their shooting (Haddad & Tremayne, 2009).

Maintain a sense of humour. Many professional comedians learned to use humour as a strategy for dealing with tension and stress in childhood. If athletes can be encouraged to maintain their sense of humour and joke with each other before a contest, they are likely to experience less tension. Athletes who are loose usually perform better than athletes who are tense.

Progressive muscle relaxation. A widely used strategy for achieving a state of deep relaxation was developed by a Chicago physician, Edmond Jacobson, and described in his book, *Progressive Relaxation*, in 1938. The technique of **progressive muscle relaxation** involves alternatively tensing and relaxing various muscle groups while attending closely to the sensations that are felt when the muscles are tensed versus when they are relaxed. One can learn to become sensitive to the relaxed state of one's muscles in contrast to the state of tension. If you wish to prepare your own relaxation CD, you can follow the instructions for achieving muscle relaxation provided in Table 9-1. It would be best to have someone with a low, even, soothing voice record the relaxation instructions. If an athlete listens to such a CD and practices the exercises at least once a day for approximately a week, then the athlete will get to the point where he/she can do the exercises without the CD. The athlete will then be able to relax in most situations in a matter of a couple of minutes. Alternatively, they can listen to the CD and practice the exercises just before competing in order to stay loose.

Table 9-1

Instructions to be Recorded on a CD and Played to Achieve Deep Musle Relaxation*

1	Listen closely to these instructions. They will help you to increase your ability to relax. Each time I pause, continue doing what you were doing before the pause. Now, close your eyes and take three deep breaths. (p) (p)
2	Make a tight fist with either hand. Squeeze it tightly. Note how it feels. (p) Now relax. (p)
3	Once again, squeeze your hand tightly and study the tension that you feel. (p) And once again, just relax and think of the tension disappearing from your fingers. (p) (p)
4	Make a tight fist with your other hand. Squeeze it as tightly as you can and note the tension in your fingers and your hand, and your forearm. (p) Now relax. (p)
5	Once again, squeeze your fist tightly. (p) And again, just relax. (p) (p)
6	Make a tight fist with one hand and bend your arm to make your biceps hard. Hold it tense. (p) Now relax totally. Feel the warmth escape down your biceps, through your forearm, and out of your fingers. (p) (p)
7	Now make a tight fist with the other hand and raise your hand to make your biceps hard. Hold it tightly, and feel the tension. (p) Now relax. Concentrate on the feelings flowing through your arm. (p) (p)
8	Now, squeeze both fists at once and bend both arms to make them totally tense throughout. Hold it, and think about the tension you feel. (p) Now relax, and feel the total warmth and relaxation flowing through your muscles. All the tension is flowing out of your fingertips. (p) (p)
9	Now, wrinkle your forehead and squint your eyes very tight and hard.** Squeeze them tight and hard. Feel the tension across your forehead and through your eyes. Now relax. Note the sensations running through your eyes. Just relax. (p) (p)
10	Okay, squeeze your jaws tight together and raise your chin to make your neck muscles hard. Hold it, bite down hard, tense your neck, and squeeze your lips really tight. (p) Now relax. (p) (p)
11	Now, all together, wrinkle up your forehead and squeeze your eyes tight, bite down hard with your jaws, raise your chin and tighten up your neck, and make your lips tight. Hold them all and feel the tension throughout your forehead, and eyes, and jaw, and neck, and lips. Hold it. Now relax. Just totally relax and enjoy the tingling sensations. (p) (p) (p)

12	Now, squeeze both your shoulders forward as hard as you can until you feel your muscles pulling tightly right across your back, especially in the area between your shoulder blades. Squeeze them. Hold them tight. Now relax. (p) (p)
13	Now squeeze your shoulders forward again and, at the same time, suck your stomach in as far as you can and tense your stomach muscles. Feel the tension throughout your stomach. Hold it. (p) Now relax. (p) (p)
14	Once more, squeeze your shoulder blades forward again, suck in your stomach as far as you can, tense your stomach muscles, and feel the tension throughout your upper body. Now relax. (p) (p)
15	Now, we are going to review all of the muscle systems that we have covered so far. First, take three deep breaths. (p) (p) Ready? Tighten up both fists and bend both of your arms to squeeze your biceps tight. Wrinkle your forehead and squeeze your eyes tight. Bite down hard with your jaws, raise your chin, and hold your lips tight. Squeeze your shoulders forward and suck in your stomach and push your stomach muscles against it. Hold them all. Feel the tremendous tension throughout. Now relax. Take a deep breath. Just feel the tension disappearing. Think about the total relaxation throughout all of your muscles--in your arms, in your head, in your shoulders, in your stomach. Just relax. (p) (p)
16	Now, let's go to your legs. Bring your heels in tight toward your chair, push them down hard, and raise your toes so that your calves and your thighs are extremely tense. Squeeze your toes up and push your heel down hard. Now relax. (p) (p)
17	One more time, bring your heels in tight toward your chair, push them down hard, and raise your toes so that your calves and your thighs are extremely tense. Push down on your heels and raise your toes. Now relax. (p) (p)
18	Now, take three deep breaths. (p) Now, tense all the muscles as they are named, exactly as you have practiced: fists and biceps, forehead, eyes, jaw, neck, lips, shoulders, stomach, legs. Hold it. (p) Now relax. (p) (p) Breathe in deeply three times. Notice how relaxed all of your muscles feel. Now one more time, tense everything! Hold it! (p) And relax. Let all the tension disappear. Breathe normally and enjoy the completely tension-free state of your body and muscles. (p) (p) (p) (p) (p) (p) Now turn the tape off.

*Each "(p)" represents a pause of five seconds. (The numerals should not be read out loud.)

**Individuals who wear contact lenses might want to remove them before doing this exercise.

Reprinted with permission from Martin & Pear (1996)

Visualize a relaxing scene. In the last chapter I described in considerable detail how athletes are able to close their eyes and mentally picture scenes that they have seen before, a process called visualization. Visualizing a relaxing scene can be an effective way to help an athlete to combat excessive nervousness. For example, Martin and Martin (2006) described how a nervous curler might use visualization to relax before an important game. Suppose that it is approximately 15 minutes until the game starts, and the curler is feeling quite nervous. The curler could sit in the locker room or in a quiet corner of the lounge in the curling rink, close his/her eyes and visualize a relaxing scene that the curler had previously experienced. The curler might imagine for example, that he/she was sitting on a deserted beach on a warm summer day, watching the waves. The curler might imagine feeling the warm sun, and seeing the waves break on shore, over and over and over. When feeling really relaxed, the curler could then open his/her eyes, and proceed to the ice to begin the curling game. Other examples of the use of visualization as a relaxation strategy to change the body's reactions to stressors are described by Williams (2010).

Choking Under Pressure

There are many examples of highly skilled, highly trained athletes who were expected to perform well in particular athletic contests, but who "blew it" under the pressure of the big game or event. It is common among members of the media to explain such an occurrence by saying that the athlete "choked." While there is no widely accepted definition of that term, a definition that is consistent with a behavioral approach is one by Mesagno, Marchant, and Morris (2009) that defined **choking** as "a critical deterioration in the execution of habitual processes as a result of an elevation of anxiety levels under perceived pressure, leading to substandard performance" (p. 131). For example, in a close football game late in the fourth quarter, a quarterback, on the way to the huddle, might think, "Everybody is depending upon me. If I blow it I'll let the whole team down." Such self-talk might cause excessive nervousness, and that nervousness may have one or more of the four effects stated on p. 127, causing the quarterback to throw a bad pass and causing the team to lose the game. In other words, the self-induced pressure caused the quarterback to "choke and blow the game."

Strategies to prevent choking can include the five guidelines for eliminating negative thoughts listed on pp. 129-130, or any of the strategies for relaxing described earlier in this chapter. Specific pre-performance routines that athletes can learn to follow just before an important competition can also decrease the likelihood of choking (Mesagno & Mullane-Grant, 2010). Pre-performance routines are discussed in considerable detail in Chapters 15 and 16.

Anger, Aggression, and Athletic Performance

As discussed previously, anger is caused by the withdrawal or withholding of rewards. A call by a tennis umpire that a serve is outside rather than inside the line, a goal that is disallowed in hockey, a missed shot in golf, a penalty in football that wipes out a yardage gain - all have been known to cause angry outbursts by the players involved. The aggressive ways that various athletes may have learned to display anger are not always problematic. An angry ice hockey player might deliver a devastating bodycheck on an opponent, and an angry football player might make a bone-crushing tackle. Moreover, "you have to play aggressively to win" is a comment that one is likely to hear from coaches and athletes of many sports. Consider, for example, the following quotes from coaches of football, ice hockey, and lacrosse, respectively:

"Hit him hard and hit him low, and if he gets up, hit him again."
"If you can't beat them in the alley, you can't beat them on the ice."
"The fans wanted violence, and we gave it to them."

The degree and type of aggression considered desirable varies from sport to sport. Boxing involves direct aggression against an opponent. Aggressive body checks in ice hockey and aggressive tackling in American football and Australian rugby are considered acceptable and desirable. Even in sports which supposedly have little body contact such as basketball and soccer, flying elbows and pushing and shoving are common. During the 1980s and 1990s, however, excessive aggression and violence in sport, both on and off the field, came to be perceived as a social problem. In the hope of reducing the incidence of aggression and violence in the athletic domain, the *International Society of Sport Psychology* published a position paper that included a series of recommendations (Tenenbaum, Stewart, Singer, & Duda, 1997). Their paper prompted a debate on issues related to aggression and violence in sport, and I highly recommend their paper and those that followed to anyone interested in the debate (Kerr, 1999; Tenenbaum, Sacks, Miller, Golden, & Doolin, 2000; Kerr, 2002). Excellent discussions of aggression and violence in sports can also be found in Cox (2007), Gee (2011), and Weinberg and Gould (2011). It is not my intention here to enter that debate. Rather, my goal here is to describe for athletes, for whom anger and aggression are considered problematic, strategies to cope with or diminish their anger and to control their aggression.

Strategies for Coping With Anger

For this section I used information contained in five studies on anger management strategies for athletes (Allen, 1998; Brunelle, Janelle, & Tennant, 1999; Connelly, 1988; Jones, 1993; Silva, 1982). All five studies followed at least three of four basic steps to teach athletes to replace anger behavior with acceptable alternative behavior in the presence of typical anger-causing situations. All five studies also reported successful results. In four of these anger-management programs, the first three steps (described below) occurred before athletes were encouraged to use the coping skills in competitive situations.

Step 1: Identify Anger-Causing Situations

The first step is to help athletes prepare a list of the situations or cues that typically cause them to display angry outbursts. In a case described by Silva (1982), for example, a Division 1 male ice hockey player attributed his excessive penalties during games to his uncontrolled anger. Through discussion, the player indicated that he experienced frustration and anger when opponents would take the puck away from him, body check him, or grab his stick, and the player typically reacted by slashing (with his hockey stick) at the skates, ankles, and legs of the opponents. As another example, Brunelle et al. (1999) found that anger-causing cues among soccer players in an intramural university league included verbal attacks by opponents, criticism by teammates, poor referee calls, and hard fouls by opponents. When identifying anger-causing situations, the athletes involved were encouraged to go beyond the preparation of general lists by outlining the details of several specific recent instances in which they experienced excessive anger.

Step 2: Teach Substitute Behaviors to Compete with the Anger

Substitute behaviors taught to athletes to displace their anger have included relaxation, focusing on specific sport skills, and focusing more generally on rational behavior or assertiveness. In the example of Seth at the beginning of this chapter, when Seth gave a sign that he was feeling angry, his parents provided a clicking sound that prompted Seth to engage in the competing response of deep center breathing.

In four of the five studies, self-talk was added to the intervention to prompt the desired substitute behavior. (Self-talk – saying things to yourself – was discussed in Chapter 8.)

General coping self-talk to stay in control. One approach to Step 2 is to teach the athlete some coping self-statements of a general sort to help the athlete to react constructively to feelings of anger in any situation. Examples might include:

- "First I'll relax, then I'll deal with the problem;"
- "Feeling relaxed is a lot more comfortable than feeling angry;"
- "I'm not going to let it get to me;"
- "I'll handle this if I stay relaxed and stay in control."

General coping self-talk was used to help a golfer with whom I worked who frequently got mad at himself on the golf course following a bad shot. Not only did the angry outbursts interfere with his performance on the next two or three shots, it took away from the general enjoyment of the game, both for the golfer and for those who were playing with him. His strategy was to write the following on a cue card:

> "Enjoy the game"
> "Make it fun for everyone"
> "I'll play better if I'm relaxed and have fun"
> "Only an idiot spoils their game by getting
>   mad, and I'm too smart for that."

Just before playing a round of golf, and frequently between shots, the golfer reviewed the contents of the cue card. Doing so helped him to prepare for situations that had evoked angry outbursts in the past, and to more effectively control his anger. (A similar strategy for helping a figure skater control excessive anger at practices is described in Chapter 12.)

Specific cue words to elicit relaxed feelings. Another approach to Step 2 - teaching substitute behaviors to compete with the anger – is to teach clients to practice relaxation strategies (Deffenbacher et al., 1986). It is also possible to provide an athlete with appropriate training so that specific cue words will come to elicit relaxed feelings. For example, in order to help an international level racquetball player control her anger, Jones (1993) taught the player to use the cue word, "R-e-l-a-x" to trigger a quick relaxation response. The athlete first learned to relax by listening to 20 minutes of taped instructions. Then, over several phases spread over two weeks, the athlete learned to relax in a shorter and shorter period of time. Eventually, the athlete was able to relax in approximately 20 seconds or less while saying to herself the word "R-e-l-a-x." Only after the athlete achieved this skill did Jones proceed to Step 3 of the anger management program (described later in this chapter).

This step could also be accomplished by practicing deep-centre breathing. As described earlier in this chapter, deep-centre breathing involves breathing down in your stomach instead of high up in your chest. If an athlete consistently pairs a word such as, "r-e-l-a-x" with exhalation during deep-centre breathing, then, eventually, reciting the word, "r-e-l-a-x" will become a CS for relaxed feelings.

Self-talk to focus on specific sport skills. A third way of accomplishing Step 2 in an anger management program is to help the athlete to improve their focus on specific sport skills. If, in the presence of anger cues, an athlete rehearses self-talk to help focus on specific sport skills, then the athlete is less likely to experience anger. This was the approach followed by Silva (1982) in the case of the Division 1 male ice hockey player described previously who took excessive penalties during games.

In situations that typically caused anger (e.g., being body checked by an opponent), the player said, "Stick to the ice", which was a partial rule that meant, "Keep your stick on the ice and you will stay on the ice and you won't get a useless penalty." Other examples of skill-focusing self-talk used by hockey players include, "Finish your checks", "Pick up your man" (in order to cover an opponent defensively), and "Find the seam" (in order to get in the opening between two opponents to receive a pass).

 Self-talk for acting rationally or assertively. Another strategy for accomplishing Step 2 - identifying substitute behaviors to compete with anger - is to teach athletes to act rationally or assertively. Angry behavior is often irrational. Sometimes it can be replaced by rational thinking. For example, in the case of the racquetball player described previously, Jones (1993) reported that a major source of the player's anger was questionable decisions by officials. When she thought about it rationally, she realized that of several hundred times that she had argued with officials during her career, they had changed their decisions only "three or four" times, and that such arguing was quite futile on her part. As another example, Connelly (1988) described the case of an NCAA Division 1 basketball player who displayed a great deal of anger and took excessive fouls. A part of the treatment involved teaching the basketball player to react assertively by never giving up, continually challenging himself to improve, and yet being respectful of opponents' skills and personal safety.

 Away from sports, assertiveness training has proven to be an effective way of dealing with anger (Rimm, Hill, Brown, & Stewart, 1974). In sports, if an athlete's anger occurs in response to frustrating or irritating opponents or what the athlete perceives as inappropriate decisions by officials, then the athlete may be able to learn to use coping self-statements to prompt assertive behavior. Suppose, for example, that an athlete frequently shows an angry outburst (that is usually costly) in response to cheap shots by opponents - such as a late hit in football, a crosscheck in hockey, an elbow in basketball, etc. How should the athlete on the receiving end be taught to handle that type of situation? The athlete might be told, "Whenever they give you a cheap shot, let them know in every possible way that it's only going to make you play harder. The way you jump up quickly, the way you get right back into the play, the body language you show, and the encouragement you give your teammates can all be used to let them know that that kind of stuff only makes you play harder. If you do that consistently, you'll be the winner, and they'll be the loser. That way, you don't have to resort to their tactics and you won't take unnecessary penalties." The athlete might also be encouraged to rehearse coping self-statements that increase the likelihood of responding assertively to cheap shots and irritating actions by opponents. Examples of such self-statements include: "I'm not going to let them get to me. I'm not going to take any dumb penalties;" "Every time they do that, I'm going to play harder and tougher;" "They're deliberately trying to throw me off my game. They're trying to intimidate me. All they're doing is giving me more incentive."

Step 3: Practice the Substitute Behaviors Using Imagery and/or Simulations and/or Role Playing

In order for substitute behaviors for angry responses to occur when they are needed, in the presence of the anger-producing cues, the substitute behaviors need to be practised. In some cases, this is done with imagery. In the case of the Division 1 hockey player, mentioned previously, for example, Silva (1982) asked the player to imagine game situations in which he experienced an encounter with an opponent that previously led to his taking a slashing penalty. In such situations, he imagined himself saying something like, "Stick to the ice." He then imagined, that, by keeping his stick on the ice, he successfully regained possession of the puck and contributed to a scoring play. In the case of the racquetball player described by Jones (1993), she also used imagery to practice the substitute behaviors. Under the guidance of Jones, she used imagery to reconstruct precise circumstances that previously evoked anger. Then, at the crucial point of the poor call or poor play that previously caused anger, she would see and feel herself rehearsing her trigger ("R-e-l-a-x"), performing the relaxation skill, and rationalizing that it made no sense to get angry. Jones also included a simulation phase in which the racquetball player engaged in practice matches refereed by an individual who was instructed to call some "debatable rulings" against the racquetball player, in order to provide opportunities for her to practice her coping skills.

An alternative to imagery and simulations is the use of role-playing sessions. In their study of anger-control strategies with soccer players, Brunelle et al. (1999) had players participate in role-playing sessions conducted for one hour per week over five weeks. During the first session, participants were given live demonstrations of alternative responses to typical anger-inducing situations in soccer. In subsequent sessions, the players formed mini groups of three or four individuals, each of whom took turns acting out common anger-inducing situations (e.g., a disagreeable referee decision), and appropriate responses to those situations (both self-talk and acceptable assertive soccer skills).An important question is: How much time should participants in an anger management program participate in the practising of coping responses with imagery and/or simulations and/or role-playing? While more research is needed to definitively answer this question, a review of the studies cited previously suggests that four one-hour sessions might be considered a minimum.

Step 4: Use the Coping Skills in Competitive Situations, with Monitoring and/or Supportive Contingencies

In Seth's case at the beginning of this chapter, Seth skipped Step 3 and began using the deep center breathing, as a competing response for anger in non-tournament and tournament matches. His parents also added supporting contingencies to ensure that Seth carried out the procedures. For athletes who include Step 3 in which they practice the coping responses with imagery and/or simulations and/or role-playing, when they are ready to use the coping strategies in competitive situations, their attempts at doing so should be monitored either by themselves or by some volunteer helpers. In Seth's case, both Seth and his parents independently monitored the outbursts across tournament and non-tournament matches. If the monitoring of an athlete's angry outbursts across several competitions does not show sufficient improvement, then the athlete could be encouraged to return to Steps 2 and 3.

Helping athletes to control their anger successfully is not only likely to improve their athletic performance, it should also increase their enjoyment of sport experiences. For additional discussion of anger management strategies for athletes, see Abrams (2010).

Study Questions

1. In a sentence each, summarize three important characteristics of our emotions, and name the type of conditioning involved in each.

2. Describe several physiological reactions experienced in a moment of fear.

3. Describe unconditioned reflexes (i.e., the USs and the URs) that appear to characterize the emotions of fear, anger, and joy.

4. In the experiment with little Albert, what was the US? The UR? The CS? The CR?

5. Using the model for respondent conditioning, diagram an example (that is not in this book) of respondent conditioning of an emotion in a sport context.

6. For each of the following emotions, identify a general cause, and illustrate each cause with an example from your own experience:

   Happiness   Anxiety
   Anger   Relief

7. Describe four effects of excessive nervousness and tension, and briefly explain why each effect might interfere with athletic performance at competitions.

8. Briefly describe two strategies for minimizing the causes of excessive nervousness and tension. Illustrate each with an example from sports that is not in this chapter.

9. What is meant by cognitive reappraisal? Illustrate with a sport example.

10. List five guidelines that athletes should be encouraged to practice in order to eliminate negative thoughts that cause them to be tense just before performing.

11. In a sentence each, briefly describe four strategies for changing the body's

reactions to stressful events.

12. Define or describe each of the following:

> Deep centre breathing
> Progressive muscle relaxation

13. Define "choking" as the term is used in sports. Describe an example that was not in this chapter.

14. Describe several strategies that might be used to minimize the likelihood of the occurrence of "choking" in sports.

15. List the four steps that have characterized successful anger management programs used with athletes.

16. Which of the four steps of successful anger management programs were used with Seth (at the beginning of this chapter)?

17. List four different types of self-talk that might be taught to athletes to displace their anger. Illustrate each with an example.

Part III
Improving Practice Performance
With Young Athletes

Chapter 10

Teaching New Skills

An Application

Using Shaping to Teach a Novice Tennis Player to Serve[*]

Mary Henderson was one of twelve students in the Juniper High School tennis class. This was the third class in a row which Coach Linda Hill had devoted to instruction on how to serve. At the start of each class, Coach Hill discussed and demonstrated the proper components for serving correctly. After her instruction session, each of the players was given a chance to practice while Coach Hill observed and pointed out errors. Most often, the coach commented on those things that the players were doing incorrectly. Rarely did Coach Hill point out correct or nearly correct components of the skill. Under the supervision of her faculty advisor, Dr. Teodore Ayllon, and with the co-operation of Coach Hill, Hillary Buzas, a doctoral candidate in Clinical Psychology at Georgia State University, began a study of a shaping strategy for improving student performance.

The first step in the study was to assess the specific components of each skill which the students had to perform. The tennis coach helped Hillary to prepare task analyses of the components of the forehand, backhand and serve. For example, the specific components that were assessed for the serve are as follows:

1. For a right-handed player, the left foot should be positioned just behind the baseline at a 45-degree angle to it, and the right foot a comfortable distance behind the left and parallel to the baseline.

2. The player should use either the Continental or an Eastern forehand grip.

3. The swing should begin with both hands and racket in front of the player. Then the hands come down past the body,

with the right hand (for the right-handed player, left for a left handed player) continuing on back until arm and racket shaft are out parallel to the ground in behind the neck, and then [the player] releases and swings forward to hit the ball with the racket (following through until face down by the player's opposite shin).

4.   As the hand with the racket swings back, the other hand goes up to toss the ball.

5.   The ball should go over the net without touching the net, and land inside or on the lines of the service court on the other side of the net.

Observations of the students' performance on the checklists revealed that, under the initial coaching strategy practiced by Coach Hill, the students averaged approximately 13% correct performance. After discussion of these results, the coach implemented the shaping program. At each practice, the coach watched for and praised components (those listed on the checklists) that were performed correctly or nearly correctly. For example, Coach Hill might say,"Good! That was much better. You transferred your weight from your back foot to your front foot at just the right time."). When an error occurred, the coach did not comment on it in any way. The shaping program showed quick and powerful effects. By reinforcing components that represented successive approximations to the topography of the correct serve, backhand, and forehand strokes, performance improved from the baseline of 13% to almost 50% correct performance in only a few sessions. Not only did they perform better, but there were many signs that they also enjoyed it more: they smiled, they made positive comments about their tennis abilities, and they were eager to practice their skills.

*This application is based on Buzas and Ayllon, (1981).

In some sport psychology consultations involving young athletes, the psychologist will interact directly with the coach rather than with the athlete, as Hillary Buzas did with Coach Hill. The consultant might be asked, for example, to develop a training program for Little League baseball coaches (e.g., Smith, Smoll, & Barnett, 1995; Smoll & Smith, 2010), to help figure skating coaches more effectively teach troublesome jumps and spins (e.g., Hall & Rogers, 1989), or to offer guidelines for swimming coaches to use videotaped feedback for improving racing turns of young swimmers (e.g., Hazen, Johnstone, Martin, & Srikameswaran, 1990). In Chapter 3, we described basic principles of operant conditioning that are important in skill development. But it's one thing to have an understanding of basic behavioral principles, and it's another to translate them into "how-to" guidelines that a coach can easily follow. In this chapter, guidelines are presented to help a coach strengthen desirable behaviors and teach basic skills to young athletes. In the next two chapters, the related topics of decreasing persistent errors and managing disruptive problem behaviors are discussed. Preparation of this and the next two chapters were influenced by the pioneering efforts of Brent Rushall and Daryl Siedentop (1972), and the excellent work of Ronald Smith and Frank Smoll and their colleagues concerning behavioral assessment and interventions in youth sports (Smith, Smoll & Christensen, 1996; Smoll & Smith, 1987).

In addition to the range of athletic skills characteristic of a particular sport, there are other types of behaviors, that, from the coaches' point of view, are valuable for young athletes to acquire. Examples include listening attentively to the coach, picking up equipment after a game, practicing an exercise as instructed, going to a particular place on the playing field when the coach blows a whistle, and practicing on their own. These are the kinds of behaviors that are frequently displayed by individuals who are often referred to as "coachable" athletes.

The teaching guidelines provided in this chapter are helpful for strengthening many kinds of behavior. They are especially helpful for teaching relatively simple skills or for refining more complex skills that have been partially mastered. They are also useful in developing the behaviors that are characteristic of coachable athletes.

Preliminary Considerations

Guidelines for teaching simple behaviors are centered around two main concerns: (a) giving the athletes a clear idea of the skills to be mastered; and (b) providing feedback to the athletes to strengthen those skills. Before discussing these two concerns, however, there are some preliminary considerations to which a coach should attend.

Determine the Developmental Level of the Beginners

Considerable research has focused on how developmental factors may influence behaviors in physical activity settings (for discussions of this research, see Weiss, 2004). Drawing on this information, the National Coaching Certification Program in Canada provides information on the kinds of things that coaches might expect from young athletes in three age groups: 6-11 years, 11-15 years, and 15-18 years. I'll refer to these three groups as the younger group, the middle group, and the older group.

In the younger group, physical development places certain restrictions on athletic activities. At the 6 to 8-year-old level, reaction time is slow, hand-eye coordination is poor, and muscle and connective tissue are quite susceptible to injury from excessive stress (such as lifting weights). However, these children are capable of considerable aerobic endurance activities. Coaches must also be sensitive to the differential growth rate of children in this age group. Toward the end of the young period (i.e., from 9-11 years of age), some children have sudden growth spurts; others will not experience this stage of growth until later. It is important for a coach to encourage the "late" growers to continue to participate. When these children catch up in size in their later years, they may do quite well.

In terms of the behavioral characteristics of this younger group, these children have a relatively short attention span. Complex, detailed instruction or complicated game strategies simply go over their heads. Also, coaches must resist tendencies to overemphasize winning, or to holler at or chastise children for mistakes. Brief instructions coupled with frequent positive reinforcement is the most effective coaching strategy. The emphasis should be on fun, fitness, and realistic skill development.

In the middle age group, physical growth still varies considerably from one individual to the next. In competitive sports, especially body contact sports, coaches must be careful about matching a 55 kg (120 lb.) youngster who has not yet had a growth spurt against someone of the same age who may be close to 2 meters (6 ft) and 82 kg (180 lbs.). Athletes in this age group are still susceptible to muscle and connective tissue injuries (such as might occur, for example, from pushing too hard too soon in weight training). Finally, coaches must be especially sensitive to the fact that this age group is in its prime years of early sexual development. Puberty can be a trying time, and both early and late developers may experience problems in adjustment to the social, psychological, and physiological changes that are occurring in their young lives.

In terms of the behavioral characteristics of the middle age group, these young people can be challenged by more detailed instructional techniques and more complex game and team strategies. It is important, though, that coaches emphasize positive reinforcement for skill development and improvement, as opposed to winning at all costs. Finally, although it is important for a coach to be a good listener at all levels, it is perhaps most important when dealing with the middle age group. Adults are often unaware as to where adolescents are coming from. Furthermore, in comparison to when they were younger, many adolescents have a new and stronger desire to be taken seriously by adults. Genuine and attentive listening on the part of the coach can be a helpful response to the teenage athlete's needs.

In the older age group, physical growth stabilizes. Muscles grow to maturity by approximately age 17, and muscular strength continues to increase into the 20s. Moreover, although girls reach full growth by the age of 15 or 16, it is not until age 18 or 19 that full growth is typically achieved in boys. Although young people in this group are capable of safely pursuing a variety of weight training and cardiovascular fitness activities, caution must still be used in heavy resistance training and in contact sports such as football. In terms of behavioral characteristics, athletes at this level can and should become more involved than ever in goal setting, decision making, self-monitoring of progress, and personal selection of reinforcers for their participation in sports.

Begin At the Athlete's Level

There is no sense in trying to teach a young ice hockey player to stick handle and make fancy passing plays if the child can't skate. On the other hand, youngsters learning about hockey will become bored if the coach spends a lot of time reviewing fundamentals that the young players can already perform. To help maximize enjoyment and progress for all, the coach should begin at the athlete's skill level. Therefore, a preliminary step is to assess the basic skills of the beginners.

Prepare task analyses of complex skills to be taught. ***Task analysis*** refers to breaking a skill into its component parts so that it can be taught effectively, and improvements can be accurately monitored. This may require the identification of both the individual behaviors in sequence and the stimuli that should control each of those behaviors. An example of a task analysis for the backstroke was shown in Figure 6-2. An example of a task analysis of a tennis serve was shown at the beginning of this chapter.

Examples of basic skills for the sport that the coach will be teaching include such behaviors as shooting foul shots in basketball, putting in golf, and blocking in football. For each sport, books and coaching articles that have already task analyzed the basic skills in considerable detail are likely available.

Prepare checklists to assess current performance and monitor progress. As described in Chapter 1, a critical component of the behavioral approach is the emphasis on specific measurement of athletic performance, and the use of such measures as the primary means for evaluating treatment or training strategies (which might be implemented by either the athlete, the coach, or the sport psychologist). Thus, after the coach has collected the task analyses, the next step is to prepare checklists to assess current performance and monitor the progress of the beginners. Often, a task analysis of a skill and a checklist to monitor progress are one and the same. Suppose, for example, that a coach wanted to improve aspects of the form shown by a young basketball player when shooting foul shots from the freethrow line. The coach might use the checklist in Figure 10-1. As another example, the task analysis of the backstroke shown in Figure 6-2 could easily be made into a checklist.

Set Mastery Criteria. When teaching a specific skill, it is helpful to set a mastery criterion. As described in Chapter 4, a **mastery criterion** is a requirement for practicing a skill such that if the requirement has been met, there is a good chance that the skill has been learned. Consider, for example, the sport of golf. Simek and O'Brien (1981) prepared a behavioral progression of 22 components for learning to play golf. Their behavioral progression and mastery criteria are presented in Figure 10-2. You will notice that the first step in the behavioral progression was to master a 10-inch putt. They started with this step for two reasons. First, it is a relatively simple response in comparison to a more complex, full golf swing, and a general rule is to start with the simple and proceed to the complex. Second, practicing a 10-inch putt was followed by a natural reinforcer - getting the ball into the hole.

Gradually, as mastery criteria for simple components were met, a beginning golfer progressed to longer putts, then to short chip shots (which is similar in many ways to a putt), to pitch shots, to middle iron shots, and eventually to hitting woods. In an experiment conducted by O'Brien and Simek (1983), six novice golfers were taught to play golf by completing the behavioral progression and mastery criteria, while a second

Figure 10-1. Assessing foul shooting in basketball

Shooting Free Throws in Basketball									
Scoring Key: **G** = Good; **I** = Needs Improvement Dates→									
1. *Foot position:* shoulder width apart, parallel and pointed toward hoop									
2. *Centering and mental rehearsal:* Shooter appears to mentally rehearse while standing erect and holding ball in both hands at about waist level									
3. *Preshot pattern:* Shooter always follows same procedure (e.g., dribbling ball three times, then positioning seams for grip)									
4. *Grip:* Same for every shot, fingers and thumb spread, ball not touching palm									
5. *Set to shoot:* Knees bent for power (approximately 45° angle), back straight, head up									
6. *Set to shoot:* Elbow under ball, bent to approximately 90° angle and pointing at basket									
7. *Follow through:* Shooter finishes up on toes, snaps wrist, points index finger at basket, and does not "pull the string"									
8. Shooter appears to be looking at basket throughout shot (not looking at ball)									

Guidelines for Recording
It is impossible to observe all of the above points on one shot. It is necessary to monitor different shots and score different components at different times. We recommend scoring components as follows:

     First shot: record components 1, 2, 3
     Second shot: record component 4
     Third shot: record component 5
     Fourth shot: record component 6
     Fifth shot: record component 7
     Sixth shot: record component 8

Prepared by Scott Martin

Figure 10-2. A task analysis and mastery criteria for learning golf

COMPLETE GOLF CHAIN AND MASTERY CRITERIA		
Step	Shot	Mastery Criterion
1	10-inch putt	4 putts consecutively holed
2	16-inch putt	4 putts consecutively holed
3	2-foot putt	4 putts consecutively holed
4	3-foot putt	4 putts consecutively holed
5	4-foot putt some break	2 holed, 2 out of 4 within 6 inches
6	6-foot putt	4 consecutively within 6 inches
7	10-foot putt	4 consecutively within 12 inches
8	15-foot putt	4 consecutively within 15 inches
9	20-foot putt	4 consecutively within 18 inches
10	30-foot putt	4 consecutively within 24 inches
11	35-foot chip, 5 feet off green, 7-iron	4 out of 6 within 6 feet
12	35-foot chip, 15 feet off green, wedge	4 out of 6 within 6 feet
13	65-foot chip	4 out of 6 within 6 feet
14	25-yard pitch	4 out of 6 within 10 feet
15	35-yard pitch	4 out of 6 within 15 feet
16	50-yard pitch	4 out of 6 within 15 feet
17	75-yard shot	4 out of 6 within 30 feet
18	100-yard shot	4 out of 6 within 40 feet
19	125-yard shot	4 out of 6 within 45 feet
20	150-yard shot	4 out of 6 within 54 feet
21	175-yard shot	4 out of 6 within 66 feet
22	200-yard shot (if within your range)	4 out of 5 within 90 feet

Reprinted with permission from Simek and O'Brien (1981).

group of six novice golfers received lessons of traditional golf instruction. Both groups had a total of eight lessons. Then all 12 novices played a complete, 18-hole round of golf. The behavioral progression group beat the traditional group by an average of 17 strokes.

Provide Instructions for the Skills to Be Mastered

Let's suppose that the coach has taken the preliminary steps suggested in the previous section. Next, the coach must give the athletes a clear idea of the behaviors to be performed. Effective techniques for doing so are described below.

Combine Modeling With Instructions

When a coach begins to teach, the best approach is to *show* and *tell* simultaneously, especially with beginners. While demonstrating (modeling) the correct skill, the coach might describe specific body movements and subtleties that the beginner would otherwise miss. For some skills, the coach may want to use pictures to help display (model) the performance, such as those showing the backstroke in Figure 6-2. A coach might also model typical errors in order to convey the differences between the correct and incorrect movements that make up the skill.

When modeling and explaining a skill, instructions should be clear and specific (you may want to review the guidelines for using rules effectively in Chapter 4). For example, if a swimming coach is modeling a component of the freestyle arm pull, the coach might say: "Your hand should enter the water *in front of your shoulder*, with your fingers and thumb like this;" "During the first part of your pull, keep *your elbows high* and bend your arm so that your *hand curves under your stomach*;" "Your *fingertips* should pass *under your bellybutton;*" "As you complete your stroke, push your hand past the *bottom of your bathing suit* at your side to get a full stroke. You can hold your thumb out to see if you can feel the skin below your suit."

Thus, instead of simply saying, "Do it like this," the coach has given the young swimmers some very specific prompts, such as: "in front of your shoulder," "elbow high," "hand curves under stomach," "fingertips near bellybutton," "hand past bathing suit," and so forth. Although the coach might model the whole skill once or twice at the start, the coach should then emphasize one or two of the components on which the swimmers should focus while practicing. Depending upon the particular errors that they exhibit, the swimmers might use the above prompts to form key words (as described in Chapter 8) to remind themselves to perform the specific movements. To prevent "paralysis by analysis", the particular components emphasized could vary across practices and from swimmer to swimmer.

Describe Consequences of Correct and Incorrect Performance

Sometimes young athletes are not sure why they are being asked to perform particular drills. Sometimes coaches don't take the trouble to explain the positive natural results that can occur from consistently following certain practice routines. For example, a coach might tell a lineman on a youth football team on a certain play to partially block a hard-charging defensive lineman, then to go down to the secondary. If the coach further explains that the play is designed to trap the defensive lineman, then the offensive lineman is more apt to manoeuvre the defensive lineman into a position vulnerable to the trap. If a coach takes the time to point out the natural reinforcers that might occur from practicing certain drills, then the chances are increased that the athletes will practice various exercises and routines diligently. (As described in Chapter 4, this strategy capitalizes on rule-governed control over behavior.)

Similarly, when a coach models incorrect components to be avoided, it is important to describe "why" the behavior is incorrect. For example, when modeling the arm-pull for freestyle swimming, the coach might explain common errors such as reaching over in front of the head (wrong because it causes the body to twist), pulling with a dropped elbow (wrong because it decreases speed), pulling with a straight arm rather than with a bent arm (wrong because it makes the swimmer tire quickly), or pulling in a straight line under water (wrong because it is not as efficient as pulling in an S pattern).

Ask Questions to Test for Understanding

A common mistake made by many coaches of young athletes is to assume that the athletes understand instructions that have been presented just once. After explaining a drill to be performed, the coach should then check the athlete's knowledge by asking specific questions. To continue with our example of teaching the arm-pull for freestyle swimming, the coach might ask, "Where does the hand enter the water?" or "Where should your elbow be during the first part of the pull?" If wrong answers to such questions are obtained, then the modeling and instruction phase should be repeated. One more consideration: in a situation like this where a coach is asking questions, silence from the young athletes often means, "I don't know."

Ask Athletes to Role-Play Skills

In many situations, it is possible for a coach to ask an athlete to role-play or walk through a particular skill before attempting to perform it in the athletic situation. A swimming coach, for example, might ask a young swimmer to role-play the freestyle stroke while standing beside the pool. A golf instructor might ask a student to role-play the motion of a golf swing without actually requiring him or her to hit a golf ball. A basketball coach might ask a young player to role-play dribbling by showing the appropriate bent arm movements, the crouch of the legs, the bent position of the body, and the head and finger positions, all of which can be demonstrated without using a basketball. This type of role-playing allows the young athlete to concentrate solely on practicing the correct form or movements of a skill without worrying about the end result. If the athlete is performing incorrectly, the coach can provide immediate corrective feedback and ask the athlete to repeat the role-playing.

Capitalize on Natural Reinforcers Whenever Possible

As described in Chapter 3, an extremely important component of the learning process is positive reinforcement: the provision of a positive reinforcer immediately following a specific behavior. Behaviors that are reinforced tend to be repeated, those that are not reinforced tend to decrease. Additional guidelines for a coach to use reinforcers effectively are provided later in this chapter. In this section, I want to emphasize the importance of initially structuring training activities in order to capitalize on natural reinforcers.

As described in Chapters 3 and 7, reinforcers that are deliberately manipulated in behavior management programs are referred to as *arbitrary, contrived, or programmed reinforcers*. Unprogrammed reinforcers that occur in the normal course of everyday living are called *natural reinforcers*. In sports, there are two types of natural reinforcers. One is the sensory feedback that is inherent in the performance of a task. This type of reward involves the visual, tactile, and auditory sensations that come from performing the task well. The "feel" of the solid contact when a golfer hits a good shot, the sight of a baseball arching to the outfield after a solid hit, the personal satisfaction (in terms of both self-talk and the internal feelings it elicits) from swimming the length of a pool the first time, the sight of a basketball dropping through the hoop and the sound of the swish of the net - all of these are naturally reinforcing consequences in that they are not deliberately programmed by the coach or teacher. Another type of natural reinforcer is the "natural" (as opposed to deliberately-planned) reaction of others. A cheer from teammates for a good play, the roar of the crowd when a touchdown is scored, another player giving a batter a "high-5" after a home run - these are examples of natural reinforcers.

In contrast to natural reinforcers in the sport environment, deliberately-programmed reinforcers are those introduced to deliberately influence the performance of athletes. In Coach Dawson's program with the Clinton Junior High Basketball team (described in Chapter 7), for example, in which points were awarded to players for showing specific practice behaviors (and the points could be cashed in for an Eagle Effort Award), the points constituted deliberately-programmed reinforcers.

As much as possible, coaches should try to structure early training experiences so that beginning athletes experience natural reinforcing consequences. For example, as described previously in their behavioral approach to teaching golf, Simek & O'Brien (1981) began by teaching beginners to make 10-inch putts. Why? Because a powerful natural reinforcer for a golfer is hitting the ball into the hole. So they started with a task that was immediately reinforced by a natural reinforcer - making 10-inch putts. Gradually the beginning golfers were taught to make longer putts, then chip shots, then pitch shots, then middle iron shots, and eventually to hitting fairway woods and a driver. Their approach was very successful. When teaching basketball to youngsters, lowering the basket and giving them a smaller ball makes it easier for them to make shots - a natural reinforcer. When teaching baseball to youngsters, starting out with T-ball in which a ball is placed on a stationary T makes it easier for the batter to hit the ball - a natural reinforcer. In most sports, it is usually possible to structure initial learning experiences in order to capitalize on natural reinforcers.

Coaches should be encouraged to structure early training environments to capitalize on available natural reinforcers for two reasons: (a) The more that beginners experience the natural reinforcers of performing a skill, the greater is the likelihood that they will practice that skill on their own (because the natural reinforcers would continue to occur); (b) As discussed in Chapter 14, capitalizing on natural reinforcers in the natural environment is an important tactic for programming generalization of a skill from practices to competitions, and for maintaining it in the long run. However, if available natural reinforcers do not appear to be sufficient for increasing and maintaining desirable behaviors, such as occurred in the beginning of the season in Coach Dawson's program with the basketball team (as described at the beginning of Chapter 7), then a coach should use deliberately- programmed reinforcers in training programs as described in the next section.

Use Deliberately-Programmed Reinforcers

After the athletes know what is expected of them, the coach must require actual performance and should reinforce the features that are correctly done. This is one of the most critical parts of the teaching process. At this point (where the athlete has to perform the actual skill) there is often a strong tendency for the coach to point out mistakes. That tendency should be resisted. This is *not* the best time to issue excessive corrective feedback. During the first few attempts, young athletes should be made to feel a sense of accomplishment and should experience positive feedback for *attempting* the skill. The following guidelines will help a coach to effectively use reinforcers to strengthen and improve desirable behaviors and new skills.

Make Sure Reinforcers Are Reinforcers From the Athletes Point of View

Technically, a reinforcer is something that, when presented immediately after a behavior, causes that behavior to be strengthened. In a practical sense, reinforcers are things that the athlete likes, wants, or enjoys. The key phrase here is "the athlete." Some coaches forget that it is the athlete who is to be reinforced, not the coach. "OK team!", said a football coach at a practice, "If y'all run the next few plays perfectly, I'll let you come into the coaches' dressing room and watch films of me when I played ball." That may be exciting for that particular coach. It is less clear that this "privilege" would be a reinforcer for the players.

One strategy for identifying reinforcers is to use the questionnaire shown in Figure 10-3. Items that the athletes identify as reinforcers might then be incorporated as consequences for improvement in various drills and training activities. You might consider this suggestion to be inconsistent with the earlier guideline of identifying

<u>Figure 10-3</u>. A reinforcer survey for young athletes.

Please answer the following questions, and return the questionnaire to the coach.

Social Rewards

Place a checkmark beside the kinds of approval that you like others to show.

___ Facial signs (e.g., smiles, nods, winks)
___ Hand and body signs (e.g., clapping hands, holding thumbs up, clasping hands overhead)
___ Physical contact (e.g., a pat on the back, a hand shake, a hug)
___ Praise about yourself (e.g., you're smart, very helpful, a nice person)
___ Praise about your athletic skills (e.g., you have a great throwing arm, backhand, jumpshot)

Activity Rewards

What are some of the activities that you would like to do more often during practice sessions?

1. _____ 3. _____
2. _____ 4. _____

(e.g.: Have free swim time; shoot baskets for fun; help the coach set up equipment; be the leader of the group for awhile; be the first to demonstrate skills; change playing positions for fun, i.e., be catcher or pitcher or quarterback, for a change

Equipment Rewards

Which pieces of sports equipment would you like to be allowed to use more often during practice?

1. _____ 3. _____
2. _____ 4. _____

(e.g.: Paddleboards, tumbling mats, diving boards, tires or tackle machine for football, ball machines for tennis or golf, a stop watch to time you own trials, an exercise bike, a pulse meter)

Outings as Rewards

Place a check mark beside the things you would like to do with the whole team.

___ See a film about a favourite sport celebrity or a special sports event
___ Tour a sports museum or hall of fame in your local area
___ Hear a lecture or have a visit from a local professional athlete
___ Go to a competition or sports event, such as a game or track meet, where professionals or high-ranking amateurs are competing
___ Visit a practice session for professional athletes
___ Have a team party or dance
___ Other events or activities? _____

Possessional Rewards

Place a check mark beside the things you would like to have or own.

___ Team sweater
___ Team crest
___ Team uniform
___ Personal chart that shows your progress from week to week
___ Particular piece of sports equipment that you could borrow for 1 week
___ Other items? _____

Unique Opportunity Rewards

Place a check mark beside the unique opportunities that you would like to have.

___ Opportunity to be an usher or helper at a special professional sports event
___ Opportunity to be a bat boy or water girl or score keeper for one game with the local pro team
___ Opportunity to play an exhibition game or play one inning, one set of tennis, one end in curling, with or against a local pro team or professional
___ Other rewards? _____

practice activities that incorporate natural reinforcers. A problem is, however, that not all young athletes experience natural reinforcers for sport participation, at least initially. A high level of entry skills, a high level of competition, a coach who expects too much too soon, and several other factors can all contribute to a situation that contains little or no reinforcement for a beginner. Deliberately-managed reinforcers are certainly better than no reinforcers at all. If reinforcers introduced by a coach can increase the chances of a beginner acquiring skills and eventually experiencing some of the natural rewards for sport participation, then the coach should not hesitate to use deliberately-managed reinforcers.

Frequently Reinforce Athletes' Desirable Behaviors

Coaches are important to a young athlete. It is a fact, however, that some coaches are more effective when dealing with their athletes than are others. What makes one coach more effective than another? In their research at the University of Washington with coaches and players in Little League baseball, Frank Smoll, Ronald Smith, and their coworkers investigated the differences between coaches to whom young baseball players responded favourably and those to whom they responded less favourably.
Their research demonstrated that an important factor was the frequency with which coaches reinforced desirable behaviors (Smith & Smoll, 1991). The young ballplayers whom they observed responded most favourably to coaches who dispensed frequent rewards. (Interestingly, they also found that young athletes preferred coaches who gave more technical instruction.)

How often should coaches provide reinforcers? Although there does not appear to be sport research to answer this question, guidelines can be obtained from research in other areas. On an absolute basis, Siedentop (1976) found that physical education teachers can easily dispense reinforcers at a rate of 4 or 5 per minute during class. On a relative basis, as indicated in Chapter 3, the reinforcer-to-reprimand ratio should favour the reinforcers by at least 4 to 1 with young athletes.

When a coach must work with a group of athletes, the coach will often provide positive feedback to one person who has correctly performed a skill, and will then immediately move on to another athlete. Although this strategy allows the coach to interact with a number of athletes, it is not always the most effective way to strengthen skills in an individual athlete. It is often more effective to observe an athlete execute a skill several times and to positively reinforce correct attempts on each occasion. After the beginner has performed correctly several times and has been reinforced for each execution, the coach can then ask the athlete to practice alone for awhile, and move on to the next athlete. The rule is simple. In the beginning, lots of reinforcers for correct behaviors. Once the new skill is learned, it can be maintained by less frequent deliberately-managed reinforcers or by natural reinforcers.

Use Contingent Versus Noncontingent Reinforcement

When a behavior must occur before a reinforcer will be presented, we say that the reinforcer is **contingent** upon that behavior. If a reinforcer is presented at a particular time, irrespective of the preceding behavior, we say that the reinforcer is **noncontingent**. Reinforcers must be contingent upon specific behaviors in order for those behaviors to improve. To illustrate this point, consider the example described at the beginning of Chapter 6 in which Coach Keedwell frequently told the young swimmers that, while swimming sets, they should practice their racing turns at each end of the pool and swim the sets without stopping in the middle. Also, during the last 10 minutes of a typical practice, the swimmers were allowed to participate in a fun activity of their choice (e.g., swimming relays, playing water polo, etc.). In spite of her frequent prompts, the young swimmers continued to show a high frequency of improper turns and unscheduled stops during sets. The mistake made by Coach Keedwell is that a potent reinforcer - a fun activity - was noncontingent. The fun activity was time-based (scheduled at the end of each practice) and was not behavior based. Scheduling a fun activity at the end of each practice was enjoyed by the young swimmers, but it did not have any effect on their practice behaviors. When the difference between noncontingent and contingent reinforcement was explained to Coach Keedwell, she made the fun activity contingent upon desirable practice behaviors by requiring the swimmers to meet a practice goal in order to earn the fun activity at the end of practice. As a result, as indicated previously, the swimmers showed approximately 150% improvement. Thus, to maximize the effectiveness of a reinforcement program, a coach should ensure that available reinforcers are contingent upon specific behaviors that the young athletes need to improve.

In addition to being contingent upon specific behavior, reinforcers are most effective for increasing a behavior if they follow that behavior immediately. The implication of this guideline is that a coach should be constantly on the alert for desirable behaviors, and should praise them as soon as possible after they occur. If reinforcers are contingent but are delayed, such as in the case of Coach Keedwell's program where the fun activity was delayed until the end of practice, then the athletes should be given clear rules describing the relationship between their performance and the reinforcers to be earned (see Chapter 4).

Use Prescriptive Praise

Praise from a coach is a powerful reinforcer for a young athlete. If an athlete performs well, a simple positive comment from the coach can have a strong effect: "Good!" "Well done!" "All right!" "Terrific!" "You're doing a lot better!" "That was great!". However, another type of praise can be especially effective when the coach is trying to get a particular behavior to occur more often. It is called prescriptive praise. When using **prescriptive praise**, the coach identifies the aspect of the athlete's performance that was desirable or that indicated improvement. A basketball coach, for example, might say something like, "Nice follow-through on your foul shot! You pointed your index finger at the basket." This coach has identified for the shooter the exact behavior that was performed well. Prescriptive praise can be especially useful when a coach wants to encourage an athlete to concentrate on a particular component of a skill (e.g., see Kladapoulos & McComas, 2001).

Use of prescriptive praise capitalizes on rule-governed control over behavior. In the above example, the basketball coach has given the player a rule, "If I follow through on my foul shots and point my index finger at the basket, I'm more likely to make the shot," and rehearsal of an abbreviated form of this rule might exert stimulus control over the desirable form on future instances of foul shooting for that player.

Reinforce Correct Approximations In Order to Shape a New Skill

As discussed in Chapter 3, shaping refers to the reinforcement of successive approximations from an initial behavior to a final desired behavior. As described at the beginning of this chapter, Coach Hill was able to use shaping with novice tennis players to strengthen successive approximations to performing the serve. Shaping can be a powerful technique for coaches to modify the topography (or form), frequency (or speed or rate), duration, latency, intensity (or force) and quality of a behavior.

Reinforce Desirable Performance when it Occurs to Correct Cues in the Environment

As athletes begin to acquire skills, the coach should encourage them to practice under close simulations of game conditions. For example, it is one thing for a basketball player to shoot baskets when he or she is all alone with nothing between him or her and the basket. It's something else again to shoot a basket when an opposing player is standing in front waving his or her arms in the air. Obviously, learning to shoot over an opposing player is an important skill for playing under game conditions. It makes sense, therefore, to arrange practice situations that approximate the "real" game situations along various dimensions. For example, junior high and high school basketball players spend a lot of time shooting baskets - from different distances, a standing shot, a jump shot, a hook shot, and so on. But how many times in a game do they get to shoot a basket with no one in front of them trying to block the shot? Not often. At the junior high and high school level, coaches might enforce the rule, "With the exception of foul shots, practice shooting baskets with someone or something in front of you at least 50% of the time" (e.g., see Figure 10-4). The players could shoot, for example, over coat racks, over coat racks with coats on them, over a player standing with arms at his or her side, over cheerleaders, over cheerleaders waving their hands, etc. The obstacles that players have to shoot over could gradually be changed to more closely approximate an opposition player trying to block the shot.

**In Basketball,
Players often have to shoot over opponents in games**

So they should shoot over obstacles when practicing

Figure 10-4. Practice skills in approximations of competitive situations

After A Behavior Has Been Well Developed, Wean the Athlete From the Initial Schedule of Reinforcers

Although behavior is learned most effectively when it is reinforced often during the initial trials, it is *not* necessary to maintain a high frequency of reinforcers. If a coach has used praise and other deliberately-managed reinforcers to increase the frequency of a new skill performed by an athlete, other reinforcers will begin to naturally support the maintenance of that skill. A swimmer with a more efficient form is more likely to swim faster races. A basketball player with good shooting form is more likely to score baskets. These are natural reinforcers that can help to maintain learned behaviors.

Although natural reinforcers will hopefully maintain newly acquired skills in most athletes, this does not mean that the coach should totally stop dispensing deliberately-programmed reinforcers to young athletes. There are several reasons for this. First, although natural reinforcers might maintain skills in competitive environments, reinforcers from the coach can help to sustain effort and performance during repetitive (and sometimes boring) practices. Second, competitive situations contain punishers as well as natural rewards. For example, overexuberant parents might yell at their child following a losing game. This may make it difficult for that athlete to focus on improvements in his/her personal skills (as a reinforcer). In such situations, positive feedback from the coach contingent upon skilled play can help maintain those skills. Third, an athlete rarely reaches the point where there is nothing left to learn. The coach should therefore continue to provide reinforcers for slight improvements to encourage individual players to continually improve and refine their skills to a higher level.

Change the Behavior of the Coach

If you recommend the preceding guidelines to help a coach more effectively teach basic skills to young athletes, you are likely asking the coach to make some changes in his/her customary way of interacting with the athletes. The strategies recommended in this chapter for changing the behavior of young athletes – conducting behavioral assessments, preparing task analyses, prompting desirable behaviors, monitoring desirable behaviors, reinforcing desirable behaviors, etc. - can also be applied to help the coach change his/her behavior (Smoll & Smith, 1987). The checklist in Figure 10-5 was designed to help a coach become more skillful at applying behavioral techniques to teach skills to young athletes. You might suggest that the coach use the attached checklist to assess his/her performance at practices. Improvements in the coach's behavioral coaching skills as revealed on the checklist will reinforce his/her efforts at applying behavioral coaching.

Study Questions

1. What types of behaviors are likely to be displayed by individuals referred to as "coachable" athletes?

2. For athletes in the younger, middle, and older developmental groups, identify several aspects of their physical development that coaches should know about.

3. For athletes in the younger, middle, and older developmental groups, identify several behavioral patterns or characteristics that coaches should know about.

4. Briefly describe two preliminary considerations to teaching new skills.

5. Define task analysis.

6. Define mastery criterion for a sport skill. Describe an example that is not in this book.

7. Briefly list four guidelines for instructing young athletes about skills to be mastered.

8. Briefly describe two strategies for ensuring that young athletes understand what it is that the coach wants them to do.

9. Describe two types of natural reinforcers. Give an example of each.

10. What are two reasons for encouraging coaches to capitalize on natural reinforcers?

11. Briefly list seven guidelines for using deliberately-programmed reinforcers to teach new skills to young athletes.

12. Using sport examples that are not in this chapter, distinguish between contingent and noncontingent reinforcement.

13. Distinguish between prescriptive praise and regular or nonprescriptive praise. Give an example of each that are not in this chapter.

14. Describe an example of prescriptive praise that Coach Hill used while shaping the serve of novice tennis players.

15. Define "shaping" (see Chapter 3) and describe a sport example that is not in this chapter.

16. Define stimulus control (see Chapter 3), and describe a sport example from this chapter.

17. State three reasons why a coach should continue to dispense deliberately-programmed reinforcers to young athletes, even after their athletic skills appear to have come under the control of natural reinforcers.

Figure 10-5. A coach's checklist for teaching new skills to young athletes.

	DATE								
Scoring Key: 2 = Performed satisfactorily 1 = Done to some extent, but room for improvement 0 = Not done									
Preliminary Considerations									
1. Determine the beginners' developmental level									
2. Begin at the athlete's level									
- Prepare task analyses of skills to be taught									
- Prepare checklists to assess performance									
- Prepare behavioural progressions and set mastery criteria									
Provide Instructions for the Skills									
1. Combine modeling with instruction									
2. Describe consequences of correct and incorrect performance									
3. Ask questions to test for understanding									
4. Ask athlete to role-play skills									
Capitalize on Natural Reinforcers									
Use Deliberately Programmed Reinforcers									
1. Make sure reinforcers are reinforcers from athlete's point of view									
2. Frequently reinforce athletes' desirable behaviors									
3. Use contingent vs noncontingent reinforcement									
4. Use prescriptive praise									
5. Reinforce correct approximations of behavior									
6. Reinforce desirable performance when it occurs to correct cues in the environment									
7. After behavior has been well developed, wean individual from initial schedule of reinforcers									

Chapter 11

Decreasing Persistent Errors

An Application

Improving Amy's Soccer Skills[*]

Amy was a mid-fielder for a female high-school soccer team in Lincoln, Nebraska. Her coach was concerned with her **movement during re-starts**. During a soccer game there are several occasions on which the game is stopped and re-started. For example, re-starts occur when a corner kick is taken, and when the ball is thrown in from the sideline. At these times, Amy's coach wanted her to move to an open space (i.e. free of defenders) in order to be in a position to receive the ball if it was kicked or thrown to her. In spite of frequent prompts from her coach, Amy showed the correct movement during re-starts less than 40% of the time during scrimmages at soccer practices and during games.

With the help of psychologist Brandilea Brobst, Amy's coach introduced a treatment package consisting of **public posting, goal setting**, and oral **feedback**. Brandilea and Amy's coach met with Amy to explain the procedure. First, the coach set a goal of 90% correct performance for Amy of movement during re-starts in practice scrimmages and games. Second, Amy was informed that the 30-minute practice scrimmages and games against other teams would be videotaped, Amy's performance would be scored from the videotape, and the results of each day's practice or game would be posted on a daily performance chart that would be located on a picnic table beside the playing field around which water breaks and on-field meetings would be held. Third, prior to each practice session or game, Brandilea met with Amy and reviewed the data on the chart. Brandilea praised Amy when the goal was met, and encouraged her to try to meet the goal when it was not met. The intervention had an immediate and powerful positive effect on Amy's performance. Her movement during re-starts exceeded 90% correct in 13 of the next 14 practices, and during 4 of the next 6 games. When the procedure was replicated with 2 other soccer behaviors of Amy, and with 3 soccer behaviors of 2 other players, the effects were very similar. All 3 players and the coach supported the use of the procedures in the coming year.

[*]This application is based on a report by Brobst & Ward(2002).

A major portion of practice time with beginning athletes will be spent helping them to acquire new athletic skills. Consistent application of the guidelines for teaching basic skills described in the previous chapter will yield positive results in most cases. Some of the young athletes, like Amy, however, will continue to make errors even after considerable practice. The reasons why errors are repeated are numerous. Consequently, an error correction strategy that might be adopted by a coach should depend, in part, on discovering the reasons behind the error. In this chapter some behavioral strategies are described that have been used successfully to decrease several types of *persistent errors* in skills made by beginners.

Decreasing Errors Related to Lack of Focus

Sometimes young athletes make errors because they do not attend to appropriate cues just before performing a skill. A coach is likely to suggest that the athlete is making errors because of a lack of concentration or lack of focus (a behavioral interpretation of concentration is presented in Chapter 15). Consider the case of Jennifer, a 13-year-old figure skater, who was training for the Provincial Championship. As the sport psychologist for the provincial figure skating team, I had the opportunity to observe Jennifer at many practices. She could land all of the double jumps, including the double axel (the most difficult of the double jumps). But she was inconsistent. At one of the practices, for example, I observed the following: after warming up her easy jumps and socializing on the ice with her friends, she casually attempted a double axel, her most difficult jump, and missed. She also missed her second attempt. Jennifer became angry, focused carefully on the double axel, and then landed three in a row. What was Jennifer teaching herself at that practice? First, it was to land her double axel on her third attempt (but at a competition she only gets one attempt); second, to land her double axel when she's mad (but at a competition she's not likely to be mad, at least not until after she has missed the double axel in her program).

Jennifer appeared to miss the first couple of attempts at her double axel because she was not attending to the proper cues. In order to improve her concentration at practices, Jennifer agreed to use goal setting before practices, key words and mental rehearsal to focus properly during practices, and self-monitoring during and after practices to motivate herself to persist with the program. Before stepping onto the ice at a practice, she briefly reviewed her self-monitoring sheet as a prompt to reach her goal of landing jumps on the first attempt (her self-monitoring sheet also included other aspects of performance to be monitored, as can been seen in Figure 11-1). Then, after warming up her jumps and before her first attempt at the double axel, she reviewed her key words for the double axel and mentally rehearsed the correct form (as described in Chapter 8). She then fully concentrated on her attempts at the double axel. This strategy of reviewing key words for a jump, mentally rehearsing it, and then attempting it was also applied to other jumps and spins during practices. Finally, during and after a practice, she self-monitored her results. Within a short period of time, this strategy helped Jennifer become much more

<u>Figure 11-1</u>. Jennifer's goal-setting and self-monitoring sheet for figure skating practices.

After each practice, place a checkmark (✓) beside the items that you completed, or write in the appropriate score.	M	T	W	Th	F	S	S
Arrived early and stretched before							
Rating of 1st camel change camel							
Rating of 1st combo spin							
Rating of 1st double axel							
Rating of best triple toe							
Did at least 4 good attempts at triple loop							
Focused on presentation when skating my program							
Stayed positive even if I had difficulty with a jump							
Worked hard during the entire practice							

<u>Rating System for Spins</u>   <u>Deductions</u>

6 =   excellent (required rotations,   -1 if fewer than required revolutions
        good speed, good position)   -1 if poor position or travelling
5 =   very good   -1 if slow revolutions
4 =   good
3 =   fair
2 =   poor

<u>Scoring for a Triple Jump or a Double Axel</u>

6 =   landed clean
5 =   landed but with a hand down or a control problem (but stayed on one foot)
4 =   landed backwards, and flipped out of it, but stayed up; or, a good 2-foot
        attempt (2-footing it was hardly noticeable)
3 =   landed backwards, but lost the edge and fell
2 =   incomplete rotation, but on one foot
1 =   poor attempt

consistent at performing previously-mastered skills.

If a young athlete shows persistent errors in a previously-learned skill because of apparent lack of focus, then a combination of goal setting, self-talk, mental rehearsal, and self-monitoring might serve to decrease the errors, especially if the errors appear to be related to the occurrence of distractions in the practice setting.

Decreasing Errors that Occur due to Lack of Reinforcement for Correct Performance

Ideally, correct performance of skills by young athletes at practices will be maintained by natural reinforcers. But that doesn't always happen. Some athletes may show errors because of a lack of reinforcement for correct performance. That appeared to be the explanation of the frequent errors observed by Coach Keedwell at swimming practices as described at the beginning of Chapter 6. You may recall that the first error was that the swimmers failed to perform racing turns at each end of the lane. The swimmers knew how to perform racing turns correctly, but often didn't. Why would improper turns occur? Let's analyse the consequences of the swimmers' actions. What happened when they executed a proper racing turn? They had to hold their breath for much longer than if they didn't. What happened when they swam up to the end of the lane, touched, looked around, and then started swimming again? They got a bit of a rest and got to see what the rest of the swimmers were doing. Maybe they even got to wave or shout at a friend in the next lane. Now let's consider the second error, frequently stopping and touching down in the middle of a set that they were swimming. What happened if they swam a set without stopping in the middle? They likely became more tired. And what happened if they touched down in the middle of a set? They got to look around, wave at someone, adjust their goggles, etc. It appears that there were some natural reinforcers contingent upon performing with errors, and there were no reinforcers contingent upon performing without errors. A possible strategy for a coach in such a situation is to make available reinforcers contingent upon improved performance. That is exactly what happened when Coach Keedwell required the swimmers to swim sets with a minimum number of unscheduled stops and missed turns in order to *earn* relays. She made an available reinforcer contingent upon improved performance rather than presenting it noncontingently at the end of practice.

If young athletes know how to perform various skills correctly, but they are making frequent errors during practices, then there may be insufficient natural reinforcement for correct performance. In such cases, the coach should assess whether or not available reinforcers are being used effectively - i.e., that reinforcers are contingent upon desirable performance (rather than occurring noncontingently). If the use of contingent reinforcers for performing without errors leads to improved performance across several practices, then the athletes could be gradually weaned from the extra reinforcers in the hope that natural reinforcers for improved performance may begin to take over.

Decreasing Persistent, Well Learned Errors

Beginners sometimes experience a great deal of success in a sport despite the fact that they are making one or two fundamental errors in performing their skills. Some young athletes learn to compensate for the errors and, initially, manage to do quite well in spite of them. For example, the star high-jumper at the local junior high school might experience a great deal of success at that level. Despite the fact that this athlete's technique may contain a flaw, such as a habit of trailing the back leg, he or she is still the best high-jumper in the school. When that athlete reaches the high school or college level, however, that same flaw might get in the way. But eliminating the error may be difficult because of those years during which the error was practiced, was not corrected, and indeed was actually rewarded by the experience of success. When a skill results in early success, all of the components of that skill are strengthened, including a flawed component that experts might consider as improper technique. The more an athlete practices with a defective component of a skill, and the more success that the athlete achieves in spite of the defective component, the more difficult it will be to eliminate the error later on. Decreasing such errors might best be accomplished through use of one of the following multiple-component treatment strategies.

Identification of Errors and Correct Behaviors, Awareness Training, Instruction with Key Words, Mastery Criteria, and Immediate Feedback

Roger LePage was one of the coaches of the Manitoba Marlins, a youth competitive swim club. Roger had identified several swimmers with two or more persistent basic flaws in their strokes. Although the usual coaching techniques had helped many of the swimmers to show considerable improvement, these particular swimmers tended to make the same errors in practice after practice. When Roger pointed out the errors, they attempted the correct form on two or three strokes, but returned to their old, incorrect form when the coach moved on to observe another swimmer. With the help of Sandra Koop, a doctoral student in psychology at the University of Manitoba, a behavioral coaching program was designed to deal with this problem (Koop & Martin, 1983).

Each of the swimmers who participated in the behavioral coaching program had been in competitive swimming for at least a year. The swimmers, ranging from 7 to 12 years of age, typically participated in four one-hour practices per week, and swam in a meet about once a month. During practice they swam approximately 2,000 meters, approximately one-quarter of which was freestyle. Five hundred meters freestyle is 20 lengths in a 25 meter pool. Thus, if the swimmers averaged 25 strokes per length, they swam approximately 500 freestyle strokes during each practice. If there was an error in the stroke, the error was repeated 500 times during each practice. If you multiply 500 by the number of practices, you discover that the error was being repeated many thousands of times in a year. No wonder it's so hard to get rid of certain bad habits! Because such errors are very resistant to change, Sandra developed a multiple-component package that incorporated awareness training, instruction, self-talk, mastery criterion, and immediate feedback.

Part of the program included training sessions in a small pool adjacent to the Marlins' regular practice pool. The training program in the small pool was designed to decrease errors to near zero. The program in the regular practice pool was designed to ensure the generality of correct performance to a typical practice. The entire program was implemented by Coach LePage and combined most of the guidelines for teaching fundamentals described in the previous chapter. Roger started with the *identification of the error and the correct behavior.* For example, while swimming freestyle, one swimmer had a habit of reaching too far across in front of the body on hand entry, as opposed to the correct behavior of the hand entering the water in front of the shoulder. Next, Roger provided *modelling and awareness training.* Roger modelled both the incorrect way that the swimmer was executing the target components, and then modelled the correct behavior. The swimmer was asked to imitate the correct and incorrect ways of performing the target behavior, while standing on the deck, until the swimmer could feel the difference. Next, Roger provided *instruction* before the swimmer entered the small pool. The instruction included *key words* for the swimmers to rehearse, such as ""shoulder entry" for the swimmer who had a habit of reaching too far across in front of the body on hand entry as opposed to his hand entering the water in front of his shoulder. As the swimmer swam 6 consecutive laps, Roger provided *praise for correct performance and immediate feedback for errors.* Specifically, he walked along the edge of the pool while carrying a long stick with a soft pad on one end. If an error occurred, he immediately tapped the swimmer lightly on the shoulder to indicate that a mistake had been made. If the swimmer completed a lap with two or fewer errors, Roger provided praise at the end of the lap. When a swimmer reached *mastery criterion* (3 consecutive practices with 2 or fewer errors on each of the 6 required laps), he or she graduated to a *maintenance program* in the regular practice pool. For a period of three typical practices in the practice pool, the coach provided a reminder, something like, "Remember what we were working on in the small pool? That's right, the way you lift your arms in freestyle. What were you doing wrong? What should you do? Right. And what do you say to yourself for each stroke? Right. Good for you. Now, I want to see nice high elbows during practice in the big pool. OK? Good for you!" Roger also deliberately provided two instances of praise for correct performance of the target behaviors during each of the first three practices in the practice pool. During maintenance practice sessions 4 to 6 in the larger pool the swimmer received a reminder only.

The program worked well. All of the swimmers showed rapid improvement in the small pool when the multiple-component error correction procedure was used. All of the swimmers transferred their improved performance to the regular practice sessions in the larger pool. Finally, all of the swimmers managed to maintain their improved skills for at least two weeks after the training program ended. At that point, some of the swimmers needed an extra reminder. When the reminder was provided, however, the swimmers showed immediate improvement. Detailed data for two of the swimmers is shown in Figure 11-2 (similar results were obtained for the other two swimmers). This data is presented to illustrate the first characteristic of a behavioral approach, namely, that it emphasizes specific measurement of athletic behaviors and the use of these measures as the primary means for evaluating the effectiveness of specific interventions. The data clearly demonstrate that, for each of the two swimmers, improvement occurred only at the point where the treatment package was used. You will also notice the staggered presentation of the treatment. That is, Swimmer 1 received the treatment for the backstroke during weeks 6 and 7; Swimmer 4, however, did not receive any treatment during that time. Because Swimmer 1 improved during weeks 6 and 7 when the treatment was applied, and Swimmer 4 did not improve under normal coaching conditions, we can conclude that the improvement was attributable to the treatment and not the result of some chance factor. When the treatment was applied to Swimmer 4 during week 9, that swimmer also improved. As discussed in Chapter 17, this type of research design is a multiple-baseline design across subjects.

Videotaped Feedback

For several years, I served as one of the coaches of the 6 to 10 year old members of the Manitoba Marlin Youth Swimming Team. The head coach of the club had purchased a portable video camera and used it once per week to provide videotaped feedback to the swimmers regarding their technique. The coach had identified six swimmers who had consistent flaws in their freestyle. Once a week they would swim a freestyle set at a practice, while the coach videotaped each of them. Then, as a group, they would watch the videotape while the coach pointed out errors in their technique. After all of the swimmers' performances had been viewed, the swimmers returned to the normal practice conditions and were encouraged to practice swimming freestyle with correct strokes. But after several weeks of this procedure, no improvements were observed.

Because previous research had suggested several conditions under which videotaped feedback might be effective for decreasing errors in athletic performance (Rothstein, 1980), we designed a videotaping feedback package and investigated it for decreasing swimming errors of young competitive swimmers. Our package included: *identification of a specific target behavior* for each swimmer (e.g., hand entering the water in front of shoulder for freestyle swimming, rather than hand entering the water in front of the swimmer's head); *explanation of and modelling the target component* to the swimmer while standing on the pool deck; *asking the swimmer to role play the target component* while standing on the pool deck; *asking the swimmer to practice the target behavior while swimming* five strokes of freestyle that were videotaped; *having the swimmer watch the videotape and receive feedback* on correct and incorrect performance of the target behavior; and *meeting a mastery criterion* of six trials of five strokes per trial performed correctly. The videotaping feedback package was very effective. All swimmers showed an immediate improvement in the first session, and some of the

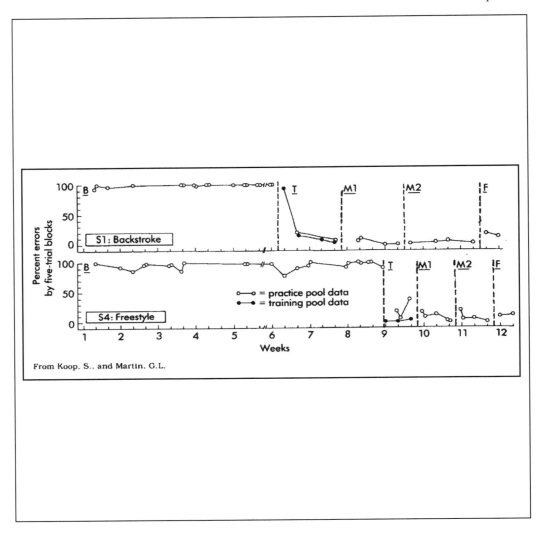

Figure 11-2. Percentage of errors in five-trial blocks made by swimmers 1 and 4 during all phases of experiment. B, baseline; T, training, M1, first maintenance phase, M2, second maintenance phase; F, follow-up. Reprinted with permission from Koop and Martin (1983).

swimmers met mastery criterion in as few as two sessions. Swimmers also generalized their improved performance to sprint trials (Hazen, Johnstone, Martin, & Srikameswaran, 1990).

Based upon this and other research (Ives, Straub, & Shelley, 2002; Templin & Vernacchia, 1995), I suggest that, if you recommend to coaches that they use videotaped replay to improve basic skills and decrease persistent errors, then they should consider doing so under the following conditions:

1.   Identify a specific skill or a specific component of a skill for improvement.

2.   When an athlete receives videotaped feedback concerning performance of a skill, the athlete should be prompted about specific environmental cues and body positions to attend to while observing the videotaped replay.

3.   Consider having two computer screens side by side so that the athlete can view his/her attempt of the skill on one screen, and then view an expert performing the skill on the second screen, for comparison purposes (Boyer, Miltenberger, Batsche, and Fogel, 2009).

4.   Within a practice, immediately after observing a videotaped replay depicting an error, an athlete should be given an opportunity to practice the correct form of the behavior and to receive positive feedback for executing it correctly. This attempt at performing the skill should also be videotaped and used to provide feedback.

5.   An athlete who exhibits a persistent error when performing a skill should be given videotaped feedback on several corrective attempts at performing that skill within a practice, repeated across several practices in a row.

Instruction, the "Freeze" Technique, and Behavior Rehearsal

Mary Allison, a doctoral student from Georgia State University, and her supervisor, Dr. Teodore Ayllon, devised and researched a behavioral error correction program that required minimal time to implement and could be used in normal practice sessions by the regular coaching staff (Allison & Ayllon, 1980). Their program combined several behavioral procedures with the "freeze" technique. One of their studies examined the possibility of decreasing errors made by 11- and 12-year old football players during blocking drills.

Instruction and the freeze technique proceeded as follows: the coach took a group of players and had them run a series of plays. During each play, one player was instructed to block. If the block was thrown correctly, the coach let the players complete the play.

On completion, the coach blew a whistle and praised the player who blocked correctly. However, if the coach noticed that some part of the block was incorrect, he immediately blew his whistle and yelled, "Freeze!"(see Figure 11-3). The player who had blocked incorrectly would freeze, that is, stop moving and hold his physical position correctly. The coach would first describe, in detail, the incorrect aspects of the player's physical position. Then the coach would describe, in detail, the correct position. Finally, the coach would model the correct position (see Figure 11-3). The player would then move from the "frozen" position and imitate the correct physical position. During this imitation, the coach would encourage the player to notice various aspects of his body position. For example, the coach might say, "OK, now, see how your leg is bent? Notice your arm position." The coach would encourage the player to "feel" the difference between the correct and the incorrect body positions. To help the player feel the difference more precisely, the coach would also encourage the player to notice how his muscles felt: "Can you feel how tense your calf muscle is now? When you're doing it correctly, the muscle should be tensed, ready to drive forward. See how it feels? Good!" The players were then allowed to complete the play (see Figure 11-3). Overall, one application of the instruction, freeze technique, and behavior rehearsal took about a minute to complete.

The procedure was researched with five different players. Each player had been averaging less than 10% correct blocks in practice. When the error correction plus the freeze technique was used, the five players showed an immediate improvement, to approximately 50% to 60% correct execution of the block. Research has demonstrated the effectiveness of this error correction package for decreasing errors in football, gymnastics, and tennis (Allison & Ayllon, 1980), soccer (Rush & Ayllon, 1984), sprinting in track (Shapiro & Shapiro, 1985), and classical ballet (Fitterling & Ayllon, 1983). In some situations, however, the freeze technique may be inappropriate because an athlete's momentum makes it impossible to freeze (such as in downhill skiing), or when freezing and listening are simply not possible (such as in teaching swimming).

Old Way/New Way Error Correction Technique

Thus far, this chapter has focused on decreasing errors of young athletes. This section describes a rapid technique-correction procedure for decreasing errors of experienced athletes (Hanin, Korjus, Jouste, Baxter, 2002).

Janice was a 19-year-old Olympic level female sprinter. For the past two years she had been experiencing a performance slump due to a problem with her starting technique. Instead of maintaining a straight back when pushing off from the blocks, her back rounded. This caused her to push off in a direction that was too upright, which caused her to lose power and speed. Janice and her coach had tried various strategies to correct the technique problem, and she was frequently able to start correctly during practices. However, during competitions, her technique repeatedly failed. With the help of sport psychologist Yuri Hanin, Janice and her coach tried the old way/new way technique. This

Player on the left is standing too erect while blocking, and coach yells, "Freeze!"

While players remain in frozen position, the coach models and explains the correct and incorrect components

The player on the left blocks from the correct, bent-knee position, and the play continues

Figure 11-3. An illustration of the "freeze" technique for error correction

technique is similar in many ways to the strategy described previously in this chapter for overcoming swimming errors of young competitive swimmers.

Preliminary Error analysis. Prior to the old way/new way training session, Janice and her coach used videotapes to prepare a detailed error analysis of the push-off from the starting blocks. They focused on three questions. What was she doing wrong? What should she be doing instead? What are the differences between the two? From watching videotapes of Janice's previous races at several competitions, and from several practices, she and the coach had a good understanding of the characteristics of both the erroneous and the correct starting techniques.

The old way/new way training session. Janice, her coach, and the sport psychologist then arranged for a training session. During the session, each start was videotaped and immediate replay was used to reveal the erroneous and correct techniques.

The warm-up. Janice went through her usual warm-up for a typical practice, which required approximately 30 minutes, including four starts.

"Feeling" the old way. Janice performed several starts using the old, erroneous technique. She was instructed to focus on the feeling and sensations while starting with the old technique. She did several of the incorrect starts with her eyes close, to help her to focus on the sensations of the erroneous technique. After each start, she was also encouraged to describe what it was that she felt. After eight starts using the erroneous technique, Janice proceeded to the next step.

"Feeling" the new way. Next, Janice attempted several starts using the correct technique, trying to feel the specific sensations associated with it. She focused on moving her left hand forward more than during the incorrect technique. Also, the left block was moved forward a bit. In addition to focusing on the sensations, after each start, Janice verbally described the correct way of starting. She practiced the correct technique for a total of nine starts.

Discriminating the old and new ways. For the next 11 starts, Janice alternated the old way and the new way. Each time focusing on the sensations and different feelings of the two types of starts, and describing those sensations after each start.

Practicing the new way. Finally, Janice practiced the new way for six more starts. Although she was becoming quite tired from such a large number of starts during a practice session, Janice performed the final six starts with very good technique, each time verbalizing the body sensations.

A review. At the end of the practice, the sport psychologist reviewed the session, summarized the progress, and provided Janice with an expectation for future starts. The psychologist indicated that in previous research, the old way/new way technique was typically followed by at least 80% of all future instances of a skill being performed the new way.

Results of the training session. Prior to the old way/new way training session, Janice had performed her starts in competitions the old way 100% of the time. In competitions during the 14 weeks following the training session, 85% of Janice's starts in competitions were performed the new way. Equally important, her times in the events started to improve. In summary, after approximately a two-hour session involving a total of 38 practice starts (some the old way and some the new way), Janice had progressed to the point where a longstanding error in technique now rarely occurred (Hanin, et al., 2002).

Additional research is need to more clearly establish the effectiveness of the old way/new way error correction technique. From a behavioural view, the old way/new way technique appears to include instruction regarding correct and incorrect techniques, awareness training to discriminate correct and incorrect techniques, key words to prompt correct technique, practicing correct technique with an approximation of a mastery criterion, and receiving immediate videotaped feedback on each practice attempt.

Decreasing Persistent Errors: Additional Comments

In this chapter, I have reviewed several strategies for decreasing persistent errors in athletic skills performed by athletes at practices. I want to remind you that the performance feedback strategies described in Chapter 5 are also frequently used to decrease errors, and those strategies have been used to decrease errors that occur during competitions, as well as practices. For additional discussion of performance feedback strategies for decreasing errors and improving athletic performance at practices and competitions, see Ward (2011).

Study Questions

1. Describe how the three components were implemented to improve Amy's movement during restarts during soccer scrimmages.

2. Is the public posting procedure described for improving Amy's soccer performance at the beginning of this chapter likely to involve positive reinforcement, punishment, or both? Justify your choice.

3. Describe the steps that Jennifer (the figure skater) followed to decrease her errors (at practices) due to her lack of focus. Describe what she did before practices, during practices, and after practices.

4. At Coach Keedwell's swimming practices when relays were noncontingent, what two behavior-consequence occurrences likely maintained improper turns by the swimmers?

5. At Coach Keedwell's swimming practices when relays were noncontingent, what two behavior-consequence occurrences likely maintained unscheduled touchdowns in the middle of sets by the swimmers?

6. If a young athlete is making errors at a practice because of a lack of natural reinforcers for correct performance, what error correction strategy might be applied?

7. When might it be necessary to use a multiple-component error correction program (such as that researched by Koop & Martin with swimmers) to decrease errors?

8. From the material in this chapter, describe three reasons why beginners might make errors or mistakes when executing a previously-learned skill.

9. Drawing on your experience, and thinking about the material in Chapter 3, describe two additional reasons (beyond those suggested in this chapter) why beginners might make errors or mistakes when executing a previously-learned skill.

10. Define key words (see Chapter 8), and describe an example from this chapter.

11. List five recommended guidelines for using videotaped replays for decreasing errors and improving skilled performance.

12. The behavioral treatment involving the freeze technique appears to involve several behavioral principles including punishment, modeling, rule-governed control over behavior, and positive reinforcement. Speculate about how each of these principles may have been involved.

13. What may be a limitation of the freeze technique? Discuss with reference to an example.

Chapter 12

Decreasing Problem Behaviors

An Application

Decreasing Non-Productive Behavior of Young Competitive Swimmers[*]

It was Thursday afternoon at 4:35 pm, and the top squad swimmers from the Thunder Bay Swim Club were in the middle of their dry land training session. The top squad included five young swimmers ranging in age from 12 to 16 years. They attended at least five practice sessions per week, each of which included 20 minutes of dry land training. But in this particular session Bill was eating a sandwich, Mark was telling Brad about his date the night before, and Steve had left the pool area to make a phone call. Coach Bill Humby was extremely concerned about the high-frequency of non-productive behaviors of the swimmers during their dry land training sessions.

With the help of psychology student Michelle Hume and her supervisor, Dr. Jane Crossman, a project was implemented to reduce the non-productive behavior of the swimmers. During an initial baseline phase of the project, non-productive and productive behaviors during dry land training were inconspicuously recorded. Across the five swimmers, non-productive behaviors averaged approximately 60% of the observation intervals per session. Next, at the beginning of the treatment phase, the swimmers were asked to indicate their music preferences. Because they all preferred similar music, it was relatively easy to select several tapes. Next, the swimmers were told that if they showed a 15% improvement in productivity compared to the baseline phase, a tape of their favorite music would be played in the following session. If anyone in the group did not demonstrate that improvement, the music would not be played in the following session. The **contingent music** led to an immediate increase in productive practice behavior and a decrease in non-productive practice behavior. Each of the swimmers showed at least a 30% improvement in performance.

[*]This example is based on a report by Hume and Crossman (1992).

Sport psychology consultants are sometimes asked for their advice concerning problems other than skill development at practices and maximizing athletic performance at competitions. One such area concerns problem behaviors exhibited by young athletes. By problem behaviors, I do not mean **skill deficiencies**, which refer to difficulties performing various athletic skills, such as not following through when throwing a baseball or making a low percentage of free throws in basketball. Those can usually be dealt with according to the techniques described in Chapters 5, 10 and 11. Rather, **problem behaviors** include a variety of disruptive, nonathletic activities that interfere with athletic performance and/or create aversiveness for others. Examples include destroying equipment or failing to put it away in its proper place, annoying and disruptive behaviors while the coach is talking to the team, excessive socializing during drills, temper tantrums, being excessively critical and aggressive toward teammates, and being disrespectful of the rights and privacy of others. This chapter describes several strategies that can be used to prevent behavior problems from occurring in the first place, and to quickly decrease those problems that do occur. Additional strategies for dealing with problem behaviors are described in Martin and Pear (2011).

It Helps to Consider the Cause

Some consideration of potential causes of problem behaviors may help a coach prevent them before they occur. Alternatively, if problems are already ongoing, some consideration of their causes will likely help to select the best treatment strategy.

Some problem behaviors stem from a lack of understanding by young athletes as to what is expected of them at practices. Some athletes may have worked with different coaches in the past who allowed them to do things that the current coach finds annoying. As described below, many problem behaviors can be prevented simply by clarifying rules and expectations at the start of a season. If the coach doesn't clarify his/her expectations, then it's likely that at least some of the young athletes will show behaviors considered to be problematic.

Some problem behaviors may occur at practices because they are immediately followed by natural reinforcers (including peer interaction), while the desirable alternative behaviors do not lead to immediate reinforcers. During the dry land training session of the Thunder Bay swimming team described previously, when Mark performed productive behaviors such as doing sit-ups and stretching, there were no immediate reinforcers. However, when he talked about his date the night before he immediately received lots of attention from Brad. If nothing positive happens when athletes perform well, and if they receive attention or other natural reinforcers for showing problem behaviors, then problem behaviors will occur. Such situations can usually be dealt with by carefully restructuring reinforcers in practice environments to make them contingent upon desirable behaviors, such as the contingent music for productive practice behavior of Mark, Brad and the other swimmers.

In some cases, athletes may show problem behaviors because they don't have the skills to earn rewards for skilled athletic performance. In such cases, it's not that reinforcers are unavailable for desirable behavior, rather, there are no skills in the individual's repertoire that enable him or her to earn those reinforcers. A young ice hockey player who has poor skating skills, poor passing skills, and poor stick handling skills, for example, might show excessive rough-housing and other problem behaviors during practices simply as a way of getting attention in the athletic environment. In such cases, the coach might carefully design a training program appropriate for the skill level of the individual so that reinforcers and recognition can be earned for showing steady improvement rather than for problem behaviors.

Still other problem behaviors may stem from the process of operant extinction. As described in Chapter 3, when the usual reinforcers are withheld following a previously reinforced behavior, that behavior is likely to decrease in frequency. In a simplified sense, if a particular behavior is ignored, it will eventually go away. However, that's the long-term effect. In the short term, withholding reinforcers following previously-reinforced behaviors may cause emotional behavior as a side-effect. Consider, for example, your reaction when a vending machine takes your money but doesn't deliver the goods. You're likely to aggressively push the button several times, bang the side of the machine, and utter a few choice words under your breath. You're showing the short-term effects of extinction - emotional behavior. This might be seen in sport when a new player joins a team. Let's suppose the new child, Cory, is a superstar. Until Cory came to town, Jason was number 1. Jason previously received lots of attention for his athletic performance on the team. Now, for approximately the same behaviors, Jason gets much less attention. Most of it now goes to Cory. It may seem to the coach that Jason has a problem. During the past week, he has shown temper tantrums, sulking and pouting, unprovoked aggression toward his teammates, and a variety of other emotional behaviors. Like your behavior toward the vending machine, Jason may be showing the short term effects of extinction. In such situations, the coach must be careful not to inadvertently provide a great deal of attention to Jason *only* following emotional outbursts. That may serve to reinforce, and worsen, the problem. Also, the coach should refrain from labelling Jason as a poor sport and blaming him for his increase of problem behaviors. What the coach might do is to talk the situation over with Jason away from the athletic environment, have Jason set personal goals (including being a good team player), encourage him to work toward self-improvement, and deliberately provide a little extra feedback for Jason contingent upon self-improvement. At all costs, the coach must avoid ignoring Jason and concentrating mainly on the new superstar.

Still other problem behaviors may stem from the dynamics of interpersonal interactions of the athletes away from the athletic environment. Suzie, for example, wasn't invited to the sleepover that most of the other girls on the team would be attending on Friday night. Scott just broke up with his girlfriend. Kim's parents are about to divorce. Michael is on the verge of failing 8th grade. Todd doesn't want to be in athletics at all; he's on the team only because his dad keeps pushing him to play. His dad also bought new sweaters for the team. All kinds of interpersonal interactions away from the athletic environment can cause problem behaviors for athletes that spill over into practices and games. Moreover, extreme anxiety, phobias, inadequate social skills, absence of problem-solving skills, sexual hang-ups, drug and alcohol dependencies, and other problems faced by many individuals may also be present in athletes. While a sport psychology consultant is not expected to treat all such problems (unless he or she is an appropriately trained clinician), the consultant must be constantly sensitive to their existence and be ever ready to refer athletes to other professionals who can help in such cases.

Strategies for Dealing With Problem Behaviors at Practices

Identify Reasonable Rules and Expectations, and Provide Feedback for Following or Not Following Rules

In the middle of one winter, I received a call from the coach of a figure skating club in a rural town. "We're having problems," she said. "Two of the girls can't get along with each other and it's affecting the whole club. The other skaters are taking sides. There are frequent arguments and nasty comments in the dressing room, and it's spilling over onto the ice. Some of the skaters are deliberately getting in the way of others who are practicing their programs. I've talked to them about it, but it hasn't done any good. Can you help us?"

The coach and I decided that we needed to go beyond the problem behaviors that occurred at practices and to look at the situation more broadly. We also focused on the behavior of the skaters at competitions, and general attitudinal behaviors away from the sporting environment. First, we prepared a checklist that identified the characteristics of a "good team-person" at figure skating practices and competitions (see Figure 12-1). Second, each of the skaters was asked individually to complete the questionnaire. Third, a meeting was held and the skaters and their parents were requested to attend. At that meeting we emphasized the importance of a positive, supportive training environment that would help all skaters to improve to the best of their ability. We also discussed those items on the checklist which most of the skaters identified as needing team improvement (interestingly, most of the skaters thought that they themselves needed little improvement, but that some other members of the team needed a lot of improvement).

Fourth, the coach indicated that she would be periodically evaluating each of the skaters on the good-team-person checklist. Knowing that they were to be evaluated, and knowing that their parents were fully aware of both the concerns of the coach and the expectations for their behaviors at practices, likely helped to exert rule-governed control over the behavior of the young skaters.

The combination of the self-evaluation on the team-person checklist, the meeting with the parents and skaters to discuss the results, and the prompts by the coach had an immediate impact. Approximately once a month during the remainder of the season, the skaters completed the checklist and discussed the results with the coach. Although no formal data were taken, the coach indicated that all of the skaters showed an increased frequency of good team behaviors at practices.

Figure 12-1. A checklist for figure skaters to assess the extent to which they are supportive of other members of their figure skating club.

Are You a Good Team Person? A Test

Read each of the items below. Place a checkmark in the column on the right beside each item for which you are a good team person most of the time. Place an "X" beside each item on which you need to improve. After you have evaluated areas where you are a good team person, and areas where you could improve, then score the rest of your teammates. For each item, place a checkmark if your teammates generally show good team performance on that characteristic, and place an "X" beside that item if one or more of your teammates need to improve on that characteristic.

AT PRACTICES, A Good Team Person: My Score   Team Score

1. Works hard at practices.

2. Encourages teammates to work hard.

3. Makes a positive comment to teammates who land a jump or
    a combo that they've been working on.

4. Approaches practices with a positive attitude and in a good mood

5. Tries to stay positive, even when things are not going well

6. Does not criticize or put down other teammates.

7. Treats all teammates with respect.

8. Treats all coaches with respect.

9. Praises teammates who work harder, rather than trying to slow
    them down.

10. Accepts responsibility for one's mistakes, loss of temper, and
    other shortcomings, and does not take it out on others.

11. Accepts coaching instructions positively and cooperatively.

12. Deals with personal disagreements with a teammate by approaching
    them privately and discussing the problem.

13. Puts in extra effort to work cooperatively with teammates following
    a disagreement.

14. Never gossips or talks negatively about teammates who are absent

---

Figure 12-1 (cont'd)

	My Score	Team Score

15. Sets a good example for teammates by trying to do their best at every practice. ____ ____

16. Is sensitive when a teammate is upset or unhappy, and offers emotional support. ____ ____

17. Never deliberately does anything to interfere with the progress of a teammate, on or off the ice. ____ ____

18. Uses more skilled teammates as models to copy (rather than trying to slow them down). ____ ____

19. Encourages less skilled teammates to improve (rather than "lording" it over them). ____ ____

20. Before, during, and after practice, praises or talks positively to a teammate about something good that the teammate did. ____ ____

AT COMPETITIONS, A Good Team Person:

21. Encourages teammates to skate proudly and do their own thing (rather than being intimidated by other skaters). ____ ____

22. Gives lots of encouragement and positive talk to teammates before, during, and after competitions. ____ ____

23. Helps teammates to stay loose, share in humour, stay relaxed, and have fun. ____ ____

24. Respects teammates' preskate plans and is sensitive to anything that might negatively affect their performance. ____ ____

25. Makes an effort to include all teammates as part of the group. ____ ____

26. Helps teammates to enjoy the experience of participating in a competition, regardless of skating performance and outcome. ____ ____

27. Never gossips or talks negatively about teammates who are absent. ____ ____

28. When teammates are "down", encourages them to think of good things, ignore bad things, and get back on track. ____ ____

In any sport, there have to be some "do"s and "don't"s at practices and competitions. Allowing young people to run free and do the things that may be acceptable at the beach or a public park does not make for effective learning in a practice session. There have to be some rules. Moreover, individuals are more likely to accept rules and consequences for rule violations when they have had input into their development, and if they have publicly committed themselves to following the rules. When formulating rules and consequences for rule violations, coaches should be encouraged to ask several questions: Are the rules reasonable? How well do particular rules contribute to the effectiveness of practices? How well do rules contribute to the instruction of individual athletes? Are there frequent positive consequences for following the rules? Are the negative consequences for rule violations fair to the individuals involved, and to the rest of the team? At the beginning of a season, if a coach: a) identifies reasonable rules concerning desirable and undesirable behaviors of athletes; b) identifies consequences for rule violations; c) obtains a commitment from the athletes to follow the rules; and d) monitors desirable and undesirable behavior during the season, and provides feedback, then the coach will have taken giant steps to minimize the chances of problem behaviors occurring.

Use Monitoring and Charting to Increase Desirable Alternative Behaviors

When a problem behavior exists, one strategy is to increase a desirable alternative behavior. Let's look in on a practice of the St. Anne's Figure Skating Club. Michelle Hume, a professional instructor and coach of the club, is in the middle of a half-hour lesson with Sally. Heather, Claudia, and Cathy are supposed to be practicing their routines and spending extra time on the difficult jumps and spins. For the last three minutes, however, Heather and Claudia have been standing along the boards, talking excitedly about the upcoming school dance. Cathy had just completed her fifth loop in a row. Coach Hume hollers at Heather and Claudia, "You're supposed to be practicing your routines, not standing around talking. Let's get at it. Cathy, you've done five loops in a row. What you really have trouble with is the double loop and the double axel. Why aren't you practicing those?"

Off-task behavior, excessive socializing, and failure to practice the really difficult routines are not uncommon problems facing coaches of various sports. Coach Hume, who was also a student in sport psychology at the University of Manitoba, decided to tackle the problem head on. Rather than continuing to nag about the off-task behavior, she set out to investigate a self-monitoring feedback system for improving desirable alternative behaviors of the skaters. Her first step was to identify specific desirable practice behaviors. These were itemized in a checklist of the jumps and spins that Heather, Claudia, and Cathy were expected to practice for 45 minutes per day while she gave lessons to the other skaters. In addition to listing them all individually, she also listed the specific combination of jumps and spins that constituted each skater's individual program.

Over the next several practices, appropriately trained university students kept track of the frequency of jumps and spins attempted, the number of times a skater practiced her program, and the amount of time spent off-task. The initial observations confirmed Michelle's suspicions. The three skaters averaged a little more than 10 minutes of off-task behavior in each 45-min. session. They averaged approximately 60 spins or jumps attempted per session, most of which were of the "easy" variety. Michelle thought that they should be averaging at least 100 per session, and should be working more on the difficult jumps and spins.

Coach Hume's second step was to devise a strategy for the skaters to self-monitor the occurrence of the desirable practice behaviors. A big chart was prepared for each skater containing the checklist of jumps and spins, the elements in the skater's program, two graphs, and appropriate instructions. Coach Hume explained the charts to the skaters: "Each practice session, I want you to do the first three elements on your chart, and then come and record them here. Then practice the next three elements and come and record them. Continue in this way until you've practiced all of the elements, which should take approximately 15 minutes. Then go through the whole routine again. After all of the elements have been checked twice, do your program and record the results. Thereafter, continue practicing those elements that you rated as poor when you were doing your program." After some discussion and an initial practice session, the skaters began using the charts.

The third step in Coach Hume's strategy was to provide feedback to the skaters for improvement (see Figure 12-2). At the end of each practice, summary bars were added to charts of off-task behavior and elements attempted so that the skaters could clearly see their progress. Progress was praised by Coach Hume.

The results can be seen in Figure 12-3. During sessions when the charts were in use, the skaters averaged more then 100 elements per practice, and from 2 to 3 minutes of off-task behavior. In other words, they improved by approximately 85% with this self-monitoring system. Once the system was implemented, the only additional time required of Coach Hume was a few minutes at the end of each practice session to review the results with the skaters, update their graphs, and praise their performance.

The basic strategy illustrated by Coach Hume's study (Hume et al., 1985) is quite straightforward. If problem behaviors occur at a practice, coaches can identify desirable alternative behaviors and reinforcers for them, and add some kind of system to keep track of whether or not such behaviors occur. Hume emphasized self-monitoring (discussed further in Chapter 13). In the study described by Siedentop (1980, see Chapter 7) in which the basketball players could earn points for showing positive comments to each other and for improved skills, team managers monitored the desirable behaviors. When there is a clear focus on improving a variety of desirable practice behaviors, problem behaviors are likely to be minimized.

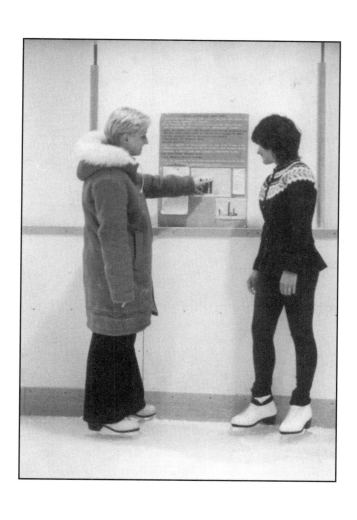

Figure 12-2. Coach Hume compliments Cathy for increasing the number of elements (jumps and spins) attempted per session.

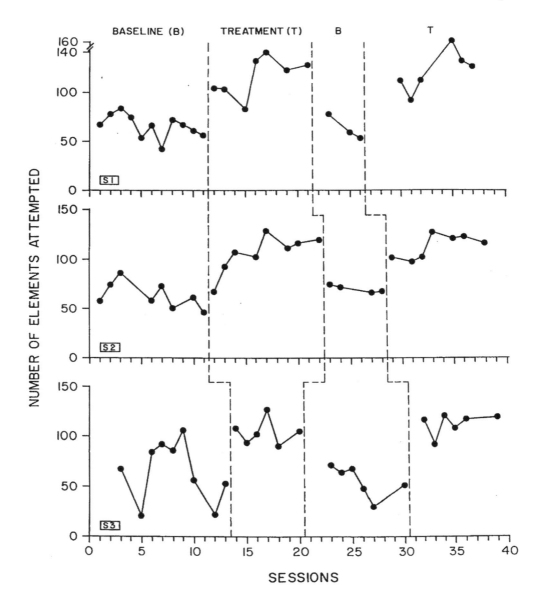

<u>Figure 12-3</u>. Number of elements attempted per 45-min. practice session by figure skaters during all experimental phases. Reprinted with permission from Hume et al. (1985).

Teach Athletes to Use Self-Talk and Cue Cards to Prompt Desirable Alternative Behavior

Sometimes when young athletes show problem behavior in a practice, they want to reduce it, but they're not sure how to solve the problem. For example, one of the young figure skaters with whom I worked frequently became extremely angry during practices when she had difficulty with a particular jump. After missing the jump two or three times the skater typically thought, "I'll never land it," "How come everybody can do this jump but me?" "I'm a terrible skater," "I can't do anything right." This negative self-talk likely exacerbated the problem. She felt unable to control her anger, and her outbursts (e.g., kicking the ice, swearing, etc.) detracted from her own ability to maximize her use of practice time and were disruptive to some of the other skaters.

The anger management strategy which she used had several components (a similar strategy used by a golfer was described in Chapter 9). First, we identified the events that typically preceded her anger. When she was practicing a jump that she had not yet mastered, that she had been working on for some time (at least 3 or 4 weeks), and on which she felt she was not making progress, she started thinking negatively and got mad at herself. Next, we developed a scoring system to help her monitor progress on such a jump so that she might more accurately assess the small progress that was sometimes made. The scoring system was the same as that described for Jennifer in Figure 11-1. Third, if, after missing the jump two or three times, she felt herself getting angry, the skater agreed to do the following:

a) Skate a "smart thinking" lap. This involved skating slowly around the rink to focus on positive self-talk.

b) Practice positive self-talk during the smart thinking lap. This involved reading the following statements from a cue card:

"I refuse to let negative emotions interfere with my practice."

"I skate because I really enjoy it. I refuse to let one specific element get me down."

"I'll work hard and try to detect small amounts of progress in this practice."

"A well-rounded skater must have good jumps, good spins, good combos and good presentation. I'll make sure that I improve in at least one of these areas in this practice."

Fourth, for three practices in a row, the coach and I prompted the skater to follow the strategy. By the fourth practice, the skater was consistently following the strategy on her own, and was able to control her anger in most situations at practices for the rest of the season.

Strategies for Dealing with Problem Behaviors at Competitions

Thus far in this chapter I have described strategies that have been successfully applied to decrease problem behaviors of athletes at practices. In Chapter 9, I described strategies for helping athletes deal with excessive anxiety or anger at competitions. I will now describe some additional strategies that have been successfully applied to decrease problem behaviors of athletes at competitions.

Use Monitoring and Charting to Decrease Problem Behaviors

Zarina Galvan, a professional tennis coach, had seen her fair share of problem behaviors on the tennis court - throwing rackets, throwing water jugs, swearing at officials, obscene gestures to fans, and so on. Such behaviors can often be seen wherever there is a tennis match, from neighbourhood courts to Wimbledon. Not only are such behaviors unsportsmanlike and against the rules, they can result in disqualification in sanctioned matches. As indicated previously in this chapter, monitoring and public posting of performance has been used to improve specific target behaviors at practices. Zarina teamed up with Philip Ward, a professor at University of Nebraska, to investigate the use of public posting to decrease problem behaviors during tennis matches (Galvan & Ward, 1998). The participants were five collegiate tennis players who had been playing tennis competitively for at least six years. In the first part of the study, data were collected on problem behaviors exhibited by the participants from videotapes of challenge matches during the season. Next, Zarina met with each of the players individually, discussed the problem behaviors that they typically displayed, asked them to try to reduce the occurrence of such behaviors, and encouraged them to practice some alternative behavior. Examples of alternative behaviors included holding the racket with two hands instead of striking the ground with it, counting to three instead of yelling, or visualizing a good shot instead of dwelling on a bad one. The players agreed that a graph of their inappropriate behaviors would be publicly posted in each of their respective locker rooms on a bulletin board that their fellow team members regularly checked for information. In each case, results were dramatic. Within one of two matches for each player, inappropriate on-court behaviors decreased from approximately 10 or more per match to approximately 5 or fewer. Equally important, when asked about the public posting procedure at the end of the study, all five players and their coaches said that the procedures were both acceptable and very helpful.

Post Signs to Prompt Desirable Alternative Behavior

In golf, when a golfer hits a ball on to a putting green, the impact of the golf ball often produces an indentation in the green, known as a "ball mark." Dickie Yu enjoyed playing golf at the local public golf course on weekends. He was dismayed, however, at the large number of ball marks on putting greens. Although ball mark repair is relatively easily accomplished using a "ball mark repairer" (a small pointed object) to repair the indentation, it was obvious to Dickie that many of the golfers playing that particular course did not take the time to repair the ball mark that their ball made when they hit it on to the green. With the approval of the golf course superintendent, Dickie launched an investigation of low-cost procedures to influence golfers to repair ball marks. During baseline observations over several weeks, data indicated an average of 20 ball marks per green per 100 golfers. Such unrepaired ball marks have long-term damaging effects on greens, in addition to being disruptive to golfers attempting to putt on a green with many indentations. Following baseline, Dickie introduced an educational sign prompt near the entrance to the clubhouse. The sign contained an explanation of, and photographs of, some unrepaired ball marks, a description of how to repair ball marks as depicted in photographs, and a request for golfers to help repair ball marks. The educational sign prompting decreased the number of unrepaired ball marks on putting greens by approximately 37% (Yu & Martin, 1987). The golf course staff were pleased with the results, and adopted the educational sign prompt as a permanent fixture. This study suggests that educational sign prompting may be a useful strategy for conserving a public sport environment.

Teach Athletes to Use Self-Reinforcement Instead of Self-Criticism

Many athletes appear to be their own worst enemies. Many golfers, for example, can be heard telling themselves, after a bad shot, "You idiot! How can you be so stupid! What a dumb shot!" But such self-criticism has no redeeming features. Moreover, there are at least four problems that occur as a result of excessive self-criticism following an athletic skill. First, research suggests that it contributes to poor performance. For example, in a study of the qualifiers and non-qualifiers for the US Olympic gymnastics team, the non-qualifiers exhibited considerably more negative self-talk than did the successful gymnasts (Mahoney & Avener, 1977). As another example, Judy Van Raalte and her colleagues (1994) studied the way in which 24 competitive junior tennis players talked to themselves during important matches. These researchers found that the eventual losers of close matches were almost twice as critical of themselves during the match as the winners. Second, it takes away from the enjoyment of the game, both for the athlete being critical and those who are playing with that athlete. Third, it interferes with the ability of that athlete to relax - a critical ingredient for success in most sports. And fourth, strong emotions increase the likelihood that the athlete will remember that bad shot or skill, and the objective should be to forget it. Remembering a bad shot or skill increases the chances that the initial bad shot will be followed by another one.

An alternative to being super-critical of a bad shot or skill is for an athlete to reinforce their good shots or skills. During one of the sport psychology classes that I taught at the University of Manitoba in which I was talking about this possibility, one of the students indicated that he thought he would try positive reinforcement on his golf game. Instead of cursing his bad shots, as he usually did, he decided to try praising his good shots. About a month after the course ended, I encountered him at the local shopping mall. "How's the golf game?", I asked. A big smile lit up his face.

"At first I was really self-conscious," he told me, "saying 'Well done,' after each good shot, and then looking around to see if anybody noticed. But after a couple of weeks my game started to get better. My handicap is down by two points, and I'm having more fun. When I was yelling at myself all the time, I was usually angry and disappointed after a game. Now, when I make a bad shot, instead of yelling, I look forward to the next shot so that I can praise myself. Some people might call it - being your own best coach. Your coach would never call you a 'dumb ass' for mishitting a golf shot. And when I see the other guys making mistakes, getting mad, and wacking their clubs into the turf, I think, 'If only they knew about self-reinforcement.'" (For additional examples of self-reinforcement, see Watson & Tharp, 2007.)

Sometimes Special Problems Require Special Procedures

The above discussion illustrates a few examples of the application of behavioral procedures to decrease problem behaviors in sport settings. Experts in behavior analysis have successfully designed programs to decrease a variety of problem behaviors of persons ranging in age from the very young to the very old, of healthy persons and of severely disturbed individuals, and in a wide variety of situations and settings (Martin & Pear, 2011). That literature provides an excellent source for additional strategies to decrease problem behaviors.

Study Questions

1. In two or three sentences, and with some examples, distinguish between skill deficiencies vs. the types of problem behaviors addressed in this chapter.

2. In a sentence of two each, describe several possible causes of problem behaviors shown by young athletes at practices.

3. What was the probable cause of non-productive behaviors of swimmers at practices, described at the start of this chapter?

4. If a young athlete shows problem behaviors at practices as a side-effect of extinction (i.e., for some reason, desirable behaviors that previously resulted in considerable attention no longer do so), what guidelines should a coach follow to appropriately deal with such problem behavior?

5. For a sport with which you are familiar (other than figure skating), list at least five desirable behaviors and five undesirable behaviors for young athletes at a typical practice.

6. When formulating rules and consequences for rule violations for a group of young athletes, what questions should coaches ask concerning the nature of those rules and consequences?

7. Briefly describe four steps that a coach might take at the beginning of a season to minimize chances of problem behaviors occurring in the first place.

8. In several sentences, describe the three steps of the strategy followed by Coach Hume to decrease off-task practice behaviors of the figure skaters.

9. Define stimulus control (see Chapter 3). How was stimulus control involved in the program with figure skaters developed by Coach Hume?

10. Define rule-governed control over behavior (see Chapter 4). How was rule-governed control used by Coach Hume in the program with figure skaters?

11. Define positive reinforcement (see Chapter 3). How was positive reinforcement used by Coach Hume in the program with figure skaters?

12. Define fixed-ratio schedule of reinforcement (see Chapter 3). How was a fixed ratio schedule applied by Coach Hume in the program with figure skaters?

13. Describe the four components of the strategy that the young figure skater followed to control excessive anger at practices.

14. What are two differences in the self-recording program with figure skaters used by Coach Hume versus the public posting program with tennis players applied by Galvan and Ward? What do you see as the relative advantages or disadvantages of the two approaches?

15. Briefly describe the educational sign prompting program applied by Yu and Martin to increase ball mark repairing by golfers. Does their program rely on natural reinforcers or deliberately managed reinforcers? Justify your choice.

16. Describe a plausible example of self-reinforcement that might be used by an athlete that is not in this chapter.

Part IV
Improving Practice Performance
With Advanced Athletes

Chapter 13

Self-Management for Quality Practices

An Application

Self-Set Goals and Public Posting to Improve Skill Execution of a Football Player[*]

Brad was a linebacker of a Division II football team at a four-year liberal arts college in the midwest. During drills and scrimmages at practices, Brad wanted to improve his "reads" (correctly positioning himself to cover a specified area on the field during a pass or a run from the line of scrimmage), his "drops" (moving to the correct position described in the playbook in response to the positioning of the offense), and his "tackles" (whether or not he tackled the ball carrier and stopped his progress). Assessments of videotapes of practices indicated that Brad averaged approximately 70% correct for each of these three, key linebacker behaviors. Brad agreed with his coach that there was room for improvement.

Brad set a goal of 90% correct performance for each of reads, drops, and tackles. He also agreed that a chart would be posted on the wall of the locker room beside the door that led to the field, and after each practice, a Y (i.e., Yes) would be placed next to his name if he met his goals, and an N (i.e., No) would be placed next to his name if he did not meet his goals. The head coach explained to the other players on the team the purpose of the chart. The results of the **self-goal-setting** and **public posting** system were dramatic. Brad immediately improved his performance to 90% or better on all three linebacker behaviors at practices, and his improved performance also generalized to games.

[*]This application is based on Ward & Carnes (2002).

Are great athletes born that way? Is it primarily innate talent that enables them to rise above their fellow competitors? Many believe that it is. Considerable research, however, suggests that differences in expert performance of elite athletes are determined primarily by differences in the amount of **focused, quality practice over an extended period of time** (at least 10 years), and much less by differences in natural talent or inherited ability (Ericsson, Charness, Feltovich, & Hoffman, 2006). That does not mean that inherited characteristics are unimportant to athletic performance. Someone who is 5 ft. 6 in. (168 cm) in height will not play centre for a professional basketball team, regardless of how much that person practices. But within the constraints that physical structure imposes on certain sports, Ericsson, Krampe and Tesch-Romer (1993) concluded, "the differences between expert performers in normal adults reflect a lifelong period of deliberate effort to improve performance in a specific domain" (p. 400). And it is not the overall amount or duration of practice that is critical. In fact, elite athletes often limit the duration of their practices to avoid exhaustion and burnout. Rather, the critical variable appears to be the amount of **deliberate, focused, quality practice**.

But what are the critical components of deliberate, focused, quality practices? Orlick and Partington (1988) studied 235 Canadian Olympic athletes representing many different sports. From these athletes, two groups were identified: those who performed at or exceeded their expectations at national, world, or Olympic competitions; and those who performed below their potential at major competitions. The athletes who performed well did the following to a greater extent than those who performed below their potential:

- had a strong commitment to get the most out of each and every practice;
- wrote out their goals before practices;
- set practice goals that included quality as well as quantity;
- thought about their goals on the way to practice so that they arrived committed to do their best to accomplish their goals;
- had ways of monitoring progress on new skills;
- kept a written record of their progress in meeting their practice goals.

Additional differences between these two groups of athletes are discussed in Chapter 15. Concerning practices, the above strategies followed by the top group of athletes provide a useful way for conceptualizing the details of "deliberate, focused, quality" practices. These strategies also fit well with a behavioral approach to self-management.

A Behavioral Approach to Self-Management

Carlos just finished jogging his second mile after wrestling practice. Although he was supposed to jog three miles each day to get his weight down, he decided to cut it short. "I've got lots of time left," he thought to himself. "I don't have to push myself yet." Later, on the way back to the dormitory, he stopped at the Dairy Queen and ordered a

Blizzard. The waitress, a friend of his, chided, "Shame on you! I thought you were in training." "But they're so delicious!" replied Carlos. "Besides, one more won't make any difference."

Many problems of self-control require responses that need to be increased - such as exercising, studying, and being assertive. Other problems of self-control require behavior change in the opposite direction - they involve learning restraint from behaviors that have immediate gratification, such as excessive eating, excessive TV watching, and excessive socializing. Carlos faced both types of problems. Many people speak as though there's some magical force within us - called **willpower** - that is responsible for overcoming such problems. As expressed by Martin and Pear (2011), you may have been told, "If you had more willpower, you could get rid of that bad habit," or "If you had more willpower, you could improve yourself and get some better habits." Unfortunately, such advice is not very helpful because the person offering it almost always neglects to tell us how we can get more of this so-called willpower.

Rather than speculate about willpower, a behavioral approach to self-management offers concrete steps that an individual can take for self improvement. An effective **behavioral model of self-management** has two parts. The first part of the model requires clear specification of the behavior(s) to be changed. In Carlos's case, he needed to increase his daily aerobic exercising, and decrease his consumption of ice cream products. The second part of the model requires that the individual apply behavioral techniques to manage the problem behavior(s). Stated differently, an individual must behave in some way that rearranges the environment to manage his or her own subsequent behavior. This approach to self-control has been referred to as self-modification (Watson & Tharp, 2007), and self-adjustment (Martin & Osborne, 1993). It provides a useful framework for helping advanced athletes to get more out of practices. But first, let's examine some of the causes of self-control problems.

Some Causes of Self-Control Problems

Why did Carlos find it difficult to resist having a Blizzard on the way home from practice? There are two reasons. For many undesirable behavioral excesses, the immediate reinforcement of the problem behavior wins out over the unnoticeable negative effects that are only cumulatively significant (Malott, 1989). For Carlos, eating the ice cream was immediately reinforced by the good taste. Second, although the negative effects (excess cholesterol, increased body weight, etc.) of the ice cream were immediate, they were too small to be noticed. Rather, it is the accumulation of extra sweets on many occasions that causes health and weight problems.

What about Carlos's behavioral deficit - the problem of cutting short his jogging? Or more generally, why do many athletes find it difficult to spend the amount of time practicing various drills that are crucial to the development of excellence? Again, there are two main reasons. For many behavioral deficits, athletes fail to engage in appropriate practice activities because doing so leads to immediate small punishers while the positive effects, though immediate, are too small to be effective until they have accumulated over many trials (Malott, 1989). For Carlos, his jogging was time-consuming and tiring. And second, while running the full three miles by Carlos may have immediate benefits (increased blood circulation, better removal of waste products, burning off of calories, etc.), and while performing a skill drill at a practice may have some immediate benefits (improvement in technique, etc.), such outcomes are often too small to be noticed. Rather, it is the accumulation of such benefits of practice activities on many occasions that is eventually noticeable. We now turn to self-management strategies that can be used to overcome such problems.

Steps in Self-Management for Quality Practices

The majority of successful, documented cases of self-management in a variety of areas (such as improving eating habits, overcoming stress, improving study habits, etc.) include the following steps: (1) set specific behavioral goals for quantity and quality; (2) increase commitment to change; (3) design monitoring data sheets for key behaviors; (4) manage antecedents to motivate desirable behaviors; (5) manage consequences to motivate desirable behaviors; (6) prevent relapse and make it last. Self-management strategies for improving performance at practices will be described in terms of these steps.

1. Set Goals for Quantity, Quality, and Game Simulations

As described in the application at the start of this chapter, Brad's goal included both quantity (90%) and quality (only correct behaviors counted). For many practice activities in many sports, it is relatively easy to set goals that have quantity and quality components (Gould, 2010; Ward, 2011). Examples include the number of successful jumps and spins at a figure skating practice, the number of backhands hit down the line in tennis, the number of over-the-head catches successfully made in football by a wide receiver, the number of grounders fielded without error in baseball, percentage foul shots made in basketball, percentage of shots into the left corner of the goal from 30 feet in soccer, and the number of wedge shots onto the green from 100 yards in golf.

Athletes practice in order to prepare for competitions. It stands to reason, therefore, that at least some goals should involve practicing under competition-like conditions. This topic is so important that I have devoted the next chapter entirely to it.

2. Increase the Athlete's Commitment to Change

As described in Chapter 4, a **commitment to change** refers to statements or actions by an athlete which imply that it is important to improve in a specific area, that he/she will work toward doing so, and that he/she recognizes the benefits of doing so. In problem areas such as eating, smoking, studying, or dating, successful self-managers had both a stronger commitment to change and used more behavior change techniques than did unsuccessful self-managers (Watson & Tharp, 2007). It is probably also true for athletes that *both* a commitment to change *and* knowledge of change techniques are important for successful accomplishment of self-modification projects.

Athletes can be encouraged to take several steps to keep their commitment strong. First, they might express their commitment to improve to friends, coaches, and/or fellow athletes. Making a public commitment to change increases the chances of success (Hayes et al., 1985). Second, they might arrange their environment to provide frequent reminders of practice goals. They could write their goals on index cards and leave them in conspicuous places, such as taped to their fridge door or on their car dashboard. Some athletes have creatively used photographs to remind them of their goals. Third, they might make a list of all of the benefits for improving their practice performance. Fourth, they should arrange for frequent reminders of the positive benefits associated with reaching their practice goals.

In Chapter 7, I outlined a behavioral approach to the topic of motivation. One strategy for motivating desirable practice behavior discussed in that chapter involved arranging antecedents to prompt desirable behaviors. The suggestions in the previous paragraph to increase an athlete's commitment to change could also be conceptualized as managing antecedents to prompt desirable behaviors. More examples of this strategy will be presented later in this chapter.

3. Design Monitoring Sheets for Key Behaviors

The next step is to design a data sheet to monitor the occurrence of the practice behaviors to be improved. (Reasons for monitoring target behaviors were listed in Chapter 6.) For example, Randy Ambrosie, All-Canadian offensive tackle with the University of Manitoba Bisons, with the help of Jody Young, a graduate student in physical education, developed the checklist shown in Figure 13-1. Randy recorded self-evaluations after practices during the week before an important game with the University of Calgary. He found the checklist to be very helpful in maintaining his concentration on various aspects of technique. Such a checklist can also help a coach provide feedback on specifics of practice performance, instead of just making vague, general comments. Other examples of self-monitoring of practice performance include components of the backstroke in swimming (Figure 6-2), rating of jumps and spins in figure skating (Figure 11-1), number of jumps and spins completed in figure skating (Figure 12-2), laps completed in swimming (Figure 5-2), shots made in golf (Johnston-O'Connor & Kirschenbaum, 1986), and scores in bowling (Kirschenbaum et al., 1982).

Figure 13-1. A self-monitoring form used by a college lineman to improve performance at football practices.

Date _____						Comments
Skill Evaluation Assess each on a scale of 1 to 5, where 1 = less than 50% of opportunities; 3 = 50% to 70% of opportunities; and 5 = almost all the time.	M	T	W	Th	F	
1. Pass blocking a. Butt down						
b. Back straight						
c. Hands out in front						
d. Foot movement, lead steps						
e. Contact on chest						
2. Run blocking a. Lead steps						
b. Quickness off the ball						
c. Explosion into man						
d. Extension and hip thrust through man						
e. Contact on body, not outside						
3. Blocking success a. One-on-one						
b. Team situations						
Contributing Factors Rate each subjectively on a scale of 1 to 5, where 1 = very poor; and 5 = super or great.						
1. Effort						
2. Concentration						
3. Physical well-being						
4. Sleeping habits (minus {-} = too little, too tired; checkmark {✓} = about right, 7½ to 8 hours; plus {+} means too much, too sluggish.)						
5. Eating habits						

If the practice areas to be improved include subjective components, such as working hard or having a positive attitude, then these can often be monitored effectively with a rating system. A sample of such a checklist used with members of the Manitoba provincial gymnastics team is shown in Figure 13-2.

4. Manage Antecedents to Motivate Quality Practices

As described in Chapter 7, one strategy for motivating desirable practice behavior is to arrange antecedents to prompt desirable behaviors. In the section in this chapter concerning an athlete's commitment to change, several suggestions were made for managing antecedents. This section provides additional examples of managing antecedents to motivate athletic behavior.

Self-Instructions. Self-instructions have been used successfully in a variety of formal self-management projects (Watson & Tharp, 2007). To illustrate a self-instructional approach, consider a problem faced by a young professional hockey player at his first major league tryout camp. During the first practice, the player was extremely nervous. He frequently experienced negative thoughts such as, "These guys are awesome," "What am I doing here?" "I'll never stick with this team." During the first practice, the player performed considerably below his potential. Before the second practice of tryout camp, we went through a modeling and role-playing session to help the player learn positive self-talk to counteract his negative thinking. Just before practice, he was taught to say to himself, "The fact that I'm nervous doesn't mean that I'm going to blow it - being nervous is just a way to prepare me to be alert and do my best." Next, he practiced self-instruction during the practice to help himself focus on his strengths. Just before various drills, he told himself things like, "I've got excellent speed, I handle the puck well, have good hands, and a hard, accurate slapshot, and I'll make the most of them." "I play my position well, I see the ice well, and I read the play well." "I'll finish my checks, play aggressive, and work hard every shift." Finally, the player was instructed to make self-reinforcing statements immediately after he had a good shift or performed well during a drill (e.g., "Great! Keep it going."). By the third practice of the tryout camp, the player was relaxed and playing well. He indicated that he continued using the self-instructions throughout the camp. At the end of camp, he was offered a contract.

Self-instructional strategies have been used in many areas of cognitive behavior modification (Brown, 2011; Martin & Pear, 2011). Before recommending self-instructions to improve practice performance with athletes, however, I suggest that you review the guidelines for using rules and goals in Chapter 4.

Modeling. Modeled behavior is another class of stimulus events that is useful in self-management programs. Here is an example of its use by a figure skater to improve practice performance. The skater had been working on a difficult jump for several weeks, and tended to get down on herself at practices for lack of progress. She frequently got so upset that it spoiled the whole practice. To deal with this problem, she agreed to try modeling a hardworking, cheerful skater. When the skater got upset, she looked around at

Figure 13-2. A self-monitoring sheet to improve practice performace of young gymnasts.

To Get the Most out of your Practices, Regularly Assess Your Practice Habits

At least two or three times per week, use the following score form to assess your practice habits. Be totally honest with yourself. Don't give yourself the highest score unless you think you've earned it. Use your scores to motivate yourself to train to be the best that you can possibly be.

For the following items, score them on a 1-5 scale:

1	2	3	4	5
Definitely No		**To Some Extent**		**Definitely Yes**

Dates→								
1. I deliberately put myself in a good mood at the start of practice								
2. I did everything that the coach asked me to do in my practice plan								
3. On the beam, I tried my hardest to stick everything								
4. I was happy with my performance on the beam								
5. On the vault I tried my hardest to stick every attempt								
6. I was happy with my performance on the vault								
7. I tried my hardest to do everything on the bars								
8. I was happy with my performance on the bars								
9. I tried my hardest to stick everything on the floor								
10. I was happy with my performance on the floor								
11. At least once during the practice, I did a serious simulation of each of my routines								
12. I practiced instant mental replays of several difficult moves just after I stuck them								
13. I used my self-talk to stay positive and feel good about myself								
14. I used my self-talk to feel confident about practicing difficult moves								
15. I worked hard for the entire practice								
16. Before leaving practice, I told the coach about one thing that I thought I did really well, and really liked about the practice								
17. I showed my rating sheet to my coach to see if my coach agreed with my ratings								

the other skaters at practice, and picked one who typically worked hard and was usually in a good mood. After watching that skater for a few seconds, the skater (who was upset) told herself, "So-and-so falls, but continues to work hard and usually stays in a good mood. If she can do it, so can I." Her coach was told about the plan, and he agreed to remind the skater to follow it when she appeared to be getting mad at herself. The strategy proved to be quite successful. The general rule is this: if an athlete wants to improve a particular behavior at practices, the athlete might identify another athlete who's good at that behavior, observe that other athlete's behavior across several practices, and try to imitate the behavior.

The immediate surroundings. Because certain behaviors are likely to occur in certain situations or settings, rearranging one's existing surroundings can be an effective strategy for changing behavior. Consider the example of a golfer who experienced difficulty following her off-season fitness routine that included weightlifting. Frequently, she couldn't seem to "get up the energy" to lift weights. To increase the likelihood of weightlifting during her fitness sessions, she placed the weights in the centre of her exercise room, turned on the TV to the local fitness channel, and opened her *Muscle Beach* magazine to the centrefold showing her favourite body builder. Rearranging her surroundings in this manner usually motivated her to do the weightlifting exercises. Other examples of rearranging the immediate surroundings include playing fast-paced music when practice drills require lots of action (Anshel & Marisi, 1978; Kodzhospirov, Zaitsev, & Kosarev, 1988), wearing a professional team jersey with the number of one's favourite player to induce one to practice to "be like that person", posting pictures of one's sport heroes to motivate one to become as skilled as such individuals, or changing the location of a practice activity to minimize various distractors.

Other people. As indicated above, modeling is one way of providing strong prompts for an individual to engage in some behavior. Another strategy is to simply change the people in the nearby vicinity. The athlete may not necessarily model these new people, but they may nevertheless exert stimulus control over improved practice performance. A strategy frequently used by figure skaters, for example, is to invite friends to practices to watch them perform.

The time of day. We've all learned to do certain things at certain times. Sometimes practice problems are related to that fact. Sometimes it's possible to achieve successful self-management by changing the time of the activity. Suppose, for example, that a member of the college golf team is most alert in the morning and early afternoon. Yet that person typically spends that time having coffee and socializing with friends, and he leaves both his golf practice and studying until late afternoon and evening when he is less alert and less focused. Successful self-management of both improved practice performance and studying for such an individual might be accomplished by moving practicing and studying to mornings and early afternoons, and socializing to evenings.

5. Manage Consequences to Motivate Quality Practices

As described in Chapter 7, an effective strategy for motivating behavior is to manage consequences.

Eliminate reinforcers for problem behavior. One strategy for manipulating consequences is to eliminate reinforcers that may be maintaining problem behavior that interferes with desired practice behavior. Consider the example of the young figure skater who had indicated on a pre-season needs assessment that she wanted to get more out of practices, but continued to show considerable off-task behavior during practices. Observations indicated that most of her off-task behavior involved socializing with other skaters. When this was pointed out to her, her strategy was to ask the other skaters to interact with her during practices only by making brief comments or words of encouragement when she worked at practicing her jumps and spins. They agreed not to converse with her about non-skating activities until after practices. As a result, her off-task behavior decreased to a much lower level.

Self-record and chart improvements. A second way of manipulating consequences is by self-recording and charting the target behavior (e.g., see Figure 13-3). Seeing a line on a graph that represents gradual improvement can serve as a prompt to think a variety of positive, self-confidence thoughts. I observed an example of this effect with a young competitive gymnast. Jody included a move in her beam routine referred to as a front sumi down. The move is kind of like a forward somersault in which the gymnast lands on one foot in a squat position with the arms pointing straight out to each side. Although she was landing the move approximately half of the time, she felt that she was making little progress and was very discouraged. She agreed to make 10 attempts on the front sumi down in three practices per week, and to chart her progress. She showed considerable improvement, and by the end of the third week, was "sticking" approximately 90% of them. During the fourth week, she participated in a competition and did a clean beam routine, including her front sumi down.

Reinforce desirable practice behaviors. A third way of manipulating consequences involves arranging for specific reinforcers to be earned by the athlete for showing improvement, or even just for sticking to the practice plan. One strategy is for the individual to apply self-reinforcement for desirable practice behavior. This was the strategy followed by Carlos to maintain his jogging program. His goal was to run three miles each day. But after the first two miles, he felt tired, and frequently talked himself out of doing the last few laps. He decided to try a self-reinforcement program to increase the frequency of "anti-fatigue" thoughts. Specifically, during the third mile, he would think an anti-fatigue thought and then follow it with a pleasurable thought. Each time he got to a quarter-mile spot on the track, he imagined himself diving into the university pool, splashing around, and having a refreshing swim - an activity that always invigorated him. After several seconds of such thoughts, he then thought about

Figure 13-3. Self-recording and self-charting can improve performance.

something enjoyable, such as watching his favourite actress in his favourite movie - Julia Roberts in *Pretty Woman*. Each time he reached a quarter-mile mark, he repeated the process. In this way, he was able to engage in a private behavior that counteracted the fatigue thoughts, and was able to strengthen that behavior by following it with reinforcing thoughts. After practicing this strategy for about two weeks, he was able to put the fatigue thoughts completely out of mind. (Although the program was effective, there may be better ways of explaining it than thinking of it as self-reinforcement. For a discussion of conceptual problems with the notion of self-reinforcement, see Martin and Pear, 2011.)

A second strategy for managing reinforcers is for the athlete to arrange for others to present reinforcers (to the athlete) contingent upon improvement. For example, Mary decided to initiate a jogging program. She made arrangements with her husband to dispense reinforcers. Each day that she jogged, she would receive money immediately after, and would later have an opportunity to engage in one of several possible social activities with her husband. The program was quite successful (Kau & Fischer, 1974).

A third strategy for managing reinforcers to motivate practice performance is for the athlete to remind him/herself of delayed natural reinforcers for specific practice behavior, and to do so immediately after the practice behavior occurs. Suppose, for example, that an ice hockey player sets a goal of increasing his/her strength and muscle mass by following a weight lifting program. Doing so could lead to sizeable natural reinforcers. With more strength and weight, the hockey player will be able to check more aggressively, push away the sticks of other players trying to check him or her, and so forth. But these consequences are long delayed after the early stages of a weight lifting program. After all, it takes a while to build up strength and muscle. A solution, therefore, is to increase the saliency of the natural reinforcers right after the behavior to be controlled. Immediately after a bench pressing exercise, for example, the hockey player might imagine how much fun it is going to be to use his/her increased weight and strength in various game situations.

Some rules of thumb for incorporating reinforcers into self-management programs include: (1) make it possible for the individual to earn specific reinforcers in each practice; (2) set up bonuses that can be earned for progress on a weekly basis; (3) vary the reinforcers from one practice to the next; and (4) if possible and desirable, have other individuals dispense the reinforcers to the athlete when the athlete meets the practice goals.

6. Prevent Relapse and Make it Last

Let's suppose that an athlete has made good progress using self-management to improve practice performance. Now the question is, will it last? Will the athlete be able to maintain desirable practice performance over the long run? Unfortunately, relapses are common in self-management programs. A *relapse* refers to going back to the unwanted behavior at approximately the same rate at which it occurred before a program was initiated. The three variables of *situations, behaviors,* and *consequences* provide a useful framework for analyzing causes of relapse and how to prevent them (Martin & Pear, 2011).

Causes of relapse in situations. One cause of relapse in self-management programs is a failure to anticipate setback situations - situations where one is at risk for returning to earlier unwanted behavior patterns. Some setback situations can simply be avoided until the individual is better able to cope with them. For example, Carlos knew that he would have difficulty resisting his visits to the ice cream store on the way back to the dormitory after practices. His solution - he changed the route that he walked to return to the dormitory so that he didn't have to walk by the ice cream store and resist his favourite dessert. If an athlete can avoid setback situations until after some success with the self-management program has been achieved, then that athlete might be better able to cope with situations that provide strong cues for the problem behavior.

Another cause of relapse is counterproductive self-talk. In Carlos's case, part way through his jogging program, he frequently thought to himself, "I don't have to push myself yet. I've got lots of time left." Recognizing such counterproductive self-talk is an important first step in preventing relapse. But such self-talk needs to be replaced by other self-talk and/or other behaviors. In Carlos's case, you will recall, he focused on swimming and Julia Roberts to take his mind off the fatigue.

Causes of relapse in the specification of the response. Some relapses occur because the response component of the self-management program is too vague. For example, Mary wanted to improve her golf skills. But after a month of regular practice at the driving range, she wasn't sure if she was improving. The problem was that "wanting to improve" was too vague. She had not specified her target behavior precisely enough. If Mary's goals had been to hit five drives in a row over 220 yards, or to hit three 9-irons in a row within 30 feet of the 100-yard marker, or to make four 3-foot putts in a row, then she would have been able to evaluate her progress more easily (Martin & Ingram, 2001). The target behavior must be phrased in a way so that it can be easily recognized when it occurs.

In some cases, relapse may occur because long-term goals have not been translated into specific short-term goals. A figure skater, for example, might set a goal of skating a clean program (with no falls or misses) at each practice. But if it is the beginning of the season, that goal is likely to be a long way away. In such cases, in order to provide specific progress checks along the way, daily and/or weekly short-term goals should be precisely stated, be realistic, and move the athlete in the direction of the long-term goal (see the discussion of goal setting in Chapter 4).

Causes of relapse in consequences. Many athletes begin self-management programs with a great deal of enthusiasm. But after awhile, the extra work from recording and graphing and rearranging the environment, along with the increase in practice activities that such self-management is likely to produce, can become quite burdensome. One way to prevent relapse is to link the self-management program to everyday activities that are rewarding. One 16-year-old figure skater, for example, had set a goal for herself of attempting at least 50 elements (jumps or spins), landing three double-axels, and landing three triple toe jumps in each practice. She also agreed with her parents that, on those days when she did not meet her practice goals, she would not be allowed to drive the family car on the following day. She rarely missed meeting her practice goals. Another effective strategy to "make it last" is for the athlete to involve supportive others in the program, both in the short term and in the long term. One strategy is to set up a "buddy system". Two athletes can initiate self-management programs at the same time, and can check each others' progress on a weekly basis. Involving supportive others has proven effective in a variety of self-management programs (Watson & Tharp, 2007).

Study Questions

1. List six components of "deliberate, focused, quality practices".

2. What do people seem to mean when they talk about "willpower"? Is willpower a useful concept? Why or why not?

3. In two or three sentences, describe the behavioral model of self-management presented in this chapter.

4. Briefly describe two causes of self-control problems that involve behavioral excesses. Illustrate with a sport example that is not in this chapter.

5. Briefly describe two causes of self-control problems that involve behavioral deficits. Illustrate with a sport example that is not in this chapter.

6. List six steps that characterize many programs in self-management.

7. Give an example of a quantity goal for a practice of a sport that is not in this chapter.

8. Give an example of a quality goal for a practice of a sport that is not in this chapter.

9. With behavioral self-management, what is meant by "commitment to change?"

10. Using an example that is not in this chapter, describe how an athlete might improve practice performance by rearranging the immediate surroundings.

11. In a sentence or two each, describe three ways of manipulating consequences in self-control programs.

12. Describe three strategies for reinforcing desirable practice behaviors. Give an example of each that is not in this chapter.

13. Describe two possible causes of relapse in situations, and indicate how each might be handled.

14. Describe two possible causes of relapse in specification of the response, and indicate how each might be handled.

15. Describe a possible cause of relapse in consequences, and indicate how it might be handled.

Chapter 14

Arrange Practice Conditions so that Practice Performance Will Transfer to Competitions

An Application

Simulating Service Returns in Tennis[*]

Returning serves in tennis requires rapid decision making. Because intermediate-level and higher-level tennis players can serve the ball at speeds of well over 100 km/hr, players are often obliged to try to predict the serving intentions of their opponents. To maximize the likelihood of a successful return, a player might try to anticipate the type of serve that is likely to be made by the server (flat, topspin, or sliced), the likely landing position of the ball (center line, middle of the receiving court, or inside tram line), and the likely depth of the ball when it lands (shallow or deep). Let's see how David Scott and his colleagues attempted to improve such anticipatory skills with intermediate-level tennis players.

First, David prepared a videotape of an elite tennis player hitting a variety of serves toward the camera. Next, an intermediate-level tennis player, with a tennis racket in hand, watched the camera, tried to anticipate where the ball would likely be hit by the server, vocalized his/her prediction, watched the serve on videotape and then physically acted out what he/she believed to be the correct returning shot. For each serve observed on videotape, the practicing returner could earn up to three points: a) one point for identifying which of the three types of serves (see above) was likely to occur; b) one point for identifying which of the three different landing positions might occur; and c) one point for identifying which of the two different depths of serve might occur. During training, serves were initially presented on the videotape at a reduced speed until the player consistently scored 45 or more points (of a maximum of 60 points) for 20 serves. Then, across five sessions, the speed of the videotape was increased until the player scored 45 points when viewing the videotape at regular speed (which represented a level of 75% accuracy in prediction).

Did this simulated practice improve the returns of the tennis player on the court? It did indeed. A total of six intermediate tennis players (3 males and 3 females) were studied

for their returns before and after they participated in the
above training program. The results demonstrated a statistically
significant improvement in performance for all participants.

*This application is based on Scott, Scott & Howe (1998).

There's an old expression that goes: "Practice makes perfect." But that expression
is misleading. A better expression is: "Practicing under conditions that are similar to
competitions helps to make one perfect." Athletes and coaches need to fully understand
the different implications of these two expressions. To illustrate, consider the sport of
golf. While practicing at the driving range, it's typical for a golfer to hit a number of balls
in rapid succession with a particular club. After a while, that same golfer will switch
clubs and hit more balls in rapid succession. In this way, the golfer practices with several
different clubs. But what happens on the golf course? Does the golfer hit balls in rapid
succession? Of course not! There is considerable time between shots. Does the golfer hit
10 or 15 shots in a row with the same club? Of course not! On the course, the golfer will
hit a driver, then perhaps a 5-iron, then perhaps a short chip shot, and then perhaps a
couple of putts. But it's much easier to hit a particular shot with a club if you have just hit
five or six shots in a row with that same club from that same spot than it is to hit a shot
with a club when you haven't used that club for several holes, and you haven't even hit a
shot for the last few minutes because you've been walking to your ball. Stated differently,
if a golfer wants to maximize the likelihood of playing well on a course, then the golfer
should devote a part of driving range practice to course-like conditions, including
alternating clubs after every shot, as would happen during a typical round of golf.

Coaches and athletes must constantly address two questions: (a) At practices, will
specific skills be learned? and (b) At competitions, will the previously learned skills
transfer effectively? To increase the likelihood of a positive answer to the second
question, athletes must devote some time to practicing under conditions that are similar to
those that exist during competitions.

Several of the earlier chapters focused on the problem of developing new skills.
This chapter focuses on the problem of transferring practice performance to competitions.
Three main strategies for doing so are: (a) simulating the competitive environment; (b)
programming a few common stimuli; and (c) varying the training conditions. Other
strategies for enhancing competitive performance are discussed in Chapters 15 and 16.

Simulate Cues from the Competitive Environment

You will recall from Chapter 3 that **stimulus control** refers to the control that a
stimulus has over a behavior as a result of that behavior having been reinforced in the
presence of that stimulus. You will recall, also, that **stimulus generalization** occurs when
a behavior becomes more probable in the presence of one stimulus or situation as a result

of having been strengthened in the presence of similar stimuli. Thus, one way to ensure transfer of athletic performance from practices to competitions is to make stimuli in the practice environment as similar as possible to the stimuli that will be encountered in the competition. Attempts at doing so are referred to as **simulations**. As illustrated in the application at the beginning of this chapter, Scott et al. (1998) were able to use videotaped presentation of tennis serves in order to simulate the variety of serves that a player might encounter during a tennis match. In their study of 235 Canadian Olympians, Orlick and Partington (1988) found that the best athletes made extensive use of simulation training. They frequently approached practices as if they were at the competition, including wearing their competition outfits and warming up like they would at a competition.

In order to simulate the typical cues at a competition, it is helpful to analyze competition stimuli into seven somewhat overlapping categories, as described below. To illustrate these categories, let's suppose that it's the week before two rival football teams meet in the championship game. It's expected to be a low scoring game that could easily be decided by a field goal. Let's see how the opposing field goal kickers use simulations at practices during the week before the most important game of the season.

Cues From the Physical Environment

At each practice, *Kicker A* kicks field goals from various places on the field. The center and the ball holder are usually the only other two players practicing in the immediate vicinity of the kicker. Since no other players are around, they don't bother wearing their helmets. *Kicker B*, on the other hand, practices kicking field goals from several places on the field under full scrimmage conditions. The defensive players wear sweaters that are the same colour as the opponents will wear during the big game. A loudspeaker blares the previously taped noise of a roaring crowd from the sidelines. A score has even been placed on the scoreboard that indicates that *Kicker B*'s team is losing by 2 points.

Obviously, *Kicker B* has done a much better job of simulating game-like conditions than has *Kicker A*. During simulations, athletes and coaches should be encouraged to identify critical aspects of the competitive environment, and to duplicate those at several practices prior to important competitions.

Cues From the Behavior of the Coach

The kicking coach for *Kicker A* occasionally stands near *Kicker A* on the field, watches a few practice kicks, and gives feedback on the kicker's form. Other than that, the kicker practices on his own, except for the person holding the ball. For *Kicker B*'s team, the kicker must run in from the sidelines to practice a kick during scrimmage conditions. Just before *Kicker B* runs on the field, the coach, while standing on the sidelines, says,

"Take your time, keep it smooth. You can do it."

At practices, coaches are typically on the playing field (or ice surface or court), providing instructions, explaining things, hollering at athletes, and are generally very intrusive. During games, however, coaches are on the sidelines. It's the athletes who must perform. And while some coaches do lots of hollering from the sidelines, it's very likely that just before the kicker went on the field for a critical field goal, the coach would be very supportive. Once again, the simulation for *Kicker B* is more realistic than for *Kicker A*.

Cues From the Behavior of Other Athletes

With *Kicker A* at practices, the center and the ball holder are relaxed and frequently joke around. Before and after each kick, they "shoot the breeze" about their courses, their girlfriends, etc. When *Kicker B* runs on the field to practice a kick during scrimmage conditions, the defensive players (wearing uniforms that are the same colour as the opponents) holler at and taunt the kicker, telling him that he's going to miss. When the ball is snapped, they charge the offensive line and the kicker full out with their hands in the air, doing essentially what the opposition will be doing. This routine is repeated several times each practice throughout the week.

The behavior of teammates at practices is often very different than the behavior of the opposition during competitions. To maximize stimulus generalization from practices to competitions, it is important that the typical behavior of the opposition at competitions be simulated during practices. Clearly, *Kicker B* will be better prepared to kick a field goal in the presence of cues provided by the opposition than will *Kicker A*.

Cues From the Level of Autonomic Arousal Or Degree of Anxiousness of the Athlete

Kicker A is very relaxed at practices, joking with the center and the ball holder in between kicks. Just before jogging on the field at a practice to kick a field goal during scrimmage conditions, *Kicker B* glances at the scoreboard that shows that his team is losing by two points. The roaring crowd from the loudspeaker elicits some nervousness. *Kicker B* practices deep center breathing, as described in Chapter 9.

As we described in Chapter 9, one effect of excessive arousal or nervousness is that it adds additional stimuli to the competitive environment that were not likely present in the practice environment, which interferes with stimulus generalization of skills from practices to competitions. *Kicker A* is obviously loose and relaxed at practices. Provided that *Kicker A* can stay loose and relaxed just before having to kick a critical field goal in the big game, then his skilled kicking displayed at practices might transfer to the big game. However, it's quite likely that the "hype" during the big game will elicit considerable arousal. *Kicker B* has duplicated some of that hype at practices, experienced increased arousal, practiced a coping strategy (deep center breathing), and practiced kicking. Once again, *Kicker B* has done a better job of simulating game-like conditions than has *Kicker A*.

One way of simulating the arousal that an athlete might feel in a pressure-packed competition is to create pressure situations at practices. Consider, for example, a golfer on the practice green preparing for an important match. A routine used by some golfers in such situations is the "money putts drill". First, the golfer picks a hole on the practice green and places four quarters around it, each quarter being about four feet from the hole. Then, using one ball, the golfer pretends that each quarter is a ballmark. The golfer must putt the ball from each of the four quarters. For each putt that is made, the golfer gets to keep that quarter. But for each putt that is missed, the golfer must leave that quarter on the putting green (for the lucky person who next practices at that hole). To increase pressure, the golfer can use four $1 bills, four $5 bills, and so on, depending on the golfer's individual wealth.

Proprioceptive Cues From the Muscles of the Athlete.

Suppose that an athlete performs a skill five times in a row. After the first four times, the proprioceptive cues and "muscle memory" are very fresh for the fifth attempt. Now suppose that an athlete waits approximately 30 minutes, and then attempts that same skill. Obviously, the chances of performing that skill after 30 minutes of sitting on the sidelines are less than the chances of performing the fifth attempt correctly (immediately following four previous attempts). The proprioceptive cues for muscles constitute a part of the stimulus conditions associated with the performance of a particular skill.

Kicker A, with the help of the center and the ball holder, practices kicking several kicks in a row. They then move over to a different spot and distance on the field and practice a few more kicks. They continue in this way throughout the practice. For *Kicker B*, a portion of the practice is devoted to making a number of kicks as described for *Kicker A*. In addition, however, several kicks in each practice are performed under game-like conditions. That is, after an offensive play is run during the scrimmage, the coach signals the field goal team to try a field goal, the kicker runs onto the field under conditions as described above, has one opportunity to kick a field goal, and then returns to the sidelines. A few minutes later, the same routine is repeated, but at a different distance from the goal line. As with all of the other categories of stimuli, *Kicker B* has done a better job of simulating the competitive conditions in this category than has *Kicker A*.

The Athlete's Imagery as Cues

If it is not possible to physically rearrange various aspects of the practice environment to simulate competitive conditions, then an alternative is to capitalize on *imagery* at practices (see Chapter 8). A golfer, for example, while at the driving range, might imagine all 18 holes of a course that she is going to play. Before actually playing the course (assuming that she is familiar with it), she can play it at the driving range. For each hole, she could visualize the general layout and the landing area for each shot. She could then hit those shots that she wants to play on those holes. She might keep track of the number of imaginary fairways that she hit with her tee shots, the number of imaginary greens that she hit in regulation, and she could try to improve on each visit to the driving range. If the golfer is able to hit the desired shots at the driving range under such imaginary, simulated conditions, then the odds are increased that she will be able to hit those shots when actually playing the course.

As another example of the use of imagery to simulate competitive conditions, consider the following statement by a world champion figure skater:

> Sometimes in a practice I get myself psyched into a program that will win the Olympics, like I won the long program last year. I step on the ice and go to my starting position and I get this feeling, "I'm at the Olympic games," and I sort of get the whole program flashed before my eyes and I get this internal feeling of how this program will be, and usually I'm fresh and usually it will be a perfect program. I don't just step out there in training and just say, "Here we go, another program." (as reported by Orlick & Partington, 1988, p. 113).

At practices, *Kicker A* does not use imagery. *Kicker B*, just before running in from the sidelines to practice a kick in the mock competition, mentally rehearses performing the perfect kick. During games, he does the same thing. Thus, Kicker B practiced game-like imagery before several kicks, *Kicker A* did not.

The Athlete's Self-Talk as Cues

While practicing with the center and the ball holder, *Kicker A* may emit some rule statements just before each kick, such as, "Keep your head down and follow through." With these exceptions, the kicker's conversation is mostly directed in a joking way at the other two teammates who are helping. Just before running in from the sidelines to practice a kick under the "almost real" game conditions, *Kicker B* practices deep center breathing, mentally rehearses performing the perfect kick, and says to himself while trotting on the field, "I've made lots of these before, and I can do it now. This is just like we practiced. I'll keep it smooth and let it happen."

As described in Chapter 8, an athlete's imagery and self-talk can affect athletic performance. Self-talk and other mental skills are like physical skills - practicing them under game-like conditions helps to perfect them. When an athlete practices physical skills for hundreds of hours, it makes no sense to leave the mental skills to chance. *Kicker B* practiced game-like imagery and self-talk before several kicks, *Kicker A* did not.

In summary, considering the seven categories of competition stimuli discussed previously in this chapter, which of the two kickers is most likely to make crucial field goals during the big game? Obviously, the practice conditions favour *Kicker B*. Analyzing the different categories of stimuli that are likely to exist at a competition and simulating those in mock competitions or in practice drills greatly increases the likelihood of stimulus generalization of athletic performance from practices to competitions.

Program A Few Common Stimuli

Simulations require the analysis of the many stimuli that typically exist in competitions, and the duplication of those stimuli at several practices. An alternative strategy is to deliberately bring desired athletic behavior under the control of a few specific stimuli in practices, and to then take those stimuli to the competition. If athletic performance occurs to a specific stimulus in practice, and if that stimulus can be introduced into a competition, then the likelihood of stimulus generalization to the competitive environment is increased. In the behavior modification literature, this strategy for programming stimulus generalization is referred to as "programming common stimuli" (Martin & Pear, 2011).

One way of programming common stimuli is for the athlete to have a consistent pre-competition routine (discussed further in Chapter 16) that can be rehearsed at practices and used at competitions. This can be especially beneficial for sports in which the timing of a skill is under the control of the athlete, such as in diving, gymnastics, figure skating, and golf. Professional golfers, for example, have more consistent pre-shot and pre-putt routines than do low handicap amateurs, and low handicap amateurs have more consistent pre-shot and pre-putt routines than do high handicappers (Cohn, Rotella, & Lloyd, 1990; Crews & Boutcher, 1986). At the beginning of Chapter 3, I described a pre-putt routine followed by a professional golfer that consisted of four steps. Practicing that routine at practices as well as during golf tournaments is an example of programming common stimuli between practice and competitive conditions (see Figure 14-1).

As discussed in Chapter 8, an athlete's self-talk can provide common stimuli between practices and competitions. An athlete can use self-talk to remind him or herself of the sorts of things that should be focused on in practice. Then, that same self-talk can be used to focus on those same things at a competition, and the skilled performances that occurred in practice are likely to transfer to the competition. A young figure skater, for example, was able to land her double axel consistently at practices, but often missed it at competitions because the jump was rushed in the excitement of the moment. To solve the problem, she added the word, "e-a-s-y", just before stepping onto her takeoff foot, as a prompt to control the speed of the takeoff. Using this key word consistently at practices and competitions improved her execution during competitions.

Appropriate use of *imagery* at practices and competitions just before performing a

Practicing a preputt routine at the practice green

Following a preputt routine during a competition

<u>Figure 14-1</u>. Having a consistent, well-practiced preshot routine can help a golfer generalize good performance from practices to competitions.

skill can also provide a common stimulus to promote generalization from practice to competition. Consider the case of a golfer who has a smooth, rhythmic swing at the driving range, but tends to rush the swing during critical shots on the course. For such a golfer, Simek and O'Brien (1981, p. 42) suggested the following:

> If you want to slow your backswing, give yourself the suggestion that you are swinging behind an imaginary swinging door. As you make your backswing, the door swings toward you following your club. Before you can begin your downswing, you must wait until the door starts to swing back in the other direction. If you start the downswing too early, you will bang into the door before it has swung out of the way. The pendulum motion of the door stopping and then swinging back forces you to pause briefly at the top while waiting for the door to swing back past the ball.

Vary the Training Conditions

This strategy for programming generalization, adopted from the behavior modification literature (Martin & Pear, 2011), involves conducting practices under a wide variety of conditions. The assumption is that if athletic skills are brought under the control of a greater variety of stimuli during training, then there is an increased probability of some of those stimuli being present during competitions. If, for example, a golfer practices putting when it is hot, cold, windy, calm, quiet, noisy, with no one around, with many people milling around, etc., and if the golfer is able to make putt under all such conditions, then some of those conditions are likely to exist during an actual match, and the golfer's putting skill is more likely to transfer. Another reason that this strategy may be effective is that the golfer may be less susceptible to distractors during a competition if the golfer has practiced successfully in the presence of a wide variety of distractors.

Other Strategies for Enhancing Competitive Performance

This chapter has described several ways for rearranging practice conditions to enhance the likelihood that athletic performance will transfer from practices to competitions. There are other strategies to enhance competitive performance, but they focus more on what an athlete can do, say, and imagine on the day of competition, rather than on ways to improve practices. These additional strategies include preparation of detailed pre-competition and competition plans to maintain confidence and concentration on the "day of the game", and conducting of post-competition evaluations to assess the areas that worked well (and should be continued) and those that need improving. These additional strategies for enhancing competitive performance are described in Chapters 15 and 16.

Study Questions

1. What two questions must coaches and athletes constantly address?

2. Define stimulus generalization. Give a sport example that is not in this chapter.

3. Define stimulus control. Give a sport example that is not in this chapter.

4. Consider these statements: "Practice makes perfect." "Practicing under conditions that are similar to playing conditions helps to make one perfect." Explain, in terms of stimulus generalization, why athletes and coaches need to understand the implications of these statements.

5. What are simulations? Illustrate with a sport example that is not in this chapter.

6. List seven categories of stimuli that are useful for analyzing competitive and practice environments.

7. Pick a sport, other than football, with which you are familiar. For that sport, for each of the seven categories of stimuli described in this chapter, describe an example from a typical competition.

8. Describe an example of how athletes might use imagery at practices to simulate aspects of a competition in order to increase the likelihood that practice performance will transfer to competitions.

9. Pick a sport with which you are familiar. For that sport, describe a plausible "pressure game" that an athlete might play at practices in order to get used to performing under conditions of increased autonomic arousal.

10. Describe the generalization strategy referred to as "programming a few common stimuli". Illustrate it with a sport example that involves a <u>precompetition</u> routine that is not in this chapter.

11. Describe the generalization strategy referred to as "programming a few common stimuli". Illustrate it with a sport example that involves <u>self-talk</u> that is not in this chapter.

12. Describe the generalization strategy referred to as "programming a few common stimuli". Illustrate it with a sport example that involves <u>imagery</u> that is not in this chapter.

13. Describe the generalization strategy referred to as "vary the training conditions." Illustrate it with a sport example that is not in this chapter.

Chapter 15

Confidence, Concentration, Mental Toughness, and Peak Performance

Consider the case of Jason, one of the top amateur golfers in the country. When Jason is playing well, he tends to focus on each shot as it comes, he follows his pre-shot routine, and he "knows" that he's going to make the shot. He feels totally confident and his concentration is automatic. Some golfers describe it as "being in the zone" (Martin & Ingram, 2001). But when Jason is not playing well, he loses that confident feeling. He begins to second-guess himself. He questions his ability. He becomes increasingly susceptible to distractions before each shot. And he wonders if he will ever return to top form. Would you describe Jason as being mentally tough?

The term "peak performance" has been used to refer to an outstanding athletic performance, when an athlete puts it all together (Krane & Williams, 2010). There is no doubt that athletes who are at the top of their game feel lots of confidence and have excellent concentration. But many athletes who are not playing well lose those confident feelings, and they are easily distracted. However, there are some athletes, despite the ups and downs of their athletic performance, who seem to have an unshakable belief that they will accomplish their long-term goals. Such athletes are likely to be described as being mentally tough. What are the critical components of confidence and concentration that contribute to peak performance? If an athlete is performing poorly, how can that athlete recapture those confident feelings and focusing skills that correlate with playing well? What are coaches, athletes, and sport psychologists referring to when they talk about mental toughness? Those are the topics of this chapter.

What is Confidence?

You've no doubt heard the following kinds of statements made about some athletes:

"Charlie is really playing with a lot of confidence."

"I've never seen Lisa play so well. She looked so confident throughout the entire game."

"I could tell before the contest started that Derek wasn't going to perform well. He just didn't look confident."

"Nicole skated well until she fell on her triple toe jump. After that, she just fell apart. I guess she lost her confidence."

These kinds of statements imply that confidence is some "thing" within us that causes outstanding athletic performance. And many research studies have reported that the factor that most consistently distinguishes highly successful from less successful athletes is "confidence" (Weinberg & Gould, 2011; Williams, Zinsser, & Bunker 2010). From a behavioral perspective, however, **confidence** is not some internal cause of successful athletic performance. Rather, it is a summary label that we use to describe athletes who have performed well in recent practices and/or competitions, and who show certain behavior patterns that would be described collectively as illustrating the belief that they will perform well in an upcoming competition. The many behaviors that make up that belief are described below under the sub-section titled "Steps to Improve Confidence, Concentration, and Peak Performance." But first, let's briefly consider the concept of concentration.

What is Concentration?

A behavioral analysis of the activities frequently discussed under the general topic of concentration suggests that two distinct behavioral processes are involved. First, concentration includes behavior that might be referred to as observational, orienting, attending, or focusing - behavior that puts the individual in contact with relevant S^Ds for further responding. Orienting behavior can include turning one's head to locate the source of a sound, focusing one's eyes on objects in the environment, or moving one's hands over a surface to detect tactile cues. Orienting behavior can also include selectively attending to one of several cues, such as when a football receiver "listens for" the numbers called by the quarterback (just before the ball is snapped) and selectively "tunes out" the roar of the crowd. The second aspect of concentration refers to the extent to which particular cues exert stimulus control over skilled performance. After a batter has focused on the pitcher, does the sight of a baseball in the strike zone exert stimulus control over a solid swing by the batter? When a basketball player steps to the free throw line and orients to the basket, does the appearance of the basket and the feel of the player's stance and the ball exert control over an accurate free throw? When the answer is "yes" in such instances, we are likely to say that the athletes involved have shown good concentration.

Steps to Improve Confidence, Concentration and Peak Performance

Unfortunately, imparting confidence to an athlete is not like putting oil in your car. Oh oh, Charlie's a little low on confidence! I guess I'd better give him a litre. No! It doesn't work that way. Similarly, the behavioral processes that make up concentration cannot be instantly developed. However, the behaviors characteristic of improved confidence and concentration can be learned, if athletes are willing to work at them. Implementation of the following steps will help athletes to improve their confidence and concentration in order to experience peak performance regularly.

Develop Confidence and Concentration at Practices

1. Develop skills to a high level with practice drills. When talking about confidence, Tiger woods stated, "the biggest thing is to have the belief that you can win every tournament going in. A lot of guys don't have that, Jack Nicklaus did." Obviously, Tiger Woods has had that belief many times. But that belief is not something that he was born with. It was something that was developed, in part, through his tremendous practice habits. For example, recall Tiger's putting drill presented at the beginning of Chapter 4 in which he would not quit the drill until he had made 100 3-foot putts in a row. Tiger stated, "I did this (drill) before and after each round and found that it really helped me on the course with my short putts" (*Golf Digest*, November, 2005). It's not surprising that Tiger would have confidence in his short-putts after completing that drill before and after every competitive round. Stated more generally, the first step toward developing confidence at practices is to use goal-setting, performance monitoring, and mastery criteria to develop basic athletic skills to a high level.

2. Teach orientation to proper cues. Let's suppose that an athlete shows inconsistent performance at practices, even though the coach describes the athlete as consistently being highly motivated. In such cases, the athlete may be experiencing difficulty orienting to the proper cues. One possible solution is to use Nideffer's (1981) four categories of stimulus control (broad vs. narrow and internal vs. external) discussed in Chapter 8. You might find, for example, that the athlete is using too much self-talk (broad-internal control) for a task (like batting in baseball) which should be under narrow-external control (watching the ball from the time it leaves the pitcher's hand until it arrives at the plate). Alternatively, an athlete might be focusing primarily on external cues when it would be more appropriate to concentrate on particular kinesthetic feelings (narrow-internal control). The latter might be illustrated by a figure skater who attends excessively to other skaters on the ice when approaching a jump, rather than focusing on the feeling of being directly over the take-off foot.

Sometimes orienting to proper cues requires an athlete to rapidly shift from one type of stimulus control to another. In soccer, for example, a player who scans the field to find an opening is exhibiting broad-external stimulus control. When the player finds an opening and rushes to it, that player must then shift to narrow-external stimulus control in order to focus on a pass from a teammate. When the ball has been received, that same player must quickly shift back to broad-external control in order to check the position of the goal-keeper, evaluate the defensive alignment, and find an open teammate to whom the ball might be passed. Ziegler (1994) devised a series of drills to help soccer players improve their ability to rapidly shift from one attentional style to another. In one drill, for example, four individuals on the soccer field held a cue card at knee level, and the color of the card was different for each individual. Ziegler would pass a ball to a subject (a Division 1 male college soccer player) and call out the name of one of the colors. The player had to listen for the color name that was called (narrow external control), then quickly scan the four individuals holding the cards (broad-external control), identify the one holding the proper cue card and kick the ball to that person (narrow-external control). The drills were quite successful in improving the shifting skills of the soccer players.

Another strategy for helping athletes to orient to the proper cues is to enhance particular aspects of those cues in practices, and then to fade those cues over time. For example, a batter in baseball learns to judge the rate of spin of an approaching curve ball thrown by a pitcher, in order to gauge his/her swing with respect to the anticipated location of the path of the ball as it nears the plate. Some batters, however, have difficulty in orienting to the proper cues, with the result that they experience difficulty hitting curve balls. To help such batters, Osborne, Rudrud, and Zezoney (1990) added orange stripes to mark the seams of baseballs. In their study, several members of the St. Cloud State University Men's Baseball team were able to hit a greater percentage of marked than unmarked curve balls. While further research is needed to demonstrate that improved hitting of curve balls can be maintained when colored markings on the seam are faded out, the Osborne et al. study nicely illustrates a strategy for enhancing orientation to proper cues.

As discussed in Chapter 8, key words can be used to help athletes orient to proper cues. In one study, for example, beginning tennis players practicing backhand shots showed little progress when simply told to "concentrate." But they showed rapid improvement when told to vocalize the word "ready" when the ball machine was about to present the next ball, the word "ball" when they saw the ball fired from the machine, the word "bounce" as they watched the ball contact the surface of the court, and the word "hit" when they observed the ball contacting their racquet while swinging their backhand (Ziegler, 1987).

3. Transfer the control of sport skills from rules to natural cues. Studies of athletes who have experienced peak performances indicate that the athletes frequently talk about experiencing "effortful performance," about "not thinking of performing," and "feeling that the performance was automatic." As described in Chapter 4, these kinds of descriptions appear to illustrate behavior that is primarily under the control of cues in the natural environment, rather than being rule-governed. Stated differently, skills that occur during a peak performance are likely to be so well mastered that the athlete does not need to think about technical aspects of the skills. As illustrated in the previous sub-section, key words can initially be helpful in mastering a skill. However, a behavior that is initially under the control of rules can, with practice, be transferred to cues in the natural environment. For example, suppose that a person taking golf lessons learns the rules for

selecting the appropriate club, how to stand before making a shot, how to swing the club, and so on. Initially, the persons' behavior looks very rigid and mechanical. For each shot, the person is likely to rehearse a series of key words (i.e. partial rules) such as, "left shoulder back" (to start the backswing for a right-handed golfer), and so on. With practice, it is possible to shorten the rules that are needed to control the behavior appropriately. Rather than saying, "left shoulder back," for example, the person might simply say, "shoulder." With further practice, the stimulus control can be transferred from the key words to subtle cues in the natural environment. For example, when the golfer sets up to hit a shot, the golfer will eventually focus on the ball and start the backswing smoothly without necessarily thinking, "shoulder." Gradually, the person's golf swing looks more "natural" and less "mechanical." In general, it is important to reduce key words for skills to a small number so that skill execution comes under the control of the cues in the practice environment and so that the skills are so well practiced that the athlete is likely to report "not having to think about them." (Also see Martens & Collier, 2011).

4. Athletes should perform well in simulations. Other than performing well in competitions, one of the most important components for eliciting confidence is for an athlete to experience in practice what he/she wants to accomplish in the competition (Weinberg & Gould, 2011). And as described in the previous chapter, a part of practices before important competitions should be structured to simulate competitive conditions. If an athlete has performed successfully many times during simulations at practices, it is then much easier for that athlete to focus their self-talk and imagery on performing successfully in a competition.

Maintain Confidence on the Day of a Competition

1. Athletes should have a restful, stress-free day prior to competing. In 2007, the University of Winnipeg Wesmen won the Canadian Inter-University Sports Men's Volleyball Championship. After the championship game Wesmen Head Coach Larry McKay stated, "In this tournament it is often the team that can settle down and be calm and relaxed that will win it. We began a little shaky against Lavalle on Friday, but fortunately we made it through that and then everyone seemed to relax" (Winnipeg Free Press, March 5, 2007). As illustrated by this statement by Coach McKay, and as will be described in the next chapter, athletes should have a game-day plan that enables them to stay loose on the day of competition. Athletes who appear confident are usually loose, and not uptight. Athletes who appear quite nervous are generally not described as "being confident." Strategies to stay loose include deep center breathing, muscle relaxation, relaxing self-talk, relaxing imagery, "tuning out," and "enjoying the setting" (see Chapters 8 and 9).

2. Athletes should relive best performances. As described in Chapter 8, many highly successful athletes have learned to mentally rehearse specific aspects of performance in considerable detail just before performing. And hundreds of athletes have

endorsed mental rehearsal as an effective technique for helping them prepare to compete to the best of their ability (Orlick & Partington, 1988). If, just before performing, an athlete is able to recapture the feelings of a recent occasion where that athlete performed well, then the athlete is likely to feel confident (Moritz et al., 1996).

3. Athletes should focus on what they can control, not on uncontrollables. Athletes can exert a degree of direct control over their behavior - what they do, say, eat, drink, look at, think, feel, etc. Uncontrollables are all of the things that they have no direct control over. Examples of uncontrollables include weather conditions, officiating, size and skill level of opponents, fans, expectations of family and friends, and so forth. To maintain confidence, athletes should focus on what they can control.

4. Athletes should focus on realistic goals for execution rather than worrying about outcome. Goal setting for competitions is somewhat different than goal setting for practices. As described in Chapter 4, practice goals should include a certain amount of stretch to encourage athletes to reach new heights. And long before a particular competition occurs, most athletes have goals for winning or being the best. Such goals are called *outcome goals,* which are goals for results. Such goals are useful to motivate one to practice diligently, and to improve all aspects of one's athletic skills. But when it comes time to participate in that important game or that important match, confident athletes are able to set aside outcome goals, and to focus realistically on taking it one step at a time, one play at a time, and on executing to the best of their ability. Such goals are called *execution or process goals.* Realistic execution goals for a competition are typically associated with confidence. And when these goals are met, the outcome takes care of itself. For example, when sport psychologists Austin Swain and Graham Jones developed a goal-setting program for games for a men's university basketball team, they didn't tell the players to set goals for winning or getting a certain score during each game. Instead, they helped the basketball players set goals for offensive rebounds, defensive rebounds, steals, and turnovers (Swain & Jones, 1995). Similarly, as described in Chapter 13, when Ward and Carnes (2002) helped linemen in American college football set goals for games, they focussed on process by setting goals for proper positioning to defend against certain types of plays, and for tackling the ball carrier.

5. Athletes should focus on their strengths, not on their limitations or their mistakes. Some athletes have a tendency to worry about their previous poor performances, or their weaknesses, or they look for reasons why they might perform poorly. Athletes should certainly work to overcome their weaknesses when practicing. But on the day of a competition, they should focus on their strengths.

6. Athletes should use "countering" and "reframing" to counteract negative thoughts. The previous steps for improving confidence focus on specific behaviors to be increased. This step describes strategies for counteracting negative thinking that is associated with lack of confidence (also see Chapter 8). Suppose that a young hockey

player, on the day of his first professional tryout, is concerned that he is a slower skater than the other players. In such situations, Bell (1983) proposes the use of **countering** - using facts and reasons to build a case against negative thinking. The hockey player, for example, might carefully restate actual evidence concerning his skating speed (e.g., "I'm not as fast as Player X, but I can skate as fast as Player Y"), rather than making general statements (e.g., "I'm too slow."). The hockey player might also take a broader view of the skills of different players, and identify specific players who had a successful NHL career even though they were not fast skaters.

Another strategy for counteracting negative thinking is referred to as **reframing** (Gauron, 1984) - examining a situation from a different perspective in order to view that situation more positively. Consider, for example, the behavior of former amateur figure skater Kurt Browning at the World Championships in Halifax. When Kurt was asked how he felt about drawing the second position to skate in the short program, he indicated that it was a good place to skate from because it was then possible to put pressure on those who followed. Later, when asked how he felt about drawing the fifth position for skating the long program, Kurt again indicated that it was a great position to skate from, because he then knew exactly what he had to do and he could lay out a great program to convince the judges that he deserved to win. When the discrepancy in his comments was pointed out to him, Kurt explained that there were advantages and disadvantages of all positions to skate from, and that it was important to view a situation in the best possible light. Although a situation may initially appear to present difficulties, it is possible to use reframing to view that situation in a manner that focuses on its advantages and/or possibilities.

From a behavioral perspective, the techniques of countering and reframing involve rule-governed control over behavior. The hockey player, for example, identified a rule (e.g., "I can skate as fast player Y"). In the example of Kurt Browning's reframing, Kurt was giving himself a rule, "Skating in the second position enables me to put pressure on the other skaters." And when capitalizing on rule-governed control over behavior, it is important to remember the guidelines from Chapter 4: a rule is most likely to exert control over behavior if the rule identifies a specific behavior, a deadline for performing it, and sizeable and probable consequences for the behavior are specified or implied. (Also see cognitive behavior therapy techniques for countering negative thinking, Brown, 2011).

7. Athletes should prepare and follow a competition plan. At the 2006 Winter Olympics, Cindy Klassen became the only Canadian to win 5 medals at a single Olympic games, including Gold, Silver, and Bronze. On the day of her first Gold-Medal win, Cindy reported, "I didn't do anything special. That's the big thing, to keep everything the same. I just woke up this morning feeling really good and really happy. I wasn't really thinking about the race too much" (*Winnipeg Free Press*, Feb. 23, 2006). Interviews with successful Olympic athletes like Cindy indicate that they have detailed time management

plans to guide their actions at competitions (e.g., what to think, how to minimize distractions, when and how to warm up, etc.). Although the preparation of competition plans will be discussed in detail in Chapter 16, it is mentioned here because it is an important strategy for maintaining confidence. It's one thing to recommend guidelines for athletes regarding focusing, as was done in several of the previous items. It's another thing for athletes to follow those recommendations. A major purpose of a competition plan is to help them to do so. As suggested by Goldberg (1998), a big part of helping athletes to focus is to teach them to control what they look at and listen to. Athletes need to learn to look at and listen to things that help them to stay calm, loose, confident and to focus on the "here and now." This process will be discussed further in Chapter 16.

Maintain Confidence and Concentration During a Competition

1. Athletes should be energized, but remain calm. In 2005-06 Osvaldo Jeanty was the Canadian Inter-University Sport Athlete of the Year, and the driving force behind University of Carleton's fourth straight men's national basketball title. When asked about dealing with the pressure of big games, Jeanty said, "Performing successfully under pressure is not about being better than normal - it's about maintaining a sense of calm so that the athlete can be as good as he is in a meaningless game" (*Winnipeg Free Press*, May 15, 2006). Reports by athletes indicate that, during peak performances, they: "feel in control of their emotions and arousal," "feel mentally relaxed," "feel physically relaxed," "are loose," and are "ready to play."

Is it possible to maintain a sense of calm and be energized at the same time? The answer appears to be "yes." Many studies support some variation of the inverted-U relationship between physiological arousal and performance (Landers & Arent, 2010; see Figure 15-1). As indicated in Figure 15-1, before a competition, an athlete should not be too laid back nor too pumped up or tense. Rather, the athlete wants to feel both loose and energized at just the right level. An *optimal level of arousal* is the level of physiological arousal associated with peak performance. However, the optimal level of arousal is likely to differ from individual to individual and from sport to sport. A sport like weightlifting is likely to have a higher optimal level of arousal for most athletes than a sport like golf. But between individual weightlifters, or between individual golfers, there would also be considerable differences in their optimal level of arousal. The frequency of competitions is another variable that can influence an athlete's level of arousal. In my experience with young figure skaters who have only a half-dozen or so competitions during the year, their main concern (in terms of arousal) is to be able to stay relaxed. Professional hockey players, on the other hand, who play an 84 game schedule during the regular season, frequently experience a lack of intensity before games. They need to know how to energize before some games, and how to relax before other games, such as before a game with a team within their conference against whom they have built up an intense rivalry (Martin, 2010). The need to energize or to relax can also vary within a competition. Before a championship ice hockey game, for example, the players are likely

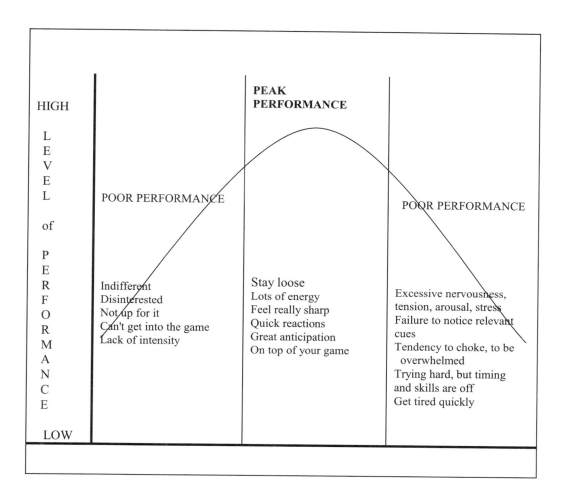

Figure 15-1. An illustration of the inverted-U relationship between level of arousal and athletic performance.

to be somewhat tense. They may need to practice strategies to stay loose. After two hard-played periods, however, the players are likely to be tired. They are likely to benefit from energizing techniques before the third period. Thus, the behavioral strategies to be recommended to help athletes achieve an optimal level of arousal would depend on the task, the athlete, the nature of the sport, the frequency of competitions, and the circumstances surrounding particular competitions.

Summary of Strategies for Staying Loose. Strategies for staying loose during a competition include deep-centre breathing, muscle tensing and relaxing, use of relaxing mood words, use of humour, and "tuning out" during breaks in the action (see Chapters 8 and 9). Some professional golfers, for example, tune out thoughts about golf between shots. Justin Leonard, winner of the British Open and many other tournaments, stated, "I just try to stay pretty brainless out there, except when I have to pull a club or make a putt. Beyond that, I'm probably thinking about some old Saturday Night Live skit that I saw on the Comedy Channel."

Summary of Strategies for Energizing. If athletes need to energize during a competition, they can use energizing imagery, energizing mood words, physical actions (such as giving each other high fives), and energizing music.

2. Athletes should focus on what they want to do, not what they don't want to do. In 1994, Nick Price was the best golfer in the world. During an interview on TSN on November 2 of that year, his caddy ("Squeeky") said, "During a round, we don't say 'don't'. If there is danger on the left, we don't say, '*don't* leave it left'. We say, 'let's keep it right'." Focusing on what one wants to do during a competition, rather than what not to do, helps to maintain confidence.

3. Athletes should focus on process, not outcome. As described earlier in this chapter, when it comes time to participate in that important game or that important match, confident athletes are able to set aside outcome goals, and to focus on one step or one play at a time, and on executing to the best of the their ability. For example, consider the sport of golf. In 2007, Zack Johnson won the Masters at Augusta, one of the most coveted titles in golf. When describing his mental approach during the last round, he said "I didn't look at the Leader Board. I really didn't know what was going on. I knew that if I just kept doing what I was doing, staying in the present and putting well, I had a chance" (Winnipeg Free Press, April 9, 2007). Confident golfers, like Zack, focus on their game plan for each hole as it comes, take it one shot at a time, and stick to their pre-shot routine.

An important component of focusing on process is attending to the proper cues. At the World Figure Skating Championship in 2006, young American Kimmie Meissner won the ladies Gold Medal. When asked what she was thinking about during her outstanding performance in the long program, she stated, "I just keep thinking of the jump coming up

– forgetting about what I just landed, forgetting about everything that I'd just done – so I could keep breathing" (*Winnipeg Free Press*, Mar. 26, 2006). When experiencing peak performance, athletes like Kimmie report such things as "being focused on the present," "not easily influenced by distractors," and "focusing narrowly on one specific thought or action." These kinds of statements strongly suggest that athletes experiencing peak performance show appropriate orienting or focusing behavior to critical cues in the athletic environment. They are not thinking about winning or losing during a peak performance (Jackson & Roberts, 1992). They are not worried about past mistakes or future outcomes, they are focused on the here and now. A defensive lineman in football is totally focused on the play as it evolves around him. An ice hockey player breaking in on the goalie is completely aware of the opening between the goalie's legs. A batter in baseball sees the seams of the ball as soon as it leaves the pitcher's hand. A swimmer is totally aware of her position relative to the end of the pool as she prepares for her tumble-turn. In such instances, the athletes are totally focused on what's important at that particular moment. Often, athletes can use self-talk during a competition to maintain appropriate attending behavior. General self-talk would include statements like "stay in the present," "focus on the moment," "keep pushing." Examples of specific self-talk for specific situations were given in Chapter 8.

Factors that Interfere with Confidence and Concentration during Competitions, and How to Control Them

When you look at the mental strengths of world-class athletes like Cindy Klassen and Tiger Woods, one of the characteristics that has set them apart from most other athletes has been their ability to stay focused and to maintain their confidence and concentration throughout a match or game or race. While the ability to concentrate during competitions seems to develop quite naturally for some athletes, all athletes can improve their concentration skills. Thus far in this chapter, I have described strategies for improving and maintaining confidence and concentration. In the remainder of this chapter, I want to alert you to several things that can interfere with an athlete's confidence and concentration during competitions, and to suggest ways to minimize their effects.

As described in Chapter 6, a **slump** is an unexpected decline in athletic performance that occurs for a sufficient length of time to be of serious concern to the athlete and coach. If the problems listed in the remainder of this chapter cause a slump, then the suggested solutions can be viewed as strategies for overcoming slumps (see Chapter 6). For additional discussion of slump-busting strategies, see Goldberg (1998).

The Problem: The athlete is easily distracted. A golfer may be bothered by excessive movements of her competitors when she is trying to line up a putt. A basketball player might be distracted by the crowd when attempting free throws. A gymnast may have difficulty concentrating on her beam routine while other gymnasts are participating in the floor exercise and the vault at the same time in other parts of the gym. In such instances, the athletes involved appear to be attending to too many cues or distractions in the environment.

A Solution: Simulations under Competition-Like Conditions. As we described in the preceding chapter, one way to ensure that an athlete will show the behavior characteristic of good confidence and concentration during competitions is to make the final stages of the practice environment as similar as possible to the conditions that will be encountered during the competition. If an athlete gets used to performing well in the face of numerous distractions at practices, then that athlete is more likely to perform to potential in the presence of distractions at competitions.

Another strategy for minimizing the effects of distractions is for the athlete to have a well-practiced competition plan to follow on the day of competition. This strategy is discussed in more detail in Chapter 16.

The Problem: The athlete experiences "paralysis by analysis". As described in Chapter 8, some athletes tend to over-analyze the particular body movements involved in executing a particular skill (e.g., see Figure 15-2). A smooth athletic performance must be under the control of the appropriate cues in the athletic environment. One or two of those cues can be key words, as described in Chapter 8. But for the most part, the athletic skill should occur naturally without excessive thinking in the middle of it. Excessive analysis of body mechanics just before or during a skilled performance can interfere with smooth execution of that performance (Martens & Collier, 2011).

The Solution: Use one or two mood words and limit technique thoughts. As described in Chapter 8, mood words are "quick thoughts" that influence the athlete's emotions and confidence, and that help the athlete to get the right feel in the athletic setting. Examples used by some golfers include "easy," "have fun," "keep it smooth," etc. If an athlete makes errors because they are too analytical, they may want to limit their thoughts to just using a few mood words.

The Problem: The athlete is too pumped or excessively nervous. If an athlete feels like she is rushing, performing skills before she is ready to do so, or trying too hard to make things happen, she should check her arousal level. Being overly aroused, or too pumped, or too nervous can throw off the timing and stimulus control of skilled activities. Instead of being patient and performing smoothly, the athlete tends to rush things.

The Solution: Relax. If an athlete makes mental errors because they are too physiologically aroused, they should practice the relaxation strategies described in Chapters 8 and 9.

The athlete might also be encouraged to assess his or her self-talk, as described later. Chances are that the athlete is experiencing negative thoughts that are creating

Figure 15-2. An example of "Paralysis by Analysis."

doubt, which in turn can elicit excessive nervousness.

The Problem: The athlete experiences interfering emotions. A golfer may get mad after making a bad shot. A basketball player may become extremely upset if a teammate does not pass the ball when that player is open. A shortstop in baseball might become extremely angry after missing an easy double play. In such instances, if the anger stays with the athlete, then it is likely to interfere with that athlete's concentration for the next few plays.

The Solution: Relax, regroup, and refocus. To eliminate concentration errors due to negative emotions, athletes should be encouraged to practice the strategies described in Chapter 8 to relax, regroup, and refocus. Also see strategies to minimize "choking" in Chapter 9.

The Problem: The athlete tends to think too far ahead. Suppose that a golfer hits several bad shots on the first couple of holes. The golfer starts thinking, "Oh no, I'm going to shoot a terrible score." Or suppose that the golfer has a great front nine and begins thinking, "If I can keep it together, I can shoot my best score ever." In such instances, the golfer is thinking too far ahead. The golfer is already thinking about the final outcome. But thinking too far ahead can affect an athlete's concentration in that the athlete is less likely to orient toward the cues in the environment that normally exert stimulus control over skilled performance.

The Solution: Use self-talk to focus on the here and now. The golfer in the above example might be encouraged to tell himself, "My goal is to take it one step at a time." "I'll follow my pre-shot routine for the next shot, and in between shots I'll enjoy a walk in the park." Athletes, as illustrated in this golf example, can use self-talk to focus on the cues that should control their behavior at that particular point in time, rather than thinking too far ahead.

Another strategy for helping an athlete to focus on the relevant cues just before and during performance of a skill is to have a well-practiced pre-performance routine (discussed further in Chapter 16). As indicated previously, for example, professional golfers have a more consistent pre-shot routine than do low-handicap amateurs, and low-handicap amateurs have a more consistent pre-shot routine than do high-handicappers (Cohn et al., 1990; Crews & Boutcher, 1986). When a professional golfer begins his or her pre-shot routine, they are essentially performing a well-practiced behavioral chain (see Chapter 3). And once the behavioral chain is initiated, relevant cues in the chain evoke the appropriate behavior. The end result is that the golfer is able to focus on the "here and now," rather than thinking too far ahead.

The Problem: Worrying about past events. All world class athletes have experienced mistakes or poor performances. A figure skater might fall on a critical jump during an important competition. A gymnast might miss her dismount from her beam routine. A football player might miss a critical field goal at the final buzzer that would win the game. Such events do occur. They become a problem when an athlete worries about past performances just before or during the current competition. If the gymnast, for example, thinks about having missed the dismount on her beam at the time that she is to begin her floor routine, then thinking about a past event will interfere with her current concentration.

The Solution: Use self-talk to regroup and refocus on the here and now. Following an error or a mistake, an athlete can use self-talk to regroup. Examples would include, "That one's history, forget about it." "Smart people don't worry about things that are in the past and that can't be changed, and I'm a smart person." "The rest of my game starts right now." The athlete can then use self-talk to focus on the cues that should control skilled performance (as described in Chapter 8).

Mental Toughness

When we try to describe top athletes in any sport that have experienced success over a considerable period of time, we can use a wide variety of descriptors and identify a wide variety of behaviors that characterize those individuals. They are very good at setting and pursuing long-term and short-term goals. They are highly motivated for spending thousands of hours practicing and overcoming setbacks. They are skilled at using imagery and positive self-talk, and at recognizing and controlling negative self-talk. They know how to rearrange their environment to manage their emotions when it is beneficial to do so, and to capitalize on the experience of various emotions that may be beneficial for athletic performance. As described in this chapter, they are skillful at designing practices to develop confidence and concentration, at performing well in simulations to transfer skilled performance to competitions, at using competition planning to maintain confidence and concentration on the day of and during competitions, and at overcoming and controlling factors that can interfere with confidence and concentration. Athletes who are likely to do all of the above at a higher level than many of their opponents, and who are able to perform at the highest level in spite of a variety of demands and pressures, are likely to be described as "mentally tough" (Connaughton, Hanton, & Jones, 2010; Gucciardi, Gordon, & Dimmock, 2009a, 2009b; Jones, Hanton, & Connaughton, 2007). In simple terms, athletes who are described as mentally tough are likely to be described as having an "unshakable belief" that they can accomplish their goals, and are likely to show consistent "never give up," "always go the extra mile" attitudes, in spite of a variety of difficulties and setbacks.

Some sport psychologists have suggested that confidence, concentration, and mental toughness are crucial in determining successful athletic performance. But we must remember that they are summary labels for behavior patterns. And although summary labels for behavior are useful for quickly providing general information about how a labeled individual might perform (e.g., athletes labeled as confident are likely to perform well in competitions), we must be cautious of the disadvantages of such summary labels (see Chapter 1). We must also remember that the strategies described in this and preceding chapters can be used to increase the behaviors that would lead us to describe an athlete as having confidence, displaying concentration, and being mentally tough.

Study Questions

1. In general, what is a peak performance?

2. From a behavioral perspective, what is confidence and what is it not?

3. Describe how concentration appears to involve two distinct behavioral processes. Illustrate each process with a sport example that is not in this chapter.

4. List four steps for developing confidence and concentration at practices.

5. Briefly describe two strategies for helping athletes to orient to proper cues.

6. List seven steps for maintaining confidence on the day of a competition.

7. What are outcome goals in the context of athletic competitions? Illustrate with two sport examples.

8. What are execution or process goals in the context of athletic competitions? Illustrate with two sport examples.

9. What is countering? Illustrate with a sport example.

10. What is reframing? Illustrate with a sport example.

11. Describe the inverted-U relationship between arousal and performance.

12. To what does an *optimal level of arousal* refer?

13. Suppose that an athlete's level of arousal is far too low for a peak performace to occur. List four things that an athlete can do to increase his/her level of arousal?

14. Suppose that an athlete's level of arousal is too high for a peak performance to

occur. List four things that an athlete can do to decrease his/her level of arousal.

15. List three strategies for maintaining confidence and concentration during a competition.

16. Using an example that is not in this chapter, illustrate a solution to the problem of an athlete being easily distracted during a competition.

17. Using an example that is not in this chapter, illustrate a solution to the problem of an athlete who experiences "paralysis by analysis".

18. Using an example that is not in this chapter, illustrate a solution to the problem of an athlete who loses concentration during a competition because of thinking too far ahead.

19. Using an example that is not in this chapter, illustrate a solution to the problem of an athlete who has difficulty concentrating during a competition because of worrying about past events.

20. In simple terms, summarize the kinds of behaviors typically displayed by athletes who are described as being "mentally tough."

21. Describe a plausible sport example of how confidence, as a summary label for behavior, might be involved in a pseudoexplanation. (You may want to review the discussion of summary labels in Chapter 1.)

Chapter 16

Preparing and Following a Competition Plan

On the day of a competition, an athlete's potential for performance has already been established by that athlete's prior preparation. It is too late to improve the athlete's level of physical fitness. It's too late for the athlete to learn new skills. The tactical strategy or game plan should be well developed and thoroughly understood. What can happen, however, is the occurrence of numerous events to distract an athlete and detract from performance. A competition plan can minimize the effects of such distractions. Studies of Olympic athletes indicate that top performers have detailed, well-developed, and well-practiced competition plans to guide them at competitions (Gould, Eklund, & Jackson, 1992; Orlick & Partington, 1988). **In general, a competition plan** refers to those things that an athlete can do, say, think about, concentrate on, and attend to on the day of, just before, and during the competition that will maximize the chances of the individual performing up to his/her potential. A competition plan includes strategies to minimize the effect of distractions, cope with distractors which can't be minimized, deal with competitive anxiety, achieve an optimal level of arousal for the particular event or competition, maintain confidence and concentration, minimize the effects of fatigue, and maximize effort.

To a large extent, the strategies to be used in a competition plan have already been discussed in earlier chapters - things like appropriately using mental imagery, practicing coping self-talk, and following strategies to maintain confidence and concentration. But it's one thing to have general knowledge of these strategies, and it's another thing to incorporate them into a carefully designed, written plan to be followed at a particular competition. In this chapter, numerous examples are presented for helping athletes to develop, use, and refine detailed competition plans in different sports.

Complete competition plans typically include five components: (a) a game day plan (from the time of awakening up to approximately an hour before the competition) to ensure that the athlete has a restful, stress-free day prior to competing; (b) a pre-competition plan for the last hour or so prior to the start of the competition in order to minimize distractions and maximize an athlete's mental readiness to perform; (c) a competition focusing plan to ensure that, once a competition begins, the athlete will experience the covert and overt behaviors associated with optimal performance (often described as maintaining confidence and concentration and being mentally tough); (d) a refocusing plan for dealing with uncontrollable distractors that might be encountered; and (e) a structured post-competition evaluation strategy for reviewing and refining the plans.

Preparing a Game Day Plan

On the day of competition, an athlete should remain positive, conserve energy, and be relatively free of stressors. A plan to ensure these outcomes should cover the time from which the athlete awakes in the morning through to approximately an hour or so before the beginning of the competition. If athletes have a detailed plan of action to follow during the day of competition, then they are determining the things that can influence them. If they don't have a detailed plan, then the things that can influence an athlete are left to chance and/or are in the hands of others.

During the day of a competition, before leaving for the competition site, some athletes spend considerable time thinking about the upcoming event. Other athletes participate in activities to tune out, such as watching a movie, reading a book, visiting a nearby shopping mall, etc. Which strategy is the best?

The answer depends both on the preferences of individual athletes and on the nature of the sport. For sports like figure skating, diving, and gymnastics, where the athlete is performing well-practiced routines, there is usually ample time at the competition site to focus on the competition. During the day of the competition, such athletes usually engage in relaxing activities that enable them to "tune out" thoughts about competing. In open-ended sports like ice hockey, football, and basketball, however, where one must react to an opponent, a part of the game day is likely to be set aside to review the mental strategies that will be used in that particular game. A form that I have used with college level and professional ice hockey players to help them with mental preparation before leaving for the rink on game day is shown in Figure 16-1 (also see Martin, 2010).

In some team sports, a coach is likely to review tactical strategies and a game plan for that particular game. This should be done at least a couple of hours before the beginning of the competition. As described in the next section, the last hour or so should be set aside for individual mental preparation of athletes. Regarding old-style pep talks or team "rah-rah" meetings, those should also be conducted (if at all) at least two hours before the game. As expressed by Rushall (1992), pep talks during the last hour or so before a competition will interfere with the individual preparation of athletes on a team, and they are more likely to be a distraction rather than an aid to performance.

After a game day plan has been prepared, it should be reviewed with the athlete to ensure that the athlete can answer "yes" to the following questions:

– Does it include a wake-up routine to start the day in a good mood and a positive frame of mind?

– Will it help the athlete stay relaxed and stress-free during the day up to the time of arrival at the competition site?

Figure 16-1. A form to help ice hockey players with their mental preparation on game day before leaving for the rink.

It's Game Day: Mentally Picture Yourself Playing Well

a. Recall what you know about the opposition.

Forwards I'll likely face; how they play and how can I beat them?
Defense I'll likely face; how they play and how can I beat them?
Goalie I'll likely face; and how can I beat him/her?

b. Think of specific situations, and visualize yourself playing well. For each of the specific situations below that apply to you, put a checkmark (✔) beside them. You may want to add to the list to suit your particular skills and the role that you play on the team.

Specific Situations	Specific Situations
___ Finishing a check ___ Anticipating & intercepting a pass ___ Forechecking and creating a turnover ___ Winning a battle for a loose puck ___ Finding the seam ___ Scoring on a one-timer ___ Tying up their player in front of our net ___ Playing the body, not the puck ___ Winning a key face-off _____ _____	___ Anticipating a rebound on the power play and scoring ___ Charging the net for a rebound and scoring ___ Taking the puck on a breakaway and scoring _____ _____ _____ _____ _____

- For each situation, visualize it for a few seconds, imagine your teammates and the opposition, feel yourself in that situation
- Imagine yourself successfully executing the move or the play really well
- In between each scene tune out for a few seconds and briefly take your mind away from the action.

c. Review self-talk to feel confident and to energize.

Choose the self-talk that will help you to energize, feel confident, be mentally tough, and be ready to play when the game starts. Write the self-talk below. Say the words to yourself while feeling yourself getting pumped and ready to go.

_____

_____

_____

_____

_____

–   Does it ensure that the athlete will eat proper foods, and that the last meal will occur at least two hours prior to the beginning of the competition?

–   Does it ensure that the athlete will consume ample fluids?

–   Does it maximize the likelihood that the athlete will enjoy the experience of preparing to compete?

–   Does it include an equipment and clothing check prior to leaving for the competition site?

–   Does it identify the appropriate times for leaving for, travelling to, and arriving at the competition site?

Preparing a Precompetition Plan

Let's assume that the athlete has arrived at the competition site, and that there is approximately an hour or so until the competition begins. A well designed pre-competition plan should ensure that the athlete: (a) is appropriately warmed up and energized; (b) is reasonably free of excessive nervousness or anxiety; (c) maintains positive self-talk; (d) focuses on realistic goals for execution; (e) mentally rehearses previous successful performances; and (f) is ready to attend to task-relevant cues at the time that the competition begins.

There are several strategies that can be followed for helping athletes to develop pre-competition plans. Each of these strategies assumes that the athlete is familiar with many of the techniques discussed in earlier chapters, such as goal setting, imagery rehearsal, positive self-talk, and emotion-control techniques.

Provide a Best/Worst Competition Questionnaire for the Athlete

If an athlete has not previously prepared a pre-competition plan, they are likely to experience difficulty in deciding where to begin and what to put into a plan. One strategy to help them get started is to provide them with a form to review one of their best and one of their worst competitions in terms of various pre-competition activities (Orlick, 1986b). An example of such a form that I have used with young competitive swimmers is shown in Figure 16-2. When completing such a form, the athletes might be prompted to pay special attention to the interval between warm-up and the entrance into competition. This is a crucial period because athletes at this point in time are maximally susceptible to distractions and/or anxiety and/or lack of arousal (Rushall, 1979, 1992).

Figure 16-2. A questionnaire to help swimmers identify activities that they might use in a precompetition plan

Swimmers: Use this form to review your best and worst events at a recent competition or competitions. If you draw on two different competitions, it is assumed that you were equally prepared, tapered, shaved, etc. for each competition. In other words, the goal is to focus on mental factors that might have played a role in causing you to swim your best vs. your worst.

A review of your best and your worst event at recent competitions

	Name of Competition Date _____ Your best event was:	Name of Competition Date _____ Your worst event was:
1. Did you plan and write out thought content for your events so that it included both mood words and technique thoughts?		
2. Did you practice the thought content for your races during at least two practices prior to the competition?		
3. Did you complete a goal setting sheet (with splits) before the competition?		
4. Did you arrive at the pool in ample time to enable you to relax before stretching before the in-pool warm-up?		
5. Did you use positive self-talk while stretching?		
6. Did some of the in-pool warm-up content occur at the same quality and intensity as that which would occur during the event?		
7. Did you have planned activities to stay relaxed after your in-pool warm-up while waiting for your event?		
8. From about 20 minutes before the event until you checked in at the marshalling area: a) What did you think about or concentrate on?		
b) Did you psych-up or psych-down?		

Figure 16-2 (cont'd)

	Name of Competition Date _____ Your best event was:	Name of Competition Date _____ Your best event was:
c) Did you use muscle relaxation?		
d) Did you use centering?		
e) Did you use coping self-statements?		
f) Did you mentally rehearse the entire race, including self-talk?		
g) Did you time the mental rehearsal?		
9. When you checked in with the coach, what did he/she say?		
10. At the marshalling area and behind the blocks: a) What did you do?		
b) What did you think about?		
c) How did you deal with nervousness?		
d) How did you deal with distractions?		
e) On a scale of 1-5, where 1 is *very relaxed*, and 5 is *very nervous*, how would you rate your nervousness?		
f) On a scale of 1-5, where 1 is *not confident* and 5 is *very confident*, how confident were you in achieving your goals?		
11. Did you mentally rehearse the start of your race during the last couple of minutes before mounting the blocks?		
12. When mounting the blocks, did you think explosive "mood" words for the start?		

Provide A Detailed Precompetition Guide with Write-in Options.

If you have worked with athletes in a particular sport, and if you are familiar with various pre-competition plans used by athletes in that sport, then you might devise a pre-competition planning form that contains suggestions for structured activities, but that also allows the opportunity for individual athletes to adapt it to their own particular styles, likes, and dislikes. A form that I have used with members of the Manitoba Synchronized Swimming team is shown in Figure 16-3.

Figure 16-3. A form to help synchronized swimmers to develop a precompetition plan. he model for this form was provided by Rushall (1979).

Planned Activities (describe your strategies below)	Possible Distractors	Coping Responses
1. **At the pool, be comfortable with the setting ahead of time.** Where will you sit and/or rest? Where do you report or check in? Where will your teammates and coach be? Where will the officials and judges be located?		
2. **Activities at the pool to maintain confidence.** Possibilities include: relaxation with positive imagery, land drill of the forthcoming activity, positive coping statements, review of realistic goal-setting.		
3. **The warm-up:** Center and/or relax and use positive imagery		
Review positive self-talk		
Rehearse deck work		
In the pool: Some of the warm-up content should be of the same quality and intensity as that which will occur in competition:		

Figure 16-3 (cont'd

	Possible Distractors	Coping Responses
4. Between the warmup and the competition Listen to music or do something to "tune out". Just before seeing the coach, stretch to achieve warmth and range of movement contained in the warmup.		
5. About 5 to 10 minutes prior to seeing the coach: Mentally rehearse the event		
Practice some positive self-talk		
6. See the coach		
7. While the swimmer(s) before you performs: Pump up if necessary		
Centering and relaxation if necessary		
Mental rehearsal, if there is time		
Use positive self-talk, if needed		
Just before starting, focus only on centering and preparation for the first element		

Provide A Questionnaire to Identify the Athlete's Current Mental Preparation Activities, and Areas in Need of Improvement

Let's assume that an athlete has competed at a high level, and has developed a way of mentally preparing to compete. However, the athlete has asked for additional help in refining his/her mental preparation plan. One strategy is to design a questionnaire to help determine their current mental preparation strengths as well as the areas in need of improvement. An example of a questionnaire which I have used with figure skaters is presented in Figure 16-4.

<u>Figure 16-4</u>. A questionnaire to help figure skaters develop a preskate plan before skating their program at competitions.

What Period Does a Preskate Plan Cover? At a competition, the time during the last hour or so before your on-ice warmup, and after your warmup while waiting for your turn to skate your program is the preskate period. **Why Have a Preskate Plan?** To plan out your activities and self-talk to maintain high confidence; To minimize distractors that affect your concentration; To eliminate negative thinking and anything that makes you nervous.		
Components of your Preskate Plan	**Yes**	**No**
1. Have you written out self-talk that helps you to: a) relax?		
b) recall your skating during your best 3 or 4 practices leading up to the competition?		
c) enjoy yourself?		
d) maintain confidence?		
e) tune out distractors?		
2. Have you memorized your self-talk?		
3. Have you planned out a specific series of stretching and physical activities for your off-ice warmup?		
4. Will you do your stretching, mental rehearsal, etc. by yourself?		
5. Have you written out the approximate times of the various activities right up until the point of putting on your skates and outfit?		
6. Have you decided how much mental rehearsal you will practice during your preskate plan (i.e., will you mentally rehearse your whole program? or just some of the elements?)?		
7. Have you planned specific relaxing activities during the preskate time (such as listening to the relaxation CD, talking with certain people about certain topics, etc.)?		
8. Have you planned specific activities for the waiting period following the 6 min. warmup to cover all the options from skating 1st through to skating 6th?		
9. Have you gone to several practices early enough in order to practice all of the above at simulations during the last couple of weeks prior to the competition?		

Refining A Pre-competition Plan

After a pre-competition plan has been prepared, you should review it with the athlete, and make adjustments where appropriate, so that the athlete can answer "yes" to the following questions:

- Does it identify the appropriate times for performing warm-up and stretching activities, changing into the competition uniform, completing the mental rehearsal or pre-performance routines, meeting with the coach, etc.?

- Does it include specific positive self-talk and other strategies to help the athlete maintain confidence (as described in Chapter 15)?

- Does it keep the athlete away from individuals (such as friends, relatives, the press) who are not familiar with mental preparation procedures, especially during the last hour or so before the competition?

- Does it include steps to minimize distractions, including interactions with other performers, especially during the last hour before competing?

- Does it include performance enhancement imagery at the competition site?

- Does it include steps to help the athlete maintain an appropriate, narrow focus on the here and now, especially during the last few minutes before competing?

- Does it ensure that the athlete will maintain an appropriate level of physiological and emotional arousal, especially during the last few minutes before competing?

- Does it ensure that thoughts that might occur about the competition are kept as simple as possible?

- Has the precompetition plan been practiced before one (and preferably several) mock competitions?

Preparing A Competition Focusing Plan

A competition focusing plan covers the period of time from the beginning to the end of the competition. For a game like ice hockey, it would be the time from the point at which the puck is dropped at the beginning of the first period through to the sound of the final buzzer at the end of the third period. For a figure skater, it would include the time that the music starts at the beginning of that skaters's program through to the completion of that specific program. The general goal of a competition focusing plan is to ensure that, once a competition begins, the athlete will experience the covert and overt behaviors that characterize optimal performance.

The nature of a competition focusing plan varies considerably from sport to sport. For controlled kicks in Australian football, an effective pre-kick focusing plan can include deep center breathing, an external focus on the scoring zone, and key words for executing the kick (Mesagno, Marchant, & Morris, 2008; Mesagno & Mullane-Grant, 2010). For a sport like figure skating, a competition focusing plan should include sufficient thought content to consume the time of the entire program. This would include key words or technique thoughts for specific jumps and spins, as well as self-talk between elements that might focus on ensuring proper concentration (e.g., "One step at a time."), presentation (e.g., "Smile, play to the judges."), staying in control (e.g., "Breathe, have fun."), and motivation to try difficult jumps (e.g., "Go for it."). As described in Chapter 14, the use of such self-talk capitalizes on the strategy of programming common stimuli in order to promote generalization of practice performance to competitions. If skaters practice such self-talk during run-throughs of their programs at practices, and if they subsequently use such self-talk at competitions, the self-talk is likely to exert stimulus control over desired performances in the "heat of the battle". Stated differently, the better rehearsed the thought content, the more likely it will occur naturally without having to think about it (a characteristic of peak performance, see Chapter 15), and the more it will exert control over a skilled performance. In such cases, the skater will likely maintain concentration and consistency during the program, and will be less likely to be influenced by distractions and pressures of competition. A checklist that I have used to help ice dancers prepare a competition focusing plan is presented in Figure 16-5 (also see Martin & Thomson, 2010).

A sport like ice hockey presents quite different problems than figure skating. Rather than programming a continuous series of thoughts that might last three or four minutes (the length of a figure skating program), an ice hockey player must deal with the shifts on the ice (each one lasting from approximately 30 seconds to a minute), the time on the bench between shifts (lasting approximately 2 to 5 minutes), the time between periods (15 minutes), and specific situations that arise on the ice (such as preparing for a face-off, getting tired near the end of the game, dealing with intimidation attempts by opponents, etc.), or on the bench (such as coping with criticism from a coach for a poor play on the ice). A competition focusing plan for a hockey player might cover any or all of these situations, depending upon the particular player and the situations that are most troublesome. Prior to taking a face-off, for example, a center might review a mental checklist concerning the positioning of the players, the stance of the opposing center, and the puck-dropping style of the particular linesman. Between shifts, a player might use self-talk to get ready for the next shift. Examples would include, "I'll use my speed," "I'll be aggressive and finish my checks," "I won't let anybody go untouched in front of our goalie."

Figure 16-5. A checklist to help ice dancers prepare a competition focusing plan.

Dance: _____ Name: _____ Approximate Duration of Dance: _____	
	Completed?
1. Draw out the pattern of the dance on a drawing of the ice surface of a typical ice skating rink. Duplicate the pattern so that each partner will have a copy.	
2. For that dance, make a list of the difficult elements (edges, steps, positions, holds) as they occur in sequence. Use numbers to identify the difficult elements as they occur and place the numbers on the pattern. Then list them on a separate sheet and number them in order.	
3. For each element that is difficult for you, identify (each partner should do this separately): a) where (in the element) you usually have a problem b) what you need to do to counteract the problem c) what key word(s) you can use to help you concentrate on what you need to do	
4. Review your pattern once again and add any key words that you think might be necessary to help you with: a) timing (e.g., "step and wait", vs. "quick, quick") b) expression and body language (e.g., "romantic" vs. "glare") c) flow (e.g., "smooth" vs. "snappy") d) form (e.g., "posture" and "body lean")	
5. Discuss all your key words with your partner and your coach and make changes where necessary. Also, remember the "paralysis by analysis" problem. You want a small number of key words and self-talk, but don't overdo it. Add just enough key words so that you will remain focused and maintain concentration throughout the dance.	
6. Walk out your program off the ice with your partner at least 3 times per day for 3 days in a row so that: a) you walk out your program to the music b) you and your partner say your key words out loud c) you and your partner make the simulation as realistic as possible in terms of paying attention to position and presenting with style and grace	
7. At each on-ice practice, use your key words and self-talk, and each time that you perform the entire dance, try to do so to the best of your ability.	

A useful strategy when helping athletes to develop competition focusing plans is to encourage them to view extended athletic performances in terms of segments (Rushall, 1992) or sequential checkpoints (Orlick, 1986b). In a swimming race, for example, the swimmers might prepare a mini competition focusing plan for each length of the pool that will be covered during the race (Rushall, 1992). In sports like diving and golf, each dive or golf shot might be considered as a segment. In American football, each play could be considered a segment (Ravizza & Osborne, 1991). Dividing a competition into segments makes it easier for the athlete to focus on one step or segment at a time.

It should be clear from the above examples that an important component of a competition focusing plan consists of planned thought content. And although more research is needed, there is evidence that planned thought content can improve performance in rowing (Rushall, 1984), swimming (Rushall & Shewchuk, 1989), cross-country skiing (Rushall et al., 1988), basketball (Hamilton & Fremouw, 1985; Kendall et al., 1990), tennis (Landin & MacDonald, 1990; Zeigler, 1987), figure skating (Ming & Martin, 1996), ice-hockey (Rogerson & Hrycaiko, 2002), bowling (Hill & Borden, 1995), Australian football (Mesagno & Mullane-Grant, 2010), soccer (Johnson, Hrycaiko, Johnson & Halas, 2004) and water-polo (Hatzigeorgiadis, Theodorakis & Zourbanos, 2004). Self-talk is likely to be especially useful in helping an athlete to mobilize his or her energy and resources during the most demanding parts of a competition. If that outcome is achieved, then the athlete stands a good chance of experiencing a peak performance.

Preparing a Competition Refocusing Plan

In spite of one's best laid plans, athletes in competition do experience uncontrollable distractions, unexpected difficulties, psych-out attempts by the opposition, occasional bad plays or missed routines or skills, emotional outbursts, uncontrollable reactions from spectators, and other events that can temporarily disrupt competitive performance. Refocusing plans enable the athlete to minimize the effects of such disruptions, and to quickly get back into a top-level competitive performance.

A general strategy that athletes can use to refocus after a variety of distracting situations is the "relax, regroup, refocus" strategy described in Chapter 8, and illustrated in Figure 16-6 for ice hockey players. With experience, athletes learn to tailor the regrouping and the refocusing self-talk to their particular situations. Consider, for example, a golfer who frequently played below her potential because of an inability to immediately refocus following each of three or four missed shots during a round. Thoughts of a missed shot and a missed opportunity tended to stay with her for several minutes, and typically interfered with the following shot. She learned to improve her refocusing after a missed shot by using the following post-shot routine. First, she relaxed by practicing deep center breathing for a few breaths, and then looking at the scenery (typically a beautiful park-like setting). Second, she regrouped by telling herself, "That one's history. No sense worrying about it. Because I can't get it back, that shot is no

<u>Figure 16-6</u>. A form to help ice hockey players with a strategy for competition refocusing between shifts.

Relax, Regroup, and Refocus between Shifts

Many players don't take advantage of the time between shifts. Some players become spectators when they sit on the bench. Their thoughts and emotions are controlled by what they see happening on the ice. That can be good if your team is playing well. But sometimes it's not good, especially when things are <u>not</u> going well on the ice. Other players let their minds wander between shifts, and they lose their concentration. Still other players get down on themselves after a bad shift, or after missing a goal. And players who are not on the specialty teams sometimes have trouble staying in the game when there are a lot of power plays or penalties, and they have to sit on the bench for quite a while. Remember, your thoughts and emotions can control you, or you can control them. To control your thoughts and emotions between shifts, to help you play the best game that you are capable of, you should practice: **Relax, Regroup, Refocus**

<u>(a) Relax</u> (during first 30 seconds or so after shift)
   − Use deep center breathing;
   − Emphasize exhalation;

<u>(b) Regroup</u> (during next 30 seconds or so after shift)
   − Rehearse general self-talk to put the last shift behind you and to get ready for the next shift
     e.g. "That one's gone forever."
        "The rest of my game starts now."
        "My immediate goal is to play well on the next shift."
        "Be pumped, be ready."

<u>(c) Refocus</u> (to get mentally ready for next shift)
   − Review some things to focus on to get ready for the next shift
     e.g. "I'll jump on loose pucks."
        "I'll finish my checks."
        "I'll jump into the openings."
        "I'll shoot quick."
        "I'm loose, I'm ready."

Write down the thoughts that will help you to regroup and refocus.
<u>To Regroup</u>:

_____

_____

<u>To Refocus</u>:

_____

_____

Remember, after a shift is over, it's history. So focus on the next one.

---

longer important, how I react to it is important. The next shot coming up is the one for me to think about." Third, when she got to her ball, she refocused by deliberately talking herself through her pre-shot routine for the next shot. After practicing this routine during several rounds, it became automatic, and her scores improved. Every golfer hits a few missed shots. Smart golfers are able to refocus and ensure that the few missed shots don't turn into many missed shots.

Another strategy to help athletes refocus is to encourage them to identify typical distractors which they might encounter during a competition, and to plan specific coping self-talk or other techniques that they can use to counteract the distractors. The form shown in Figure 16-3 that serves as a guide for synchronized swimmers to develop a precompetition plan includes columns on the form for the swimmers to list various distractors that they might encounter, and coping responses that they can make to offset the distractors. A general form to prompt athletes concerning such distractors is presented in Figure 16-7. Depending on the sport, additional potential distractors or disrupting influences can be added to the list.

Implementing the Plans

Mental skills are like physical skills; to be effective, they must be practiced. After an athlete has developed the various components of a competition plan, the entire plan should be practiced at mock competitions. Also, before using a competition plan in important competitions, the athlete should test it and refine it in less important competitions. Young figure skaters in the Canadian province of Manitoba, for example, compete in competitions at the regional, provincial, divisional, and national championship level. Their most important competition is the Canadian Championship, and only a few of our young skaters typically make it to that level in any given year. Those who do participate experience the hoopla of a national championship, and they encounter other competitors and coaches speaking in French. They notice different routines in the dressing room, during stretching, during warm-ups, and just before competing. But just because it's different, doesn't mean that it's better. Our skaters are able to tell themselves, "My routines are well practiced, they've proven successful, and I feel comfortable with them. The mental preparation strategies that I have learned and will follow are used by many of the best athletes in the world, and I'm going to stick with my plan." This type of self-talk, coupled with the components of confidence described in Chapter 15, and the experiences from having a well-rehearsed competition plan, enables the skaters to approach their most important competition with considerable confidence that they can perform up to their potential.

Figure 16-7. A form to prepare refocusing strategies for dealing with distractors at competitions.

Write in examples of the specific distractors that you have encountered (or expect to encounter), and examples of negative self-talk that you sometimes make to those distractors.	Write in examples of specific alternative positive self-talk (including possible technique thoughts) and/or other techniques that you can use to counteract the distractors
Psych-out attempts by opponents (e.g., specific comments, body language, disruptions, etc.) _____ _____ _____	_____ _____ _____ _____ _____
Thinking negatively about a skill (e.g., falling on a jump or a move, missing a shot, etc.) _____ _____ _____	_____ _____ _____ _____ _____
Feeling nervous or anxious before a competition or a shot or a routine _____ _____	_____ _____ _____ _____ _____
Feeling tired or starting to hurt during a competition _____ _____ _____	_____ _____ _____ _____ _____
Thinking negatively about facilities (e.g., the course, field, rink, etc.) _____ _____ _____	_____ _____ _____ _____ _____
Other possible distractors _____ _____ _____	_____ _____ _____ _____ _____

Post-Competition Evaluations

In a study of 235 Canadian Olympic athletes, Orlick and Partington (1988) found that the best athletes had developed a strategy for evaluating their mental approach after every competition, and used that information to continually refine their mental preparation for future competitions. Orlick (1986b) has described a competition evaluation form that can be used by athletes in any sport. My own consulting experiences suggest that such forms are more helpful for athletes if they are sport specific. Moreover, post-competition checklists should enable an athlete to self-assess their athletic performance as well as their mental performance and readiness. An example of a post-game self-assessment checklist that I have used with professional hockey players (defensemen) is shown in Figure 16-8 (also see Martin, 2010). An example of a post-competition checklist that we (Martin & Thomson, 2010) have used with figure skaters is shown in Figure 16-9.

How often must a total competition plan be practiced before it will help an athlete perform to his/her potential on a consistent basis during important competitions? At this point, formal research has not been done to answer this question. Based on his consulting experiences, Terry Orlick suggested that it takes from one to three years of consistent practice of mental skills and use of competition plans by highly committed athletes to get to the point where their psych plans are refined enough to affect performance consistently (Orlick, 1986b, 1989). Although this is a reasonable yardstick to present to athletes, we must remember that their progress in benefiting from use of a competition plan will depend on the extent to which they incorporate mental training into their regular practices, the extent to which they consistently follow their plans at numerous competitions, and the extent to which they refine their plans after each competition.

Figure 16-8. Checklist used by a defenseman for self-assessment after ice hockey games.

Score each item as follows:				
Excellent Average Needs Improvement				
+3 +2 +1 0 -1 -2 -3 Date				
Opposition				
Home/Away				
Mental Skills During the Game				
1. Pumped up about right (+3) vs. too laid back or too tight (-3)				
2. Lots of energy, good legs (+3) vs. sluggish (-3)				
3. Good concentration (+3) vs. dopy (lost focus) (-3)				
4. Played aggressive (intensity) (+3) vs. lacked intensity (-3)				
5. Confident throughout (+3) vs. lacked confidence (-3)				
Skills During the Game				
OPPONENTS HAVE POSSESSION				
Our End				
- Cleared front of net for shots from point				
- Tied up his stick, eye contact with puck				
- Communicated with goalie and D-partner at all times				
- Finished checks, got back to front of net after hit				
- Attacked aggressively, but under control				
Neutral Ice				
- Played with the blue line behind, "gap control"				
- 3 on 2, reduced their time and space, belly to belly when they crossed the blue line				
- Communicated and called out read at all times				
Their End				
- When "pinching", result was to take the forward out of the attack				
- When retreating, faced the play with "gap control"				
- Played with blue line behind me				
WE HAVE POSSESSION				
Our End or Neutral Zone				
- Set screens for puck carrying partner				
- Looked before I passed, froze the puck rather than give it up				
- When partner carried puck, was available for pass (went to vacated area for back pass)				
Their End				
- Shot low with quick release and on the net				
- Put the puck in deep if pressured				
- Kept dump-ins away from the goalie				
+/- in Game				
Things to work on at practice or to focus on for the next game				

Figure 16-9. A post-competition form for figure skaters.

EVALUATION OF MY PSYCH PLAN AFTER A COMPETITION

Complete this form as soon as possible after the competition. In all cases, 5 is the best rating, and 1 is the worst rating.

Name _____

Date _____ Competition Site _____

1. How did you feel during the last week or so before this competition?

Sick, injured, and/or tired	1 2 3 4 5	Healthy and rested
Not confident that I could skate a clean program	1 2 3 4 5	Confident that I could skate a clean program
Worried a lot about other skaters	1 2 3 4 5	Thought mainly about my own skating
Thought or worried a lot about where I would place	1 2 3 4 5	Thought mainly about having a good skate, like at a good practice
Felt nervous or worried about participating	1 2 3 4 5	Eagerly looked forward to participating

2. How did you feel at the competition (at the practice rink, at the competition rink, and during times in between)?

Sick, injured, and/or tired	1 2 3 4 5	Healthy and rested
Not confident that I could skate a clean program	1 2 3 4 5	Confident that I could skate a clean program
Worried a lot about other skaters	1 2 3 4 5	Thought mainly about my own skating
Thought or worried a lot about where I would place	1 2 3 4 5	Thought mainly about having a good skate, like at a good practice
Felt nervous or worried about participating	1 2 3 4 5	Eagerly looked forward to participating

3. At practices at the competition:

Did you have specific strategies (or a plan) to:		Did you use them?	Rate the results (5 is excellent)
Stay relaxed?	Yes No	Yes No	1 2 3 4 5

Figure 16-9 (cont'd)

			Rate				
Stay confident?	Yes No	Yes No	1	2	3	4	5
Think positive?	Yes No	Yes No	1	2	3	4	5
Minimize negative effects of other skaters?	Yes No	Yes No	1	2	3	4	5
Do your own thing?	Yes No	Yes No	1	2	3	4	5
Be energized?	Yes No	Yes No	1	2	3	4	5

4. During the last 45 minutes or so before your program:

Did you have specific strategies (or a plan) to:		Did you use them?	Rate the results				
Get used to the setting and the surroundings?	Yes No	Yes No	1	2	3	4	5
Do off-ice stretching?	Yes No	Yes No	1	2	3	4	5
Stay relaxed?	Yes No	Yes No	1	2	3	4	5
Stay confident?	Yes No	Yes No	1	2	3	4	5
Think positive?	Yes No	Yes No	1	2	3	4	5
Tune out when needed?	Yes No	Yes No	1	2	3	4	5
Mentally rehearse your program?	Yes No	Yes No	1	2	3	4	5
Minimize negative effects of other skaters?	Yes No	Yes No	1	2	3	4	5
Think about enjoying the opportunity to skate your program?	Yes No	Yes No	1	2	3	4	5
Focus mainly on skating like at a good practice?	Yes No	Yes No	1	2	3	4	5
Stay energized?	Yes No	Yes No	1	2	3	4	5
Have a minimum of unplanned sit-around or stand-around time?	Yes No	Yes No	1	2	3	4	5

5. After the on-ice warmup for your program, and while waiting for your turn:

Did you have specific strategies (or a plan) to:		Did you use them?	Rate the Results				
Stay relaxed?	Yes No	Yes No	1	2	3	4	5

Figure 16-9 (cont'd)

Stay confident?	Yes No	Yes No	1 2 3 4 5
Think positive?	Yes No	Yes No	1 2 3 4 5
Tune out for awhile, if needed?	Yes No	Yes No	1 2 3 4 5
Do a mini off-ice warmup if needed?	Yes No	Yes No	1 2 3 4 5
Not be affectively negatively by events happening around you?	Yes No	Yes No	1 2 3 4 5
Do your own thing?	Yes No	Yes No	1 2 3 4 5
Stay energized?	Yes No	Yes No	1 2 3 4 5
Look forward to skating your program?	Yes No	Yes No	1 2 3 4 5

6. During your program:

Did you have specific strategies (or a plan) to:		Did you use them?	Rate the Results
Feel positive and loose while waiting for the music to start?	Yes No	Yes No	1 2 3 4 5
Focus on each element?	Yes No	Yes No	1 2 3 4 5
Stay confident?	Yes No	Yes No	1 2 3 4 5
Think positive?	Yes No	Yes No	1 2 3 4 5
Sell the artistic presentation?	Yes No	Yes No	1 2 3 4 5
Stay energized?	Yes No	Yes No	1 2 3 4 5
Refocus after a miscue?	Yes No	Yes No	1 2 3 4 5
Enjoy the experience?	Yes No	Yes No	1 2 3 4 5

7. After your program, did you think that you had skated like at a good practice (or better)?	1 2 3 4 5

8. Is there anything about your psych plan that you need to change or improve upon for the next competition?

_____
_____
_____
_____
_____
_____
_____

Study Questions

1. In general, what is a competition plan?

2. In a sentence each, list and describe the purpose and the time-frame of each of the five components typically included in a complete competition plan.

3. What six outcomes should a well-designed pre-competition plan ensure in terms of athletic readiness to perform?

4. List three strategies that can be followed for helping athletes to develop precompetition plans.

5. What period of time is covered by a competition focusing plan? Describe an example for a sport.

6. What is the general goal of a competition focusing plan?

7. Briefly discuss the demands of two different sports to illustrate how the nature of a competition focusing plan varies from sport to sport.

8. A useful strategy when helping athletes to develop competition focusing plans is to encourage them to view extended athletic performances in terms of segments. Describe plausible segments of a particular sport in order to make it easier for an athlete to focus on each segment.

9. Competition focusing plans are likely to include self-talk to relax, key words for skills, and mood words. Pick a sport with which you are familiar and give plausible examples of these three different types of self-talk (you may want to review Ch. 8).

10. Pick a sport with which you are familiar (other than ice hockey) and describe a disruption to competitive performance for which an appropriate refocusing strategy would be to "relax, regroup, and refocus". Also, describe the details of the self-talk that might characterize the regroup and refocus components of the strategy.

11. For a sport with which you are familiar (and that is different from the sport you used to answer question #9), identify a typical distractor that an athlete might encounter during a competition. For that distractor, describe specific coping self-statements and/or other techniques that the athlete might use to counteract the distractor.

12. What two aspects of an athlete's performance should a post-competition evaluation assess?

Part V

Functioning As An Effective Practitioner-Scientist

CHAPTER 17

Single-Subject Research Designs to Evaluate your Interventions

As described in Chapter 1, an important characteristic of a behavioral approach is a strong emphasis on defining problems in terms of behavior that can be measured in some way, and using changes in the behavioral measure of the problem as the best indicator of the extent to which the problem is being helped. And in Chapter 6, I indicated that a minimal behavioral program should have at least three phases: a baseline phase, for determining the initial level of the behavior prior to the intervention; a treatment phase, in which the intervention strategy is applied; and a follow-up phase, for evaluating the persistence of the desirable behavior change following the termination of the intervention. But when a treatment is introduced for the purpose of modifying behavior of some individual, it is quite possible for some uncontrolled or interfering variable or condition to occur concurrently with the treatment, such that the change in the behavior is due to the uncontrolled variable rather than the treatment itself. Consider, for example, the case of the gymnast described in Chapter 13 who experienced difficulty landing her front sumi down at practices. You might recall that she used a self-recording program to monitor her frequency of "sticking" that particular move. And you might also recall that she showed considerable improvement during the self-monitoring phase. But was the improvement really due to the self-monitoring intervention? Perhaps the gymnast improved because she was invited to compete at a competition, and she knew that she had to improve at practices in order to be able to perform well at the competition. Or perhaps a new, hardworking gymnast joined the club at the time that the intervention began, and the other gymnasts were simply imitating her hard work. Or perhaps something else was responsible for the improved performance. The point is, when there are only the three minimal phases of a behavioral program, it may be difficult to conclude that an observed improvement was really due to the intervention.

Many sport psychology consultations consist of the three minimal phases of a behavioral program. But sometimes a sport psychology consultant will have the luxury of adding an additional phase or phases to a behavioral program to scientifically demonstrate that a particular treatment (rather than some uncontrolled variable) was responsible for a particular change in athletic behavior. This chapter describes research designs that have proven to be effective for evaluating sport psychology interventions, and that are likely to be acceptable to many coaches and athletes.

Single-Subject vs. Group Research Designs

In research projects in psychology, the behavior of the subjects is referred to as the dependent variable, and the treatment or intervention is referred to as the independent variable. There are two main approaches or methodologies for conducting experimental research in psychology; control group designs and single-subject designs. A control group experiment typically involves at least two groups, one that receives the treatment (called the treatment group) and one that does not (called the control group). The average performance of the two groups is then compared according to appropriate statistical procedures. Zaichkowsky (1980), Bryan (1987) and Hrycaiko and Martin (1996) have outlined several limitations of group designs for research in applied sport psychology. First, it is often difficult to locate enough subjects with the same performance problem to form the different groups. Second, coaches and athletes may resist participating in a no-treatment control group. Third, group designs require assumptions that may not be valid. More specifically, group designs assume that the dependent variable of concern is distributed in the population at large (from which the samples were drawn) in some specific fashion (usually normally), and that the samples are randomly selected from that population. However, assumptions concerning the population distribution are rarely assessed, and random samples in applied sport research are extremely rare. Fourth, because control group designs focus on the average performance of groups as they exist at a particular point in time, researchers who use them rarely use data obtained from continuous monitoring of an athlete's performance over time. Rather, they typically provide a pre-post assessment - a comparison of average performance at some point in time before treatment, to average performance at some point after treatment. A coach and an athlete, however, are often concerned with repeated measurement of that athlete's performance across several practices and/or competitions. Group-design researchers typically do not provide information on the individual variation in the performance of a given athlete over time.

An alternative methodology for evaluating interventions is referred to as single-subject designs. Such designs have several salient characteristics (Hrycaiko & Martin, 1996; Luiselli, 2011). Two of these characteristics are also characteristics of control group designs. First, both types of designs require interobserver reliability (IOR) assessment of the dependent variable to ensure that the records of the athletes' behavior are accurate. During a portion of observation sessions, two trained observers independently record the dependent variable of a subject in such a way as to not influence each other. Following the session, their assessments are compared. If the assessments compare favorably, it is assumed that the data on the dependent variable is reliable. One common strategy for computing an IOR score is to divide the smaller total of the dependent variable (recorded by one observer) by the larger total (recorded by the other observer) and to multiply the dividend by 100% (Martin & Pear, 2011). By convention, IOR scores of 80% or greater are considered acceptable. Second, steps are typically taken to ensure that the treatment was applied as intended and as described (Billingsley, White, & Munson, 1980). This characteristic is referred to as assessment of treatment integrity, and sometimes takes the form of a procedural reliability assessment. The experimenter typically prepares a checklist of the critical components of treatment. Throughout the research project, two observers (or the experimenter and one observer) regularly assess whether or not the treatment was applied as outlined on the checklist, and a reliability assessment is obtained in the manner described previously for IOR on the dependent variable. If the treatment involves some form of mental practice, then the procedural reliability assessment should include monitoring of the athlete's practice of the mental skills to ensure that they occur as intended (Martin, 1993; Wollman, 1986). Adequate procedural reliability assessments of treatment components help to ensure treatment integrity, increase research replicability, and enhance interpretation of results.

Three additional characteristics differentiate single-subject designs from control group methodology. First, single-subject designs typically require repeated measurement of the main dependent variable throughout the duration of the study, as opposed to pre/post assessments. Examples include laps completed in swimming practices (McKenzie & Rushall, 1974), setting accuracy across practices in volleyball (McKenzie & Liskovych, 1983), and successful application of a defensive basketball skill across games (Kendall et al., 1990). Other examples can be found in a review paper by Martin, Thomson and Regehr (2004). Ongoing monitoring of critical aspects of the performance of individual athletes across practices and games is one of the features that makes these designs potentially valuable for coaches and athletes. Second, although single-subject designs include control conditions in which behavior is studied in the absence of treatment, they do not typically include control groups. Instead, all subjects studied, at one time or another, are studied under all conditions of the experiment. In some of these designs, each subject acts as his or her own control in the sense that changes in a subject's behavior during treatment are compared against that subject's baseline performance before and after treatment.

Third, researchers who use single-subject designs typically rely on visual inspection of data to assess the effects of treatment. When judging whether or not the treatment was responsible for producing a reliable effect on the dependent variable, the experimenter typically proceeds through three phases of judgement (Martin & Pear, 2011). First, the experimenter ensures that the IOR measures on the dependent variable have met acceptable standards, and that the treatment procedures have been precisely specified as indicated by acceptable procedural reliability assessments. Second, the experimenter visually examines graphs of the dependent variable to determine if the intervention has clearly improved the athlete's performance. When inspecting one's data to judge whether or not the treatment had an effect on the dependent variable, one has greater confidence that an effect has been observed: (a) when baseline performance is stable or in a direction opposite to that observed for the effects of treatment; (b) the greater the number of times that an effect is replicated both within and across subjects; (c) the fewer the overlapping data points between baseline and treatment phases; (d) the sooner the effect is observed following the introduction of treatment; and (e) the larger the effect in comparison to baseline. These guidelines are illustrated in the following pages. Statistical techniques are also available for analyzing data from single-subject experiments (Hrycaiko & Martin, 1996; Parker, 2006; Parker & Hagan-Burke, 2007; Shambrook & Bull, 1996), and Kazdin (1984) suggested that visual inspection and statistical analyses of single-subject data should be viewed as complementary rather than competing strategies. Nevertheless, the majority of published reports using single-subject designs rely on visual inspection. Finally, in the third phase of judgement, one has more confidence that an experimental effect has occurred if results are consistent with existing data and accepted behavioral theory.

Types of Single-Subject Designs

There are three main types of single-subject designs: the reversal replication design, multiple-baseline designs, and the alternating treatments design. These are described in subsequent pages. Although they are referred to as single-subject designs, such investigations typically include three to five subjects. Such designs are not to be confused with a case study. The best possible scenario that a case study can achieve would include the three phases of a minimal behavior modification program. Although a case study can provide useful information (Virués-Ortega & Martin, in press; Smith, 1988), it is always possible that a change in behavior during the intervention may be due to some uncontrolled variable that happened to occur concurrently with the intervention. Single-subject designs include additional phases to convincingly demonstrate that observed performance improvements are really due to the treatment. Examples of the use of single-subject designs to study the behavior of athletes were reviewed by Luiselli (2011) and Martin et al. (2004).

The Reversal Replication (ABAB) Research Design

You may recall from Chapter 12 the problem faced by Coach Hume at figure skating practices. Three of the skaters showed considerable off-task behavior and a low frequency of practicing various jumps and spins. Coach Hume introduced a goal-setting and self-monitoring package to attempt to improve the practice performance of the skaters. Coach Hume used a reversal replication design to evaluate the effects of the intervention. First, the practice performance of each subject was studied during a *baseline phase* - sessions conducted during which performance was monitored without the intervention. The results of this phase for each of the subjects can be seen in Figure 17-1. Next, each subject was introduced to an *intervention phase* in which they utilized the self-management package. As can be seen in Figure 17-1, when the treatment was first

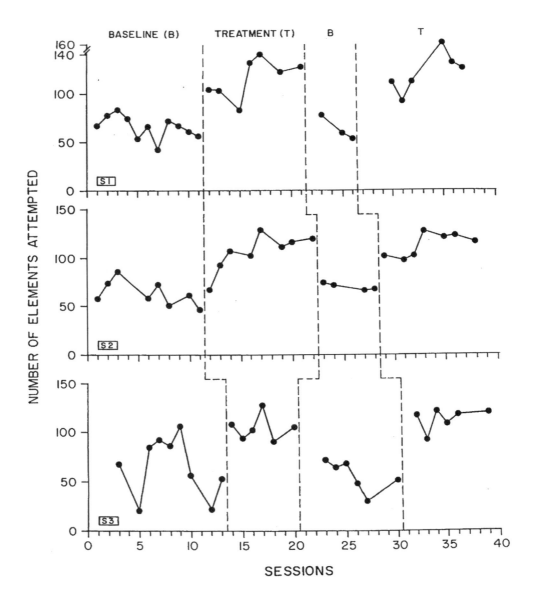

<u>Figure 17-1</u>. Performance of three figure skaters across practices. Reprinted with permission from Hume et al. (1985).

introduced, performance improved for all three skaters. Was this due to some uncontrolled variable? To assess whether or not the improvement was due to treatment, a *reversal to baseline phase* was conducted in which treatment was withdrawn. In each case, performance quickly decreased to pre-treatment levels. This result makes it less probable that some uncontrolled variable was mysteriously occurring and not occurring at the exact same time that treatment was introduced and then withdrawn. To further assess the effects of treatment, a *replication phase* was conducted in which the treatment was again applied to each of the skaters. Once again, performance improved in all three subjects. This suggests that the treatment (and not some uncontrolled variable) was responsible for the improved performance of the skaters. A finding is said to have **internal validity** if the independent variable did, in fact, cause the observed changes in the dependent variable.

As previously indicated, there are five commonly used guidelines for visually inspecting data to determine whether a treatment has had a consistent effect. First, the last few data points of the baseline should be reasonably stable or in a direction opposite to that predicted for the effects of treatment. The first two subjects in Figure 17-1 meet this criterion. Second, one has greater confidence that an effect has been observed the more times that it is replicated. In Figure 17-1, clear replication occurred in all six treatment phases (i.e., during treatment and replication for all three subjects). Third, one has greater confidence that an effect has been observed when there are few overlapping data points between adjacent baseline and treatment phases. Comparison of the first baseline and treatment phase for Subject 1 in Figure 17-1 shows only one overlapping data point (the highest data point in baseline overlapped with the lowest data point during the first intervention). An assessment of adjacent baseline and treatment phases across all three subjects in Figure 17-1 shows few overlapping data points. The fourth guideline is that one has greater confidence that an effect has been observed the sooner the effect is observed following the introduction of the treatment. For all three subjects in Figure 17-1, there was an immediate and clear experimental effect. The final guideline is that one has greater confidence that an effect has been observed if the effect is large. The intervention had a large effect for all three subjects in Figure 17-1.

A limitation of the reversal replication design is that it may be undesirable or impossible to obtain a reversal. Once a golf pro has taught a novice golfer to hit a golf ball over 200 yards, for example, it is unlikely that the golfer would deliberately return to his original, unorthodox swing, which produced a 150-yard drive. Additional single-subject designs for demonstrating the control imposed on behavior by a particular treatment, and that do not require a reversal phase, are referred to as multiple-baseline designs.

A Multiple-Baseline Design Across People

To examine the effects of a treatment package (imagery rehearsal, relaxation, and self-talk) on the performance of a defensive basketball skill (cutting off the baseline) during games, Kendall et al. (1990) used a multiple-baseline design across people, as described in the Application at the beginning of Chapter 8. With this design, baseline data is taken across several subjects concurrently (see Figure 17-2). The intervention is then introduced to the first subject while the other subjects remain on baseline (see Figure 17-2). Although Subject 1 by herself would essentially be a case study, the ongoing concurrent assessment of the other three subjects provided controls for comparison purposes. Then, in a staggered fashion across the remaining subjects, the intervention was introduced. Because each subject improved at the point where they experienced the intervention, it is plausible to assume that the improvements were due to the treatment and not due to some uncontrolled variable.

In experimental research, a finding is said to be **externally valid** to the extent that it can be generalized to other behaviors, individuals, settings, or treatments. Often, single-subject designs tend to be weak on external validity. However, in the study by Kendall et al., there was a demonstration that the treatment had external validity across individuals in the sense that results were demonstrated with all four subjects. A potential research limitation of the multiple-baseline design across people is that the first subject might explain the treatment or model the desirable behavior to the other subjects, causing them to improve in the absence of treatment. Also, it is not always possible to find two or more subjects, nor the additional observers to gather the necessary data.

A Multiple-Baseline Design Across Behaviors

Consider the case of Bob, a coach of an age-group competitive swimming team. Bob solicited help from Brent Rushall, a well-known sport psychologist, to become a "better" coach. Observations of Bob's performance as a coach at practices indicated that he displayed a low frequency of three categories of behaviors: dispensing positive reinforcement to the swimmers, providing instructional feedback to the swimmers concerning aspects of swimming technique that they were performing correctly, and the combination of reinforcement and feedback together. These three behavioral categories were recorded across several baseline sessions. Then, in a staggered fashion, a treatment program was introduced in sequential fashion to each of those behaviors. The treatment focused primarily on prompting and self-recording the target behaviors. When the treatment was introduced to the reinforcing behaviors, they improved while the remaining two categories continued at baseline levels. When the treatment was applied to instructional feedback, it, too, improved. And when the treatment was applied to the reinforcing and feedback behaviors together, the coach showed an increased frequency of the two behaviors as a package (Rushall & Smith, 1979).

This design, known as a multiple-baseline design across behaviors, follows a similar logic to a multiple-baseline design across people except that data are collected on several behaviors of a single individual rather than on a single behavior of several

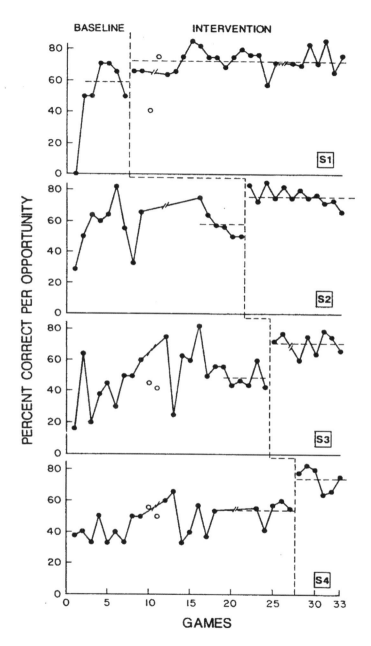

Figure 17-2. Performance of a defensive basketball skill by four female university players across games. Reprinted with permission from Kendall et al. (1990).

individuals. As illustrated in the study by Rushall and Smith (1979), this design has the potential to demonstrate external validity of a treatment to other behaviors. The application of this design assumes that the behaviors that are studied are relatively independent. If Bob had improved in all categories when the treatment was applied to just the first behavior, then Rushall and Smith could not have confidently attributed the improvement to the treatment itself. Other limitations are that it may not be possible to find two or more suitable behaviors, or sufficient observers to gather the necessary data on several behaviors.

A Multiple-Baseline Design Across Situations

Another variety of multiple-baseline design studies the effects of a treatment on a single behavior of an individual that occurs in several situations. Thus far, I have not encountered a published study of a multiple-baseline design across situations with athletes. Consider, therefore, an example of such a design applied to Mike, an eight-year old boy with minimal brain damage who was attending a summer camp. Frequently during the day, Mike fantasized out loud about his imaginary pet penguins. His verbalizations interfered with Mike's interactions with his peers and the camp counsellors. During the initial baseline phase of a program to change Mike's behavior, the frequency of verbalizations was monitored in four situations: during trail walks in the evening, in the dining hall, in Mike's home cabin, and during education classes. Next, treatment was introduced in the first situation (trail walking) while the remaining three situations continued in baseline. The treatment involved an extinction program in which verbalizations were ignored. Then, sequentially across the remaining situations, treatment was introduced. In each instance, the frequency of bizarre verbalizations decreased to near zero only when treatment was applied to that particular situation (Allen, 1973).

This design examines the external validity of a treatment across different settings. A potential research limitation is that when the treatment is applied to the behavior in the first situation or setting, it may cause subsequent improvement in all settings. When this happens, the experimenter is not able to conclude that the improvement was necessarily a result of the treatment. Other potential limitations are that the behavior may occur in only one setting, or there may not be sufficient observers to gather the necessary data.

Alternating-Treatments (or Multi-Element) Design

The preceding research designs are ideally suited for demonstrating that a particular treatment was indeed responsible for a specific behavioral change. But what if you wanted to compare the effects of different treatments for a single behavior of a single individual? An appropriate design for such a task is the alternating-treatments design (Martin & Pear, 2011). This design involves measuring a behavior as it occurs during two or more alternating treatments. One treatment per session is typically applied, and treatments are alternated across sessions. Presenting each treatment for only one session at a time and alternating the treatments in a randomized or counterbalanced fashion are common manipulations to minimize sequence effects (Hrycaiko & Martin, 1996).

Wolko et al. (1993) used the alternating-treatments design to compare the effects of standard coaching (as a baseline condition) versus standard coaching plus public self-regulation (Treatment 1) versus standard coaching plus private self-regulation (Treatment 2) on the frequency of completed skills by young gymnasts during practice on the balance beam. Each condition was in effect for six sessions, with the conditions randomly alternated across a total of 18 sessions. The data for one of the subjects is shown in Figure 17-3. As indicated in Figure 17-3, private self-regulation (Treatment 2) appeared to be the most effective intervention. Note that the data in Figure 17-3 are plotted cumulatively across sessions (rather than as a frequency graph). When small effects are obtained from an alternating-treatments design, plotting the data as a frequency graph results in frequent overlap of data points, which makes it difficult to visually detect differences between treatment conditions. However, when results are plotted cumulatively, small effects gradually accumulate over time to the point where there is a clear separation of the effects of the different treatments, as can be seen in Figure 17-3.

The alterating-treatments design has several advantages over the reversal replication and multiple-baseline designs. First, it allows for the comparison of the effects of treatments within an individual over time and is ideally suited to detect delayed treatment effects because it can include an ongoing baseline as one of the conditions for comparison. As illustrated in Figure 17-3, results began to emerge by the fourth session. Second, when an ongoing baseline is one of the conditions, the design is able to be used with behaviors (such as athletic performances) that occur at unstable rates (e.g., McKenzie & Liskevych, 1983). Third, because all conditions can be introduced concurrently, it avoids the need for lengthy baseline or treatment conditions that commonly occur with reversal replication designs. This is possible because the conditions are alternated rapidly within a short period of time. Fourth, the design also makes it possible to terminate less effective treatments early because the effects of different treatments can be detected quickly (McKenzie & Liskevych, 1983).

There are two noteworthy limitations to the alternating-treatments design. First, generalization may occur because of similarities between the conditions. Second, contrasting effects may enhance differences between the alternating-treatment conditions. In other words, if just one of the treatments is applied, the effects observed may be different than when several treatments are alternated (Hains & Baer, 1989). There are two possible solutions to these problems. First, it would be possible to observe the behavior during several baseline sessions prior to the introduction of the alternating-treatments. A comparison of performance during an initial baseline to later baseline performance when baseline is alternated with treatment conditions would at least enable one to judge whether or not an interaction occurred between the baseline and one or more of the treatment conditions. A second alternative is to conduct a few additional sessions

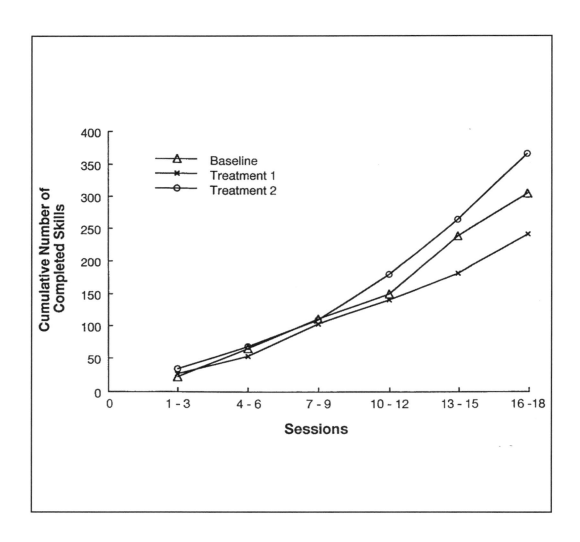

Figure 17-3. Performance of a gymnast across practices. Only one condition was applied per practice. Adapted from Wolko et al., (1993).

with just the most effective treatment at the end of the study. If performance continues at the same level as when that treatment was alternated with other conditions, then it is less likely that an interaction occurred.

Summary of Single-Subject Designs

Single-subject designs have a number of features that render them "user friendly" for practitioners to evaluate the effects of interventions on athletic performance at practices and during competitions (Virués-Ortega & Martin, in press). They require only a small number of subjects to demonstrate internal validity (and sometimes, external validity) of treatments, athletic performance is monitored continuously across practices or competitions, and all subjects are typically exposed to both baseline and treatment conditions. In a review of 30 years of research (1974-2003), 40 studies were identified that used single-subject designs in sport psychology (Martin et al., 2004). Those studies clearly indicate that such designs have considerable potential for demonstrating the effectiveness of our interventions to consumers of sport psychology services.

Judging whether or not a significant effect has occurred from a scientific point of view is one thing; evaluating the practical importance of behavior change to the client, or the significant individuals in the client's life, and society in general, is something else again. Evaluating the practical significance of a behavioral treatment is referred to as an assessment of social validity (Wolf, 1978), and is discussed further in Chapter 18.

Study Questions

1.   Briefly describe the three minimal components of a behavior modification program.

2.   In two or three sentences, explain why we cannot necessarily claim that a change in behavior during a minimal behavior modification program was due to the treatment.

3.   What is a dependent variable? Describe an example from a sport psychology research project.

4.   What is an independent variable? Describe an example from a sport psychology research project.

5.   In two or three sentences, summarize the strategy of control group research methodology.

6.   List four limitations of the control group methodology for conducting research in applied sport psychology.

7. Describe two characteristics that are common to both group designs and single-subject designs.

8. Describe three characteristics of single-subject designs that distinguish them from group designs.

9. When visually inspecting single-subject data to determine if the treatment had an effect on the dependent variable, what five factors influence the judgement of the experimenter?

10. Describe briefly, with reference to a sport example, the four components of the reversal replication design.

11. Ideally, how long should the baseline phase of the reversal replication design continue?

12. Identify a limitation of the reversal replication design, and illustrate it with a sport example.

13. What is meant by internal validity? Illustrate with a sport example.

14. Describe briefly, with reference to a sport example, a multiple-baseline design across people.

15. Briefly describe three potential limitations or problems of the multiple-baseline design across people.

16. What does it mean to say that a finding is externally valid? Illustrate with a sport example.

17. Briefly describe, with reference to a sport example, a multiple-baseline design across behaviors.

18. What are three limitations of a multiple-baseline design across behaviors?

19. Briefly describe, with reference to a sport example, a multiple-baseline design across situations.

20. What are three limitations of a multiple-baseline design across situations?

21. Briefly describe, with reference to a sport example, the characteristics of an alternating-treatments design.

22. List four advantages of an alternating-treatments design over reversal replication and multiple-baseline designs.

23. What are two limitations of the alternating-treatments design?

Chapter 18

Ethical and Professional Issues

In general, a profession is an occupation for which an individual must master significant educational material, receive extensive training or supervised experience, be recognized or licensed by a professional society or state/provincial professional group, provide a valued service, and follow an established code of ethics (Ziegler, 1987). During the past 45 years, sport psychology has acquired professional status. In 1965, the International Society of Sport Psychology was established to disseminate information about sport psychology throughout the world. In 1967, the North American Society for the Psychology of Sport and Physical Activity was formed. In 1969, the Canadian Society for Psychomotor Learning and Sport Psychology was established. Since the late 1970s, sport psychology has experienced considerable growth in North America, as evidenced by the development of several journals (e.g., *Journal of Sport Behavior*, 1979; *Journal of Sport Psychology* now called *Journal of Sport and Exercise Psychology*, 1979-; *The Sport Psychologist*, 1986-; *Journal of Applied Sport Psychology*, 1989-; and *Journal of Clincial Sport Psychology*, 2007-), the appearance of sport psychology articles in other journals (e.g., *Behavior Modification*, *Journal of Applied Behavior Analysis*), the publication of numerous books, frequent national and international conferences, and the establishment of the Association for the Advancement of Applied Sport Psychology (AAASP, 1986-), which, in 2006, became the Association for Applied Sport Psychology (AASP). AASP is dedicated to the development and professionalization of the field of sport psychology, and its professional and student members are working in both academic and private settings. There now exists a number of sport and exercise psychology organizations around the world, and entering sport-related psychology associations in Google produces websites for many such organizations.

In our society, being considered a professional implies that such individuals have specialized knowledge that enables them to provide a needed service. From a behavioral perspective, the service provided by behavioral sport psychology consultants involves influencing the behavior of athletes and coaches. Ideally, such applications would always be in the best interests of the individuals who are treated. But, human nature being what it is, simply resolving to treat various individuals and groups in ethical ways is not a sufficient guarantee that they will be so treated. One way to increase the likelihood that an individual will behave responsibly as a professional is to require that individual to follow ethical guidelines set out by the individual's professional organization. A code of ethics is a set of rules or principles that help to guide practical behavior in everyday situations. From a behavioral perspective, ethics refer to certain standards of behavior that are developed by a culture and that promote the survival of that culture (Skinner, 1953, 1971). In 1995, AAASP published a set of ethical principles to guide the actions of sport psychologists. These principles are based in large part on the ethical principles of psychologists developed by the American Psychological Association, and are summarized in Table 18-1. This chapter provides additional discussion of the ethics and practice of behavioral sport psychology consulting. The following discussion is directed toward individuals who would offer themselves to the public in a professional capacity as a behavioral sport psychology consultant. For additional discussion of education and training requirements in sport psychology, see Silva, Lerner, and Metzler (2007). For additional discussion of ethics in sport psychology, see Whelan, Meyers, and Elkin (1996).

Qualifications of the Behavioral Sport Psychology Consultant

Academic Training

Behavioral sport psychology consultants should receive appropriate academic training that would include a solid grounding in basic behavioral principles (such as described by Martin & Pear, 2011), detailed knowledge of the field of sport psychology (such as described by Weinberg & Gould, 2011), and a thorough appreciation of the application of behavioral principles in sport settings (such as described in this book). Individuals who are so trained should also receive appropriate supervised practicum experiences to ensure competence in behavioral assessment, designing and implementing treatment programs, evaluating their results, and ensuring a thorough understanding of professional ethics (for a description of graduate programs in applied sports psychology, see Burke, Sachs and Gomer, 2008). In 1991, AAASP established a model for individuals to become certified sport psychologists by AAASP. Their model included a doctoral degree from an accredited institution of higher education. However, in 2002, AAASP also approved standards and a process for certifying individuals with a Masters degree (see the website, http://www.aaasponline.org),or http://www.appliedsportpsych.org). In Canada, the Canadian Sport Psychology Association was formed in 2006, and it also certifies sport psychology practitioners (see www.en.cspa-acps.ca).

Some degree of accountability is also ensured by meeting recognized criteria for professional status provided by membership in the local state or provincial psychological (or other appropriate professional) association. It should also be pointed out that the title *Psychologist*, is restricted by law in the United States and Canada. Only those who are licensed or certified by the local state or provincial association can use the term *psychologist*, *psychology*, or *psychological* in private practice. Individuals who are not so licensed but whose primary job description is that of a psychologist in a university or government setting can also use the term in their job title (however they may not do so in private practice). This presents a problem for individuals whose Ph.D.s are from sport science programs in physical education faculties. Although many such individuals cannot legally call themselves sport psychologists in private practice, they are nevertheless highly qualified service providers in the area of sport psychology. Because of legal constraints,

Table 18-1

Ethical Principles of Sport Psychologists

Principle A: Competence

Sport psychologists recognize the boundaries of their particular competencies and the limitations of their expertise. They provide only those services and use only those techniques for which they are qualified.

Principle B: Integrity

Sport psychologists are honest, fair, and respectful of others. In describing or reporting their qualifications, services, products, fees, research, or teaching, they do not make statements that are false, misleading, or deceptive.

Principle C: Professional and Scientific Responsibility

Sport psychologists uphold professional standards of conduct and accept responsibility for their behavior. When appropriate, they consult with colleagues in order to prevent or avoid unethical conduct.

Principle D: Respect for People's Rights and Dignity

Sport psychologists respect the fundamental rights, dignity, and worth of all people. They respect the rights of individuals to privacy, confidentiality, self-determination, and autonomy.

Principle E: Concern for Others' Welfare

Sport psychologists seek to contribute to the welfare of those with whom they interact professionally. When conflicts occur among psychologists' obligations or concerns, they attempt to resolve those conflicts in a reasonable fashion that avoids or minimizes harm.

Principle F: Social Responsibility

Sport psychologists are aware of their professional and scientific responsibilities to the community and the society in which they work and live. They apply and make public their knowledge of psychology in order to contribute to human welfare.

Note: Adapted with permission from the Ethical Principles of the Association for the Advancement of Applied Sport Psychology.

they must offer their services in private practice under other titles such as Sport Psychology Consultant, Performance Enhancement Specialist, Peak Performance Trainer, and Mental Training Consultant.

Knowledge of Sport Environments and Sport Language

There is a consensus among successful sport psychology consultants that detailed knowledge of sport environments is critical for success (Simons & Andersen, 1995). This would include: having detailed knowledge of one or more sport environments; initially spending lots of hours doing voluntary work with athletes, especially with youth athletes, and hopefully while in graduate school; communicating often with athletes, coaches, and parents of younger athletes; arriving before practices and staying after practices; spending time with all types of individuals associated with sports, such as trainers and managers; and spending time with athletes throughout competition days. If you hope to consult to athletes in sports which you have not played yourself, you can read technical descriptions of the skills involved, attend practices and competitions, and talk with athletes who play that sport. You must also understand the specific demands that confront athletes in closed-ended individual sports like figure skating, diving, and gymnastics, versus open-ended team sports such as basketball, football, and hockey. Similarly, you must understand the different demands placed on athletes by contact sports (like ice hockey and football) versus non-contact sports (like baseball and volleyball).

An important part of preliminary preparation is to be familiar with the jargon used by athletes and coaches in sports in which you hope to consult. Ravizza (1988) identified lack of sport specific knowledge on the part of the consultant as a common barrier which makes it difficult for a sport psychologist to gain entry to the athletic world. Spending sufficient time familiarizing yourself with a sport to ensure that you can "speak the language" of that sport will help you to eliminate that barrier.

In addition to being comfortable with the jargon of particular sports to which you would like to consult, you should also be adept at quickly translating behavioral analyses into the "language of the sport". The jargon of behavior analysis (e.g., contingencies, rule-governed behavior, S^Ds, S^Es, CSs, etc.) is useful for enabling us to conduct behavioral assessments, analyze performance problems, design effective interventions, conduct research, communicate precisely with colleagues, and publish our research. It is nevertheless foreign to most athletes, coaches, parents, and others in the athletic world. When describing your service and your interventions, your language must be "user friendly" and make sense to your consumers.

Establishing Credibility and Support during Initial Meetings

In Chapter 6, I suggested that, if you are a sport psychologist in your first meeting with an athlete, you might: explain confidentiality, briefly describe your background, provide information on sport psychology, and clarify some misconceptions about sport psychology. I encourage you to review those topics in Chapter 6. In this section I would like to describe additional strategies that a sport psychologist might follow to gain interest, credibility, and support from potential recipients of his/her service during initial presentations and/or meetings.

One strategy is to be flexible regarding meetings, and not expect all meetings to take place in your office. An important part of gaining support is for you to be prepared to become a part of the sport environment, to attend early and late practices, and to arrange your meetings to adapt to the very busy schedules of athletes and coaches.

A second strategy, as expressed previously, is to be able to speak the "sport language" of the athletes with whom you are dealing, and to communicate effectively in a way that makes sense to coaches and athletes (Yukelson, 2010). Sport psychology consultant Ken Ravizza recommends the KISS principle - keep it simple and smart (Simons & Andersen, 1995). Similarly, sport psychologist Bob Rotella suggested, "Everything I know that works, and is good, is logical and makes common sense, and has been around for a long time. It's just a matter of whether you can get people to do it." (Simons & Andersen, 1995).

A third strategy during initial meetings is to try to be aware of vested interests of all involved, including coaches, assistant coaches, trainers, administrators, alumni, friends, and parents. There may be some hidden agendas concerning your involvement, and not knowing of them could hinder your success. In one case, for example, I was asked by a gymnastics coach to develop a mental preparation program for one of his young gymnasts. After several meetings, however, it became clear that what the coach really wanted was someone to take the brunt of frequent demands from the gymnast's overly-aggressive parents. When I refused to accept that role, the consultation was terminated.

A fourth strategy is to take the time to establish rapport with coaches, which can increase the likelihood that coaches will support your suggestions to athletes, and increase the likelihood that athletes will follow your suggestions. In my work as the Sport Psychologist for the Manitoba Provincial Figure Skating team over many years, for example, I met with individual coaches at the beginning of each season to obtain their views on the mental preparation needs of their skaters. During each season, with permission of a skater, I sent copies of that skater's homework assignments to the skater's coach. At competitions, I discussed elements of a competition plan with the coach and the skater. As a consequence of such efforts, the coaches became knowledgeable about aspects of mental training, and encouraged the skaters to incorporate mental training into practices and competitions. At practices, for example, I frequently observed coaches ask skaters about their key words, prompt them to do instant mental replays, and encourage them to rehearse their positive self-talk just before skating their programs.

A fifth strategy for establishing support is to thoroughly explore the athletes' concerns and problems, as discussed in Chapter 6, and to tailor your program to meet their particular needs. None of a group of leading American sport psychology consultants endorsed a "cook book" approach to mental skills training in which the same "recipe" is applied to all athletes (Simons & Andersen, 1995). There are many different types of problems and many possible ways of effectively dealing with them.

A sixth strategy for establishing support is to identify and express appreciation for current skills that the athletes already possess (Orlick, 1989). A part of this process is to determine whether or not the athletes have worked with sport psychologists in the past. If they have, you should recognize their current skills and focus on helping them to refine those skills.

A seventh strategy to gain support is to suggest ways to incorporate mental skills training into existing practices, rather than presenting them as something separate that's taught in your office (Ravizza, 1987). For example, in figure skating, when a figure skater's name is announced at a competition, it is important for the skater to think positively and to control their arousal and anxiety when skating to their starting position prior to the beginning of their program. I suggested to figure skaters that they accomplish this by rehearsing positive self-talk and practicing deep-center breathing during that time. But to ensure that such mental skills were well-practiced and would be used at competitions, I encouraged skaters to incorporate them into simulations at practices. During a particular practice session, even though there were other skaters on the ice, when the time came for a particular skater to skate his/her program, I would announce loudly, for example, "Our next skater, from the Brandon Figure Skating Club, Suzie Haldon." While Suzie was skating to her start position, she practiced her positive self-talk and deep-center breathing.

It is important to approach your initial sessions with athletes with a dose of realism. Not all of your interventions will be successful. And if you are consulting to a team, not all of the athletes will be receptive to your program. I once asked one of the professional ice hockey players with whom I worked, "How many guys on the team do you think would be interested in a mental training program?" He answered, "About a third of them would be interested and might be willing to do homework assignments, about a third might express an interest but probably wouldn't do any homework, and the remaining third wouldn't want any part of it." Ken Ravizza expressed a similar view based on years of experience consulting to professional baseball players (Simons & Andersen, 1995).

Definition of the Problem and Selection of Goals

As discussed in Chapter 6, target behaviors selected must be the most important for the client. Goals selected are most likely to be achieved when the sport psychologist, athlete, coach (and perhaps parents and others) agree on the same goals and work together to achieve them. But occasionally, conflicts can arise, especially in situations where the psychologist is paid by management to work with individual athletes on a team. Following an injury, for example, management might expect a player to play in an important game, while the player may feel that it is in his/her best interest to delay return until the injury has completely healed. If the psychologist is expected to play a role in the early return of the athlete in such a situation, then it is essential for the psychologist to communicate his or her responsibilities clearly to everyone involved. My own approach is to communicate to all concerned that my first allegiance is to the athlete, and that I will not communicate information to management or the coach concerning an athlete without obtaining that athlete's prior permission to do so.

From an ethical perspective, goals must be consistent with the basic rights of the athlete to confidentiality, dignity, and humane care, and must also be consistent with the short-term and long-term health and well-being of the athlete. There is evidence, for example, that eating disorders are commonplace among gymnasts, long-distance runners, and ballet dancers (Johns, 1993; Kerr, Burman, & De Souza, 2006). If a sport psychologist is approached by athletes or over-zealous coaches, managers, or parents with the request that the psychologist help the athlete to pursue target behaviors that put the athlete at risk (even though they may be accepted in the sport), then the psychologist must take the ethical high ground. As expressed by Hughes and Coakley (1991), psychologists must help athletes understand the consequences of their decision to accept or reject training regimens as part of the sport ethic, rather than buying into such training regimes and developing into "high tech pimps" (p. 323).

When selecting target behaviors, psychologists must be wary of an overemphasis on winning, especially when working with youth athletes. No matter what some coaches of kids say about winning, their behavior implies a "win-at-all costs" philosophy. In the heat of the battle, such coaches are likely to use only the best players, despite prior statements that everyone will get a chance to play; scream at officials and referees, despite prior suggestions that such behavior is unsportsmanlike; or play an injured "star" player, even though aggravating the injury may have severe long-term consequences for the youngster. With such coaches, you might find youngsters in tears while being screamed at by the coach, or youngsters whose self-image is destroyed at the ripe old age of 10 years because they were cut from the team or never got to play in the "big" game. Some parents also place far too much emphasis on winning. Some parents force their children to live, sleep, eat, and drink a particular sport, even though the child would rather do other things. Some parents have been known to "encourage" a son to repeat one of the early grades so that he'll be bigger and stronger for high school football, presumably with images of an illustrious college career and a lucrative professional contract somewhere in the future. At competitions involving their kids, parents of opposing teams have been known to scream obscenities at each other across the playing field or rink, or heap abuse on and sometimes punch out referees because a call went against their child. Most people would agree that such examples represent the worst in youth sports. To counteract a win-at-all-costs philosophy, the psychologist should: a) encourage everyone to focus on individual and team development and improvement, independent of the outcome of a contest; b) encourage young athletes to pursue performance goals that can be achieved regardless of the score at the end of the game; and c) help young athletes to feel a sense of pride for playing up to their potential. After all, in athletic contests, many participants will play up to their potential and still lose. Excellent discussions of these issues can be found in Ginsburg, Durant, and Baltzell (2006), and Smoll and Cumming (2006).

Selection of Treatment

Sport psychologists should use the most effective, empirically validated methods with the least discomfort and least negative side-effects. When helping coaches to improve the performance of young athletes, as described in earlier chapters, the emphasis should be on positive reinforcement strategies rather than techniques involving aversive control. When treatment focuses on the development of a competition plan (see Chapter 16), the emphasis should be on self-management strategies (Rushall, 1992). Just before and during the competition, it is the athlete who must get ready to perform and compete to the best of his or her ability.

A recommended strategy to help ensure ethical behavior by the sport psychologist in private practice is the inclusion of a **treatment contract-** a written agreement between the athlete and the sport psychology consultant that indicates how the consultant will help the athlete achieve certain behavioral goals, and the contingencies for reumeration that may be forthcoming to the consultant. The contract should identify: the aim of the project; the services to be provided by the consultant; the nature of the treatment strategies; the homework expectations for the athlete; the form of performance monitoring to be used and who will have access to the data; the form of progress reports provided by the consultant, and who will have access to them; and guidelines for remuneration to be paid to the consultant. Procedural matters should also be clarified, such as when and where you can call the athlete and the coach, and vice-versa. When the agreement is signed, both the client and the psychologist have secured basic protections of their rights. Use of a treatment contract also increases the likelihood of a client being able to give *informed consent*, that is, consent by the athlete for the psychologist to proceed with a program based on the athlete's knowledge of the procedures to be used and their probable effects.

Recognizing Potential Boundary Issues

You must be sensitive to potential boundary issues, and be prepared to deal with them in an up-front fashion. If you are trained as a performance enhancement specialist and not as a counsellor or clinician, and if serious clinical issues arise, then of course you must refer to a counsellor, clinical psychologist, or psychiatrist. Even if you were trained as a counsellor or clinician as well as a performance enhancement specialist, if you are to be effective in providing service as a sport psychology consultant, then I believe that it is necessary to keep those roles separate. When you are working with an athlete as a performance enhancement specialist, and serious clinical or counselling issues arise, I recommend that you refer the athlete to someone else for the latter problems.

Another boundary issue can arise if you have played a particular sport and you know a great deal about it. You must remember that you are providing a sport psychology service, and not a coaching service. Interviews with Canadian Olympic athletes indicated that some sport psychology consultants lost their service contract because they could not refrain from giving advice in areas traditionally covered by the coach (Orlick & Partington, 1987).

It is also important for you to examine any biases and assumptions that you may have concerning athletes from racially, culturally, and ethnically diverse backgrounds. Working with diverse athletes may present unique challenges, and understanding any prejudgements that you might have is important in providing good service for these athletes. While it is beyond the scope of this book to pursue this topic, excellent discussion of relevant boundary issues can be found in Cox (2007), Hanrahan (2005), Martens and Mobley (2005), Parham (2005), and Barber & Krane (2005).

Record Keeping and Ongoing Evaluation

An important component of ensuring ethical treatment of clients is the maintenance of accurate data throughout a program. This includes a thorough behavioral assessment before the intervention is developed, ongoing monitoring of target behaviors as well as possible side-effects, and appropriate follow-up evaluation after the treatment is concluded. As described in Chapter 1, an important characteristic of behavioral sport psychology consulting is its strong emphasis on defining problems in terms of behavior that can be measured in some way, and using changes in the behavioral measure of the problem as the best indicator of the extent to which the problem is being helped. Providing frequent opportunities throughout a program for a client to discuss with the sport psychologist the data that assesses progress is an important accountability mechanism. Of course, confidentiality with respect to such data must be respected at all times.

Monitoring Consumer Satisfaction

Let's suppose you've completed a project with an athlete. Was it successful? One way of answering this question is to look at objective measures of behavioral improvement. Such measures have been discussed repeatedly throughout this book, and Chapter 17 describes single-subject research designs to assess the extent to which objective measures of improvement in performance were due to your interventions. A second aspect of program evaluation consists of subjective judgements by clients of the practical value of your program. As indicated in Chapter 1, these evaluations are referred to as judgements of **social validity**. In general, social validation helps to ensure that practitioners do the best job that they can in helping consumers of their service function to the best of their ability. In sport psychology, social validity evaluations will help you to become more effective in helping athletes, which, in turn, is likely to enhance your consulting practice.

Although several strategies might be followed to socially validate your service (Kazdin, 1977; Wolf, 1978), the most common approach involves a questionnaire evaluation in which athletes or other significant individuals are asked about their satisfaction with the procedures that were used, the results that were obtained, and personal characteristics of the sport psychologist. Partington and Orlick (1987) have developed the Sport Psychology Consultant Evaluation Form to assess consumers' reactions to consultant characteristics, as well as their view of the overall effectiveness of the service (see Table 18-1). However, their form does not provide an evaluation of treatment components. An alternate approach that can provide useful feedback from athletes is to design your own personalized form to suit the characteristics and service for a particular sport, rather than to attempt to use a standardized form across all sports. Table 18-2 shows an evaluation form that was used by the Manitoba Section of the Canadian Figure Skating Association to evaluate the sport psychology service that I provided for them (Martin & Toogood, 1997). Table 18-3 describes an evaluation form that I prepared for the Assistant General Manager of a professional hockey team to evaluate a service that I provided for four of the players during a season.

Behavior analysis has great potential for enhancing the performance and satisfaction of athletes and others associated with sports. Ongoing objective measures of sport performances provide the yardstick by which we must judge the effectiveness of our interventions. Subjective performance evaluations by consumers of our service will tell us whether or not athletes, coaches, and others are happy with our efforts and our effects.

Study Questions

1. In general, what are the defining features of a profession?

2. Name three sport psychology journals.

3. What do the letters "AASP" stand for? To what is AASP dedicated as an association?

4. Briefly, what is a code of ethics?

5. List the names of the six ethical principles of sport psychologists adopted by AAASP (now AASP).

6.   According to the author, what should be included in the training for someone to be a behavioral sport psychology consultant?

7.   What are the legal constraints on the use of the title "psychologist"?

8.   List four strategies that a sport psychologist could follow to establish credibility and support with clients during initial meetings (any four of the seven that were listed).

9.   What is the KISS principle recommended by Ken Ravizza?

10. From an ethical perspective, by what yardsticks should a sport psychologist judge goals that he/she might set for athletes?

11. What types of behaviors are likely to imply that a "win-at-all-costs" philosophy is held by: a) coaches of kids? b) the kids' parents?

12. List three strategies that a sport psychologist might follow to counteract a "win at all costs" philosophy held by some coaches and parents?

13. What is a treatment contract?

14. What is meant by informed consent in the context of sport psychology consulting?

15. Describe two boundary issues that are likely to be faced by a sport psychologist.

16. What is an important accountability mechanism for sport psychology consultants?

17. List three areas that might be assessed in a questionnaire evaluation of consumer satisfaction.

Table 18-2

The Sport Psychology Consultant Evaluation Form

Name _____   Consultant's Name

Sport _____   _____

Please rate your sport psychology consultant on each of the following characteristics by using a number from 0 to 10 as seen on the scale below.

Not at all										Yes definitely
0	1	2	3	4	5	6	7	8	9	10

1. Consultant characteristics   Ratings

Had useful knowledge about mental training that seemed to apply directly to my sport.   _____

Seemed willing to provide an individual mental training program based on my input and needs.   _____

Seemed open, flexible, and ready to collaborate/cooperate with me.   _____

Had a positive, constructive attitude.   _____

Proved to be trustworthy.   _____

Was easy for me to relate to (e.g., I felt comfortable and that he/she understood me).   _____

Fitted in with others connected with the team.   _____

Tried to help me draw upon my strengths (e.g., the things that already worked for me) in order to make my best performance even better and more consistent).   _____

Tried to help me overcome possible problems, or weaknesses, in order to make my best performance even better and more consistent.   _____

Provided clear, practical, concrete strategies for me to try out in an attempt to solve problems, or improve the level and consistency of my performance.   _____

2. How effective was this consultant?

	hindered/ interfered									helped a lot
effect on you:	-5	-4	-3	-2	-1	0	+1	+2	+3	+4	+5
effect on team:	-5	-4	-3	-2	-1	0	+1	+2	+3	+4	+5

3. Do you have any recommendations to improve the quality or effectiveness of the sport psychology consultation service being offered (write suggestions on back of this evaluation sheet)?

Reprinted with permission from Partington & Orlick (1987).

Table 18-3

Evaluation of a Sport Psychology Service Provided for Figure Skaters

Dear Skater:
Please complete this questionnaire without discussing it with others (e.g., coaches, athletes, parents etc.). We are interested in how you feel. Your answers will be kept confidential and will not affect your position with the team in any way.

A. The first thing we would like to find out is to what extent you found the sport psychology service helpful. For the following questions, circle the number on the right that best applies to you.	
Did the sport psychology service help you to...	Don't Know No Somewhat Yes
1. Get more out of practices?	____ 1 2 3 4 5
2. Improve your confidence at competitions?	____ 1 2 3 4 5
3. Improve your concentration at competitions?	____ 1 2 3 4 5
4. Stay relaxed and not get too nervous at competitions?	____ 1 2 3 4 5
5. Improve your overall skating at competitions?	____ 1 2 3 4 5

B. Concerning the individual components of the program, please rate the following on the two scales on the right.	Did you use this component?	Did you feel that this component was helpful?
i) At Practices	Don't Know No A Few times A lot	Don't Know No To Some Extent Yes
1. Talking to Dr. Martin at practices	____ 1 2 3 4 5	____ 1 2 3 4 5
2. Goal setting for practices	____ 1 2 3 4 5	____ 1 2 3 4 5
3. Recording % landed on practice run-throughs	____ 1 2 3 4 5	____ 1 2 3 4 5

Table 18-3 (cont'd)

4. Doing serious simulations at practices	____ 1 2 3 4 5	____ 1 2 3 4 5
5. Using self-talk at practices to stay more relaxed, not worry about other skaters, not get mad if having a bad practice etc.	____ 1 2 3 4 5	____ 1 2 3 4 5
6. Using imagery at practices to improve jumps	____ 1 2 3 4 5	____ 1 2 3 4 5
ii) At practices and at competitions 1. Doing off-ice walkouts or mental rehearsals of programs	____ 1 2 3 4 5	____ 1 2 3 4 5
2. Using key words for elements	____ 1 2 3 4 5	____ 1 2 3 4 5
3. Practicing self talk for programs in between elements	____ 1 2 3 4 5	____ 1 2 3 4 5
iii) At competitions 1. Using relaxation tape for competitions	____ 1 2 3 4 5	____ 1 2 3 4 5
2. Using positive self talk tape for competitions	____ 1 2 3 4 5	____ 1 2 3 4 5
3. Talking to Dr. Martin at competitions	____ 1 2 3 4 5	____ 1 2 3 4 5
4. Using precompetition plan for last half-hour before 6 minute warmup	____ 1 2 3 4 5	____ 1 2 3 4 5
5. Using precompetition plan for waiting period after 6 minute warmup	____ 1 2 3 4 5	____ 1 2 3 4 5
6. Completing postcompetition evaluations	____ 1 2 3 4 5	____ 1 2 3 4 5

Table 18-3 (cont'd)

D. Regarding Dr. Martin's characteristics: Did Dr. Martin...	Don't Know	No	To Some Extent		Yes
1. Have useful knowledge about mental preparation strategies?	____	1 2	3	4	5
2. Seem willing to provide an individual program based on your input and needs?	____	1 2	3	4	5
3. Seem easy for you to relate to?	____	1 2	3	4	5
4. Provide clear and practical ways to help improve your skating?	____	1 2	3	4	5
5. Treat all the skaters fairly?	____	1 2	3	4	5
6. Help you to overcome weaknesses in order to make your performance even more consistent?	____	1 2	3	4	5
7. Prove to be trustworthy and treat your concerns confidentially?	____	1 2	3	4	5
8. Help you to draw upon your strengths in order to make your performance more consistent?	____	1 2	3	4	5
9. Seem open, flexible, and willing to cooperate with you?	____	1 2	3	4	5
10. Have a positive and constructive attitude?	____	1 2	3	4	5

E. Regarding the sport psychology program: Would you...	Don't Know	No	Somewhat		Yes
1. Recommend a sport psychology program for next year?	____	1 2	3	4	5
2. Recommend Dr. Martin for next year?	____	1 2	3	4	5
3. Recommend keeping the sport psychology program but with a different sport psychologist?	____	1 2	3	4	5

F. Are there any additional questions or comments that you would like to make regarding the sport psychology program?

_____

_____

_____

_____

_____

Table 18-4
Evaluation of Sport Psychology Service
Provided for Several Members of a Professional Hockey Team

Please indicate your honest opinion of the sport psychology service that you received from Garry Martin by marking the number that best indicates how you feel about the following questions, or by checking the right-hand column for items that don't apply.

Concerning the components of the sport psych program	Definitely Not Helpful 1 2	A Little Helpful 3 4	Very 5 Helpful 6 7	Didn't Really Use It ___
1. The sport psychology manual that was given to me was:	1 2	3 4	5 6 7	___
2. The sessions with Garry were:	1 2	3 4	5 6 7	___
3. The telephone contacts with Garry to review games and strategies were:	1 2	3 4	5 6 7	___
4. The mental preparation tape that Garry prepared was:	1 2	3 4	5 6 7	___
5. The relaxation tape that Garry prepared was:	1 2	3 4	5 6 7	___
6. The deep center breathing strategy was:	1 2	3 4	5 6 7	___
7. The mood words were:	1 2	3 4	5 6 7	___
8. The strategy of relax, regroup, refocus in between shifts was:	1 2	3 4	5 6 7	___
9. Mentally rehearsing my skills checklist (or positive self-talk) before games was:	1 2	3 4	5 6 7	___
10. Mentally rehearsing my skills checklist (or positive self-talk) in between shifts was:	1 2	3 4	5 6 7	___
11. Mentally rehearsing my skills checklist (or positive self-talk) in between periods was:	1 2	3 4	5 6 7	___
12. Scoring my psychological factors after every game was:	1 2	3 4	5 6 7	___
13. Scoring my on-ice skills after every game was:	1 2	3 4	5 6 7	___

(Cont'd)

Table 18-4 (cont'd)

Concerning Garry's Personal Qualities	Definitely Not Helpful 1 2	A Little Helpful 3 4	Very Helpful 5 6 7	Didn't Really Use It ___
14. He was very approachable, easy to relate to.	1 2	3 4	5 6 7	___
15. He was very knowledgeable about sport psychology.	1 2	3 4	5 6 7	___
16. He explained sport psych in a way that made it easy to understand.	1 2	3 4	5 6 7	___
17. He was able to adapt the mental prep program to meet my personal needs.	1 2	3 4	5 6 7	___
18. He was very accessible.	1 2	3 4	5 6 7	___
19. He proved to be trustworthy.	1 2	3 4	5 6 7	___

Concerning the Overall Effects of the Sport Psych Program

20. It helped my concentration during game.	1 2	3 4	5 6 7	___
21. It helped my self-confidence before games.	1 2	3 4	5 6 7	___
22. It helped my self-confidence during games.	1 2	3 4	5 6 7	___
23. It helped me to play more consistently.	1 2	3 4	5 6 7	___
24. It improved my overall level of play.	1 2	3 4	5 6 7	___

Concerning a sport psychology service in the future

1. Would you recommend that Garry Martin continue as our sport psychologist?	Yes	No	No Opinion
2. Would you recommend that we seek the services of a different sport psychologist?	Yes	No	No Opinion
3. Would you recommend that we not have a sport psychology service?	Yes	No	No Opinion

Any Comments?

_____
_____
_____

References

Abrams, N. (2010). *Anger management in sport: Understanding and controlling violence in athletes.* Champagne, IL: Human Kinetics.

Allen, G. J. (1973). Case study: Implementation of behavior modification techniques in summer camp settings. *Behavior Therapy, 4,* 570-575.

Allen, K. D. (1998). The use of an enhanced simplified habit-reversal procedure to reduce disruptive outbursts during athletic performance. *Journal of Applied Behavior Analysis, 31,* 49-492.

Allison, M. G., & Ayllon, T. (1980). Behavioral coaching in the development of skills in football, gymnastics, and tennis. *Journal of Applied Behavior Analysis, 13,* 297-314.

Andersen, G., & Kirkpatrick, M. A. (2002). Variable effects of a behavioral treatment package on the performance of inline roller speedskaters. *Journal of Applied Behavior Analysis, 35,* 195-198.

Anshel, M. H., & Marisi, D. Q. (1978). Effect of music and rhythm on physical performance. *The Research Quarterly, 49,* 109-113.

Baldwin, J. D., & Baldwin, J. I. (2001). *Behavior principles in everyday life*, 4th ed. Englewood Cliffs, NJ: Prentice-Hall.

Bandura, A. (1986). *Social foundations of thought and action: A social-cognitive theory.* Englewood Cliffs, NJ: Prentice-Hall.

Barber, H. & Krane, V. (2005). The elephant in the locker room: Opening the dialogue about sexual orientation on women's sport teams. In M. B. Andersen (Ed.), *Sport Psychology in Practice* (pp. 265-286). Champagne, IL: Human Kinetics.

Beck, A. T. (1991). Cognitive therapy: A thirty-year retrospective. *American Psychologist, 46,* 368-375.

Beck, A. T., Emery, G., & Greenberg, R. L. (1985). *Anxiety disorders and phobias: A cognitive perspective.* New York: Basic Books.

Bell, J. J. & Hardy, J. (2009). Effects of attentional focus on skilled performance in golf. *Journal of Applied Sport Psychology, 21,* 163-177.

Bell, K. F. (1983). *Championship thinking: The athlete's guide to winning performance in all sports.* Englewood Cliffs, NJ: Prentice-Hall.

Berkowitz, L. (1990). On the formation and regulation of anger and aggression: A cognitive-neoassociationistic analysis. *American Psychologist, 45,* 494-503.

Billingsley, F., White, O. R., & Munson, R. (1980). Procedural reliability: A rationale and an example. *Behavioral Assessment, 2,* 229-241.

Botterill, C. (1988). *Visualization: What you see is what you get.* A videotape produced by the Coaching Association of Canada, 333 River Road, Ottawa, ON K1L 8H9.

Boyer, E., Miltenberger, R. G., Batsche, C., & Fogel, V. (2009). Video modeling by experts with video feedback to enhance gymnastic skills. *Journal of Applied Behavior Analysis, 42,* 855-860.

Braam, C., & Malott, R. W. (1990). "I'll do it when the snow melts": The effects of deadlines and delay outcomes on rule-governed behavior in preschool children. *Analysis of Verbal Behavior, 8,* 67-76.

Brobst, B., & Ward, P. (2002). Effects of public posting, goal setting, and oral feedback on the skills of female soccer players. *Journal of Applied Behavior Analysis, 35,* 247-257.

Brown, J. (2011). Cognitive-behavioral strategies. In J. K. Luiselli & D. D. Reed (Eds.) *Behavioral sport psychology: Evidenced-based approaches to performance enhancement.* New York: Springer.

Brunelle, J. P., Janelle, C. M., & Tennant, L. K. (1999). Controlling competitive anger among male soccer players. *Journal of Applied Sport Psychology, 11,* 283-297.

Bryan, A. (1987). Single-subject designs for evaluation of sport psychology interventions. *The Sport Psychologist, 1,* 283-292.

Burke, K. L., Sachs, M. L., & Gomer, S. (Eds). (2008). *Directory of graduate programs in applied sport psychology,* 8th ed. Morgantown, WV: Fitness Information Technology Inc.

Butler, R. J., & Hardy, L. (1992). The performance profile: Theory and application. *The Sport Psychologist, 6,* 253-264.

Butler, R. J., Smith, M., & Irwin, I. (1993). The performance profile in practice. *Journal of Applied Sport Psychology, 5,* 48-63.

Buzas, H. P., & Ayllon, T. (1981). Differential reinforcement in coaching skills. *Behavior Modification, 5,* 372-385.

Cameron, J., Banko, K. M., & Pearce, W. D. (2001). Pervasive negative effects of rewards on intrinsic motivation: The myth continues. *The Behavior Analyst, 24,* 1-44.

Cohn, P. J., Rotella, R. J., & Lloyd, J. W. (1990). Effects of a cognitive behavioral intervention on the preshot routine and performance in golf. *The Sport Psychologist, 4,* 33-47.

Connaughton, D., Hanton, S., & Jones, G. (2010). The development and maintenance of mental toughness in the world's best performers. *The Sport Psychologist, 24,* 168-193.

Connelly, D. (1988). Increasing intensity of play of nonassertive athletes. *The Sport Psychologist, 2,* 255-265.

Cover-Jones, M. (1924). The elimination of children's fears. *Journal of Experimental Psychology, 7,* 383-390.

Cox, R. H. (2007). *Sport psychology: Concepts and applications*, 6th ed. New York: McGraw-Hill.

Cracklen, C., & Martin, G. L. (1983). Earning fun with correct techniques. *Swimming Technique, 20,* 29-32.

Crews, D. J., & Boutcher, S. H. (1986). An exploratory observational behavior analysis of professional golfers during competition. *Journal of Sport Behavior, 9,* 51-58.

Critchfield, T. S., & Vargas E. A. (1991). Self-recording, instructions, and public graphing: Effects on swimming in the absence of coach verbal interaction. *Behavior Modification, 15,* 95-112.

Deci, E. L. (1975). *Intrinsic motivation.* New York: Plenum Press.

Deci, E. L., Koestner, R. & Ryan, R. M. (1999). A meta-analytic review of experiments examining the effects of extrinsic rewards on intrinsic motivation. *Psychological Bulletin, 125,* 627-668.

Deci, E. L., & Ryan, R. M. (1985). *Intrinsic motivation and self-determination in human behavior.* New York: Plenum.

Deffenbacher, J. L., Demm, P. M., & Brandon, A. D. (1986). High general anger: Correlates and treatment. *Behavior Research and Therapy, 24,* 481-489.

Donohue, B., Dickens, Y. L., & Del Vecchio III, P. D. (2011). Cognitive assessment in behavioral sport psychology. In J. K. Luiselli & D. D. Reed (Eds.), *Behavioral sport psychology: Evidenced-based approaches to performance enhancement.* New York: Springer.

Doyle, J., & Parfitt, G. (1997). Performance profiling and construct validity. *The Sport Psychologist, 11,* 411-425.

Ekman, P. (1993). Facial expression and emotion. *American Psychologist, 48,* 384-392.

Ericsson, K. A., Charness, N., Feltovich, P. J., & Hoffman, R. R. (Eds.) (2006). *The Cambridge Handbook of expertise and expert performance.* New York: Cambridge University Press.

Ericsson, K. A., Kramp, R. T., & Tesch-Romer, C. (1993). The role of deliberate practice in the acquisition of expert performance. *Psychological Review, 100,* 363-406.

Fitterling, J. M., & Ayllon, T. (1983). Behavioral coaching in classical ballet: Enhancing skill development. *Behavior Modification, 7,* 345-368.

Flora, S. R. (1990). Undermining intrinsic interest from the standpoint of a behaviorist. *The Psychological Record, 40,* 323-346.

Flora, S. R., & Flora, D. B. (1999). Effects of extrinsic reinforcement for reading during childhood on reported reading habits of college students. *The Psychological Record, 49,* 3-14.

Gallimore, R., & Tharpe, R. (2004). What a coach can teach a teacher, 1975-2004: Reflections and reanalysis of John Wooden's teaching practices. *The Sport Psychologist, 18,* 119-137.

Galvan, Z. J., & Ward, P. (1998). Effects of public posting on inappropriate on-court behaviors by collegiate tennis players. *The Sport Psychologist, 12,* 419-426.

Garza, D. L., & Feltz, D. L. (1998). Effects of selected mental practice on performance, self-efficacy, and competition confidence of figure skaters. *The Sport Psychologist, 12,* 1-15.

Gauron, E. F. (1984). *Mental training for peak performance.* Lansing, NY: Sport Science Associates.

Gee, C. J. (2011). Aggression in competitive sports: Using direct observation to evaluate incidents and prevention-focused intervention. In J. K. Luiselli & D. D. Reed (Eds.), *Behavioral sport psychology: Evidenced-based approaches to performance enhancement.* New York: Springer.

Ginsberg, R. D., Durant, S., & Baltzell, A. (2006). *Who's game is it anyway?* Boston: Haughton-Mifflin.

Goldberg, A. S. (1998). *Sports slump busting.* Champagne, IL: Human Kinetics.

Gould, D. (2010). Goal-setting for peak performance. In J. M. Williams (Ed.), *Applied sport psychology: Personal growth to peak performance,* 6th ed. (pp. 211-220). New York: McGraw-Hill.

Gould, D., & Damarjian, N. (1996). Imagery training for peak performance. In J. L. Van Raalte & B. W. Brewer (Eds.), *Exploring sport and exercise psychology* (pp. 25-50). Washington, DC: American Psychological Association.

Gould, D., Eklund, R. C., & Jackson, S. A. (1992). 1988 U.S. Olympic wrestling excellence: I mental preparation, precompetitive cognition, and affect. *The Sport Psychologist, 6, 358-*

382.

Greenspan, M. J., & Feltz, D. L. (1989). Psychological interventions with athletes in competition situations: A review. *The Sport Psychologist, 3,* 219-236.

Greenspoon, J. (1951). *The effect of verbal and nonverbal stimuli on the frequency of numbers of two verbal response classes.* Unpublished Ph.D. dissertation, Indiana University.

Gucciardi, D. F., & Gordon, S. (2009). Revisiting the performance profile technique: Theoretical underpinnings and application. *The Sport Psychologist, 23,* 93-117.

Gucciardi, D. F., & Gordon, S., & Dimmock, J. A. (2009a). Evaluation of a mental toughness training program for youth-aged Australian footballers: I. A quantitative analysis. *Journal of Applied Sport Psychology, 21,* 307-323.

Guicciardi, D. F., & Gordon, S., & Dimmock, J. A. (2009b). Evaluation of a mental toughness training program for your-aged Australian footballers: II. A quantitative analysis. *Journal of Applied Sport Psychology, 21,* 324-339.

Haddad, K., & Tremayne, P. (2009). The effects of centering on the free-throw shooting performance of young athletes. *The Sport Psychologist, 23,* 118-136.

Hains, A. H., & Baer, D. M. (1989). Interaction effects in multi-element designs: Inevitable, desirable, and ignorable. *Journal of Applied Behavior Analysis, 22,* 57-69.

Hall, C., Schmidt, D., Durand, M., & Burcholz, E. (1994). Imagery and motor skills acquisition. In A. A. Sheikh, & E. R. Korn (Eds.), *Imagery in sports and physical education* (pp. 121-134). Amityville, NY: Baywood.

Hall, C. R., & Rogers, W. M. (1989). Enhancing coaching effectiveness in figure skating through a mental skills training program. *The Sport Psychologist, 3,* 142-154.

Halliwell, W. (1990). Providing sport psychology consulting services in professional hockey. *The Sport Psychologist, 4,* 369-377.

Hamilton, R. A., Scott, D., & MacDougall, M. P. (2007). Assessing the effectiveness of self-talk interventions on endurance performance. *Journal of Applied Sport Psychology, 19,* 226-239.

Hamilton, S. A., & Fremouw, W. J. (1985). Cognitive behavioral training for college basketball free-throw performance. *Cognitive Therapy and Research, 9,* 479-483.

Hanin, Y., Korjus, T., Jouste, T., & Baxter, P. (2002). Rapid technique correction using old way/new way: Two case studies with Olympic athletes. *The Sport Psychologist, 16,* 2002.

Hanrahan, S. (2005). Able athletes with disabilities: Issues and group work. In M.B. Andersen

(Ed.), *Sport psychology in practice* (pp. 223-248). Champagne, IL: Human Kinetics.

Hardy, J., Gammage, K., & Hall, C. (2001). A descriptive study of athlete self-talk. *The Sport Psychologist, 15,* 306-318.

Harris, B. (1979). What happened to Little Albert? *American Psychologist, 34,* 151-160.

Hastie, P. A. (1999). An instrument for recording coaches' comments and instructions during time-outs. *Journal of Sport Behavior, 14,* 467-478.

Hatzigeorgiadis, A., Theodorakis, Y., & Zourbanos, N. (2004). Self-talk in the swimming pool: The effects of self-talk on thought content and performance on water polo tasks, *Journal of Applied Sport Psychology, 16,* 138-150.

Hayes, S. C. (Ed.) (1989). *Rule-governed behavior: Cognition, contingencies, and instructional control.* New York: Plenum Press.

Hayes, S. C., Rosenfarb, I., Wulfert, E., Munt, E. D., Korn, Z., & Zettle, R. D. (1985). Self-reinforcement effects: An artifact of social standard setting. *Journal of Applied Behavior Analysis, 18,* 201-214.

Hazen, A., Johnstone, C., Martin, G. L., & Srikameswaran, S. (1990). A videotaping feedback package for improving skills of youth competitive swimmers. *The Sport Psychologist, 4,* 213-227.

Heward, W. L. (1978). Operant conditioning of a .300 hitter? The effects of reinforcement on the offensive efficiency of a barnstorming baseball team. *Behavior Modification, 2,* 25-40.

Hildebrand, R. G., Martin, G. L., Furer, P., & Hazen, A. (1990). A recruitment of praise package to increase productivity levels of developmentally handicapped workers. *Behavior Modification, 14,* 97-113.

Hill, K. L., & Borden, F. (1995). The effects of attention cueing scripts on competitive bowling performance. *International Journal of Sport Psychology, 26,* 503-512.

Hrycaiko, D., & Martin, G. L. (1996). Applied research with single-subject designs: Why so few? *Journal of Applied Sport Psychology, 8,* 183-199.

Hume, K. M., & Crossman, J. (1992). Musical reinforcement of practice behaviors among competitive swimmers, *Journal of Applied Behavior Analysis, 25,* 665-670.

Hume, K. M., Martin, G. L., Gonzalez, P., Cracklen, C., & Genthon, S. (1985). A self-monitoring feedback package for improving freestyle figure skating performance. *Journal of Sport Psychology, 7,* 333-345.

Hughes, R., & Coakley, J. J. (1991). Positive deviance among athletes: The implications of overconformity to the sport ethic. *Sociology of Sport Journal, 8,* 307-325.

Ives, J. C., Straub, W. F., & Shelby, G. A. (2000). Enhancing athletic performance using digital video in consulting. *Journal of Applied Sport Psychology, 14,* 237-245.

Izard, C. E. (1991). *The psychology of emotions.* New York: Plenum Press.

Jackson, S. A., & Roberts, G. C. (1992). Positive performance states of athletes: Toward a conceptual understanding of peak performance. *The Sport Psychologist, 6,* 156-171.

Jacobson, E. (1938). *Progressive relaxation.* Chicago: University of Chicago Press.

Johns, D. P. (1993). Nutritional need or athletic overconformity: Ethical implications for the sport psychologist. *The Sport Psychologist, 7,* 191-203.

Johnson, J. J. M., Hrycaiko, D. W., Johnson, G. V., & Halas, J. M. (2004). Self-talk and female youth soccer performance, *The Sport Psychologist, 18,* 44-59.

Johnston-O'Connor, E. J., & Kirschenbaum, D. S. (1986). Something succeeds like success: Positive self-monitoring in golf. *Cognitive Therapy and Research, 10,* 123-136.

Jones, G. (1993). The role of performance profiling in cognitive behavioral intereventions in sport. *The Sport Psychologist, 7,* 160-172.

Jones, G., Hanton, S., & Connaughton, D. (2007). A framework of mental toughness in the world's best performers. *The Sport Psychologist, 21,* 243-264.

Josephson, W. L. (1987). Television violence and children's aggression: Testing the priming, social script, and disinhibition predictions. *Journal of Personality and Social Psychology, 53,* 882-890.

Kau, M. L., & Fischer, J. (1974). Self-modification of exercise behavior. *Journal of Behavior Therapy and Experimental Psychiatry, 5,* 213-214.

Kazdin, A. E. (1977). Assessing the clinical or applied importance of behavior change through social validation. *Behavior Modification, 1,* 427-451.

Kazdin, A. E. (1984). Statistical analyses for single-case experimental designs. In D. H. Barlow, & M. Hersen (Eds.), *Single-case experimental designs: Strategies for studying behavior change.* Oxford: Pergamon Press.

Kendall, G., Hrycaiko, D., Martin, G. L., & Kendall, T. (1990). The effects of an imagery rehearsal, relaxation, and self-talk package on basketball game performance. *Journal of Sport and Exercise Psychology, 12,* 157-166.

Kenrick, D. T., & MacFarlane, S. W. (1986). Ambient temperature and horn-honking: A field study of the heat/aggression relationship. *Environment and Behavior, 18,* 179-191.

Kerr, G., Burman, E., & De Souza, M. J. (2006). Disorded eating in womens' gymnastics: Perspectives of athletes, coaches, parents, and judges, *Journal of Applied Sport Psychology, 18,* 28-43.

Kerr, J. H. (1999). The role of aggression and violence in sport: A rejoinder to the IISP position stand. *The Sport Psychologist, 13*, 83-88.

Kerr, J. H. (2002). Issues in aggression and violence in sport: The IISP position stand revisited. *The Sport Psychologist, 16*, 68-78.

Kirschenbaum, D. S., Ordman, A. M., Tomarken, A. J., & Holtzbauer, R. (1982). Effects of differential self-monitoring and level of mastery of sports performance: Brain power bowling. *Cognitive Therapy and Research, 6,* 335-342.

Kirschenbaum, D. S., Owens, D., & O'Connor, E. A. (1998). Smart golf: Preliminary evaluation of a simple, yet comprehensive, approach to improving and scoring the mental game. *The Sport Psychologist, 12*, 271-282.

Kladopoulos, C. N., & McComas, J. J. (2001). The effects of form training on foul-shooting performance in members of a women's college basketball team. *Journal of Applied Behavior Analysis, 34*, 329-332.

Kodzhaspirov, Y. G., Zaitsev, Y. M., & Kosarev, S. M. (1988). The application of functional music in the training sessions of weight lifters. *Soviet Sports Review, 23,* 39-42.

Kohn, A. (1993). *Punished by rewards: The trouble with gold stars, incentive plans, A's, praise, and other bribes.* New York: Houghton Mifflin.

Komaki, J., & Barnett, F. T. (1977). A behavioral approach to coaching football: Improving the play execution of the offensive backfield on a youth football team. *Journal of Applied Behavior Analysis, 7,* 199-206.

Koop, S., & Martin, G. L. (1983). A coaching strategy to reduce swimming stroke errors with beginning age-group swimmers. *Journal of Applied Behavior Analysis, 16,* 447-460.

Krane, V., & Williams, J. M. (2010). Psychological characteristics of peak performance. In J. M. Williams (Ed.), *Applied sport psychology: Personal growth the peak performance,* 6th ed. (pp. 169-188). New York: McGraw Hill.

Landers, D. M., & Arent, S. M. (2010). Arousal-performance relationships. In J. M. Williams (Ed.), *Applied sport psychology: Personal growth the peak performance,* 6th ed. (pp. 221-246). New York: McGraw Hill.

Landin, D., & Hebert, E. P. (1999). The influence of self-talk on the performance of skilled female tennis players. *Journal of Applied Psychology, 11,* 163-282.

Landin, D. K., & MacDonald, G. (1990). Improving the overheads of collegiate tennis players. *Journal of Applied Research in Coaching and Athletics, 5,* 85-90.

Langer, E. J., Janis, I. L., & Wolfer, J. A. (1975). Reduction of psychological stress in surgical patients. *Journal of Experimental Social Psychology, 11,* 155-165.

Laraway, S., Snycerski, S., Michael, J., & Poling, A. (2003). Motivating operations and terms to describe them: Some further refinements, *Journal of Applied Behavior Analysis, 36,* 407-414.

Lattal, K. A., & Metzger, B. (1994). Response acquisition by Siamese fighting fish with delayed visual reinforcement. *Journal of the Experimental Analysis of Behavior, 61,* 35-44.

Leslie-Toogood, S. A., & Martin, G. L. (2003). Do coaches know the mental skills of their athletes? Assessments from volleyball and track, *Journal of Sport Behavior, 26,* 56-68.

Lines, J. B., Schwartzman, L., Tkachuk, G. A., Leslie-Toogood, S. A., & Martin, G. L. (1999). Behavioral assessment in sport psychology consulting: Applications to swimming and basketball. *Journal of Sport Behavior, 22,* 558-569.

Locke, E. A., & Latham, G. P. (2002). Building a practically useful theory of goal setting and task motivation: A 35-year odyssey. *American Psychologist, 57,* 705-717.

Luiselli, J. K. (2011). Single-case evaluation of behavioral coaching interventions. In J. K. Luiselli & D. D. Reed (Eds.), *Behavioral sport psychology: Evidenced-based approaches to performance enhancement.* New York: Springer.

Madsen, C. H., Jr., & Madsen, C. R. (1974). *Teaching discipline: Behavior principles towards a positive approach.* Boston, MA: Allyn & Bacon.

Mahoney, M. J., & Avener, M. (1977). Psychology of the elite athlete: An exploratory study. *Cognitive Therapy and Research, 1,* 135-141.

Mahoney, M.J., Gabriel, P. J., & Perkins, T.S.I. (1987). Psychological skills and exceptional athletic performance. *The Sport Psychologist, 1,* 181-199.

Mallett, C. J., & Hanrahan, S. J. (1997). Race modeling: An effective cognitive strategy for the 100m sprinter? *The Sport Psychologist, 11,* 72-85.

Malott, R. W. (1989). The achievement of evasive goals: Control by rules describing contingencies that are not direct-acting. In S. C. Hayes (Ed.), *Rule governed behavior: Cognition, contingencies, and instructional control* (pp. 269-324). New York: Plenum.

Malott, R. W. (1992). A theory of rule-governed behavior and organizational behavior management. *Journal of Organizational Behavior Management, 12,* 45-65.

Malott, R. W., & Whaley, D. L. (1983). *Psychology.* Holmes Beach, FL: Learning Publications.

Martens, B. K., & Collier, S. R. (2011). Developing fluid, efficient, automatic repertoires of athletic performance. In J. K. Luiselli & D. D. Reed (Eds.), *Behavioral sport psychology: Evidenced-based approaches to performance enhancement.* New York: Springer.

Martens, N. P., & Mobley, M. (2005). Straight guys working with gay guys: Homophobia and sport psychology service delivery. In M. B. Andersen (Ed.), *Sport psychology in practice,* (pp. 249-264). Champagne, IL: Human Kinetics.

Martin, G. L. (1992). Applied behavior analysis in sport and physical education: Past, present, and future. In R. P. West & L. A. Hamerlynk (Eds.), *Designs for excellence in education: The legacy of B. F. Skinner* (pp. 223-257). Longmont, CO: Sopris West.

Martin, G. L. (1993). Research on mental practice techniques: Comment on Palmer's study. *The Sport Psychologist, 7,* 339-341.

Martin, G. L. (2010). *Sport psychology manual for hockey players.* Winnipeg, Canada: Sport Science Press.

Martin, G. L., & Hrycaiko, D. (1983). Effective behavioral coaching: What's it all about? *Journal of Sport Psychology, 5,* 8-20.

Martin, G. L., & Ingram, D. (2001). *Play golf in the zone: The psychology of golf made easy.* San Francisco: Van der Plas Publications.

Martin, G. L., Le Page, R., & Koop, S. (1983). Applications of behavior modification for coaching age-group competitive swimmers. In G. L. Martin & D. Hrycaiko (Eds.), *Behavior modification and coaching: Principles, procedures, and research* (pp. 147-174). Springfield, IL: Charles C. Thomas.

Martin, G. L., & Martin, T. (2006). *Curl in the Zone: The psychology of curling made easy,* Winnipeg, Canada: Sport Science Press.

Martin, G. L., & Pear, J. J. (1996). *Behavior modification: What it is and how to do it,* 5th ed. Upper Saddle River, NJ: Prentice-Hall

Martin, G. L., & Pear, J. J. (2011). *Behavior modification: What it is and how to do it,* 9th ed. Upper Saddle River, NJ: Prentice-Hall.

Martin, G. L., & Osborne, J. G. (1993). *Psychology, adjustment, and everyday living,* 2nd ed. Englewood Cliffs, NJ: Prentice-Hall.

Martin, G. L., & Thomson, K. (2010). *A sport psychology self-instructional manual for figure skaters.* Winnipeg, Canada: Sport Science Press.

Martin, G. L., & Thomson, K. (2011). Overview of behavioral sport psychology. In J. K. Luiselli & D. D. Reed (Eds.), *Behavioral sport psychology: Evidenced-based approaches to performance enhancement.* New York: Springer.

Martin, G. L., Thomson, K., & Regehr, K. (2004). Studies using single-subject designs in sport psychology: 30 years of research, *The Behavior Analyst, 27,* 123-140.

Martin, G. L., & Tkachuk, G. A. (2000). Behavioral sport psychology. In J. Austin & J. E. Carr (Eds.), *Handbook of applied behavior analysis* (pp. 399-422). Reno, NV: Context Press.

Martin, G. L., & Toogood, A. (1997). Cognitive and behavioral components of a seasonal psychological skills training program for competitive figure skaters. *Cognitive and Behavioral Practice, 4,* 383-404.

Martin, G. L., Toogood, A., & Tkachuk, G. (1997). *Behavioral assessment forms for sport psychology consulting.* Winnipeg, Canada: Sport Science Press.

Martin, K. A., Moritz, S. E., & Hall, C. R. (1999). Imagery use in sport: A literature review and applied model. *The Sport Psychologist, 13,* 245-268.

Masser, L. S. (1993). Critical cues help first-grade students' achievement in handstands and forward rolls. *Journal of Teaching in Physical Education, 12,* 301-312.

McKenzie, T. L., & Liskevych, T. N. (1983). Using the multi-element baseline design to examine motivation in volleyball training. In G. L. Martin & D. Hrycaiko (Eds.), *Behavior modification and coaching: Principles, procedures, and research* (pp. 187-202). Springfield, IL: Charles C. Thomas.

McKenzie, T. L., & Rushall, B. S. (1974). Effects of self-recording on attendance and performance in a competitive swimming training environment. *Journal of Applied Behavior Analysis, 7,* 199-206.

Mellalieu, S. D., & Juniper, S. W. (2006). A qualitative investigation into experiences of the role episode in soccer. *The Sport Psychologist, 20,* 399-418.

Mesagno, C., Marchant, D., & Morris, T. (2009). Alleviating choking: The sounds of distraction. *Journal of Applied Sport Psychology, 21,* 131-147.

Mesagno, C., & Mullane-Grant, T. (2010). A comparison of different pre-performance routines as possible choking interventions. *Journal of Applied Sport Psychology, 62,* 343-360.

Michael, J. (1986). Repertoire-altering effects of remote contingencies. *The Analysis of Verbal Behavior, 4,* 10-18.

Michael, J. (1993). Establishing operation. *The Behavior Analyst, 16*, 191-206.

Ming, S., & Martin, G. L. (1996). Single-subject evaluation of a self-talk package for improving figure skating performance. *The Sport Psychologist, 10,* 227-238.

Moritz, S., Hall, C. R., Martin, K. A., & Vadocz, E. (1996). What are confident athletes imaging? An examination of image content. *The Sport Psychologist, 10,* 171-179.

Murphy, S. M. (1994). Imagery interventions in sport. *Medicine and Science in Sports and Exercise, 26,* 486-494.

Nicklaus, J. (1974). *Golf my way.* New York: Simon & Schuster.

Nideffer, R. M. (1981). *The ethics and practice of applied sport psychology.* Ithaca, NY: Mouvement Publications.

Nideffer, R. M. (1985). *Athlete's guide to mental training.* Champaign, IL: Human Kinetics Publishers.

O'Brien, R. M., Mellalieu, S., & Hanton, S. (2009). Goal-setting effects in elite and nonelite boxers. *Journal of Applied Sport Psychology, 21,* 293-306.

O'Brien, R. M., & Simek, T. C. (1983). A comparison of behavioral and traditional methods for teaching golf. In G. L. Martin & D. Hrycaiko (Eds.), *Behavior modification and coaching: Principles, procedures, and research* (pp. 175-186). Springfield, IL: Charles C. Thomas.

Orlick, T. (1986a). *Coach's training manual to psyching for sport.* Champaign, IL: Human Kinetics.

Orlick, T. (1986b). *Psyching for sport.* Champaign, IL: Leisure Press.

Orlick, T. (1989). Reflections on sport psych consulting with individual and team sport athletes at summer and winter Olympic games. *The Sport Psychologist, 3,* 358-365.

Orlick, T., & Partington, J. (1987). The sport psychology consultant: Analysis of critical components as viewed by Canadian Olympic athletes. *The Sport Psychologist, 1,* 4-17.

Orlick, T., & Partington, J. (1988). Mental links to excellence. *The Sport Psychologist, 2,* 105-130.

Osborne, K., Rudrud, E., & Zezoney, F. (1990). Improved curveball hitting through the enhancement of visual cues. *Journal of Applied Behavior Analysis, 23,* 371-377.

Parham, W. D. (2005). Raising the bar: Developing an understanding of athletes from racially, culturally, and ethnically diverse backgrounds. In M. B. Andersen, (Ed.), *Sport psychology in practice* (pp. 201-216). Champagne, IL: Human Kinetics.

Parker, R. I. (2006). Increased reliability for single-case research results: Is the bootstrap the answer? *Behavior Therapy, 37,* 326-338.

Parker, R. I., & Hagan-Burke, S. (2007). Useful effect size interpretations for single case research, *Behavior Therapy, 38,* 95-105.

Partington, J., & Orlick, T. (1987). The sport psychology consultant evaluation form. *The Sport Psychologist, 1,* 309-317.

Pavlov, I. P. (1927). *Conditioned reflexes: An investigation of the physiological activity of the cerebral cortex.* Trans. G. V. Anrep. London: Oxford University Press.

Pear, J. J. (2001). *The science of learning.* Philadelphia, PA: Psychology Press.

Ravizza, K. (1987). The integration of psychological skills training into practices. In J. Salmela, B. Petoit, and T. Blaine (Eds.), *Psychological nurturing and guidance of gymnastic talent* (pp. 5-12). Montreal: Sport Psych. Editors.

Ravizza, K. (1988). Gaining entry with athletic personnel for season-long consulting. *The Sport Psychologist, 2,* 243-254.

Ravizza, K., & Osborne, T. (1991). Nebraska's three R's: One-play-at-a-time, preperformance routine for college football. *The Sport Psychologist, 5,* 256-265.

Reifman, A. S., Larrick, R., & Fein, S. (1988). The heat-aggression relationship in major league baseball. Paper presented at the American Psychological Association Convention.

Rimm, D. C., Hill, G. A., Brown, N. N., & Stewart, J. E. (1974). Group assertive training in the treatment of expression of inappropriate anger. *Psychological Reports, 34,* 791-798.

Roberts, R. N. (1979). Private speech in academic problem solving: A naturalistic perspective. In G. Zevin (Ed.), *The development of self-regulation through private speech* (pp. 295-323). New York: John Wiley.

Roberts, R. N., & Tharp, R. G. (1980). A naturalistic study of children's self-directed speech in academic problem solving. *Cognitive Research and Therapy, 4,* 341-353.

Rogerson, L. J., & Hrycaiko, D. W. (2002). Enhancing competitive performance of ice hockey goal tenders using centering and self-talk. *Journal of Applied Sport Psychology, 14,* 14-26.

Rothstein, A. L. (1980). Effective use of videotape replay in learning motor skills. *Journal of Physical Education and Recreation, 51,* 59-60.

Rush, D. B., & Ayllon, T. (1984). Peer behavioral coaching: Soccer. *Journal of Sport Psychology, 6,* 325-334.

Rushall, B. S. (1975). A motivational device for competitive swimming training. *Swimming Technique, 11,* 103-106.

Rushall, B. S. (1979). *Psyching in sport: The psychological preparation for serious competition in sport.* London: Pelham Books.

Rushall, B. S. (1983). Coaching styles: A preliminary investigation. In G. L. Martin & D. Hrycaiko (Eds.), *Behavior modification and coaching: Principles, procedures, and research* (pp. 299-319). Springfield, IL: Charles C. Thomas.

Rushall, B. S. (1984). The content of competition thinking. In W. F. Straub & J. M. Williams (Eds.), *Cognitive sport psychology* (pp. 51-62). Lansing, NY: Sport Science Associates.

Rushall, B. S. (1992). *Mental skills training for sports: A manual for athletes, coaches, and sport psychologists.* Spring Valley, CA: Sport Science Associates.

Rushall, B. S., Hall, M., Roux, L., Sasseville, J., & Rushall, A. C. (1988). Effects of three types of thought content instructions on skiing performance. *The Sport Psychologist, 2,* 283-297.

Rushall, B. S., & Shewchuk, M. L. (1989). Effects of thought content instructions on swimming performance. *Journal of Sports Medicine and Physical Fitness, 29,* 326-334.

Rushall, B. S., & Siedentop, D. (1972). *The development and control of behavior in sport and physical education.* Philadelphia: Lea & Febiger.

Rushall, B. S., & Smith, K. C. (1979). Coaching effectiveness of the quality and quantity of behavior categories in a swimming coach. *Journal of Sport Psychology, 1,* 138-150.

Schunk, D. H. (1987). Peer models and children's behavioral change. *Review of Educational Research, 57,* 149-174.

Scott, D., Scott, L. M., & Howe, B. L. (1998). Training anticipation for intermediate tennis players, *Behavior Modification, 22,* 243-261.

Shambrook, C. J., & Bull, S. J. (1996). The use of a single-case research design to investigate the efficacy of imagery training. *Journal of Applied Sport Psychology, 8,* 27-43.

Shapiro, E. S., & Shapiro, S. (1985). Behavioral coaching and the development of skills in track. *Behavior Modification, 9,* 211-224.

Shaw, G. A., & Belmore, S. M. (1983). The relationship between imagery and creativity. *Imagination, Cognition and Personality, 2,* 115-123.

Shelton, J. L., & Levi, R. L. (1981). *Behavioral assignments and treatment compliance: A handbook of clinical strategies.* Champaign, IL: Research Press.

Siedentop, D. (1976). *Developing teaching skills in physical education.* Boston: Houghton-Mifflin Co.

Siedentop, D. (1980). The management of practice behavior. In W. F. Straub (Ed.), *Sports psychology: An analysis of athletic behavior* (pp. 49-71). Ithaca, NY: Mouvement Publications.

Siedentop, D., & Tannehill, D. (2000). *Developing teaching skills in physical education,* 4th ed. Mountainview, CA: Mayfield.

Silva, J., Lerner, B., & Metzler, J. (2007). *Training professionals in the practice of sport psychology,* Morgantown, WV: Fitness Information Technology, Inc.

Silva, III, J. M. (1982). Competitive sport environments: Performance enhancement through cognitive intervention. *Behavior Modification, 6,* 443-463.

Simek, T. C., & O'Brien, R. M. (1981). *Total golf: A behavioral approach to lowering your score and getting more out of your game.* New York: Doubleday. (Now available from B-Mod Associates, Suite 109, 4230 W. Hempstead Turnpike, Bethpage, NY 11714.)

Simons, J. P., & Andersen, M. B. (1995). The development of consulting practice in applied sport psychology: Some personal perspectives. *The Sport Psychologist, 9,* 449-468.

Skinner, B. F. (1953). *Science and human behavior.* New York: McMillan.

Skinner, B. F. (1957). *Verbal behavior.* New York: Appleton-Century-Crofts.

Skinner, B. F. (1969). *Contingencies of reinforcement: A theoretical analysis.* New York: Appleton-Century-Crofts.

Skinner, B. F. (1974). *About behaviorism.* New York: Knopf.

Smith, P. J. K., & Johnston, D. (2000). A comparison of augmented verbal cues and self-talk regimes in learning a tennis volley. *Journal of Sport and Exercise Psychology, 22,* 92-101.

Smith, R. E. (1988). The logic and design of case study research. *The Sport Psychologist, 2,* 1-12.

Smith, R. E. (2010). A positive approach to coaching effectiveness and performance enhancement. In J. M. Williams (Ed.), *Applied sport psychology: Personal growth to peak performance,* 6th ed. (pp. 42-58). New York: McGraw-Hill

Smith, R. E., & Little, L. M. (1998). A review of *Behavioral Assessment Forms for Sport Psychology Consulting. The Sport Psychologist, 12*, 104-105.

Smith, R. E., Schutz, R. W., Smoll, F.L., & Ptacek, J. T. (1995). Development and validation of a multi-dimensional measure of sport-specific psychological skills: The Athletic Coping Skills Inventory-28. *Journal of Sport and Exercise Psychology, 17,* 379-398.

Smith, R. E., & Smoll, F. L. (1991). Behavioral research and intervention in youth sports. *Behavior Therapy, 22,* 329-344.

Smith, R. E., Smoll, F. L., & Barnett, N. P. (1995). Reduction of children's sport performance anxiety through social support and stress reduction training for coaches. *Journal of Applied Developmental Psychology, 16,* 125-142.

Smith, R. E., Smoll, F. L., & Christensen, D. S. (1996). Behavioral assessment and interventions in youth sports. *Behavior Modification, 20,* 3-44.

Smith, R. E., Smoll, F. L., & Curtis, B. (1979). Coach effectiveness training: A cognitive-behavioral approach to enhancing relationship skills in youth coaches. *Journal of Sport Psychology, 1,* 59-75.

Smoll, F. L., & Cumming, S. P. (2006). Enhancing coach-parent relationships in youth sports: Increasing harmony and minimizing hassle. . In J. M. Williams (Ed.), *Applied sport psychology: Personal growth to peak performance,* 5th ed. (pp. 192-206). New York: McGraw-Hill.

Smoll, F. L., & Smith, R. E. (1987). *Sport psychology for youth coaches: Personal growth to athletic excellence.* Washington, DC: National Federation for Catholic Youth Ministry.

Smoll, F. L., & Smith, R. E. (2010). Conducting psychologically oriented coach-training programs: A social-cognitive approach. In J. M. Williams (Ed.), *Applied sport psychology: Personal growth to peak performance,* 6th ed. (pp. 392-416). New York: McGraw-Hill.

Staats, A. W. (1968). *Learning, language, and cognition.* New York: Holt, Rinehart, & Winston.

Staats, A. W., Staats, C. K., & Crawford, H. L. (1962). First order conditioning of meaning and the parallel conditioning of a CSR. *Journal of General Psychology, 67,* 159-167.

Stokes, J. V., Luiselli, J. K., & Reed, D. D. (2010). A behavioral intervention for teaching tackling skills to high school football athletes. *Journal of Applied Behavior Analysis, 43,* 509-512.

Stokes, J. V., Luiselli, J. K., Reed, D. D., & Fleming, R. K. (2010). Behavioral coaching to improve offensive line pass-blocking skills of high school football athletes. *Journal of Applied Behavior Analysis, 43,* 463-472.

Stuart, R. B. (1971). Assessment and change of the communication patterns of juvenile delinquents and their parents. In R. D. Ruben, H. Fernsterheim, A. A. Lazarus, & C. M. Franks (Eds.), *Advances in behavior therapy* (pp. 183-196). New York: Academic Press.

Sundberg, M. L. (2004). A behavioral analysis of motivation and its relation to mand training. In W. L. Williams (Ed.), *Advances in developmental disabilities: Etiology, assessment, intervention, and integration* (pp. 199-220). Reno, NV: Context Press.

Swain, A., & Jones, G. (1995). Effects of goal-setting interventions on selected basketball skills: A single-subject design. *Research Quarterly for Exercise and Sport, 66,* 51-63.

Taylor, J. (1988). Slump-busting: A systematic analysis of slumps in sports. *The Sport Psychologist, 2,* 39-48.

Templin, D. P., & Vernacchia, R. A. (1995). The effect of highlight music videotapes upon the game performance of inter-collegiate basketball players. *The Sport Psychologist, 9,* 41-50.

Tenenbaum, G., Stewart, E., Singer, R., Duda, J. (1997). Aggression and violence in sport: An ISSP position stand. *The Sport Psychologist, 11,* 1-7.

Tenenbaum, G., Sacks, D. N., Miller, J. W., Golden, A. S., & Doolin, N. (2000). Aggression and violence in sport: A reply to Kerr's rejoinder. *The Sport Psycholgist, 14,* 315-326.

Tingstrom, D. H., Sterling-Turner, H. E., & Wilczynski, S. M. (2006). The good behavior game: 1969-2002, *Behavior Modification, 30,* 225-253.

Tkachuk, G., Leslie-Toogood, A., & Martin, G. L. (2003). Behavioral assessment in sport psychology. *The Sport Psychologist, 17,* 104-117.

Van Raalte, J. L., Brewer, B. W., Rivera, P. M., & Petitpas, A. J. (1994). The relationship between observable self-talk and competitive junior tennis players' match performance. *Journal of Sport and Exercise Psychology, 16,* 400-415.

Vealey, R. S., & Greenleaf, C. A. (2010). Seeing is believing: Understanding and using imagery in sport. In J. M. Williams (Ed.), *Applied sport psychology: Personal growth to peak performance,* 6th ed. (pp. 267-304). New York: McGraw Hill.

Virués-Ortega, J., & Martin, G. L. (in press). Guidelines for sport psychologists to evaluate their interventions in clinical cases uses single-subject designs. *Journal of Behavioral Health and Medicine.*

Vygotsky, L. S. (1978). *Mind and society.* Cambridge: Harvard University Press.

Wanlin, C., Hrycaiko, D., Martin, G. L., & Mahon, M. (1997). The effects of a goal setting package on the performance of young female speed skaters. *Journal of Applied Sport*

Psychology, 9, 212-228.

Ward, P. (2011). Goal setting and performance feedback. In J. K Luiselli & D. D. Reed (Eds.), *Behavioral Sport Psychology: Evidence-based approaches to performance enhancement.* New York: Springer.

Ward, P., & Carnes, M. (2002). Effects of posting self-set goals on collegiate football players' skill execution during practice and games. *Journal of Applied Behavior Analysis, 35,* 1-12.

Watson, D. L., & Tharp, R. G. (2007). *Self-directed behavior: Self-modification for personal adjustment,* 9th ed. Belmont, CA: Wadsworth/Thompson Learning.

Watson, J. B. (1930). *Behaviorism.* Chicago: The University of Chicago Press.

Watson, J. B., & Rayner, R. (1920). Conditioned emotional reactions. *Journal of Experimental Psychology, 3,* 1-14.

Weinberg, R. S., & Gould, D. (2011). *Foundations of sport and exercise psychology,* 5th ed. Champaign, IL: Human Kinetics.

Weiss, N. R. (2004). *Developmental sport and exercise psychology: A lifespan perspective.* Morgantown, WV: Fitness Information Technology, Inc.

Whelan, J. P., Meyers, A. W., & Elkin, T. D. (1996). Ethics and sport and exercise psychology. In VanRaalte, J. L., & Brewer, B. W. (Eds.), *Exploring sport and exercise psychology* (pp. 431-445). Washington, DC: American Psychological Association.

Williams, J. M. (Ed.) (2010). *Applied sport psychology: Personal growth to peak performance,* 6th ed. New York: McGraw Hill.

Williams, J. M. (2010). Relaxation and energizing techniques for regulation of arousal. In J. M. Williams (Ed.), *Applied sport psychology: Personal growth to peak performance,* 6th ed. (pp. 247-266). New York: McGraw Hill.

Williams, J. M., Nideffer, R. M., Wilson, V. E., Sagal, M., & Pepper, E. (2010). Concentration and strategies for controlling it. In J. M. Williams (Ed.), *Applied sport psychology: Personal growth to peak performance,* 6th ed. (pp. 336-358). New York: McGraw Hill.

Williams, J. M., Zinsser, N., & Bunker, L. (2010). Cognitive techniques for building confidence and enhancing performance. In J. M. Williams (Ed.), *Applied sport psychology: Personal growth to peak performance,* 6th ed. (pp. 305-335). New York: McGraw Hill.

Wolf, M. M. (1978). Social validity: The case for subjective measurement or how applied behavior analysis is finding its heart. *Journal of Applied Behavior Analysis, 11,* 203-214.

Wolko, K. L., Hrycaiko, D. W., & Martin, G. L. (1993). A comparison of two self-management packages to standard coaching for improving practice performance of gymnasts. *Behavior Modification, 17,* 209-223.

Wollman, N. (1986). Research on imagery and motor performance: Three methodological suggestions. *Journal of Sport Psychology, 8,* 135-138.

Wolpe, J. (1958). *Psychotherapy by reciprocal inhibition.* Stanford, CA: Stanford University Press.

Wolpe, J. (1990). *The practice of behavior therapy,* 4th ed. New York: Pergamon.

Yu, D., & Martin, G. L. (1987). Low-cost procedures to conserve a public sport environment. *Behavior Modification, 11,* 241-250.

Yukelson, D. P. (2010). Communicating effectively. In J. M. Williams (Ed.), *Applied sport psychology: Personal growth to peak performance,* 6th ed. (pp. 149-166). New York: McGraw Hill.

Zaichkowsky, L. D. (1980). Single-case experimental designs and sport psychology research. In C. H. Nadeau, W. R. Halliwell, K. M. Newell, & G. C. Roberts (Eds.), *Psychology of motor behavior and sport - 1979* (pp. 171-179). Champaign, IL: Human Kinetics.

Ziegler, E. F. (1987). Rationale and suggested dimensions for a code of ethics for sport psychologists. *The Sport Psychologist, 1,* 138-150.

Ziegler, S. G. (1987). Effects of stimulus cueing on the acquisition of ground strokes by beginning tennis players. *Journal of Applied Behavior Analysis, 20,* 405-411.

Ziegler, S. G. (1994). The effects of attentional shift training on the execution of soccer skills: A preliminary investigation. *Journal of Applied Behavior Analysis, 27,* 545-552.

Author Index

Subject Index

Permissions Acknowledgements

Appreciation is expressed for permission granted by the following individuals and organizations for use of illustrations, data, or text.

Parts of Chapters 1, 2, 3, 4, and 13 were paraphrased, with permission from Prentice-Hall, from Martin, G. L., & Pear, J. J. (1996). *Behavior modification: What it is and how to do it*, 5th ed.

Parts of Chapters 8 and 9 were paraphrased, with permission from Prentice-Hall, from Martin, G. L., & Osborne, J. G. (1993). *Psychology, adjustment, and everyday living*, 2nd ed.

Table 9-1. Instructions for achieving deep muscle relaxation. From *Behavior modification: What it is and how to do it*, 5th ed., Table 25-2, by Garry Martin & Joseph Pear. Copyright © 1996 by Prentice-Hall, Inc. Reprinted by permission.

Figure 6-2. A checklist for the backstroke. From "Effective behavioral coaching: What's it all about?" by Garry Martin, & Dennis Hrycaiko, *Journal of Sport Psychology (Vol. 5, No. 1)*, p. 12. Copyright © 1983 by Human Kinetics Publishers. Reprinted by permission.

In the Application, Chapter 10. Components of the serve in a shaping program with novice tennis players. From "Differential reinforcement in coaching tennis skills" by H. P. Buzas & T. Ayllon, *Behavior Modification (Vol. 5)*, pp. 375, 376. Copyright © 1981 by Sage Publications, Inc. Reprinted by permission.

Figure 10-2. From *Total golf: A behavioral approach to lowering your score and getting more out of the game* by Tom Simek and Richard O'Brien, Huntington, NY: B-Mod Associates, p. 2. Copyright © 1981 by Thomas C. Simek and Richard M. O'Brien. Reprinted by permission.

Figure 11-2. From "Evaluation of a coaching strategy to reduce swimming stroke errors with beginning age-group swimmers," by Sandra Koop and Garry Martin, *Journal of Applied Behavior Analysis (Vol. 16)*, p. 455. Copyright © 1983 by Society for the Experimental Analysis of Behavior, Inc. Reprinted by permission.

Figure 5-2. From "A motivational device for competitive swimming training," by Brent Rushall, *Swimming Technique (Vol. 11)*, pp. 103-104. Copyright © 1979 by Sports Publications, Inc. Reprinted by permission.

Figure 12-3. From "A self-monitoring feedback package for improving freestyle figure skating practice," by K. Michelle Hume, et al., *Journal of Sport Psychology (Vol. 7, No. 4)*, p. 340. Copyright © 1985 by Human Kinetics Publishers. Reprinted by permission.

Part of Chapter 17 was paraphrased, with permission from the Association for the Advancement of Applied Sport Psychology, from "Applied research studies with single-subject designs: Why so few?" by D. Hrycaiko & G. Martin, *Journal of Applied Sport Psychology* (Vol. 8, pp. 183-199).

Figure 17-1. From "A self-monitoring feedback package for improving freestyle figure skating practice," by K. Michelle Hume, et al., *Journal of Sport Psychology (Vol. 7, No. 4)*, p. 340. Copyright © 1985 by Human Kinetics Publishers. Reprinted by permission.

Figure 17-2. From "The effects of an imagery rehearsal, relaxation, and self-talk package on basketball game performance," by Gail Kendall, Dennis Hrycaiko, Garry Martin, & Tom Kendall, *Journal of Sport and Exercise Psychology (Vol. 12, No. 2)*, p. 162. Copyright © 1990 by Human Kinetics Publishers. Reprinted by permission.

Table 18-1. From "Ethical principles of AAASP" by Andrew Meyers, *Association for the Advancement of Applied Sport Psychology Newsletter (Vol. 10, No. 1)*, pp. 15, 21. Copyright © 1995 by Association for the Advancement of Applied Sport Psychology. Reprinted by permission.

Table 18-2. From "The Sport Psychology Evaluation Form" by John Partington and Terry Orlick, *The Sport Psychologist (Vol. 1, No. 4)*, p. 312. Copyright © 1987 by Human Kinetics Publishers. Reprinted by permission.

About the Author

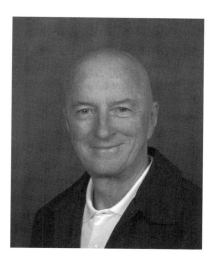

A native of Manitoba, Canada, **Garry Martin** attended Colorado College on a hockey scholarship, where he received his BA degree. After receiving his MA and Ph.D. degrees at Arizona State University, he began teaching psychology at the University of Manitoba, where he is currently a Distinguished Professor Emeritus. His co-authored books on behavioral psychology are used as primary texts at many universities in many countries, and have been translated into Spanish, Italian, Portuguese, Chinese, and Korean. During his career, he has received numerous honors and awards, including an Honorary Doctorate from Colorado College, Distinguished Service Awards from the Canadian Psychological Association and the Brazilian Association of Psychotherapy and Behavioral Medicine, induction into the Royal Society of Canada, and the 2010 Award for Distinguished Contributions to Education and Training in Psychology from the Canadian Psychological Association. During the past 35 years, Garry has been a sport psychology consultant to scores of athletes, from beginners to professionals, in gymnastics, swimming, diving, tennis, ice hockey, field hockey, golf, football, basketball, curling, and figure skating.